LIBRARY OF HEBREW BIBLE/
OLD TESTAMENT STUDIES

739

Formerly Journal for the Study of the Old Testament Supplement Series

Editors
Laura Quick, Oxford University, UK
Jacqueline Vayntrub, Yale University, USA

Founding Editors
David J. A. Clines, Philip R. Davies and David M. Gunn

Editorial Board
Sonja Ammann, Alan Cooper, Steed Davidson, Susan Gillingham,
Rachelle Gilmour, John Goldingay, Rhiannon Graybill, Anne Katrine Gudme,
Norman K. Gottwald, James E. Harding, John Jarick, Tracy Lemos, Carol Meyers,
Eva Mroczek, Daniel L. Smith-Christopher, Francesca Stavrakopoulou,
James W. Watts

INTRODUCING A HERMENEUTICS OF CISPICION

Reading Sarah and Esau's Gender (Failures) Beyond Cisnormativity

Jo Henderson-Merrygold

LONDON • NEW YORK • OXFORD • NEW DELHI • SYDNEY

T&T CLARK

Bloomsbury Publishing Plc, 50 Bedford Square, London, WC1B 3DP, UK
Bloomsbury Publishing Inc, 1359 Broadway, New York, NY 10018, USA
Bloomsbury Publishing Ireland, 29 Earlsfort Terrace, Dublin 2, D02 AY28, Ireland

BLOOMSBURY, T&T CLARK and the T&T Clark logo are trademarks of Bloomsbury Publishing Plc

First published in Great Britain 2024
Paperback edition published 2026

Copyright © Jo Henderson-Merrygold, 2024

Jo Henderson-Merrygold has asserted her right under the Copyright, Designs and Patents Act, 1988, to be identified as Author of this work.

All rights reserved. No part of this publication may be: i) reproduced or transmitted in any form, electronic or mechanical, including photocopying, recording or by means of any information storage or retrieval system without prior permission in writing from the publishers; or ii) used or reproduced in any way for the training, development or operation of artificial intelligence (AI) technologies, including generative AI technologies. The rights holders expressly reserve this publication from the text and data mining exception as per Article 4(3) of the Digital Single Market Directive (EU) 2019/790.

Bloomsbury Publishing Plc does not have any control over, or responsibility for, any third-party websites referred to or in this book. All internet addresses given in this book were correct at the time of going to press. The author and publisher regret any inconvenience caused if addresses have changed or sites have ceased to exist, but can accept no responsibility for any such changes.

A catalogue record for this book is available from the British Library.

A catalog record for this book is available from the Library of Congress.

ISBN: HB: 978-0-5677-1308-7
PB: 978-0-5677-1312-4
ePDF: 978-0-5677-1309-4
eBook: 978-0-5677-1311-7

Series: Library of Hebrew Bible/Old Testament Studies, volume 739, ISSN 2513-8758

Typeset by RefineCatch Limited, Bungay, Suffolk

For product safety related questions contact productsafety@bloomsbury.com.

To find out more about our authors and books visit www.bloomsbury.com and sign up for our newsletters.

CONTENTS

Introduction
MAKING SENSE OF FAILURE AND FAILING TO MAKE SENSE   1

Chapter 1
GENDER FAILURE AND INDECENCY   17

Chapter 2
FROM HERMENEUTICS OF HETERO-SUSPICION TO CISPICION   67

Chapter 3
SARAI AND THE PROBLEM OF CISNORMATIVE EXPECTATIONS   113

Chapter 4
ESAU: MORE THAN JUST A BODY THAT FAILS   151

Conclusion   187

Glossary   201
Bibliography   211
Index of References   223
Index of Authors and Key Themes   227

Introduction

MAKING SENSE OF FAILURE AND FAILING TO MAKE SENSE

Diverse presentations of gender in stories from bygone ages frequently go hand in hand with accounts of failure. That is not to say that to be gender nonconforming *is* to fail, but in a world of binary, mutually exclusive, either/or categories, to say 'none of the above' or 'it's not that simple' is to cause confusion. As readers, then, our presuppositions inform our capacity to make sense of that confusion. In turn that frequently leads us to force narratives to conform to those preconceptions. Where that is possible a character may only appear to succeed once those aspects of confusion are diminished sufficiently, or even erased entirely. Where that is not possible failure beckons, and the character in question is likely to be denigrated for their shortcomings. Even in such stories it is possible to see that there is more going on than a fleeting glance reveals. In fact, lives are so rarely categorizable into either/or options, yet they remain particularly prevalent in the understanding of gender.[1]

Binaries predominate in the conceptualisation of gender and sex. They are also largely treated as immutable – masculine *or* feminine; male *or* female; man *or* woman; and even trans *or* cis; binary *or* nonbinary.[2] Some of us will have a strong identification with one option or the other in each pair, while for other people things are less clear. In that lack of clarity complications emerge, frustrating our presuppositions about what it is to be gendered.[3] Certainly, where those

---

1. Alex Iantaffi and Meg-John Barker, *Life Isn't Binary: On Being Both, Beyond and In-Between* (London: Jessica Kingsley Publishers, 2019). Iantaffi and Barker address this explicitly throughout *On Being Both*. The short volume offers a helpful introduction to nonbinary thinking, throughout many facets of life, especially in the contexts of therapy and popular gender theory.

2. Iantaffi and Barker, *Life Isn't Binary*, 75–82. Iantaffi and Barker emphasize the importance of trying to move away from the creation of new binaries, especially in trans and gender theory. Instead, they argue for a more pluralistic understanding of gender, including transness, that recognizes a richly populated genderscape. See also Alex Iantaffi and Meg-John Barker, *How to Understand Your Gender: A Practical Guide for Exploring Who You Are* (London: Jessica Kingsley Publishers, 2017).

3. Such complications emerge quickly in citational practice, as well as in analysing narratives. Throughout this project I seek to use the appropriate name and pronouns for

preconceptions are significantly informed by cisnormativity, the dominant expectation will be that someone is only ever either male and masculine or female and feminine – and that those labels will correspond with the sex assigned at birth. That sex is presumed to only ever be male *or* female. In other words, we ordinarily expect everyone we encounter to be cisgender (i.e., fixed in a binary gender identity/expression; hereafter cis) and we trust that assumption to be true even though it is not so. So, we need to find ways of navigating a richer genderscape, where it becomes possible to identify a multitude of gender expressions that are not wedded to cisnormative binaries. That does not require a rewriting of existing stories, just an openness to recognize small details about a character's gender or sex that may ordinarily seem inconsequential.

Following Jack Halberstam, I argue that these tiny details seem irrelevant or anachronistic precisely because we are skilful in disregarding anything that challenges a fixed, binary notion of a character's gender.[4] We are also likely to treat such facets of identity as an inescapable indication of a character's failure, to justify maligning them, or at least that part of their personhood. Those models certainly feature in my case studies, found in Chapters 3 and 4, but such insights do not begin in or end with texts from antiquity. So, with that in mind I turn to a far more recent tale of a bygone age, albeit one that just creeps into the earliest days of the twenty-first century.

Of Manly Men, Womanly Women – and Me

Back at the beginning of this new millennium, I embarked on a path that turned out to be punctuated by failure. Having dropped out of further education, I grabbed a copy of the local apprenticeship guide, scanned the pages, and picked the one that paid most: Fleet Sales Trainee. I had never given a thought to selling cars, but I bloody loved driving and that seemed as good a reason as any. So, after a brief interview, I found myself in a mid-range, mid-size dealership trying to sell cars to businessmen all over the country. Almost universally my clients were men. Then again, so was everyone else doing sales both in the dealership and in my training course. This provided me with an immersive course in masculinity. The salesmen around me played up to their role and took any opportunity to man-off

---

each author. This follows the *Chicago Manual of Style* recommendation to follow the preferences of living authors where possible. Where differences occur from a published name this is reflected in square brackets in the bibliographic information only to aid tracing the original publication. The body text refers only to an author's current name. Some have expressed a desire for one pronoun or another, primarily through their publication records or personal correspondence. Where no preference is recorded, I have relied upon assumptions or best guesses. I acknowledge that such methods are only of limited value and hope not to have misgendered or misnamed anyone in the process.

4. Jack [Judith] Halberstam, *The Queer Art of Failure* (Durham, NC: Duke University Press, 2011).

against each other in the showroom, especially when there were no customers around. The competitions were brutal and those who lost were routinely pilloried in front of the entire staff: the showroom was the epitome of toxic masculinity. The workshops and service bays were a more muted version of the same old story, although the men based in them had neither the power nor the visibility of their sales colleagues. Meanwhile, the women were kept behind the scenes, behind the service desk or office doors. Ladies should be seen only if necessary, and were rarely heard, whether those women were staff or customers. In a dealership so clearly demarcated on grounds of gender I stood somewhere in the middle, not quite fitting in either gendered camp. Like Esau, whose story features in Chapter 4, I had been set up to fail although I did not know it yet.

As part of my apprenticeship training, I learned alongside three other trainees most of the time. The classroom mirrored the dealership in large part, especially with the habit of manning off against each other. There was one key difference: whereas in the dealership I was expected to turn up in heels and skirt, and be the good little salesgirl, in the classroom I was as much of a lad as everyone else there. In the classroom, the four of us learned together what it meant to be car sales*men* under the tutelage of a wonderfully seasoned retired salesman. He taught us all the same skills to prepare us for a career in sales and enabled us to grow into our manhood as much as hone our knowledge and expertise. Outside the classroom, rivalries thrived, although not with the brutal masculinity of the showroom. We variously out-raced, out-sold, out-achieved and otherwise outmanned each other whenever the opportunity arose. In this environment I thrived.

My status as one of the guys was fragile. My similarities and differences from the other men became clearest when another trainee joined us. Her arrival changed the group dynamics. She embodied the stereotypes the other trainees had of a young woman and she appeared to appreciate their paternalistic yet sexualized treatment. The guys relished having a girl to fawn over. She typified femininity that was otherwise alien on a course which served to nurture masculinity. Though she soon moved on, her short tenure made one thing particularly apparent: in the strictly binary gendered world I did not fit. She made visible that I was neither sufficiently one of the lads nor one of the girls.

After mere months in the role, my situation at the dealership became untenable: to stay I needed to be the sales*woman* I had been hired to be. However, donning skirts and heels no more made me a saleswoman than did the course that trained me in the manly art of sales. Kate Bornstein persuasively notes that sales roles demand markedly different gender roles and skills. Bornstein realized that all the things that made them so successful as a salesman undermined their reception as a saleswoman. 'I knew how to sell ... as a man. As a woman, the clients did not want to hear my "expert opinion". As a woman, the clients wanted to hear me say, "Well, you know better than me, Mr. Jones – what do **you** think?"'[5] Bornstein

---

5. Kate Bornstein, *Gender Outlaw: On Men, Women, and the Rest of Us*, Revised & Updated ed. (New York: Vintage, 2016), 146.

absolutely describes the disconnection between my training and life at college, and the reception and expectations held by colleagues in the dealership. I had worked hard to gain my expert status. I had honed and tested my skills against the other guys on my course. I was certainly not going to set it aside in order to conform to the narrowly gendered expectations of my colleagues even if they could not have envisaged anything more horrifying than unwomanly me in their clearly demarcated male space. In the face of such carefully constructed and policed gender spaces, I frustrated my colleagues' presuppositions about what it meant to be both man and woman, masculine and feminine. Rather than deal with that uncertainty, they removed me, and the discomfort I brought with my presence.

Too often, confronting gendered preconceptions is met with violence or erasure, but it need not be that way. The disconnection between the showroom and the learning environment showed me that inherited expectations need not constrain what it means to be a gendered person. For different futures to emerge it can be helpful to consider the ways those foundational ideas are modelled for us. That is particularly the case when it comes to exploring the powerful, well-known narratives that have long informed our perception of human experience – and which continue to impact our world today. For some this desire takes the search for representative forebears through history and culture.[6] In my case, I turn to a collection of texts that had a profound effect on shaping my understanding not only of the world, but also, with a far wider impact, the Bible. It is the foundational text that underpins the North Atlantic Christian and academic context which has had – and continues to have – a colonising influence when treated as historically authoritative. From within that collection of texts Genesis is my object of scrutiny: where better to start the search for a suitable model than in a book synonymous with beginnings?

Suspicious Encounters with Genderscapes in Genesis and Beyond

The genderscape of Genesis has wide-reaching implications for contemporary understandings of what it means to be sexed and gendered.[7] But the Bible is not just an ancient text speaking only of bygone eras; it is one that continues to be

---

6. See, for example, Leslie Feinberg, *Transgender Warriors: Making History from Joan of Arc to Dennis Rodman* (Boston, MA: Beacon Press, 1997).

7. Steven Greenberg argues that 'among the most enduring social, political, and psychological legacies of the Genesis stories are their grounding of sex and gender'. Steven Greenberg, *Wrestling with God and Men: Homosexuality in the Jewish Tradition* (Madison, WI: University of Wisconsin Press, 2004), 1–2. Philip Davies also rightly points out that 'there is, of course, more to Genesis than gender, but gender pervades the whole book nevertheless'. Philip R. Davies, 'Genesis and the Gendered World', in *The World of Genesis: Persons, Places, Perspectives*, ed. Philip R. Davies and David J. A. Clines, Journal for the Study of the Old Testament Supplement Series (Sheffield: Sheffield Academic Press, 1998),

interrogated for each generation.⁸ The Bible is a religious and culturally significant document that has a profound, enduring impact on gender norms, expectations and presuppositions. It contributes to what we consider natural and normal, acceptable, and authentic, and is even identified as a notable factor in 'the cisgendering of reality'.⁹ That is, it presents a divinely authorized model of humanity that *only* includes cisgender characters within its narrative scope. The effect on today's adherents to those religious texts is that the only possible modes for human existence, let alone flourishing, are similarly constrained to a cisgender framework. For those of us who question our own location within the framework, who identify beyond it, who seek capaciousness,¹⁰ and for those who dispute the validity of the whole genderscape, we are rendered at best unintelligible and, at worst, something other than a divinely-created human. The interpretative model I advocate here has real-world implications because the very experiences that inform it are carefully, although cautiously, offered to challenge long-established doctrine, received knowledge, and trusted wisdom about the perceived immutability of cisnormativity. Our preconceptions of what *is* possible for the genders of both living people and biblical characters must be reconfigured to pursue new insights. In embarking on this journey of exploration, the potential remains for any individual – from the real world or in mnemohistory¹¹ – to emerge at a new, perhaps previously unrecognised, point within the genderscape. Reader and text can then enter into a new dialogue through which a richer and more diverse genderscape appears, and in turn new points of resonance and dissonance can be discovered.

7–15, 8. Phyllis Trible addresses the links between the Genesis gender stories and androcentrism: see Phyllis Trible, *God and the Rhetoric of Sexuality* (Philadelphia, PA: Fortress Press, 1978). Meanwhile Ken Stone addresses the relationship between Genesis and heteronormativity, with a focus on heterosexuality: see Ken Stone, 'The Garden of Eden and the Heterosexual Contract', in *Bodily Citations: Religion and Judith Butler*, ed. Ellen T. Armour and Susan M. St Ville (New York: Columbia University Press, 2006), 48–70.

8. Biblical texts are taken from the New Revised Standard Version, unless otherwise stated.

9. J. E. Sumerau, Ryan T. Cragun and Lain A. B. Mathers, 'Contemporary Religion and the Cisgendering of Reality', *Social Currents* 3, 3 (2016), 293–311. For further discussion of significance of biblical and Christian teaching in restrictive approaches to gender and sexuality, see Ken Stone, 'Bibles That Matter: Biblical Theology and Queer Performativity', *Biblical Theology Bulletin* 38, 1 (2008), 14–25; Jo Henderson-Merrygold, 'Queer(y)ing the Epistemic Violence of Christian Gender Discourses', in *Rape Culture, Gender Violence, and Religion: Christian Perspectives*, ed. Caroline Blyth, Katie B. Edwards and Emily Colgan, Religion and Radicalism (London: Palgrave, 2018), 97–117.

10. I am grateful to one of the reviewers for introducing me to the idea of gender capaciousness.

11. Recognizing the Bible as mnemohistory makes apparent the intersection of cultural, collected, remembered history through which the stories reach their readers. The Bible presents an image of all those collated meanings that today's readers can engage with as a

To engage creatively and actively with the genderscapes found in biblical texts I have devised a hermeneutical approach I call cispicion. The hermeneutics of cispicion treats cisnormativity in literature, society and culture with suspicion. The hermeneutics of cispicion proposed here plays with a phrase most associated with Paul Ricoeur: the hermeneutics of suspicion.[12] He advocates for a greater recognition of the dialectics between author and reader, with reference to Karl Marx, Friedrich Nietzsche and Sigmund Freud.[13] Ricoeur demonstrates that the dialectic involves multiple levels of cognition and self-reflection for author and reader alike. Reflection is key to the dialectical process as it requires us to integrate ourselves into interpretation.[14] For Ricoeur, Freudian reflectiveness enables readers to identify new relations between 'the patent and the latent' that recognizes the differences 'between appearances and the reality of things'.[15] Words can be understood for their multifaceted symbolic function, rather than a single literal or historical meaning. Even then those symbols work in different ways: reflecting back only on the past and appearing so common place they barely warrant a second thought; useful and frequently utilized symbols that translate from one era to the next; and the multifaceted symbols that 'serve as the vehicles of new meaning'.[16] Interrogation of texts, then, requires suspicion to aid our creativity in interpreting the symbols we encounter.

credible historical account; one that draws together the divine, religious and cultural through diverse (and divergent) interpretations. Mnemohistory, a term coined by Jan Assmann, offers a way to recognize a history that is remembered and through that memory gains power and authority. It includes cultural, collective memory that brings richness and depth to an historical record which, in turn, adds to its ongoing significance. See Assmann, 'Collective Memory and Cultural Identity', *New German Critique* 65, Cultural History/Cultural Studies (1995), 125–133: 129: 'Cultural memory has its fixed point; its horizon does not change with the passing of time. These fixed points are fateful events of the past, whose memory is maintained through cultural formation (texts, rites, monuments) and institutional communications (recitation, practice, observance). We call these "figures of memory"'. He later explains more about the interplay between that memory and the present when he writes, 'Our theory of cultural memory attempts to relate all three poles – memory (the contemporised past), culture and the group (society) – to each other' (129).

12. Paul Ricoeur. *Freud and Philosophy: An Essay on Interpretation.* Translated by Denis Savage. (New Haven, CT: Yale University Press, 1970); *The Conflict of Interpretations: Essays in Hermeneutics,* edited by Don Ihde. Northwestern University Studies in Phenomenology & Existential Philosophy. (Evanston, IL: Northwestern University Press, 1974).

13. Ricoeur, *Freud and Philosophy*, 32–33.

14. Ricoeur, *Freud and Philosophy*, 494.

15. Ricoeur, *Freud and Philosophy*, 33.

16. Ricoeur, *Freud and Philosophy*, 504.

Tracing a Genealogy from Suspicion to Cispicion

The journey between Ricoeur's hermeneutics of suspicion and my reconfiguration here takes a somewhat circuitous path. The first step is to make a shift from Ricoeur's philosophical interest in texts encountered through a phenomenological approach to religion. His dialogue with Marx, Freud and Nietzsche continues to provide a helpful rationale for new approaches to reading. Then comes attention to the practical, political application of Ricoeur's insights with their view towards liberation. For that to become apparent, the Bible becomes the central focus for such explorations – not least because it sits at the intersection of phenomenological, theological, political and cultural discussions. Ricoeur's work was adopted and adapted as part of the move to shape intentionally liberational biblical hermeneutics in the liberation theology movement of the 1970s and 1980s.[17] Juan Luis Segundo, for example, focuses on Ricoeur's recognition of Marx 'as one of the great masters of "suspicion"' before asking how such a Marxist suspicion could aid biblical interpretation.[18] In response he brings in James Cone's black liberation theology to emphasize the need to critique ideology in the biblical hermeneutical process.[19] Segundo recreated an intentionally theological hermeneutical circle – an image taken from Martin Heidegger, via Rudolf Bultmann – where suspicion of ideology could then lead to liberation. Yet the description of such an approach as a hermeneutic of suspicion did not carry over directly.[20]

---

17. Marcella Althaus-Reid, 'Paul Ricoeur and the Methodology of the Theology of Liberation: The Hermeneutics of J. Severino Croatto, Juan Luis Segundo and Clodovis Boff'. (PhD University of St Andrews, 1993).

18. Juan Luis Segundo, *The Liberation of Theology* (Maryknoll, NY: Orbis Books, 1976), 17.

19. Segundo, *Liberation of Theology*, 25–32.

20. Instead, it is the commitment to liberation shared with Cone's black theology in combination with an overt attention to the politics of biblical hermeneutics from Ricoeur that are reflected in the enduring influence of the central and South American liberation hermeneutics. For further examples of such dialogue between Ricoeur, Cone and liberation theologians; see Leonardo Boff, *Jesus Christ Liberator: A Critical Christology of Our Time*, translated by Patrick Hughes (London: SPCK, 1980); Gustavo Gutiérrez, *A Theology of Liberation: History, Politics and Salvation*, trans Sister Caridad Inda and John Eagleson, (London: SCM Press, 1974). Gutiérrez focuses his argument on Ricoeur's attention to interpersonal (and human-divine) relationships and its relationship to utopia (47. 232, 237). Nevertheless his awareness of Ricoeur's work on hermeneutics is apparent throughout *A Theology of Liberation* and his later work, *We Drink from Our Own Wells* (London: SCM Press, 2012 [1984]). Indeed, in her preface to the SCM Classics edition of *We Drink from Our Own Wells*, Althaus-Reid makes this lineage more explicit through referencing tracing Gutiérrez's genealogy through Segundo, Sobrino, Boff, and Croatto's liberation hermeneutics. See Althaus-Reid, 'Preface' in *We Drink from Our Own Wells*, ed. Gustavo Gutiérrez, SCM Classics, (London: SCM Press, 2012), xxiii–xxix, xxv–xxvii; cf. 'Paul Ricoeur and the Methodology'.

The journey back to a named hermeneutics of suspicion then winds through feminist theology and biblical scholarship. Feminists such as Phyllis Trible were drawing on new approaches to interpretation with liberation at the heart of their hermeneutical endeavour. Like Segundo, Trible draws on Cone's work to address systems of oppression.[21] She also integrates the work of Segundo's contemporaries working in liberation theology.[22] As the second wave of feminist theology and biblical scholarship grew, it increased interest in drawing on the hermeneutics of liberation theologians such as Segundo, and Gustavo Gutiérrez, to shape their own engagement with oppressive ideology.[23]

For feminists such as Trible, the ideology that most warranted suspicion was patriarchy. Her work led to further attempts to 'depatriarchalize' biblical interpretation.[24] Later Elisabeth Schüssler Fiorenza became most associated with the hermeneutics of suspicion in biblical studies. Both women, along with many other feminist scholars, sought to free the biblical texts from the ideological influences of patriarchy. Works like Trible's paradigm-shifting interpretation of

---

21. Trible, *God and the Rhetoric*, 5.

22. Trible, *God and the Rhetoric*, 5–23. She specifically highlights the contributions of black and liberation theologies. She writes, 'When set in a context of the poor and powerless, the Bible critiques every culture of injustice to proclaim the good news of liberation' (p.5). While she cites Cone explicitly, she does not include reference to Segundo. Instead, she refers to José Profirio Miranda, Gustavo Gutiérrez and Ernesto Cardenal.

23. The adaptation of liberation theology for feminist hermeneutics features heavily in Trible's *God and the Rhetoric*, and Elisabeth Schüssler Fiorenza, *Bread Not Stone: The Challenge of Feminist Biblical Interpretation*. (Boston, MA: Beacon Press, 1984). Rosemary Radford Ruether, like Trible and Schüssler Fiorenza, draws on liberation theology to argue that women are an impoverished group who need to benefit publicly from God's preference for the poor. See Rosemary Radford Ruether, *Womanguides: Readings toward a Feminist Theology, with a new preface* (Boston, MA: Beacon Press, 1996), 158, 261–262. Carter Heyward draws heavily from Gutiérrez, in particular, for her development of embodied feminist theologies; see [Isabel] Carter Heyward, *The Redemption of God: A Theology of Mutual Relation* (Lanham, MD: University Press of America, 1982), 39, 205–208; *Our Passion for Justice: Images of Power, Sexuality, and Liberation* (New York: Pilgrim Press, 1984), 103–111. She emphasises the contribution for a preference for the poor and the possibilities and limitations for transferring that commitment to new contexts such as her feminist and lesbian endeavour. See also Carter Heyward, *Touching Our Strength: The Erotic as Power and the Love of God* (San Francisco, CA: Harper and Row, 1989). For a critique of the commodification and appropriation of liberation theology see, Marcella Althaus-Reid, 'Gustavo Gutiérrez Goes to Disneyland: Theme Park Theologies and the Disapora of the Discourse of the Popular Theologian in Liberation Theology', in *Interpreting Beyond Borders*, ed. Fernando F. Segovia, The Bible and Postcolonialism (Sheffield: Sheffield Academic Press, 2000), 36–58.

24. Phyllis Trible, 'Depatriarchalizing in Biblical Interpretation'. *Journal of the American Academy of Religion* 41, 1 (1973): 30–48.

the creation story of Genesis 2, where God creates the first humans from the ground, freed the text from a male-centric reading. Trible offered a nuanced reading of gender dynamics rather than one simply of male primacy.[25] Similarly her *Texts of Terror* showcased how the texts themselves can – and do – perpetrate violence against women through their portrayal of neglect, abuse, and sexual violence.[26] Yet it was Schüssler Fiorenza who revolutionized feminist biblical scholarship when she proposed multiple, carefully crafted hermeneutics designed to address specific aspects of the erasure and abuse of women. Like Ricoeur, she specifically addresses the complexities of implicit and explicit themes, although her work is not as immediately indebted to his as it is to the liberation theologians he inspired.[27] Indeed she calls out those who have criticized her for not making the links to her 'great "masters" of hermeneutics' explicit enough while she is never expected to trace the genealogies through any 'foresisters'.[28] Nevertheless, as Schüssler Fiorenza traces her hermeneutics through the work of liberation theologians, the legacy of Ricoeur's hermeneutics of suspicion becomes apparent in new ways.

When Schüssler Fiorenza employs liberation theologians, her central commitment is that 'their methodological starting point is that all theology

25. Trible, *God and the Rhetoric*, 72–143.

26. Phyllis Trible, *Texts of Terror*. SCM Classics. (London: SCM Press, 2002).

27. Schüssler Fiorenza, *Bread Not Stone* (1984), 43–63. Schüssler Fiorenza attends to the complexity in drawing from liberation theology for her feminist endeavour: 'To discuss the relationship between liberation theology and biblical interpretation in general, and to consider the function of the Bible in the struggle of women for liberation in particular, is to enter an intellectual and emotional mine field' (43). She persuasively dismisses possible objections to the engagement by noting that 'women and children represent the majority of the "oppressed," and poor and Third World women must bear the triple burden of sexism, racism, and classism. If liberation theologians make the "option for the oppressed" the key in their theological endeavors, then they must articulate that "the oppressed" are women' (44).

28. Elisabeth Schüssler Fiorenza, *Bread Not Stone: The Challenges of Feminist Biblical Interpretation; With a New Afterword* (Boston, MA: Beacon Press, 1995). She notes in the afterword to the second edition of *Bread Not Stone* that her framework is, in some ways, coincidental with the work of the 'great "masters" of hermeneutics such as Bultmann, Ricoeur, the Frankfurt School...'. She later adds 'such an evaluation of feminist work only in terms of malestream hermeneutical discourses neglects the fact not only that feminists have independently raised many of the questions theorized by postmodern epistemology or critical theory, but also that, as a critical theoretical inquiry, feminist biblical hermeneutics must be evaluated in terms of its own theoretical frameworks and practical goals which determine its selective use and bricolage of supporting hermeneutical theories' (178).

I want to acknowledge my appreciation of Schüssler Fiorenza's commitment to selective inclusion. I make similar decisions throughout this project. Therefore, some of the 'foresisters' who shaped feminist biblical hermeneutics but whose work contributes to trans exclusion are intentionally omitted. See also p. 67 n.1, below.

knowingly or not is by definition always engaged for or against the oppressed'.[29] She proposes a series of targeted hermeneutics which form the basis of distinctly *feminist* hermeneutics of suspicion.[30] Describing her model she writes, 'a *hermeneutics of suspicion* does not presuppose the feminist authority and truth of the Bible, but takes as a starting point the assumption that biblical texts and their interpretations are androcentric and serve patriarchal functions'.[31] Here she articulates clearly the integration of a specific ideology that warrants critique through dialectical reflection.[32] These tools then enable a recognition and questioning of 'the underlying presuppositions, androcentric models and

---

29. Schüssler Fiorenza, *Bread Not Stone* (1984), 45. She also asserts that 'intellectual neutrality is not possible in a historical world of exploitation and oppression' thus reflecting back a Ricoeurian recognition of the complexity of interpretation and the need for suspicion.

30. Schüssler Fiorenza, *Bread Not Stone* (1984), 15-17. In *Bread Not Stone* Schüssler Fiorenza proposed a hermeneutics of consent; creative actualization; proclamation and remembrance alongside that of suspicion. She has continued to develop a hermeneutics of experience; domination and social location; critical evaluation; creative imagination; re-membering and reconstruction; and transformative action for change. See Elisabeth Schüssler Fiorenza, *Wisdom Ways: Introducing Feminist Biblical Interpretation* (Maryknoll, NY: Orbis Books, 2001), 165-189.

In addition to *Bread Not Stone* and *Wisdom Ways*, see also Elisabeth Schüssler Fiorenza, *In Memory of Her: Feminist Practices of Biblical Interpretation* (New York: Crossroad, 1983); *But She Said: Feminist Practices of Biblical Interpretation* (Boston, MA: Beacon Press, 1992).

31. Schüssler Fiorenza, *Bread Not Stone* (1984), 15.

32. She later refined her suspicion to address specific ideologies (after Segundo), and she makes clear those she attends to are those of the 'kyriarchy'. Schüssler Fiorenza's neologism is 'derived from the Greek words for "lord" or "master" and "to rule or dominate" (*archein*) which seeks to redefine the category of patriarchy' to recognize multiple intersecting structures of power and domination. Laura Beth Bugg, 'Explanation of Terms (Glossary)', in *Wisdom Ways: Introducing Feminist Biblical Interpretation*, ed. Elisabeth Schüssler Fiorenza (Maryknoll, NY: Orbis Books, 2001), 207-216, 211. Bugg continues, 'Kyriarchy is a socio-political system of domination in which elite educated propertied men hold power over wo/men and other men. Kyriarchy is best theorized as a complex pyramidal system of intersecting multiplicative social structures of superordination and subordination, of ruling and oppression.' It is then enabled through 'kyriocentrism – the cultural-religious-ideological systems and intersecting discourses of race, gender, heterosexuality, class, and ethnicity that produce, legitimate, inculcate, and sustain kyriarchy'.

The enduring presentation of kyriarchy is also visible throughout Raewyn Connell's exploration of the multitude of masculinities present today. Connell identifies that hegemonic masculinity sits at the top of the very pyramid that Bugg and Schüssler Fiorenza identify. See, R. W. Connell, *Masculinities*. (Cambridge: Polity Press, 1995).

unarticulated interests of contemporary biblical interpretation.³³ Such suspicion affects all areas of interpretation, with Schüssler Fiorenza identifying its impact on translation choices and the resultant representation. 'If it is "the limits of our language that are the limits of our world," then androcentric biblical language and translation become a feminist issue of the utmost importance. Such language not only makes women marginal but also makes us invisible in the written classics of our culture, among which the Bible is preeminent'.³⁴

This assertion lies at the heart of my rationale for adopting and adapting Schüssler Fiorenza's approach. She recognizes that erasure and omission have a profound effect on who is recognized as 'the paradigmatic human being' and who becomes the Other.³⁵ Schüssler Fiorenza's form of suspicion draws on Ricoeur's approach, as well as liberation and political theologians, since she applies her strategy to biblical texts specifically. In so doing, she offers a form of advocacy and political engagement that challenges the very preconceptions and assumptions of which she encourages suspicion. Yet she also clearly invites further adaptation to address new facets of oppressive ideologies – suspicious biblical hermeneutics thus become inherently political and liberational. To be most effective, a hermeneutic must be able to name, critique and respond to an identifiable ideology that oppresses.

Schüssler Fiorenza's work on a suspicious hermeneutic continues to shape biblical interpretation, including this project. It is a de facto part of much queer biblical scholarship, where heteronormativity becomes the ideology under scrutiny. Queer interpretations, such as those discussed in Chapter 2, demonstrate the flexibility of Schüssler Fiorenza's frameworks to create space for a recognition of diverse expressions of sexuality beyond those solely associated with heterosexuality. However, the need to adapt her approach and recontextualize it for a different context requires that we recognize its limitations. Neither does a suspicion of kyriarchy or androcentrism adequately serve the aims of queer politics, nor does it sufficiently recognize the intersectional nature of the oppression of women who do not conform to heteronormative expectations.³⁶ Althaus-Reid, for example, noted that neither feminist nor liberation theologians spoke to the

---

33. Schüssler Fiorenza, *Bread Not Stone* (1984), 16.
34. Schüssler Fiorenza, *Bread Not Stone* (1984), 17.
35. Schüssler Fiorenza, *Bread Not Stone* (1984), 16.
36. See for example, Deryn Guest, *When Deborah met Jael: Lesbian Biblical Hermeneutics* (London: SCM Press, 2005); 'Looking Lesbian at the Bathing Bathsheba', *Biblical Interpretation* 16, 3 (2008), 227–262; *Beyond Feminist Biblical Studies*, Bible in the Modern World, (Sheffield: Sheffield Phoenix Press, 2012). Guest shows throughout their collected works that feminist scholarship does not address the experiences of lesbians and other women who love women. Indeed sometimes the supposedly universal experiences of the (straight) feminist subject is antithetical to the queer woman. For further discussion, see Chapter 2.

highly sexual, indigenous women of her Argentine homeland.[37] Their apparent 'indecency' provided the basis for an intentionally queer and postcolonial 'indecent theology'.[38] Althaus-Reid takes insights from feminists and the liberation theologians whose work features in her analysis of the influence of Ricoeur while also critiquing the limits of each approach. Meanwhile Deryn Guest developed a hermeneutics of hetero-suspicion that continues directly from Schüssler Fiorenza's work.[39] Guest draws directly from their feminist foresisters, as well as queer scholars, to reshape a hermeneutics of suspicion that is specifically queer in remit and approach. Guest rightly argues, as Schüssler Fiorenza did before them, that it must be a specific and appropriate ideology that is subject of suspicion in biblical interpretation.

The question at the heart of this project, then, is what specific ideology must readers be suspicious of when exploring the apparent lack of gender diversity in Genesis? Just as feminist scholarship is not sufficient for Guest's queer and lesbian endeavours, and just as liberationist and feminist approaches are not close enough fits for Althaus-Reid's indecent theology, I argue that there is not yet an approach that can adequately serve the needs of gender diverse scholarship. For that, as Schüssler Fiorenza persuasively argues, suspicion is foundational. But the question remains: which ideology must we name, enter into dialectal reflection with, and treat with an intentional suspicion? I, therefore, name cisnormativity as that ideology, and so embark on a journey to recognize (Chapter 1), confront (Chapter 2), and then read against its influence in biblical texts (Chapters 3 and 4).

Introducing a Hermeneutics of Cispicion

The hermeneutics of cispicion remains suspicious that a given individual is necessarily cisgender. It provides a frame of reference through which to engage with gendered presuppositions and to explore gender diversity. Here, I apply that perspective to biblical characters drawn from the ancestral narratives in Genesis in order to explore examples of gender diversity and nonconformity. Approaching the texts in the final form, I re-encounter Sarai/h (Genesis 11:27–23:2) and Esau (25:25–33:17) through an approach informed by trans and queer theories. I shape a cispicious hermeneutic that builds on queer suspicious approaches, most notably those developed and deployed by Guest, in order to focus specifically on the impact of cisnormativity on the reading experience.

Like patriarchy and heteronormativity, cisnormativity names a set of norms and cultural expectations that establish parameters around what is normal, natural,

---

37. Marcella Althaus-Reid, *Indecent Theology: Theological Perversions in Sex, Gender and Politics* (London: Routledge, 2000); *The Queer God* (London: Routledge, 2003). This is discussed further in Chapter 1.

38. Althaus-Reid, *Indecent Theology*.

39. Guest, *When Deborah Met Jael*.

and preferable within human life.⁴⁰ Cisnormativity expresses the idea that it is natural and normal to be either male or female, based almost solely on an observation of genitals at birth. From then on, each individual is expected to identify only with the gender that corresponds with that assignation of sex. The result is a privileging of individuals who are cisgender, whose gender (including identity, expression and performance), is at least largely consistent with the sex assigned at birth, so that male-identified infants grow into boys and men, while female-assigned babies become girls then women. However, there is a far richer diversity of gender and sex than such a model allows for, but it faces challenges for recognition and acceptance. Gender diverse people include those who are intersex, gender nonconforming, genderqueer, nonbinary and trans, to give but a few examples. Such perspectives are rarely recognized, unless explicitly stated, and the enduring preconception of another is that they are, and always have been, the gender and sex we perceive them to be now.⁴¹

The endurance of this presumption presents problems when encountering characters in narrative, such as in the Bible. The hermeneutic of cispicion treats with scepticism such preconceptions that restrict characters to a fixed gender binary. My approach focuses on gender diversity specifically, which both differentiates the cispicious method from its queer and feminist counterparts while also complementing them. There is also a need to address trans-specific experiences, capaciousness within gender categories, and the relationship with constrictive gender norms. Such perspectives add much needed richness to biblical interpretation. In this project I am primarily interested in using insights from trans and queer scholars to build an understanding of how to identify gender diversity in texts where it initially appears hidden. To ensure these voices are central I use the first half of this volume to explore how and why this can be done. Once the hermeneutical framework has been outlined carefully, then I move on to close readings of two relevant biblical narratives featuring Sarai/h and Esau.

To construct the hermeneutics of cispicion, I begin by shaping an approach I call indecent whimsy. I find inspiration in the work of Jack Halberstam and Marcella Althaus-Reid. They each address how nonconforming gender is obscured through systems and norms that make it a particular challenge to identify. Halberstam's 'low theory' integrates and privileges underrepresented perspectives, small details, and idiosyncrasies which, in turn, contribute to the creation of a different vision for gendered life. The approach is somewhat whimsical, but as Halberstam evocatively shows, such irreverence and playfulness are necessary to confront preconceptions as pervasive as those tied to cisnormativity. Althaus-Reid's 'indecent theology' confronts and challenges the idea that only decency is natural, normal and divinely favoured. She privileges playful, indigenous,

---

40. A glossary of definitions, including patriarchy, heteronormativity and cisnormativity, can be found at the end of this project, starting on p. 201.

41. Julia Serano, *Whipping Girl: A Transsexual Woman on Sexism and the Scapegoating of Femininity*, Second ed. (Berkeley, CA: Seal Press, 2016).

decolonised perspectives treated as indecent: without them the theological and biblical landscape is impoverished.[42] Together these perspectives contribute a commitment to irreverently challenge norms and expectations, especially those associated with gender.

I then bring these voices into dialogue with insights from queer and trans gender theorists. These allow me to sharpen my gaze on cisnormativity and the privileges that accompany it. After a brief exploration of queer perspectives on gender, centred on the work of Judith Butler, I turn to trans theorists. Jay Prosser identifies the need for an engagement with trans experience that holistically embeds embodiment in identity. Viviane Namaste argues that trans perspectives represent a form of indigenous knowledge. By using this designation, she stresses the importance of elevating trans voices, whilst also recognizing the impact of living under the imposition of unwelcome and repressive (cisgender) gender norms. Julia Serano takes this further by identifying a specific problem that exacerbates transphobia and marginalization of trans people; this she calls cissexism. Her attention to the privilege and assumption that comes with being cis is invaluable in conceptualizing cisnormativity.

After establishing the need to address cisnormativity I conduct an analysis of Deryn Guest's portrayal of gender. Over a period of eleven years Guest addresses gender nonconformity through the hermeneutics of hetero-suspicion. Their approach is initially shaped as a lesbian-identified hermeneutic, but one that includes gender within its remit. I argue that there is profound value in Guest's model, but ultimately there remains space for a more gender-attentive framework. Guest adapts their hetero-suspicious approach to the differing contexts of elevating the perspectives of lesbians, butches, genderqueer and, most recently, trans readers. Throughout their focus remains on heteronormativity, through use of predominantly queer rubrics, and sexuality never quite disappears from their analytic lens. I argue that this is where the cispicious approach steps in and takes exploration of gender diversity further. My project builds on Guest's, whilst also making explicit that the primary frame of reference for this work is gender diversity, against the backdrop of cisnormativity. I also take forward Guest's passionate commitment to engaging deeply with the biblical texts in order to see how today's experiences of sex and gender can reveal new insights into familiar stories. From the foundations set in these first two chapters I am then able to explore the biblical narratives anew.

With that in mind, I turn to the stories, first of Sarai/h, then of Esau. Both are prominent characters within the narrative, but each fades in and out of focus, struggling to assert the fullness of their identities in the face of the gendered

---

42. Althaus-Reid and Namaste make evocative use of the term 'indigenous' in their writings about gender. Both emphasize the way that gender norms, particularly those I associate with cisnormativity, have had – and continue to have – a colonising effect. While using the same term cautiously, it is this aspect of their work I take forward in my own use of the term in this project.

expectations placed upon them. Sarai/h is subject to the expectations placed upon *her* by being Abraham's wife. They must conform, especially when parenthood is on the cards. However, when Sarai/h has space to demonstrate agency, their nonbinary-esque gender nonconformity becomes recognizable. Sarai/h displays confident, persistent examples of masculinity, something not expected of someone presumed to be a woman, no matter how carefully *her* motherhood is curated. Sarai/h's story demonstrates Halberstam's point that gender diverse lives are stuck in a cycle of fading in and out of focus, which in this case culminates with Sarai/h's excision from the narrative.[43] By seeing only a woman, so much of the rich nonbinaryness of Sarai/h's life is overlooked.

Esau, meanwhile, is a character treated less favourably than his grandparent, Sarai/h. Esau is portrayed as one of life's failures, especially when contrasted with his narratively (and maternally) favoured twin, Jacob. Esau's birth is hotly anticipated, and immediately his body is placed under scrutiny. He persistently fails to live up to the expectations placed on his hypermale body. Through treating his failures as indications of gender discontinuity I identify ruptures through which his shortcomings reveal agency otherwise withheld from him. Esau's sibling and parents seek to emphasize his otherness, including by treating him as incomprehensible. This translates into gender-based violence intended to malign Esau and render him a less than desirable character. It is only as an established (gender) failure that Esau is ultimately freed of the constraints that bind him for most of his story.

These readings demonstrate the value of this cispicious approach to overcome presuppositions about gender conformity and diversity in the Hebrew Bible. Esau and Sarai/h demonstrate through their prominent status that gender diversity is not only recognisable but frequently occurs in the lives of central members of the covenantal family. This insight embeds a more varied genderscape right at the start of the Hebrew Bible.

---

43. Jack [Judith] Halberstam, *In a Queer Time and Place: Transgender Bodies, Subcultural Lives* (New York: New York University Press, 2005), 76–96.

Chapter 1

GENDER FAILURE AND INDECENCY

Before beginning to read with cispicion, we need to recognize what we should be suspicious of. This chapter focuses on what makes my cispicious approach distinctive within a well-established line of feminist and queer hermeneutics of suspicion, as outlined in the introduction.¹ Suspicion has long been used to reveal aspects of gender and sexuality that have remained unacknowledged in malestream scholarship.² I draw on these traditions and bring them into dialogue with gender and trans theorists who further elaborate on the complexities of gender found when recognizing the impact of cisnormativity. It is a rich genderscape that I seek to illuminate through developing a cispicious reading strategy which can be applied to biblical texts. In so doing I will be extending theological and liberational hermeneutics of suspicion to address the underlying system of gender norms that make such recognition difficult. I therefore encourage a healthy scepticism of the apparent lack of gender diversity amongst the Bible's many characters.

Transforming a latent scepticism into a strategy for reading biblical narratives requires recognition of our own presuppositions and their impact on the reading process. Here I focus on exploring how the 'cis' component of 'cispicion', which relates to cisnormativity, is best understood. At its core, cisnormativity is quite simple. It is the privileging of those who consistently present as fixed and binary in their gender and sex. That, in turn, is in continuity with the sex assigned to them at birth – typified by manly, masculine men, and womanly, feminine women. Men will grow from the boys assigned male at birth, while (only) women and girls were assigned female. Such are the only natural and normal – therefore privileged –

---

1. As discussed in the introduction, Elisabeth Schüssler Fiorenza is particularly associated with the development and refinement of suspicious hermeneutics; see Schüssler Fiorenza, *In Memory of Her*; *Bread Not Stone [1984]*; *But She Said*; *Wisdom Ways*. See also Esther Fuchs, *Feminist Theory and the Bible: Interrogating the Sources* (New York: Lexington Books, 2016). For an example of queer approaches, see Guest, *When Deborah met Jael*; 'Looking Lesbian at the Bathing Bathsheba'; 'From Gender Reversal to Genderfuck: Reading Jael Through a Lesbian Lens', in *Bible Trouble: Queer Readings at the Boundaries of Biblical Scholarship*, ed. Teresa J. Hornsby and Ken Stone, Semeia Studies (Atlanta, GA: SBL Press, 2011), 9–43. I explore Guest's hermeneutics of (hetero)suspicion in Chapter 2.

modes of gendered being. It is a specific, nameable ideology and thus can be recognized within an appropriate, contextually determined hermeneutics of suspicion. This perspective then fails to recognize the validity of intersex, nonbinary, trans, and other gender transgressing people. Where recognition of any diversity occurs, it remains largely within the mutually exclusive categories of man and woman.[3] Yet the genderscape is far richer and more diverse than such presuppositions indicate. It is those cisnormative presuppositions that merit suspicion.

To illuminate how cisnormative presumptions inform our understanding of gender, I initially draw on the work of Jack Halberstam. Halberstam persuasively reveals that a more diversely populated genderscape is present, but our preconceptions render it, and those who populate it, incomprehensible. The result is that to be gender nonconforming – that is, to not fit within cisnormative expectations – is to fail.[4] Sometimes shortcomings, such as those I shared in the introduction, are accompanied by clearly identifiable failures. On other occasions the individuals in question appear unrecognizable, invalid, or otherwise unintelligible, meaning that even when present they get overlooked. Halberstam proposes low theory to recognize failure as a sign of discontinuity with expectations about what it is to be good, or laudable – or successful. He then argues for an irreverent playfulness that uses even the smallest of details as a way to reveal and make sense of such disregarded perspectives. It is the combination of Halberstam's attention to both failure and whimsy that make his work so invaluable in this project.

Halberstam's low theory finds a helpful conversation partner in the work of Marcella Althaus-Reid. Althaus-Reid, like Halberstam, uses approaches that confront the presuppositions associated with norms of gender and sexuality. She develops an indecent theology in recognition of the need for a postcolonial, queer approach that is profoundly influenced by liberation theologies and a preference for the poor.[5] She is particularly insightful as she argues that marginalization and erasure are both the cause and the effect of poverty. Poverty, she recognizes, need not solely be economic but does go hand in hand with being an outsider. She sees an essential part of theology to be a preference for the poor, that must address these omitted, impoverished perspectives. Althaus-Reid argues for the need to

---

2. Bugg, 'Explanation of Terms (Glossary)', 212. Malestream is 'a term marking the fact that history, tradition, theology, church, culture, and society have been defined by men and have excluded wo/men. Frameworks of scholarship, texts, traditions, language, standards, paradigms of knowledge, and so on, have been and are male-centered and elite male dominated'.

3. Connell, *Masculinities*, 66–80. Connell, for example, argues that there are multiple forms of masculinity, of which there is frequently a hegemonic, aspirational form for men to model themselves on.

4. Halberstam, *Queer Art of Failure*, 76–96.

5. Althaus-Reid, *Indecent Theology*, 4.

privilege indigenous perspectives particularly when they confront and provoke the certainty of malestream biblical interpretation and theology. She advocates for the value of a playful approach, something she describes as villainous, to develop new insights that share much in common with Halberstam's low theory.[6]

Together Halberstam and Althaus-Reid present a persuasive account of how and why gender diversity can and should be addressed in text and theology. Their commitment to challenging dominant ideologies, centring marginalised voices, and offering provocative commentary is inspiring. It provides a necessary continuation from the political aims inherent in biblical hermeneutics of suspicion. However, the cispicious model still requires a familiarity with gender as presented in queer theory to address and acknowledge its limitations for this project. I provide a brief overview of Judith Butler's contribution to the understanding of gender as socially constructed and performative.[7] Butler has rightly been critiqued for overplaying the social function of gender and its potential for deconstruction, with insufficient regard for an individual's life-context or the value of identity markers. As such I recognize the need to recognize the limited contribution of Butler's work and also integrate insights from some of their noteworthy critics in trans studies. Jay Prosser, Vivian Namaste and Julia Serano provide voices of dissent from trans perspectives and offer alternative insights into non-cisnormative gender expression.[8]

Serano uses her experiences as a trans woman to bring clarity to the cis assumption and privilege that underpin cisnormativity. It is through her work that I begin to conceptualize the gendered presuppositions and norms that so effectively – and insidiously – constrain biblical interpretation. Once cisnormativity becomes apparent, Prosser and Namaste's work adds invaluable insight into aspects of trans experience that particularly struggle for recognition. Prosser's area of interest is life writing, and he notes the importance of somatic experiences in trans autobiography. He argues that attention to bodies as part of the fullness of a person is essential, especially when encountering individuals in textual form. He reveals how such

---

6. Althaus-Reid, *Indecent Theology*; *Queer God*, 23–24.

7. Judith Butler, *Gender Trouble: Feminism and the Subversion of Identity*, Tenth Anniversary ed. (London: Routledge, 1999), xiv–xv. 'In the first instance, then, the performativity of gender revolves around this metalepsis, the way in which the anticipation of a gendered essence produces that which it posits as outside itself. Secondly, performativity is not a singular act, but a repetition and a ritual, which achieves its effects through its naturalization in the context of a body, understood, in part, as a culturally sustained temporal duration'.

8. Jay Prosser, *Second Skins: The Body Narratives of Transsexuality* (New York: Columbia University Press, 1998), 21–61; Viviane Namaste, *Invisible Lives: The Erasure of Transsexual and Transgendered People* (Chicago, IL: The University of Chicago Press, 2000), 9–23; 'Undoing Theory: The "Transgender Question" and the Epistemic Violence of Anglo-American Feminist Theory', *Hypatia* 24, 3 (2009), 11–32; Serano, *Whipping Girl*, 319–340.

accounts of trans experience and bodies struggle for recognition. This is particularly problematic when clear presuppositions about what trans bodies and experiences look like for a cis audience shape the presentation of those stories. He privileges self-articulated insights of transness and argues against seeking to place arbitrary and inappropriate divisions between mind, body and self. Prosser's insight, then, emphasizes the importance of a bodily sense of the sexed self, not just an assertion of gender through performative means. Namaste's work complements Prosser's, and she takes further the need to elevate trans perspectives, something she calls indigenous knowledge. For Namaste, trans people have been on the receiving end of a colonising discourse of (cisnormative) gender that seeks to undermine and invalidate identity. Trans perspectives are frequently overshadowed in favour of queer ones when it comes to theoretical engagement. Meanwhile cis voices are treated as authoritative when speaking of trans experiences they have studied with little or no reference to the perspectives they seek to represent. To counter that she advocates for trusting in the inherent authority of trans-authored personal and corporate narratives *and* she acknowledges that such voices speak against colonising powers that render the perspectives unacceptable. Those voices frequently will not resonate with those perspectives that speak over and for them – but that is what makes them so important. Such indigenous perspectives and body narratives are essential in recognizing a more diverse genderscape. By bringing these six authors – Halberstam, Althaus-Reid, Butler, Serano, Prosser and Namaste – into dialogue with one another I reveal the existence of cisnormative presuppositions *and* provide tools necessary to read beyond such presuppositions in biblical interpretation.

To set the scene I want to focus on *how* to reveal and understand gender failure through an indecently whimsical approach. Halberstam emphasizes that this is not about any individual's failure directly, but concerns a failure of intelligibility. Through the works that feature here he above all shows that there is a greater diversity of gender than our preconceptions ordinarily enable us to recognize. Althaus-Reid's indecent theology then complements Halberstam's reflections as she directs her attention to the erasure of certain gendered and sexed perspectives in Christian doctrine. Taken in combination, Althaus-Reid and Halberstam offer what I call an indecently whimsical approach to gender, that forms an essential component of my cispicious approach.

Whimsy: Jack Halberstam

Halberstam's work influences this project profoundly. He develops effective ways of revealing a complexity within today's genderscapes that is rarely acknowledged. Initially he begins by recognizing the presence of female masculinities before moving on to explore the challenges facing recognition of gender diversity, especially in the face of ubiquitous presuppositions that enable us to look beyond any apparent discontinuity. This work culminates in his low theory, which challenges dominant preconceptions and invites a playful, provocative response.

In *Female Masculinity* (1998) Halberstam writes evocatively of ways masculinity amongst female-coded and -identified people is overlooked, erased and excused in contemporary anglophone society.[9] A spectrum of butch identities gives Halberstam multiple vantage points from which to demonstrate non-male masculinities.[10] While Halberstam treats 'butch' as his primary frame of reference, he acknowledges it is a category in which lesbianism and female masculinity overlap significantly.[11] He reminds us how intertwined gender and sexuality are and how difficult it remains a challenge to neatly distinguish between one and the other. Nevertheless, sexuality shapes his masculine continuum, especially in the first half of *Female Masculinity*, with gender matters becoming more apparent in latter half.[12] He does,

9. Jack [Judith] Halberstam, *Female Masculinity* (Durham, NC: Duke University Press, 1998).

10. José Esteban Muñoz, *Disidentification: Queers of Color and the Performance of Politics* (Minneapolis, MN: University of Minnesota Press, 1999), 58. Muñoz offers a powerful commendation of Halberstam's *Female Masculinity*, when he writes that 'Halberstam dislodged masculinity from biological maleness, and in doing so opens up and reterritorializes the concept'. His commendation of Halberstam follows an equally pertinent reflection on the problematic power of masculinity when it remains intertwined with 'normalised heterosexual and masculinist privilege'. He writes: 'Masculinity is, amongst other things, a cultural imperative to enact a mode of "manliness" that is calibrated to shut down queer possibilities and energies. The social construct of masculinity is experienced by far too many men as a regime of power that labors to invalidate, exclude, and extinguish faggotry, effeminacy, and queerly coated butchness' (58). It is exactly Halberstam's ability to reveal gender beyond these 'regimes of power that labor to invalidate, exclude, and extinguish' gender diversity that makes his work so powerful and relevant for my project.

11. Halberstam, *Female Masculinity*, 152. Butch 'obviously refers to some form of dyke masculinity and refers to a historical equation of female homosexuality with female masculinity.' He continues with this caveat: 'But this history of overlap between sexual reference does not mean that female masculinity has not often been cast as a thorn in the side of contemporary lesbian definitions' – but the parallel recognition is not made about the problems for contemporary trans definitions.

12. Halberstam, *Female Masculinity*, 151. Halberstam provides a masculinity scale with reference to butchness, where androgyny is considered 'not masculine' and 'FTM' is very masculine. In the sliding scale, 'Soft Butch', 'Butch', 'Stone Butch' and 'Transgender Butch' fill in the gaps, with each progressively more masculine than its predecessor. This indicates scales of gender that complexify the male/female, masculine/feminine dichotomy as well as the cis/trans split. Joseph Marchal argues that Halberstam's 'continuum' is more effectively understood as 'a constellation [of female masculinity and ancient forms of androgyny] arrayed in relation to each other, but not in terms of progression or a hierarchy of value'. Joseph A. Marchal, *Appalling Bodies: Queer Figures Before and After Paul's Letters* (New York: Oxford University Press, 2020), 61. Marchal's non-linear model is a helpful clarification of how to understand Halberstam's continuum as it clearly emphasizes multiple locations each of which have equal validity. This maps on well to the more richly populated genderscape central to my cispicious model.

however, evocatively trace the history of pre-butch masculinities before moving to address contemporary butchness within a 'masculine continuum'.[13] Halberstam asserts that male masculinities rely upon other forms of masculinity for their structural stability, recognition and authority. Yet they also erase and marginalize those other forms in asserting their hegemonic dominance.[14] The idea that female masculinities are in some way subordinated, fake or rejected is *the* primary perception that Halberstam seeks to change. Rather, 'female masculinity actually affords us a glimpse of how masculinity is constructed as masculinity'.[15] His multiple examples clearly demonstrate the validity and authenticity of masculinity in its female forms *and* the construction of that masculinity.

As gender rather than sexuality become more dominant in Halberstam's narrative, different themes emerge of note for this endeavour. Diversity of butch identities and the interplay between male, female and butch comes to the fore in 'The Transgender Butch: Butch/FTM Border Wars and the Masculine Continuum'. Halberstam highlights the complex, and sometimes fraught, relationship between butch and FTM (female-to-male) identities. Both are sometimes included within the umbrella term of 'trans', but FTM indicates that the person in question is

---

The first half of his case studies (chapters 2–4) focus on masculine women and their sexual relationships with other women; see Halberstam, *Female Masculinity*. 'Perverse Presentism: The Androgyne, the Tribade, the Female Husband, and Other Pre-Twentieth-Century Genders' (45–73); '"A Writer of Misfits": John Radclyffe Hall and the Discourse of Inversion' (75–109); 'Lesbian Masculinity: Even Stone Butches Get the Blues' (111–139). However, in the second half, there is a shift. When Halberstam turns his attention to 'The Transgender Butch', 'Looking Butch' and 'Drag Kings' (chapters 5–7) the complex interplay of butch sexuality *and* gender becomes clear. In these chapters gender is more apparent with sexuality becoming only a secondary theme.

13. Halberstam, *Female Masculinity*, 141–173. The description of the masculine continuum refers to the title of the fifth chapter, 'Transgender Butch: Butch/FTM Border Wars and the Masculine Continuum'.

14. Halberstam, *Female Masculinity*, 1–43. Halberstam's assertion warrants consideration in the light of Raewyn Connell's explorations of the multiplicity of masculinities found amoungst (cis) men. See Connell, *Masculinities*, 66–80. Connell's exploration of hegemonic, subordinate, and marginalised masculinities is really helpful for establishing the dominance of masculinity. She acknowledges that it need not be limited to men, but sees that masculinity contributes to the subjugation of women associated with what she calls a 'patriarchal dividend'.

Connell's *Masculinities* was first published in 1995 but is not named in Halberstam's volume. Despite this her ideas resonate with Halberstam's description of the reliance on dominant or heroic masculinities on 'the subordination of alternative masculinities' (Halberstam, *Female Masculinity*, 1).

15. Halberstam, *Female Masculinity*, 1.

male.[16] Halberstam notes his choice for the term 'transgender butch' as one that acknowledges that 'there are a variety of gender-deviant bodies under the sign of non-normative masculinities and femininities, and the task at hand is not to decide which represents the place of most resistance but to begin the work of documenting their distinctive features.'[17] The permeability of boundaries between man, woman and butch can elicit tension between people who may get mistaken for each other, resulting in a lack of recognition or abuse due to misgendering. In other words, butches, trans men, nonbinary people and other gender nonconformers face a systemic lack of social acceptance. That can render invisible the differences between those very categories due to the absence of recognition of the diversity of genders beyond the binary. Nevertheless those borders remain important, even if the biggest border of all is that of social acceptability, but that is already antithetical to butchness. So, his attention to the 'border wars' highlights how there is at times a closely watched and policed boundary between the two groups, and one that may appear barely visible or even invisible to outsiders.

The discussion of border wars and identities is a necessary precursor to Halberstam's exploration of the ways in which butchness is (mis)represented in film. Here intentional performances of masculinity by women can and do draw attention to maleness and masculinity whilst also revealing just how endemic the problems of a lack of representation and recognition are. This, he argues, is why female masculinities in culture require attentive interpretation. How and why someone is represented in culture matters, especially when it confronts norms. Halberstam highlights how in films a butch's masculinity is softened, undermined, or erased to make *her* masculinity and gender palatable. Under the Hays Hollywood Production Code, which banned 'sex perversion' in films between 1932 and 1962, queerness was coded rather than made explicit.[18] In such films 'the masculine woman prowls the film as an emblem of social upheaval and as a marker of sexual disorder. She wears the wrong clothes, expresses aberrant desires, and is very often associated with clear markers of a distinctly phallic power.'[19] In adaptations from literature, however, the errancy of butchness is often 'barely' present as a veneer of femininity is added to make her more socially acceptable. That acceptability not only makes them recognizable as women to the viewer, but it makes them sufficiently decent to delink them from depravity. So, gender nonconformity becomes associated with perversity and must be diluted or erased in order to

---

16. Since publication of *Female Masculinity*, AFAB has developed as a more inclusive abbreviation than FTM for those assigned a female sex at birth but who later identify as trans, nonbinary or gender-nonconforming. When referring to Halberstam's use of FTM here (and Guest's in Chapter 2) I recall their chosen terminology; otherwise I opt for AFAB throughout. (Similarly, AMAB, assigned male at birth, supersedes use of MTF, Male to Female.)

17. Halberstam, *Female Masculinity*, 148.

18. Halberstam, *Female Masculinity*, 177.

19. Halberstam, *Female Masculinity*, 186.

preserve the dominant gender norms. Halberstam's 'barely' butch characters reveal how aspects of femininity are used to downplay masculinity in order to try and force someone into the identity of woman.[20] As I will show in Chapter 3, this approach is not limited to the Hays era films of the twentieth century but can also be found in the story of Sarai/h (Genesis 11:27–21:12). The emphasis on Sarai/h's femininity serves the same purpose, although I choose to argue for their nonbinariness rather than Halberstam's preferred language of butchness.

Where gender transgression and female masculinity cannot be diluted or erased is in the performances of drag kings. The performances are so overt that there is no opportunity to overlook genderfuckery taking place.[21] Here Halberstam identifies playful subversion in the art of the drag king. He describes 'kinging' as the core components of a drag king's gender performance. *Contra* the camp, excess performances of drag queens, kinging is typified by understatement, hyperbole and layering (allowing multiple genders to show at the same time).[22] These characters and performances then become exemplary revelations of the constructedness of (male) masculinity (in parallel with the effect of drag queens on femininity). They hold a particular value for their ability to deconstruct the link between maleness and masculinity. This will become particularly apparent in my analysis of Esau and Jacob in Genesis 27, as discussed in Chapter 4.

Female Masculinity is an invaluable resource in drawing attention to the diversity of genders and gender expressions. It emphasizes how important it is to be able to name and recognize others with similar experiences of gender to your own. Halberstam's examples do not conform to cisnormative expectations that

---

20. He later juxtaposes everyday female masculinity and its representation on stage and in film in the final chapter. In 'Raging Bull (Dyke): New Masculinities' (267–277) Halberstam uses photographs and self-reflection from his own involvement in the butch and lesbian communities to explore how everyday lives are lived. He concludes this chapter by reflecting on the value of forebears' stories to shape and affirm female masculinity in the array of forms he presents. The historical case studies and attention to different modes of butchness offer both a necessary counterpoint to the assertion that all masculinity is found in men and provides exemplars for those seeking to affirm AFAB masculinities.

21. Genderfuckery refers to the largely intentional 'mixing of masculine and feminine gender codes in ways that subvert the present bipolar gender system'. Erin Runions, 'Zion is Burning: Genderfuck and Hybridity in Micah and *Paris Is Burning*', in *How Hysterical: Identification and Resistance in the Bible and Film* (New York: Palgrave Macmillan, 2003), 93–114: 93. Runions traces this use back to Vern L. Bullough and Bonnie Bullough who argue that genderfuck is a politicised form of 'gender-bending'; see their *Cross-dressing, Sex, and Gender* (Philadelphia: University of Pennsylvania Press, 1993), 246. This political, playful approach to gender nonconformity is nicely encompassed by the term 'genderfuck'. In Chapter 2 I explore how Deryn Guest uses this concept in their exploration of biblical gender diversity.

22. Halberstam, *Female Masculinity*, 259–261.

purport that maleness is synonymous with masculinity on one side of a coin, and on the other are femaleness and femininity. These themes continue to focus Halberstam's attention throughout his subsequent works.

In *In a Queer Time and Place* (2005), Halberstam expands his work on representations of gender diversity in culture.[23] In moving beyond *Female Masculinity*, he theorizes ways to identify genderqueer and trans characters. Central to this, he imagines them 'outside those paradigmatic markers of life experience – namely, birth, marriage, reproduction, and death'.[24] Halberstam reads against dominant interpretations and envisages different presents and futures, free from a focus on the obligations of family and reproduction, and coherence to social norms. These are particularly valuable points of reflection for this endeavour, where the case studies are taken from ancestral narratives. In those stories 'paradigmatic markers of life experience' are at the forefront of the drama. Yet Halberstam shows that it is not only possible but important to look beyond those markers. His interpretations are frequently playful, informed by a clear articulation of the effects of a lack of social recognition. His primary example comes from the portrayal of Brandon Teena in biography and film.[25] Brandon Teena was trans masculine, and their brutal rape and murder has become synonymous with transphobic violence.

Halberstam provides a powerful caution when considering biographic accounts of trans people, such as Brandon Teena, and the subsequent representations of their stories in different forms:

> their lives were dismantled and reassembled through a series of biological inquires.... [T]ransgender biography [is] a sometimes violent, often imprecise project that brutally seeks, retroactively and with the benefit of hindsight, to erase the carefully managed details of the life of a passing person, and that recasts the act of passing as deception, dishonesty, and fraud.[26]

Here Halberstam seeks to disentangle their lives – and the authentic genders rendered deceptive – from accounts proffered by biographers writing for cisnormative audiences. He wisely notes that 'none of the transgender subjects whom I examine here can be definitively identified as transsexual, and none can be read as lesbian; all must be read and remembered according to the narratives they

---

23. Jack [Judith] Halberstam, *In a Queer Time and Place: Transgender Bodies, Subcultural Lives* (New York: New York University Press, 2005).

24. Halberstam, *In a Queer Time*, 2–3.

25. Halberstam, *In a Queer Time*, 22–75. See 'The Brandon Archive' (22–46) and 'Unlosing Brandon: Brandon Teena, Billy Tipton, and Transgender Biography' (47–75). Following their death, several biographies of Brandon Teena were published and their life was dramatized in the Oscar winning film, *Boys Don't Cry* (1999). Both the biographies and the film feature in Halberstam's analysis.

26. Halberstam, *In a Queer Time*, 49.

meticulously circulated about themselves when they were alive'.[27] It is striking and important for the reclamation of diversity of gender and sexuality in the past. However, it applies only where the individual is already recognized as having articulated (or otherwise recognizably expressed) their nonconformity.[28] For Halberstam, like Deryn Guest in Chapter 2, the interplay between gender nonconformity and sexuality is an enduring theme. While understandable it is something I seek to disentangle further throughout this chapter and the next. For now, however, I value Halberstam's recognition of self-asserted nonconformity even if it does not directly map on to today's terminology.

The challenge that results from Halberstam's analysis is how best to make such identifications where there is no self-articulated account. The problem is complicated when the story you do have is inextricable from the gender norms embedded in the transmission of that narrative. In other words, some characters are so influential that they contribute to the construction of our very perception of what it means to be gendered. Those characters then exemplify gender norms – especially when they appear to conform to cis and heteronormative expectations. Indeed, characters from Genesis such as Adam and Eve continue to be held up as exemplars for heteronormativity and bifurcated sex and gender norms.[29] For Halberstam, heteronormativity has a powerful effect on shaping the negative representation and reception of trans characters throughout time. He even notes that queerness presents an alternative way of considering the passing and flow of time within a given narrative, which challenges the dominance of such normative and normalizing ideas.[30]

In A Queer Time and Place offers useful techniques for identifying key differences between cis and trans gaze, which highlight the impact of gendered presuppositions and expectations. Halberstam shows a stark difference in how gender is understood between the ostensibly serious attempts to present trans individuals to predominantly cis audiences and comedic portrayals of gender

---

27. Halberstam, *In a Queer Time*, 49–50. Once again, the interplay between gender and sexuality comes to the fore in this quote. Halberstam posits both trans *and* lesbian possibilities for the subjects of his gender nonconforming subject.

28. See Jay Prosser, *Second Skins*, 9–12; CN Lester, *Trans Like Me: A Journey For All of Us* (London: Virago, 2017), 137–149. Prosser and Lester also acknowledge that historical figures do not easily map on to today's identities or labels. They both emphasize the value in finding individuals with whom it is possible to find points of resonance with today's trans experiences. Meanwhile Feinberg and Susan Stryker, in particular, demonstrate their strong desire for identifying trans forebears in their popular histories. Leslie Feinberg, *Transgender Warriors: Making History from Joan of Arc to Dennis Rodman* (Boston, MA: Beacon Press, 1997); Susan Stryker, *Transgender History* (New York: Seal Press, 2008). Despite the challenges facing such identification amongst historical figures, it is Halberstam's techniques for reclamation that make his work so evocative for my project.

29. Stone, 'Bibles that Matter', 14–25; 'The Garden of Eden', 48–70.

30. Halberstam, *In a Queer Time*, 1, 6.

nonconformity. Accounts such as the retellings of Brandon Teena's story serve as stoic, cautionary tales about the consequences of gender nonconformity. Halberstam argues that there are 'three different and often competing motivations' for the representation of trans life for cis audiences. One he identifies is 'stabilization', where the 'strange, uncharacteristic, and even pathological' features are stressed to reinforce a sense of wrongness and otherness.[31] Another is 'rationalization'. Here gender nonconformity is explicated through reliance on external sources that justify the errant behaviour; once those external factors have been removed the subject will, no doubt, return to the hetero- and cisnormative world.[32] The final category, 'trivialization', treats trans people and their lives as 'nonrepresentative and inconsequential' in order to keep them as perpetual outsiders.[33] Halberstam's recognition of the three problems builds powerfully on his work in *Female Masculinity*. He has moved from chronicling the way gender nonconformity appears on screen to offering insight into why those portrayals are so problematic. Central is his recognition of how ubiquitous these tropes are in the portrayal of gender nonconforming characters. Indeed, if these tropes can be found in accounts of biblical characters – whether in the narratives themselves or in subsequent interpretation – it further demonstrates the dominance of these forms of representation. As such a cispicious reading strategy must be attentive to them and aim not to reproduce them in biblical interpretation.

Halberstam's book gives clear examples of the way gender nonconformity is still rendered as subordinate to that of gender conformity. Mockery or violence remain likely, but Halberstam offers hope through queer renderings such as his. Counternarratives emerge and meaningful representations may still be found even when they appear paradoxical. It is 'paradoxical because it represents the desire to narrate lives that may wilfully defy narrative, but necessary because without such histories, we are left with only a bare trace of a life lived in defiance of gender norms'.[34] Thus Halberstam's trans gaze is typified by characters who seem anachronistic. They are affected by 'complex relations in time and space between seeing and not seeing, appearing and disappearing, knowing and not knowing' which then become invaluable in reading gender nonconformity.[35] In reclaiming those stories Halberstam emphasizes the importance of recognizing trans or gender nonconforming protagonists who speak for themselves and are given their own narrative within the broader story.[36] This, in turn, informs my own search for biblical characters who can be recognized in a similar way.

31. Halberstam, *In a Queer Time*, 54.
32. Halberstam, *In a Queer Time*, 55.
33. Halberstam, *In a Queer Time*, 55.
34. Halberstam, *In a Queer Time*, 50.
35. Halberstam, *In a Queer Time*, 78–79.
36. Halberstam, *In a Queer Time*, 87. Halberstam argues that 'the transgender character will be evoked as a metaphor for flexible subjecthood, but will not then be given a narrative in his/her own right'.

While *In A Queer Time and Place* is of significant value, some of the most meaningful insights are developed further in *The Queer Art of Failure* (2011).[37] Halberstam continues to address the way cultural artefacts can provide insights into how gender is understood, and how those same objects can disrupt our assumptions. The assumptions he is keen to disrupt include some from queer theory as well as those dominant in heteronormative contexts. In particular, *The Queer Art of Failure* offers a rebuttal to the antiheteronormative polemic by Lee Edelman, *No Future: Queer Theory and the Death Drive*.[38] Halberstam draws on his own earlier work to look for ways to reject heteronormativity without the overt antisocial and almost nihilistic approach of Edelman. This creates a space for Halberstam to envision ways for queerness to become identifiable as an already apparent rejection of heteronormativity. In doing so he moves away from recognizing problematic tropes such as stabilization, rationalization, and trivialization to identify opportunities for different possibilities.

The most noteworthy contribution for my work is Halberstam's articulation of low theory.[39] From the outset he asserts the importance of trusting in the authority of those whose voices have been overlooked, ignored or otherwise maligned. He then amplifies those perspectives. His chosen cultural sources similarly reflect underrepresented subjects. Halberstam describes it as 'a stroll out of the confines of conventional knowledge and into the unregulated territories of failure, loss, and unbecoming, [which] must make a long detour around disciplines and ordinary ways of thinking'.[40] Allying high culture (and theory) with hegemonic ideas of capitalist, heteronormative success, Halberstam finds celebration in myriad failures. Halberstam is compelled by Fred Moten and Stefano Harney's call to be a subversive intellectual, highlighting their recommendation to 'refuse professionalization, forge a collectivity, and retreat to the external world beyond the ivied walls of the campus'.[41] He adds his own encouragement to 'resist mastery' including through 'investing in counterintuitive modes of knowing such as failure and stupidity', privileging the 'naïve or nonsensical (stupidity)', and 'suspect[ing] memorialization ... because memorialization has a tendency to tidy up disorderly histories (of slavery, the Holocaust, wars, etc.)'.[42] Now counterintuitive, forgetful

---

37. Halberstam, *Queer Art of Failure*.

38. Lee Edelman, *No Future: Queer Theory and the Death Drive*. (Durham, NC: Duke University Press, 2004). For an alternative rebuttal, see José Esteban Muñoz, *Cruising Utopia: The Then and There of Queer Futurity* (New York: New York University Press, 2009). Where Halberstam argues for finding ruptures in the present, Muñoz advocates for fighting for a better, queer future in distinction from heteronormativity. Muñoz's future is almost eschatological in vision and is overtly political and relational in its creation.

39. Halberstam, *Queer Art of Failure*, 1–25.

40. Halberstam, *Queer Art of Failure*, 7.

41. Halberstam, *Queer Art of Failure*, 11.

42. Halberstam, *Queer Art of Failure*, 11–15.

and nonsensical interpretations can be privileged in seeking gender diversity and queerness. Halberstam sums up his approach, evocatively, by stating:

> I believe in low theory in popular places, in the small, the inconsequential, the antimonumental, the micro, the irrelevant; I believe in making a difference by thinking little thoughts and sharing them widely. I seek to provoke, annoy, bother, irritate, and amuse; I am chasing small projects, micropolitics, hunches, whims, fancies.[43]

I take this call to arms to be the central imperative in developing my cispicious approach as it will call into question established norms and truths in biblical studies. In turn this impacts the perception of sex and gender contained within the Bible.

The Queer Art of Failure serves as a culmination of Halberstam's work for this project as it draws together his desire to showcase gender nonconformity through history and culture with a strong, compelling theory for identification. It also demonstrates Halberstam's commitment to the (micro)political components of his work: 'The queer art of failure turns on the impossible, the improbable, the unlikely, and the unremarkable. It quietly loses, and in losing it imagines other goals for life, for love, for art, and for being.'[44] Here failure, and all that symbolizes for Halberstam, provides not only a new way of considering life but also makes space for that ordinarily considered implausible.

That the impossible, improbable, unlikely and unremarkable become the playground for whimsical interpretations offers great value for a cispicious reading strategy. It is such an evocative way to challenge the ubiquity of cisnormative and heteronormative forms of sex and gender. While I want to focus explicitly on cisnormativity as the ideology to which my cispicious strategy responds, Halberstam demonstrates the power of failure to reveal norms and presuppositions. In so doing I can retain the attention to failure, rupture and low theory but to move away from the focus on heteronormativity. Nevertheless, trans and queer theories, then, call into question the asserted universality of truths about sex and gender but are sometimes dismissed for being inconceivable or unrealistic. Thus, Halberstam's encouragement to naïvely make space for that perceived to be implausible not only enables readers to encounter gender diversity in the Bible, but also allows for unfamiliar interpretations aside from those propagated in the high forms of biblical interpretation. Halberstam's work provides the foundation for this project: his encouragement to seek and identify gender nonconformity, to pay close attention to the ways gender conformity and diversity are presented (and for whom), and to take a playful, irrelevant (and irreverent) approach to the dominant rules of possibility, success and high art provide essential components of what I call a whimsical approach to reading (for) gender. It is this whimsical approach that will form the basis of a cispicious reading strategy.

43. Halberstam, *Queer Art of Failure*, 21.
44. Halberstam, *Queer Art of Failure*, 88.

Across the three volumes discussed here, Halberstam demonstrates the need for a nuanced awareness of gender that extends beyond the binary model that aligns masculinity with men and femininity with women. His recognition of a masculine continuum is a powerful example of the way that there is a spectrum of gender expressions possible. Yet that does not necessarily provide an authoritative indicator of any one person's gender identity. What matters in the first place is making visible the way that gender is multifaceted and cannot be constrained merely to simple binaries. In response he indicates the ways diverse genderscapes are present but occluded and offers strategies for identification of that diversity. The way Halberstam reveals how gender diversity is made marginal – through trivialization, rationalization and stabilization – is particularly pertinent for biblical characters, especially as they struggle to hold the gaze, or attention, of the narrator. Meanwhile, Halberstam's attention to failure provides a way to recognize how small acts or experiences can serve to rupture presuppositions. This is helpful where biblical characters struggle to assert their agency through the more established models of speech, action, and location.[45] Here Halberstam offers tangible benefits to biblical scholarship because his approaches allow a way to closely read texts, paying attention to the small, micro, inconsequential details precisely to identify patterns of *non*conformity. In this way, the greatest contribution from Halberstam's work is the low theory itself. The cispicious approach developed here relies upon a willingness to be whimsical and to follow hunches in order to explore idiosyncrasies in biblical narratives. Where quirks have been long acknowledged but struggle for adequate explanation, Halberstam's low theory creates space for credible alternatives.

This approach is particularly powerful when brought into dialogue with voices who portray, represent and elevate those missing voices. This project engages with three such perspectives. The first is Althaus-Reid, whose queer, indecent theology complements Halberstam's low theory. The second voice is a chorus of contributions from queer approaches to gender. Third and finally, trans insights contribute a productive dialogue partner for my cispicious approach. It is to Althaus-Reid I turn next.

Indecency: Marcella Althaus-Reid

Complementing Halberstam's work, and sharing many similar aims, is the work of Marcella Althaus-Reid (1952–2009). Where Halberstam's focus on cultural studies does not engage with questions of religion, Althaus-Reid directs her attention to

---

45. This also applies to whether a character is granted a name. All the characters featuring in this project are, by design, narratively significant named characters. For further exploration of the significance of speech, action, location, and name in facilitating subjectivity for biblical characters, see Mieke Bal, 'Introduction', in *Anti-Covenant: Counter-Reading Women's Lives in the Hebrew Bible*, ed. Mieke Bal, The Library of Hebrew Bible/Old Testament Studies (Sheffield: Sheffield Academic Press, 1989), 11–24.

Christianity and the norms of gender, sex and sexuality it enculturates through Christian imperialism and the 'North Atlantic' academic hegemony.⁴⁶ She responds with a postcolonial and queer 'indecent' theology. Her insights reveal differences between rich depths of 'indecent' lives and the dimensionless theological motifs forcefully bequeathed on marginalized people.⁴⁷

Althaus-Reid's commitment to addressing exclusion with reference back to biblical and theological motifs comes through clearly throughout all her writing. Two of her works feature here because each offers a point of reflection for the development of the hermeneutics of cispicion. *Indecent Theology* (2000) opens discussion of a theology that is inherently provocative, queer and suspicious in its remit. It asks the reader to acknowledge, then challenge, differences between normalising perspectives on gender and sexuality and the everyday experiences of those who neither are treated as authoritative nor live within the parameters of the Christian North Atlantic.⁴⁸ In the second volume, *The Queer God* (2003), Althaus-Reid draws together taboo, highly sexual texts and concepts from the North Atlantic academic context with her indecent theology.⁴⁹ This work intentionally

46. Marcella Althaus-Reid, *Indecent Theology: Theological Perversions in Sex, Gender and Politics*, (London: Routledge, 2000b), 1–9.

47. Althaus-Reid, *Indecent Theology*, 72. She holds that 'a religious myth can become a mystification supporting an elite in power and hegemonic control instead of bringing symbolic elements of liberation to the community'. She traces the routes of her indecent theology through an interrogation of her male-dominated liberation theology. Of particular note is her exploration the genealogy of that theology which she traces back to Ricoeurian hermeneutics in her doctoral work, see Althaus-Reid, 'Paul Ricoeur and the Methodology'.

48. See Althaus-Reid, *Indecent Theology*, 11–86. A particular focus for much of her work is indigenous South American perspectives that have been silenced by Christianizing colonisation; women living in poverty provide particular case studies as they typify a group (class) perpetually excluded from discussions of theology *and* gender, sex and sexuality. Althaus-Reid suggests that the exclusion of such women contributes to the perpetuation of an erroneous belief that theology and sexuality can be separated. These women who live and work in sustained poverty regularly do not wear underwear under their skirts, something that also serves to emphasize their sexuality. She contrasts their day-to-day life, which is richly embodied and dirty, with the virginal, white, sparklingly clean representations of the Virgin Mary. Mary is received as an alien, parachuted in to be a universalizable role model for (Latin American) women, with no understanding of those women's lives. What differentiates the Argentine women from Mary is unrecognized. Althaus-Reid argues that the lemon sellers have little time or patience for the sanitized virgin Mary, instead finding female divinity and spirituality amongst the indigenous gods. Amongst the wealth of deities are tricksters, who enjoy sex and are vividly embodied in ways that resonate with these lemon sellers in a way that the cold, frigid, inanimate Mary cannot. Representation and recognition matter – and these long-held indigenous beliefs hold a living history that the imposed, narrow Christian biblical motifs can just not match.

49. Althaus-Reid, *Queer God*.

pushes at the perceived limits of acceptability and decency in order to show the construction of those concepts and the potential value of intentionally engaging with that which causes consternation.

Althaus-Reid's *Indecent Theology* evocatively highlights the disconnection between depersonalized theological motifs and everyday lived experience, including her own. Her interrogation of indigenous beliefs and practice in contrast with 'North Atlantic' Christianity and its imposition on her home country provide the basis for her call for indecent theology.[50] Althaus-Reid argues that insights offered by a rich diversity of human voices that can and should unpick Christianity and its beliefs. Those that do not find easy recognition within the dominant Christian imaginary are particularly important as they shine a light on the limits around what is acceptable. In turn those dominant Christian beliefs she calls decent because decency encapsulates a hetero-patriarchal and capitalist conception. Yet decency works by rendering those who are not decent as inherently indecent, and therefore unacceptable. The unacceptable, the indecent, are the frequently unnamed and unacknowledged victims of the violence of decent theology which is written 'over the dead bodies, the bodies of people who suffered and felt their life to be intolerable'.[51] For Althaus-Reid this culminates in hegemonic theologies that render diverse sexualities, genders and sexes (especially those not associated with cis and hetero-normalizing patriarchy) as abnormal. She responds by undertaking a process she calls the 'de-hegemonisation of theology as a sexual normative ideology'.[52]

Throughout *Indecent Theology* and *The Queer God*, Althaus-Reid includes diversity of gender and sex within the remit of her interrogation of the sexual. She describes that 'her task may be to deconstruct a moral order which is based on a heterosexual construction of reality, which organises not only categories of approved social and divine interactions but of economic ones too'.[53] When it constructs reality, to use Althaus-Reid's term, it does so through only affirming the validity of these different sex relationships. There is no meaningful social recognition or acceptance of sexual relationships between individuals of the same or similar gender. However this framework also does not give due credence to those who transition as they are not deemed as suitable partners for this reproductive sexual economy.[54] Here it is possible to see how heterosexuality

---

50. Althaus-Reid, *Indecent Theology*, 11–86. In a particularly evocative example she contrasts the diversity of gender and sexuality associated with indigenous stories and beliefs and the lives of those who continue to be excluded by the dominant Christian narratives or teachings. She offers the story of a group of lemon sellers as a quintessential example to establish her argument.

51. Althaus-Reid, *Indecent Theology*, 27.

52. Althaus-Reid, *Indecent Theology*, 7.

53. Althaus-Reid, *Indecent Theology*, 2.

54. For further discussion of the reproductive imperative at the heart of heteronormativity, see Michael Warner, 'Introduction: Fear of a Queer Planet' *Social Text* 29 (1991): 3–17, 9.

coalesces with social, divine, and economic interactions to create and maintain power dynamics. This, in turn, forms the basis of heteronormativity, where heterosexuality is the central point of reference for understanding human and divine interaction.[55]

Althaus-Reid's focus on the power of a reality built around a heterosexual construct is enormously illuminating. In fact, queer approaches, including those used by Althaus-Reid are committed to deconstructing those things valorised by heteronormativity. However, that also means that when she addresses gender diversity, it is done with an enduring focus on the impact of heteronormativity.[56] Cisnormativity, by contrast, is based on a social order constructed around the assumption that everyone is, or should be, cisgender. Sexuality is a secondary factor, rather than the primary one as in the case of heteronormativity. And, just as 'queer' is aligned with deconstruction heteronormativity, an alternative approach is needed to respond to cisnormativity. Nevertheless, her explorations of indecent sexuality and gender are enormously instructive. She offers alternative ways of understanding gender and sex through embracing indecent theology and methodologies. These three components cohere into the single category of the decent for Althaus-Reid. Her indecent theology then occurs beyond the constraints of hegemonic 'decency'. Although her remit is more wide-ranging than mine, her attention to language and the normalising power of hegemonic theologies of gender is persuasive. Through her use of the term 'decency', with reference to the norms of politics, sexuality, and theology, she shows how moves to challenge those norms are considered indecent, abnormal and shocking. In this project, I advocate recognizing the impact of such norms on our perception of acceptability – and then to intentionally look beyond those preconceptions.

With its focus on political, sexual and theological hegemonies, indecent theology continues in the legacy of South American liberation theologies. Althaus-Reid notes the shared heritage of indecent and liberation theologies, but remains cautious about uncritically aligning the former with the latter. She particularly critiques the theological tourism that accompanied liberation theology in the

---

Warner proposes the term 'reprosexuality' to account for 'the interweaving of heterosexuality, biological reproduction, cultural reproduction, and personal identity'. It 'involves more than just reproducing, more even than compulsory heterosexuality; it involves a relation to self that finds its proper temporality and fulfilment in generational transmission'.

55. As I continue to build a picture of heteronormativity I will address its benefits and limitations for this project. I will address Adrienne Rich's observations about the compulsory nature of heterosexuality and Susan Stryker's recognition of the emphasis placed on object choice, or choice of sexual partner. For further discussion, see pages 41–55 and the glossary, beginning on page 201.

56. She is not alone in this. In Chapter 2 I will discuss how this is apparent in Deryn Guest and Teresa Hornsby's work, even where they intentionally direct their attention to trans biblical interpretation.

1980s and 1990s.⁵⁷ Nevertheless, she firmly locates indecent theology within the liberation tradition that shaped her own theology. In doing so, she stresses the importance of a preferential option for the poor.⁵⁸ In contrast with her liberation theology forefathers, Althaus-Reid's understanding of poverty is intentionally broad; she emphasizes marginalization as the primary defining feature of poverty. Here the link between the economic and the sexual comes to the fore: erasure and marginalization make people poor; poverty is the result of marginalization as well as its cause. Here there are parallels between the strands of in/decent theology and the three groups of individuals who typify poverty in the Hebrew Bible: widow, orphan and stranger. While orphans do not explicitly feature in *Indecent Theology*, Althaus-Reid uses the motif of the stranger to symbolize the 'other' whose status as indecent keeps us from exerting a dominant, decent voice and leaves us on the outside. It is her attention to widows that epitomizes how individuals are made poor through the combination of (hetero)sexuality, politics and Christian theology.

Althaus-Reid reflects on the institution of levirate marriage as something intended to provide (limited) support to widows. She concludes that it is nevertheless oppressive, and widows become symbolic examples of those rejected by a Christianity – especially due to gender – because it cannot understand them or find a place or purpose for them. For a Christian woman, widowhood renders her

> a redundant Christian too ... [as] she has become socially excluded, an outcast, reduced to invisibility and hardship in the midst of the wealth she is creating. ... The woman is violated by a religious hegemony which invades the community's legislation on widowhood, and more than that, because gender categorisation, as in globalisation processes, deregulates and overrules women's lives leaving little if any space for autonomy to live.⁵⁹

Here Althaus-Reid shows how the cumulative effects of not being treated as having a voice worth hearing condemn individuals and classes of people, rendering them 'poor'. The preferential option of the poor enabled her to privilege the voices of those who are marginalised on the grounds of gender and sexuality. She calls

---

57. Althaus-Reid, *Indecent Theology*, 125–164; 'Gustavo Gutiérrez Goes to Disneyland', 36–58. Gustavo Gutiérrez features heavily in Althaus-Reid's critique, see Gustavo Gutiérrez, *A Theology of Liberation: History, Politics and Salvation*, trans. Sister Caridad Inda and John Eagleson, (London: SCM Press, 1974). Gutiérrez is particularly associated with the move in liberation theology to embed this principle as core to the (South American) liberation movement. He has become a notable figure in the internationalisation of South American liberation theologies.

58. Althaus-Reid, *Indecent Theology*, 2–4, 125–134.

59. Althaus-Reid, *Indecent Theology*, 191. Althaus-Reid's case study is drawn from Wamue, G. 'Gender, violence and exploitation: the widow's dilemma', in G. Wamue and M. Getui (eds). *Violence Against Women. Reflections by Kenyan Women Theologians* (Nairobi: Acton, 1996).

such perspectives 'unusual', highlighting the way in which unfamiliar perspectives are counter to the dominant norm.[60] In this project, I share the same aim. Althaus-Reid serves to encourage us to actively engage with underrepresented people as an essential part of working for liberation.

This example indicates the way Althaus-Reid acknowledges the power of hermeneutics. We encounter a deeply suspicious approach that necessitates a break with the past: 'The continuousness of the hermeneutical circle of suspicion and the permanent questioning of the explanatory narratives of reality implies, precisely, a process of theological discontinuity.'[61] She advocates for the need to trust in the fully developed, human experiences of those who do not fit within the hegemonic idea of decency. This, in turn, leads her to an intentionally queer focus. This emerges most clearly when she calls out readers who infer (only) heteronormativity in the Bible. She challenges the assertion that God is heterosexual based on the impregnation of Mary.

> Having sex with a woman cannot be taken as a proof of God the Father's heterosexuality, nor should Mary's pregnancy be related to a heterosexual conception of womanhood.... The fact that we know about the gender roles of God (the aggressive God of Israel, or the tender God of the New Testament) does not entitle us to homologise such gender performances with his sexuality.[62]

She returns to this idea frequently, consolidating her desire to disentangle assumptions about gender and sexuality with her commitment to integrate indecent (and thus omitted) perspectives. When discussing her queer, indecent approach, she directly challenges the perception that queering is synonymous with searching for oddities. She responds,

---

60. Althaus-Reid, *Indecent Theology*, 5. She reflects, 'The life experiences of poor urban women have the toughness of the struggle for survival in the dangerous and chaotic conditions of big cities. Not only does their economic struggle test them every day but there is a mixture of poverty and sexuality which makes of these women sometimes *unusual* poor women, and *unusual* Christian believers too. This unusualness is the condition of their indecency, that is, of the subversion of sexual and gender codes in their lives as a result of their struggle for life and dignity'.

61. Althaus-Reid, *Indecent Theology*, 4. For an example of where use of discontinuity is helpful in trans and intersex-informed theology, see Susannah Cornwall, 'Apophasis and Ambiguity: The "Unknowingness" of Transgender', in *Trans/Formations*, ed. Lisa Isherwood and Marcella Althaus-Reid, Controversies in Contextual Theology (London: SCM Press, 2009), 13–40. Cornwall's chapter provides helpful insight into the relationship between divine unknowingness and trans unknowingness through attention to God and God's (lack of) gender. Rather than directing my attention to the divine my interest is primarily in considering the gender of the human characters of the biblical texts in order to find points of resonance and dissonance with today's understandings of gender and sex.

62. Althaus-Reid, *Indecent Theology*, 67.

Queer is precisely the opposite: it is the very essence of a denied reality that we are talking about when we speak of 'Queering' or Indecenting as a process of coming back to the authentic, everyday life experiences described as odd by the ideology – and mythology – makers alike.[63]

Her observation is powerful and resonates with my cispicious aims to closely, carefully engage with what the text says. Althaus-Reid champions experiences as the basis for authentic insights into theology and biblical scholarship. This is, in part, because the ideology that informs heteronormative (and cisnormative) readings of the text become established and ubiquitous. Such ideology functions as both default and supremely valid in guiding our understanding, particularly of gender and sexuality.[64] When Althaus-Reid implores us to acknowledge the presence and impact of those norms – in the storyscape and around us today – she shows it is critical to work beyond the parameters of decency. For her indecent approach, and for my cispicious hermeneutics, there is a consistent understanding that we can look beyond the 'sexual organs, reproductive sexuality and expectations related to biology' when making definitive claims about the gender, sex and sexuality of biblical figures.[65] We must look beyond immediate assumptions and read beyond dominant ideologies in biblical interpretation and theology.

In *The Queer God* (2003), Althaus-Reid develops her indecent theology further by placing it in discussion with sexual ideas and experiences that are rarely considered 'decent'.[66] Amongst the themes she addresses are sodomy, libertinism, S&M, voyeurism and promiscuity. She uses these topics to provocatively destabilize the assumptions of decency that continue to render these sexual experiences as taboo or counter to Christianity. Meanwhile she clarifies what she means by quintessential decent theology, naming it T-Theology. This stands for Tradition and Theology, both of which are capitalized to highlight their asserted, unchanging power. T-Theology is the very North-Atlantic theology she decried in *Indecent Theology*, but here she also reaffirms her recognition of its restrictive and unchanging modality. '[T-Theology] seldom lets us perceive the historical presence of God in different, unfamiliar surroundings'.[67] While her aims in *The Queer God* are largely consistent with those of *Indecent Theology*, it is her attention to gender diversity and ways to interpret the Bible that are particularly relevant for this project. In the interplay between these two topics, she offers important critiques of

---

63. Althaus-Reid, *Indecent Theology*, 67.
64. See Sumerau, Cragun and Mathers, 'Cisgendering of Reality'. A fixed, binary gender model in religious teaching leads to the perception of a similarly fixed genderscape in the contemporary world. They particularly direct their critique to address the problems of cisnormativity. This is a notable and welcome distinction from those projects that continue to only address heteronormativity.
65. Althaus-Reid, *Indecent Theology*, 74.
66. Marcella Althaus-Reid, *The Queer God* (London: Routledge, 2003).
67. Althaus-Reid, *Queer God*, 33.

the language and understanding of embodied experiences, especially where they do not conform to dominant, decent gender norms.

Althaus-Reid continues to direct her attention to the plight of the impoverished. She builds on her earlier, briefer, exploration of the biblical figure of the stranger as the symbolic poor other, now with a compelling playfulness. In *The Queer God* she draws on another model of an outsider: the stranger. Not only is the stranger a typical example of the other, but a quintessential stranger also becomes the villain. '[A] villain was a rustic villager, an evil and at the same time a poor person, and as such, is the representation of what today we would call the dangerous stranger at our gates,'[68] she says. T-Theology has tamed 'the villainous vocation,' making poverty and sexuality evil strangers.[69] She posits indecent theologies that would seem villainous through 'sexual storytelling, traditions of sexual (and not just gender) rebelliousness in the church and also in queer literature and even films.'[70] The interpretations Althaus-Reid provides are intentionally scandalous; she uses polemical examples to incite further discussion of the limits we place on gender, sex and sexuality through her idea of the theologian-villain. The sexual stories she plays with are not primarily drawn from the Bible, however she deftly weaves biblical themes and motifs into her argument.

One way Althaus-Reid centralizes biblical imagery in her theology is in clarifying further the aims of her project: 'In the biblical sense, a theology which aims (as only Queer Theology can) to scandalise, that is, to be a stone on the road to force theologians to stop, fall down, while pausing in their pain and thinking in the pause.'[71] Here the Bible and the theology it inspires are essential to queer interpretative practice; in combination queer theory and practice coalesces with the Bible to aid theological insights – but not without discomfort for many. The readings Althaus-Reid advocates break away – indeed liberate – from 'oppressive reading [that] weakens us and even "robs" us of our sense of identity'.[72] To achieve such reading she encourages a multiplicity of interpretations, including those that find insight through interpretative perspectives that are overlooked or deemed too shocking, hyperbolic, or polemic for decent audiences. To use Althaus-Reid's terms, they should be queer, villainous and definitely indecent.

Where the juxtaposition between overtly shocking, provocative and villainous readings comes to the fore for a cispicious reader is in Althaus-Reid's exploration of bodies. She consolidates her approach by referencing the quotidian experiences of gender and sex. She reminds readers that indecency is part of everyday life for so many people who do not conform to hetero- or cisnormative expectations. Bodies, particularly transgressive ones, are sites of knowledge, enjoyment, and observation (including voyeurism): 'these bodies are not the usual ones: they are

---

68. Althaus-Reid, *Queer God*, 23.
69. Althaus-Reid, *Queer God*, 23–24.
70. Althaus-Reid, *Queer God*, 24.
71. Althaus-Reid, *Queer God*, 35.
72. Althaus-Reid, *Queer God*, 79.

libertine bodies, these bodies are unsettled and also produce tentative, unsettled reflection. We may call them nomadic bodies.'[73] These nomadic bodies highlight the potential for movement, change and transition. They can find homes in multiple locations – or through multiple gendered interpretations – and are in marked contrast to the immovability of T-Theology. However, eventually we and they fade into and out of coherence, especially in a context where they seem offset at an angle to everything (and everyone) else around them.[74] Indecent bodies are stuck in a perpetual cycle of being recognizable and unrecognizable which emphasises their strangeness and nomadic movement.

Stranger and nomad connote the potential to move, to cross borders, beyond (human, decent) limits, and correlate with my own sense of being an unsettled dweller in a gendered space not sufficiently my own.[75] In my case, I find myself feeling like an interloper in the category 'woman', fearful that I will be discovered to have neither right nor desire to be here but equally having no strong pull to any other discernible location. The language of nomad and stranger – on the move, not fixed or familiar, and (at least slightly) othered – offers points of recognition. Althaus-Reid evocatively describes the value of identifying such nomadic and migratory patterns as influencing text and interpretation. She then argues that we must be willing to play with and find meaning in 'interpretative clues and perspectives [that] may appear and disappear (and re-appear again).'[76] These glimpses may be fleeting, and offer a tantalizing possibility for one reader, but not another. Or they serve a limited purpose and need not always present characters favourably through our chosen lens. She encourages a willingness to engage in interpretations that may appear incoherent. Do they reveal, and revel in sites of gender, sex and sexuality, and reconsidering/reconceiving interrelationships and inbetweenness?[77] For Althaus-

---

73. Althaus-Reid, *Queer God*, 48.

74. Yannik [Annika] Thiem, 'No Gendered Bodies without Queer Desire: Judith Butler and Biblical Gender Trouble', *Old Testament Essays* 20, 2 (2007), 456–470: 457. Thiem writes, 'Our becoming sexed and gendered takes place at the intersections of relations of power and trajectories of desires. When bodies become sexed and gendered at an angle to the culturally normative, they in effect become "queered". Equally, social practices and expectations are queered when we inhabit them in ways that do not fully conform to social norms, and so mobilize bodies and practices as sites for renegotiating these norms'. I find this particularly helpful imagery when discussing the sense of being at odds with the norms encompassing us.

75. See Rebecca E. Wiegel, 'Trans Historiography and the Problem of Anachronism: Eunuchs and other Non-Men in Matt 19:1–14' (Society of Biblical Literature Annual Meeting, Denver, CO, 19 November 2018). Wiegel's work complements the idea of the nomadic, moving, transitory nature of biblical and theological transness. She persuasively argues that there is significant potential for finding trans representation in amongst biblical characters who move between modes of intelligibility within their narrative.

76. Althaus-Reid, *Queer God*, 81.

77. Althaus-Reid, *Queer God*, 81–84.

Reid, like Halberstam, a reader's challenge is to revel in the implausible and to place interpretative value in indecent indications of gender, sex and sexuality. This is most effective when done whilst recognizing that inherited interpretations and implied narrative links are as open to reinterpretation as the texts themselves.

Althaus-Reid offers an exciting, albeit challenging, way to re-approach texts starting from the position that gender, sex and sexuality are fluid and exist in ways long understood to be improbable. Althaus-Reid brings these themes together when she presents the patriarchs of Genesis as 'you and me figures', rich in sexuality and sensuality, in secrets and closets, and in diversity of experiences far beyond those constrained and contained in the biblical texts.[78] Within those stories, she encourages readers to explore queer (and by extension trans) traces in the lives of the characters. Such traces can and should inform the interpretations we make when looking to identify (with) literary and historical forebears, she argues.[79] She highlights the ancestral narratives as a suitable playground for her approach. She initially writes, 'I am tempted to think that the patriarchs were also people like Marx and Eleanor, "people like you and me", people of passions and contradictions, of awareness and innocences, people of closets and secrets'.[80] Rather than offering a close reading, she treats the biblical characters as figures who represent us, and others like us. She que(e)ries whether the patriarchs were like us in their loves and in their lives, inviting readers to consider the extent to which they left 'queer traces of their lives in their stories and times'.[81] She posits a pertinent but whimsical question when she asks whether the patriarchs were 'trans-sexuals in the sense that they were trans-border travellers, that is patriarchs in a journey of crossing (or desiring to cross) the borders of the law of sexuality in their times?'[82] Again we see the link between the nomad and stranger, who lives at the border, crossing between known and unknown, from the familiar, safe, acceptable to the alien, dangerous and indecent. The use of 'trans-sexual' to refer to 'borders of the law of sexuality' is noteworthy for its resonance with transness and their relationship with borders of cisnormative sex and gender. By drawing on the familiarity of the patriarchal figures, Althaus-Reid also emphasizes the significance of the characters in the Hebrew Bible along with their link to subsequent patriarchy and T-Theology: 'Queering the Scriptures will always be a project related to rereading the patriarchs, for patriarchy is not a transcendental presence but has agents responsible for its order. To deconstruct the patriarchs means to deconstruct the law, for justice requires the vigilant revision (new visions) of the ideological construction of the divine and the social.'[83] There are few characters more appropriate for an indecent,

78. Althaus-Reid, *Queer God*, 77–79.
79. Althaus-Reid, *Queer God*, 78.
80. Althaus-Reid, *Queer God*, 77–78.
81. Althaus-Reid, *Queer God*, 78.
82. Althaus-Reid, *Queer God*, 78.
83. Althaus-Reid, *Queer God*, 107.

or for that matter cispicious, interpretation than those of the ancestral narratives. These reflections do not provide detailed readings of these texts, but Althaus-Reid offers an enticing provocation to return and read these familiar stories more closely in the light of her indecent approach.

Indecent Whimsy

The contributions from Althaus-Reid, through *Indecent Theology* and *The Queer God*, provide a fascinating, sometimes joyfully provocative companion to those of Halberstam. While Althaus-Reid demonstrates the need to play with language and concepts in her encouragement to be villainous and indecent, libertine, voyeuristic, incoherent or submissive, none of her chosen terms map directly on to my project. I follow her encouragement to break rules, to look beyond human concepts such as decency and normality to open up possibilities for biblical interpretation, but I feel compelled by Althaus-Reid to find language that works for my purposes. My project is informed by queer theories, biblical studies and indecent theologies, and is directed primarily to matters of gender and sex. Similarly, it is informed by trans theories, which I discuss in the next section, but it is not bound solely to any of those approaches. Rather I draw from Althaus-Reid in order to focus on reading against cisnorms specifically and to find appropriate language for this context.[84]

When Althaus-Reid advocates for theological discontinuity, she is arguing in parallel with Halberstam's approach in *The Queer Art of Failure*. Both Althaus-Reid and Halberstam find value in breaking with traditional understandings of texts and suggest an inherent value in ruptures in continuity. Sometimes, as in Althaus-Reid's examples, breaking the cycle of recitation and re-inscription of gendered theologies or biblical interpretations can lead to a new appreciation of older sources, such as the indigenous divinities. Althaus-Reid draws from lives rendered indecent to ask questions of biblical interpretation and theology. In doing so she actively considers – and integrates – ideas that seem counterintuitive, hostile or antithetical to earlier interpretations. Halberstam makes similar observations when advocating for use of his low theory. Even where breaks in the continuity of a narrative are subtle, Halberstam argues that the value of characters is found in their rejection of cisnormative and heteronormative modes of understanding. Both Halberstam and Althaus-Reid encourage a disregard for the

---

84. I use the term cisnorms to describe the everyday presence of cisnormativity. Foundational is the expectation that there are only two, opposite sexes. Genders must correspond with the sex assigned at birth and neither can be changed with any sense of authenticity. Gender expression must also follow the same lines: men must be masculine and women feminine. While there are spectrums of socially acceptable gender behaviour, such as those outlined by Connell in *Masculinities*, those spectrums have limits. Crossing those limits leaves the person at risk of discrimination or erasure, as outlined by Halberstam, above. For an expanded definition of cisnorms, please see the glossary, p. 202.

apparent immutability of historical or genealogical context setting and instead advocate a break with traditional modes of being. For Althaus-Reid this is symbolized by decent, T-Theology and its colonising power. It is then through a playful, provocative theology and biblical interpretation that marginalised voices can become apparent. When reading with cispicion, such discontinuity is valuable as characters can be freed to move beyond previous interpretations through setting aside the need to conform or be easily contextualized.

Both Halberstam and Althaus-Reid acknowledge the profound differences between privileged perspectives and their marginalized counterparts. Each emphasizes the threat of unintelligibility for those who are outside: the indecent and the failures. However, failure and indecency reflect back on the presuppositions that inform our conceptualisation of success and decency. None of the individuals who feature in Halberstam's case studies or Althaus-Reid's stories are failures – each has been failed. The whimsical indecency inherent to both responses powerfully emphasizes the limitations of the very presuppositions Halberstam and Althaus-Reid critique. I share their commitment to irreverently play with these norms and adopt their indecent whimsy as a central piece of the hermeneutics of cispicion.

Despite the value of the indecently whimsical approach, both Halberstam and Althaus-Reid address the complexity of gender *and* sexuality. In the next section I briefly explore the complex interplay between gender and sexuality within the queer paradigm that is so central to Althaus-Reid and Halberstam's approaches. However there remains a need to integrate real-life experiences of those most directly and negatively impacted by the effects of cisnormativity. I then turn to Serano, Prosser and Namaste, who each advocate for a more narrowly focused approach to engaging with gender. They emphasize the importance of privileging trans insights when applying low theory, with each contributing to the understanding of what is important when reading accounts of gender diversity.

Building a Diverse Genderscape

Recognizing gender diversity is a central component of both queer and trans modes of scholarship. Different aspects of that diversity are privileged in each case. In order to respond with appropriate suspicion to cisnormativity it is helpful to clarify what that specific ideology encompasses. That begins with identifying core differences between queer and trans approaches to gender. At the core these relate back to the distinctions between cisnormativity and heteronormativity.

Through a queer paradigm gender and sex are most likely to be understood as socially constructed and can – and frequently should – be deconstructed. Gender and sex form parts of a trifecta alongside sexuality and all coalesce in heteronormativity. Heteronormativity privileges opposite sex relationships and enables heterosexuality and cisnormativity to be seen as the only normal, natural ways of being. A queer response pulls apart the propriety and stability of such objects – gender, sex, sexuality; heterosexuality, heteronormativity.

Trans, meanwhile, is not so inherently deconstructive. Prosser and Serano emphasize that it is important to be able to be the man, woman, or nonbinary person you know you are, and to be recognized and affirmed in that personhood by others. The problem that limits the recognition of such gender diversity then comes primarily through cisnormativity. It becomes almost impossible to gain understanding for those experiences precisely because gender diversity is not treated as natural or normal. There is less overt interest in sexuality when approaching gender through a trans paradigm. Susan Stryker, for example, argues that queer defaults towards matters of sexuality over those of gender, and there is a need to address trans experiences in history and in contemporary society that are not contingent on an individual's sexuality.[85]

Through the contributions of Halberstam and Althaus-Reid, queer approaches have a profound influence on the hermeneutics of cispicion. However, I want to make explicit three limitations of a queer model that become clear through engaging with trans voices.[86] First, queer's deconstructive engagement with gender illuminates the problems of gender norms, but frequently remains divorced from the lives and contexts of those it seeks to serve. Second, cisnormativity is a specific problem in its own right. It may be heavily intertwined with heteronormativity, but also functions in distinct ways that need to be recognized. Finally, the theories and experiences that contribute to a cispicious reading strategy must acknowledge the importance of trans embodiment, social and textual location, and personal identity in understanding (trans) sex and gender.

Beyond Que(e)rying Gender

Halberstam and Althaus – Reid highlight the problems inherent within hegemonic norms of gender, sex and sexuality. Each term requires close attention before addressing how they coalesce in heteronormativity. Sex and gender have a complex and highly intertwined history, making it almost impossible to disentangle one from the other. In shorthand terms, sex relates to the body, including the primary and secondary sex characteristics. Gender, by contrast, represents social and interpersonal expressions, identities and performances. Each relates to and shapes the other and neither can nor does exist in isolation. I consider each to be socially

---

85. Stryker, *Transgender History*; '(De)Subjugated Knowledges: An Introduction to Transgender Studies', in *The Transgender Studies Reader*, ed. Susan Stryker and Stephen Whittle (New York: Routledge, 2006), 1–17.

86. For further discussion of the need to address trans perspectives directly and to integrate an intentionally trans approach to rhetorical study see GPat Patterson and Leland G. Spencer 'Towards Trans Rhetorical Agency: A Critical Analysis of Trans Topics in Rhetoric and Composition and Communication Scholarship', *Peitho* 22, 4 (2020). While the centrality of their argument aligns with my own, their encouragement for more sustained attention to rhetorical study and agency extends beyond the scope of this work.

and contextually constructed. However, each also relates to integral parts of selfhood and identity that cannot be solely recognized by an exclusively social matrix. In this project sex translates into references to the observable body: that which is visible to someone beyond yourself. In the interpretations I posit in Chapters 3 and 4, gender relates to expressions of the self: making our own sense of ourselves apparent, especially through action and speech. That is a necessary simplification of these difficult concepts. While it is helpful to identify the core function of each term for the later cispicious interpretations, it is also valuable to understand some of the complexity and debate surrounding the terms.

I follow Thomas Laqueur's recognition that the apparent authenticity, immutability and truth of sex changes throughout time and context.[87] Laqueur provides a helpful account of key changes in the scientific perception of sexed bodies, focussing on European history. He argues that until the eighteenth century an enduring perception had lingered 'that women had the same genitals as men except that, as Nemesius, bishop of Ernesa in the fourth century, put it: "theirs are inside the body not outside it".[88] Only much later came the discovery that female bodies were significantly different anatomically from their male counterparts. He traces stories of those who have confounded the dominant perceptions of sex in their own era too. He includes examples such as Queen Elizabeth I, who intentionally channelled her masculinity as regent. In another case he draws from cases discovered by Ambrose Paré (1510–1590) and Michel de Montaigne (1533–1592). Each discovered a man who, at birth, has been named Marie and treated as female but unexpectedly presented with male genitalia in their teenage years.[89] Thereafter each was known as a man, as they had been seen to be in possession of the necessary attribute: a penis. Throughout both these sets of examples he recognizes that sex is understood to be a sociological system – something that continued until the seventeenth century.[90] Laqueur begins to show the power of sex to create someone's identity, not solely to assign a social status. Equally his recognition of the power of sex *only* reflects its social function, not an internal, personal or psychological sense of identity.[91]

---

87. Thomas Laqueur, *Making Sex: Body and Gender From the Greeks to Freud*. (Cambridge, MA: Harvard University Press, 1990).

88. Laqueur, *Making Sex*, 4. Laqueur cites Nemesius of Ernesa, *On the Nature of Man*, ed. William Tefler (Philadelphia: Westminster Press, 1955), 369. These beliefs follow Galen's teachings from two centuries earlier. Laqueur clarifies 'in this world the vagina is imagined as an interior penis, the labia as foreskin, the uterus as scrotum, and the ovaries as testicles'.

89. Laqueur, *Making Sex*, 7, 125–127.

90. Laqueur, *Making Sex*, 8.

91. It is important to note that Laqueur's recognition of sex as an ontological category is contemporaneous with Butler's work on gender performativity, discussed further below. Both Butler and Laqueur recognize the power of sex to construct identity but Butler will take this further by indicating ways to trouble the relationship between it and gender.

Most recently, within the scope of Laqueur's work, comes the arrival of psychoanalysis via Freud. For the first time, the mind – notably the ego, superego and id, along with the subconscious, preconscious and conscious – could be recognized as having an impact on sex, sexual identity and selfhood. Laqueur, like Ricoeur, draws on Freud to emphasize complexity.[92] While Ricoeur emphasizes the importance of suspicion, Laqueur highlights how the understanding of sex changed following Freud's psychoanalysis. Meanwhile, in the 1930s, came the scientific discovery of hormones. Psychology and hormones had always shaped sex, even though the recognition of each is very much a feature of modernity. Yet at the same time sex became both part of identity and something that can be pathologized. Sex *and* identity became medicalized for the first time, with the result that scientific or medical knowledge was treated as authoritative for both. Laqueur's concluding remarks about Freud – and his commitment to the scientific method – emphasize how much complexity there continues to be in the understanding of sex:

> With all [Freud's] passion for biology, this preeminent thinker showed how difficult it is for culture to make the body fit into the categories necessary for biological and thus cultural reproduction. Two sexes are not the necessary, natural consequence of corporeal difference.... The ways in which sexual difference have been imagined in the past are largely unconstrained by what was actually known about this or that bit of anatomy, this and that physiological process, and derive instead from the rhetorical exigences of the moment.[93]

Such recognition really does highlight the striking disconnection between sexual diversity across bodies and the understanding of those differences in society. His clearly asserted recognition that the sexual dichotomy is neither necessary nor natural cannot be overstated.[94]

Yet the cultural construction of sex becomes apparent when gender comes into the mix too. Butler recognizes the importance of observation of genitalia when first encountering a person: at birth an assignation is made and that sets the trajectory for life thereafter.[95] While Butler argues this is the start of the process of forming someone's gender, it is also the formalized recognition of sex. That assignation is made on a visual appraisal and those observations are treated as authoritative. Yet, as Prosser and Serano emphasize so powerfully, sexed bodies matter. Prosser emphasizes the importance of resolving a disconnection between

---

92. Ricoeur, *Freud and Philosophy*. For further discussion see p. 6–7.
93. Laqueur, *Making Sex*, 243.
94. Anne Fausto-Sterling argues that natural variation can be categorised across at least five sexes. She suggests that recognition of a plurality of sexes beyond just male and female aids understanding of intersexuality. Anne Fausto-Sterling, 'The Five Sexes: Why Male and Female Are Not Enough'. *The Sciences* 33, 2 (1993): 20–24.
95. Butler, *Gender Trouble*, 180.

one's physicality and one's sense of (gender) identity to allow the body to become a more recognizable representation of the self.[96] Meanwhile Serano openly shares her recognition of the powerful influence of hormones, particularly on her psychological self, as she began hormone therapy.[97] While she partially anticipated the physical changes the hormones provided, the internal changes to her psychology and sense of self were not as clearly foreseen. She remarks that as a biologist by background, she does not want to dismiss the significance of sex – and the differences between maleness and femaleness. She summarizes her perspective when she argues 'that certain aspects of femininity (as well as masculinity) are natural and can both precede socialization and supersede biological sex'.[98] It is then possible (and indeed necessary) to provide biological nudges to shape bodies more appropriately for the individual.

Gender, meanwhile, encompasses many internal, social and experiential aspects of identity and interpersonal relationships. As psychologist Meg-John Barker writes, 'a person's bodily sex, their psychological experience of gender, and the cultural norms and ideas of the gender in the world around them, are so inextricably linked that it is probably impossible to ever fully tease them apart'.[99] While sex markers are a common indicator of someone's gender, it is helpful to see this as a matter of correlation rather than causation. Like sex, gender is socially and historically contextual – it becomes socially constructed through interactions and the influence of social norms. The identification of the ways in which gender becomes apparent, and then can be troubled, come through Butler's work. However there is much to gender that warrants consideration before addressing Butler's key contributions.

As a social and cultural phenomena that impacts our sense of selfhood, gender is a multifaceted concept. Barker, for example, provides an inclusive and overlapping discussion of sex *and* gender that includes chromosomes, hormones, bodies, brains, identity, expression, role *and* experience.[100] The inclusion of sex markers like chromosomes, hormones and bodies emphasizes how much interplay there is between the two aspects of sex/gender. Yet it is important to recognize that our brains provide a psychological basis for our gender as well as having an impact on our sexed bodies. Such a psychological underpinning then provides the foundation for our identity, expression, role and experience. For Barker, sex/gender is best understood as a unified concept informed by interlinking biology (body, brain), psychology (personal experience, reflection) and social (cultural messages, life circumstances).[101] While there is a profound value in uniting these

    96. Prosser, *Second Skins*, 67.
    97. Serano, *Whipping Girl*, 65–76.
    98. Serano, *Whipping Girl*, 6.
    99. Meg-John Barker, *Gender, Sexual, and Relationship Diversity (GSRD)*, BACP Good Practice across the Counselling Professions, (Lutterworth, Leics: British Association for Counselling and Psychotherapy, 2017), 19.
    100. Barker, *Gender, Sexual, and Relationship Diversity*, 19–20.
    101. Barker, *Gender, Sexual, and Relationship Diversity*, 21.

terms, I continue to value the slight distinction that comes with keeping sex and gender apart. To map Barker's framework on to my own, the biological is associated with sex while the other two aspects remain with gender. Despite the overlap, recognizing gender and sex as distinct allows me to address how one area has warranted significantly more attention than the other.

One of the problems, explored in more detail below, came with the recognition of gender as a social construction. Much of the early responses, particularly (gender)queer ones, were to work to destabilize all gender under the auspices of destroying the gender binary and accompanying abusive ideologies (including patriarchy and heteronormativity). In turn such deconstructive approaches have led to a greater focus on what gender *is* and how it can be understood in more useful ways. Serano is largely consistent with Barker when she writes that gender is 'an amalgamation of bodies, identities, and life experiences, subconscious urges, sensations and behaviors, some of which develop organically, and others which are shaped by language and culture'.[102] Yet that umbrella still includes numerous ways gender works itself out in personal and public life. The first of those is gender *status*, namely whether we are most usefully described as trans, cis, intersex or nonbinary. Next there is gender *identity*, of which there are an array of identities including male, female, nonbinary, demigender, agender, genderfluid, bigender, androgynous.[103] Then comes gender *expression*, which relates to the social expectations aligned to masculinity or femininity. It can include social role, behaviour, mannerisms, hobbies and pastimes, attire, and adornment. Again, expression is a wide-reaching term that covers a range of our gendered lives but is acutely attuned to the social outworking of our gender identity and status, in combination with our sexed bodies. These gendered indicators provide the necessary context for making sense of our whole selves – including our sex. That, in turn, means that gender can appear to become the preeminent force in shaping sex – especially where the sexed designations applied to us at birth diverge from our gender. In other words, it is inordinately valuable for some people to pursue transition (including through hormones and/or bodily interventions) so bodies can be changed to better reflect gendered identity and self-identified ontology. This context, thus, serves as a helpful point to return to the broader framework in which sex and gender coalesce with sexuality. This is not least because sexuality – the intimate desires and interrelationships between people – functions as a marker for gender expression when it is underpinned by heteronormative *and* cisnormative expectations.

So, to heteronormativity, which is

---

102. Julia Serano, *Excluded: Making Feminist and Queer Movements More Inclusive* (Berkeley, CA: Seal Press, 2013), 107.

103. Barker includes all genders other than male and female under the umbrella term of 'nonbinary', however I provide an indicative list of examples to emphasise the plurality of identities. See Barker, *Gender, Sexual, and Relationship Diversity*, 28–29.

the dominant belief system that relies on fixed and binary genders and the certainty that heterosexuality is the norm that occurs naturally, that is, apart from cultural influences. All other sexual relationships are deemed culturally produced (unnatural), are regulated and defined in relation to heterosexuality, and are thus devalued. In this system, females and males (whose bodies are produced naturally) are assumed to be the only appropriate sexual partners.[104]

Here Teresa Hornsby brilliantly explains the link between gender, sex and sexuality as built upon the idea of compulsory heterosexuality. Through compulsory heterosexuality, sexual relations, between individuals of different (frequently described as opposite) sexes and genders, are celebrated as the only natural and valid expression of sexuality and become the regulatory system for gender, sex and sexuality. Adrienne Rich, who coined the term compulsory heterosexuality, notes that failure to conform renders an individual unintelligible, through removing recognition of gender, sex *and* sexuality.[105] For Rich, lesbians, in particular, become invisible as they conform neither to heteronormativity's model of opposite sex/gender relations and sexuality nor to androcentrism's male primacy. This renders such women as genderless and sexless, and therefore unintelligible. Here we encounter ways gender, sex and sexuality are immediately and essentially intertwined through both compulsory heterosexuality and heteronormativity. In turn, such a conceptualisation of heteronormativity is instrumental in queer theory, which seeks to respond to those norms by deconstructing them – frequently with a level of mocking, playful discontent that renders the norms asinine. Queer theory is political, confrontational and uncompromising, where binaries are resisted through 'subverting, undoing, deconstructing the normalcy of sex/gender regimes, cracking them open, focusing on the fissures that expose their constructedness'.[106]

Within queer studies of gender, Judith Butler's work is particularly prominent and represents something of a paradigm shift. It is also largely in response to Butler's work that trans theory sought to differentiate itself more effectively from its queer sibling. While Butler's work indirectly shapes the interpretative tools developed in this project, their contributions to the understanding of gender and the growth of trans theory are important.

Butler draws on Rich's work and argues that gender and sex are socially constructed. They become tangible through the outworking of a model of

---

104. Teresa J. Hornsby, 'Introduction: The Body as Decoy', in *Transgender, Intersex and Biblical Interpretation*, ed. Teresa J. Hornsby and Deryn Guest (Atlanta, GA: SBL Press, 2016a), 1–12, 2.

105. Adrienne Rich, 'Compulsory Heterosexuality and Lesbian Existence', in *Feminism and Sexuality: A Reader*, ed. Stevi Jackson and Sue Scott (Edinburgh: Edinburgh University Press, 1996), 130–142.

106. Guest, 'From Gender Reversal', 9.

compulsory heterosexuality into which we all become unwitting participants.[107] This, they argue, becomes consolidated through performativity and recitation and reiteration.[108] Their ideas continue to have a profound and enduring impact on the study of gender. While sex and gender are socially constructed, Butler emphasises their meaning for the intelligibility of bodies, individuals and the self. Performativity is the name they give to the way gender is constructed, repeated and reinscribed throughout an individual's life. It frequently, even usually, corresponds with the sex assigned at birth. Both sex and gender rely upon and reify one another to ensure apparently inscrutable stability. A new-born child has their gender and sex ascribed on (or even before) arrival, they are named accordingly and socialized in such a way that they perform gender according to those expectations.[109] The very performance itself is rarely conscious or intentional. Rather it is shaped, informed and enacted according to the nebulous prompts and cues encountered (and affirmed) by each one of us.

By asserting that gender is performatively and socially constructed, Butler provides an evocative way to 'trouble' gender, using their term and to move away from problematic, restrictive (especially hegemonic) norms. Reconceiving modes of gender performativity gained traction within queer theory as a way to deconstruct and reimagine modes of gendered being free from the constraints of compulsory heterosexuality. Yet Butler's *Gender Trouble* is criticized for being too ephemeral and theoretical, especially where it appears to disregard the bodily aspects of being both sexed and gendered.[110] Following concern that they overlooked embodiment, they published *Bodies that Matter* (*BTM*) as a corrective or clarification. In *BTM* they move to the language of citation, reiteration and (re) inscription, explicitly including bodies within the parameters of gender's social construction.[111] However, for some trans theorists this rather infamously misuses trans lives as idiomatic examples of gender *de*construction.[112] Namaste argues that

---

107. Judith Butler, 'Against Proper Objects', *Differences: A Journal of Feminist Cultural Studies* 9, 4 (1991), 387–407; *Gender Trouble*.

108. Judith Butler, *Bodies that Matter: On the Discursive Limits of 'Sex'* (New York: Routledge, 1993); *Gender Trouble*, 33. 'In this sense, *gender* is not a noun, but neither is it a set of free-floating attributes, for we have seen that the substantive effect of gender is performatively produced and compelled by the regulatory practices of gender coherence. Hence, within the inherited discourse of the metaphysics of substance, gender proves to be performative – that is, that is constituting the identity it is purported to be. In this sense, gender is always a doing, though not a doing by a subject who might be said to pre-exist the deed.... There is no gender identity behind the expression of gender; that identity is performatively constituted by the very "expressions" that are said to be its results'.

109. Butler, *Gender Trouble*.

110. For example, Prosser, *Second Skins*; Viviane Namaste, *Invisible Lives*; 'Undoing Theory', 11–32.

111. Butler, *Bodies that Matter*.

112. Butler, *Bodies that Matter*, 121–140.

Butler erases transgender subjectivity. Butler makes use of multiple case studies drawing from trans experience to justify their claim that the gender binary should be deconstructed. However Namaste sees this as Butler decontextualizing and disregarding the experiences of trans people who so clearly assert a clear, binary gender identity.[113] In other words, Butler identifies examples who do not wish gender to be deconstructed, they just want to get on with living their lives in a different sex to that assigned at birth without fuss or hassle. Namaste is not alone in critiquing Butler's appropriation of drag and transness to further their arguments. Prosser offers an insightful exploration of the benefits and limitations of Butler's work, concluding their approach to be too theoretical and divorced from lived experiences.[114] Meanwhile Serano highlights a distinction between Butler's more recent work and enduring queer (mis)appropriations of their earlier publications as the basis for explorations of gender that are cissexist. Her use of the term cissexist emphasizes the relative dismissal of trans, especially binary trans, perspectives while privileging cisgender voices critical of gender dynamics. Cissexism is a corollary to transphobia, but Serano highlights how this is about power dynamics rather than fear: cis (or at least apparently cis) voices continue to speak over and interrogate gender without due respect for, or engagement with, trans voices.[115]

Butler subsequently sought to backtrack from the difficulties associated with their case studies and has repeatedly declared their support for trans-inclusive and -affirmative gender theory and feminism.[116] They have subsequently published a more accessible and inclusive version of their gender theory. *Undoing Gender*

---

113. Namaste, *Invisible Lives*, 9–23. Namaste gives the example of Venus Xtravaganza, a sex worker and trans woman of colour who features in the 1990 documentary *Paris is Burning*. Xtravaganza makes clear that she wants nothing more than a 'sex change to make myself complete' and to settle comfortably into the role of wife. She is, however, murdered during the course of the filming (Jennie Livingston, 'Paris is Burning' (USA: Off-White Productions, 1990)). Namaste argues that Butler appropriates Xtravaganza and, in doing so, loses sight of the intersecting facets of her context such as poverty, race, status as a sex worker, and her clearly articulated binary gender.

114. Prosser, *Second Skins*.

115. Serano, *Whipping Girl*, 336–337. Serano opts for the language of sexism, including cissexism, rather than transphobia throughout her writing. She argues, persuasively, that the emphasis should be placed on the way one group are privileged to the cost of another. She also points out that transphobia is a misnomer in that violence directed towards trans people and people considered not to conform to cisnormative expectations is rarely, if ever, based on fear.

116. Judith Butler, 'My Life, Your Life: Equality and the Philosophy of Non-Violence' (The Gifford Lectures, University of Glasgow, 1–3 October 2018). They have subsequently made their own nonbinariness more explicit, especially in response to an upswing in high profile transphobia and hostility which tries to appropriate some of Butler's ideas about gender, see Alona Ferber, 'Judith Butler on the Culture Wars, JK Rowling and Living in

(2004) is largely a clarification – and simplification – of many of their earlier ideas.[117] It provides their clearest indication of the importance of having a gender that is intelligible to ourselves and others. They discuss the way that gender, especially in its most familiar, recognizable forms, provides a framework for acceptance and recognition of the humanity of another person. Where someone does not appear intelligible – i.e., they cannot be easily categorized as a cis- and heteronormative man or woman – that individual is othered and marginalized.[118] Here their argument finds agreement with Halberstam, who argues that representation (of trans people) only amongst marginal characters perpetuates rather than undermines abuse. Butler shows that there is a proximity to acceptability and recognition that gender conformity facilitates. Othering based on gender (nonconformity) has the power to render someone so socially unintelligible they are no longer deemed a living human being. They describe this social, figurative death and note that it can – and does far too often – precede a physical, literal death for individuals and groups of people. Through their 2004 volume, Butler advocates for close attention to the way gender is understood, and they argue that patterns of undoing can and should be challenged.

Butler has rightly been criticized for so focusing on gender, to the cost of sex and embodiment. However their success in drawing attention to the social construction and potential malleability of gender is also invaluable for this project. For me this comes back to the emphasis on compulsory heterosexuality and the corresponding ideology of heteronormativity. Butler's focus remains on these even when addressing gender diversity. As such the questions about performativity and social construction relate back to queer identity and politics. This leads to a key problem for this project: that is Butler's emphasis on deconstruction. When they draw on the experiences of trans and gender nonconforming people, especially in *Gender Trouble* and *BTM*, they focus on deconstruction. That destabilization is not only of the system of heteronormativity but also of the gender binary as a lynchpin of heteronormativity. In turn, Butler then treats their case studies as exemplars of deconstructing that binary rather than disassembling certain (cisnormative) privileges. It is not a case of diversifying what is already there, seeking capciousness or even understanding the pull of a clear location in the genderscape but dismantling

---

"Anti-Intellectual Times"', *New Statesman* 2020, 22 September, https://www.newstatesman.com/international/2020/09/judith-butler-culture-wars-jk-rowling-and-living-anti-intellectual-times. (In her interview of Butler, Ferber offers an idiomatic example of the very perception of gender that Butler and I argue against through the framing of her questions. Butler's response throughout emphasises the importance in recognizing and publicly validating trans and nonbinary individuals).

117. Judith Butler, *Undoing Gender* (New York: Routledge, 2004).

118. Butler, *Undoing Gender*. Butler describes this experience as being 'undone'. Undoing someone's gender ultimately leads to dehumanisation as gender is such an essential aspect of being human. Here Butler includes both social construction and embodiment in their exploration of gender.

the whole thing. The subsequent adoption of Butler's work as a cornerstone of queer praxis exacerbates the problem. A queer interrogation of gender frequently comes back to Butler to emphasize the importance of dismantling the oppressive gender binary – as encountered through heteronormativity. The result, as we will see in Chapter 2, is an enduring emphasis on sexuality alongside gender for one remains inseparable from the other. That, in turn, can lead to a consideration of gender diversity that overlooks the influence of cisnormativity.

My sense of the practical differences between a Butlerian, queer approach to gender diversity, and the one I advocate for in this project can be briefly summarized: a cispicious approach seeks to deconstruct cisnormativity and a constrictive genderscape. It is the restricted, binary options that I challenge, not the validity of a gender and sexed identity. In other words I want to recognize the importance of an understandable gender identity which may be that of a masculine man or feminine woman, or any of a multitude of other locations. Gender itself is not inherently flawed and so does not need to be removed. The categories of man and woman, male and female, masculine and feminine do not need to be deconstructed but there needs to be much greater recognition of an array of sexes, genders and identities. While I think Butler is getting closer to that point in *Undoing Gender*, until they shift their critical attention to cisnormativity specifically these problems are likely to endure.

A particularly insightful contribution comes through Butler's work on undoing and othering, as they understand that intelligibility is key to recognizing the humanity of another person. In fact, it is when Butler appropriated the life stories of individuals they did not understand well enough that they and their work has been most problematic. In that regard they represent a cautionary tale. Trans perspectives must be treated as authentic and authoritative. Yet this ties back, once again, to considering heteronormativity as a sufficiently adequate ideological framework to address the complexities of gender and sexuality. Butler has shown repeatedly that there is insufficient space for both. This leads me to argue more passionately for the need to recognize cisnormativity in distinction from its sexuality-focus and queer-attuned counterpart.

From critiquing established understandings of gender norms through to highlighting how a lack of gender intelligibility renders someone not recognizably human, the development of Butler's ideas corresponds with the different components of their legacy. Where Butler sought to differentiate their understanding of gender from those that preceded them, the trans theorists who follow seek to make further refinements. The primary concern of those scholars is to disentangle matters of gender from those of sexuality, including compulsory heterosexuality. A secondary concern seeks to employ trans theory (and experience) to broaden the genderscape and to reduce the risk of gender unintelligibility.

Recognizing Cisnormativity

While Butler's attention to gender is shaped by compulsory heterosexuality it remains important not to reduce people to their sexual desirability. It is not just object choice, recalling Susan Stryker's description, that ensures someone's gender is intelligible to those around them.[119] Sexuality need not feature in that appraisal at all. For that reason, Stryker also calls for a clearer distinction between queer approaches to gender, typified by Butler, and those that emerge within trans studies.[120] This then brings cisnormativity into sharper focus. Cisnormativity gives a name to the privileging of fixed, bifurcated and unchanging genders. This presupposition becomes particularly apparent in Serano's reflections on her experiences of traditional (misogynistic) sexism and its transphobic counterpart cissexism.

Serano, a trans writer and advocate, is associated with popularizing the language of 'cis' as a counterpoint to 'trans'.[121] She proposes this in order to move away from 'not-trans' or similar terms as it does not offer any sense of equivalency between being trans and cis. Rather 'cis-' is the antonym of the Latin prefix 'trans-' and signifies being on the same (as opposed to different) side. She adopts, and popularises, this language in order to try to level the power balance. For that task, cissexual provided a useful juxtaposition to transsexual.[122] Through this linguistic shift she effectively articulates the difference in treatment associated with being cissexual rather than transsexual. The latter is considered fake, less authentic and subordinate to the primacy of the former through a system she calls 'cissexism'.[123] She highlights the endemic and structural foundations of a system that privileges cisness to the exclusion of all else. She writes:

> While all transgender people experience transphobia, transsexuals additionally experience a related (albeit distinct) form of prejudice: cissexism, which is the belief that transsexuals' identified genders are inferior to, or less authentic, than those of cissexuals (i.e., people who are not transsexuals and who have only ever experienced their subconscious and physical sexes as being aligned). The most common expression of cissexism occurs when people attempt to deny the transsexual the basic privileges that are associated with the trans person's self-identified gender.... The justification for this denial is generally founded on the assumption that the trans person's gender is not authentic because it does not

---

119. Stryker, '(De)Subjugated Knowledges', 1.
120. Stryker, '(De)Subjugated Knowledges'.
121. Serano, *Whipping Girl*.
122. Serano, *Whipping Girl*, 33. While Serano preferred the term cissexual, she noted that since the initial publication of *Whipping Girl* cisgender has gained greater prominence and social recognition. She notes that she was first introduced to cis language which 'name[s] the unmarked dominant majority' through the work of Emi Koyama. Serano cites Koyama's website http://www.eminism.org/interchange/2002/20020607-wmstl.html. See also Julia Serano, 'Cissexism and Cis Privilege Revisited. Part 1: Who Exactly Does "Cis" Refer To?', Whipping Girl, 2014, accessed 1 October 2019, http://juliaserano.blogspot.co.uk/2014/10/cissexism-and-cis-privilege-revisited.html.
123. Serano, *Whipping Girl*, i–xxi.

correlate with the sex they were assigned at birth. In making this assumption, cissexists attempt to create an artificial hierarchy. By insisting that the trans person's gender is 'fake', they attempt to validate their own gender as 'real', or 'natural'. This sort of thinking is incredibly naive, as it denies a basic truth: we make assumptions every day about other people's genders without ever seeing their birth certificates, their chromosomes, their genitals, their reproductive systems, their childhood socialization, or their legal sex. There is no such thing as a 'real' gender—there is only the gender we perceive others to be.[124]

Serano's attention to the privileges and assumptions that go hand in hand with being cis has a profound impact on this project. She paves the way for a recognition of cisnormativity. The privileges she describes contribute to the perception that cisness needs no name or identity as it is natural, normal, and the true way of being, especially when being trans is portrayed as unnatural, other, and fake.[125] This belief contributes to, and justifies, cissexism. Cissexism includes cissexual assumption, a process where enduring presuppositions about gender ensure that when first encountering someone, we will seek immediately to gender them, namely, to label them as a cis man or woman.[126] The almost instinctive process implies that these are the only two possible options.[127] To challenge the status quo is to reveal the problem of cissexism. For those who speak their transness (or have it revealed by others), they openly challenge the cisnormative narrative, likely causing them to be considered as other – as trans – from then on. Meanwhile those who confront the assumptions visually, who are *seen* to deviate from the gendered

---

124. Serano, *Whipping Girl*, 12–13.

125. A. Finn Enke, 'The Education of Little Cis: Cisgender and the Discipline of Opposing Bodies', in *Transfeminist Perspectives in and beyond Transgender and Gender Studies*, ed. A. Finn [Anne] Enke (Philadelphia, PA: Temple University Press, 2012), 60–77. Finn Enke shows that without significant attention to cisnormativity, adoption of the language of cisness is problematic. It solidifies transness and reifies it into the most abjected and inescapable form of being. Despite these concerns Enke commends Serano for drawing attention to the structural and systemic privileging of cisness which, in turn, form the basis for the conceptualization of cisnormativity used in my project.

126. Serano, *Whipping Girl*, 162–164.

127. Serano, *Whipping Girl*, 165. 'While cissexual assumption remains invisible to most cissexuals, those of us who are transsexual are excruciatingly aware of it. Prior to our transitions, we find that the cissexual majority simply assumes that we fully identify as members of our assigned sex, thus making it difficult for us to manage our gender difference and to be open about the way we see ourselves. And after our transitions, many of us find that the cissexual majority simply assumes that we have already been members of our identified sex, making it impossible for us to be open about our trans status without constantly having to come out to others. Thus, while most cissexuals are unaware that cissexual assumption even exists, those of us who are transsexual recognize it as an active process that erases trans people and their experiences'.

norms, frequently experience even less favourable treatment. In the first case, it matters little how much the individual conforms to (or coheres with) the social expectations of their gender identification. Simply being trans keeps them othered. In the second case, self-identification, or articulation of gender, including whether each of us is cis, trans or somewhere in between, is secondary to its social reception and the resultant treatment.[128] Given the consistency of differential treatment and marginalization faced by those who do not conform to cisgender expectations, Serano argues for use of the term cissexism rather than transphobia. The use of cissexism helpfully focuses on differing treatment associated with not being cis rather than asserting that there is a problem with being trans. It also recognizes a context where to be cis is to be privileged and indicates that such privilege warrants critique and, hopefully, deconstruction. Since Serano introduced this conceptualization, the language and framework she provides have gained greater prominence. Cissexism is now recognized as an outworking of cisnormativity. While she does not get as far as naming it as such in *Whipping Girl*, Serano later acknowledges cissexism and cisprivilege are indicators of cisnormativity that are wide-reaching in gender discourse.[129] Serano's work, and her recognition of the components of cisnormativity, further emphasize the need to privilege voices who can most effectively highlight ways to move, and live, beyond the narrow constraints of such norms.

Serano's volume is not intended as an academic text but rather finds its value in showcasing her personal insights. She is most persuasive when she looks at the systematic problems and ties her own experiences in with those. Her use of language is particularly helpful for this project as it gives a name and context to her experiences. She recognizes that her first-person writing is just that – one person's perspective. That, too, is the limitation of her work. It must be brought into further dialogue with other perspectives, including those Stryker, Prosser and Namaste. Together they are able to expand on trans experience, not least through their engagement with multiple voices. That said, it is helpful to contextualize those experiences through Serano's recognition of cis assumption and privilege.

128. For example, Shannon Power, 'Lesbian Kicked Out of the Bowling Alley Because She Used the Women's Restroom', *GayStarNews*, 22 October 2018, https://www.gaystarnews.com/article/lesbian-kicked-out-of-bowling-alley-because-she-used-the-womens-restroom/σ.6QJqWNvx.

129. Julia Serano, 'Julia's Trans, Gender, Sexuality, & Activism Glossary!', JuliaSerano.com, [no date], accessed 3 June 2020, http://www.juliaserano.com/terminology.html. 'Cisnormativity, Cis Assumption: related concepts that enable trans erasure and invisibility. "Cisnormativity" describes a societal mindset wherein cis/cisgender/cissexual are presumed to be the norm, while trans/transgender/transsexual people and experiences are deemed "abnormal" by comparison (if they are even considered at all). "Cis assumption" is a concept I forwarded in *Whipping Girl* (pp. 164–170) to describe instances wherein people (because of cisnormativity) automatically presume that every person they meet must be cis/cisgender/cissexual (unless they are provided with evidence to the contrary)'.

Serano effectively differentiates trans experience and the problems of cis privilege and assumption which enables a move away from the realms of queer theory. Stryker reminds us that there is more to transness and gender diversity than either the destruction of the gender binary or a persistent interest in an individual's sexual desirability. Instead, it is more appropriate to respond to the normative system that privileges being fixed and binary (m/f) in both sex and gender. This is best understood as cisnormativity, and that concept is entirely reliant on the imagery established through Serano's exploration of transness and her encouragement to critically engage with the systems that bolster cisprivilege.

Gender from Trans Perspectives

Serano's exploration of cissexism allows us to see that aspects of gender and sex thought to be natural, immutable and divinely mandated are not. That makes them no less problematic, especially when the sexisms of which Serano writes remain somewhere between prevalent and endemic. Yet cisnormativity is contextual and recognizing that creates an opportunity to look at alternative ways of being sexed and gendered. In this section I draw out contributions from trans theorists in order to better understand gender in the face of cisnormativity. These perspectives speak into a context where cisnormativity is ubiquitous but invisible and unacknowledged. Both Prosser and Namaste integrate an understanding of, and differentiation from, the queer model associated with Butler. Their insights also reveal the impact of treating lives as unintelligible through cisnormativity. Prosser addresses trans experience through considering physicality and embodiment, psychology, and self-description or self-articulation. Namaste emphasizes the importance of engaging with a person's full identity and context without an overreliance on either queer's deconstructivist theories or sociological objectivity. In combination, these perspectives begin to add a richness and depth to a genderscape that is not solely reliant on cisnormativity nor on the misplaced assumption that anyone we encounter must be cisgender.

Prosser opens *Second Skins* (1998) by distancing his scholarship from that which sees transness as inherently subversive or as part of a predominantly queer agenda to destroy gender.[130] He rejects the suggestion that transness is necessarily

---

130. Prosser, *Second Skins*, 29. Prosser particularly takes Butler to task for their use of transness and drag as exemplars for radical gender conformity which is inherently subversive. He writes, 'although it never makes such an argument, *Gender Trouble* does set up the conditions for this syllogism: transgender = gender performativity = queer = subversive'. Later he returns to the syllogism, reflecting that its antithesis is equally problematic: 'non-transgender = gender constativity = straight = naturalising' (33). There are two noteworthy issues that Prosser highlights. First is the desire to claim all trans and gender nonconforming people as queer. A second issue is to implicitly compel people who identify as queer to perform gender in such a way as to be perceived as trans even irrespective of our gender.

(or even inherently) subversive; rather it is just part of the array of human gender and sex. He highlights everyday aspects of trans life by directing attention to physicality, psychology and neurology, and life – writing and autobiography. Through these themes he illustrates a richness to transness that has been hitherto overlooked, particularly through queer's emphasis on subversion. Prosser passionately advocates for an understanding that transness forms part of the quotidian genderscape – we just need to find better ways to recognize and understand it without becoming too reliant on either cisgender norms or a queer/straight dichotomy.

The somatic aspects of gendered and sexed identity feature strongly. Prosser notes that while gendered becoming is complex 'the investment of sex in the flesh is undeniable'.[131] He rightly critiques queer theorists for putting so much store in the importance of gendered performativity that the sexed body is erased. Prosser's criticism is primarily targeted at performativity, which he treats as almost synonymous with gender itself. He sees this as one of the most fundamental distinctions between queer and trans approaches. Queer theory, according to Prosser, cannot 'sustain the body as a literal category'.[132] In challenging the erasure of the body in the queer commitment to gender performativity, Prosser makes an important distinction between sex and gender. He argues that sex is synonymous with embodiment, while gender is socially constructed. It is this distinction that is at the heart of queer's aims to deconstruct the system of opposite sexes and compulsory heteronormativity. He is right to critique queer and Butlerian approaches to gender performativity which do not provide a holistic view of sex and gender. In doing so he overlooks many of the aspects of gender that I include within the term. Notably the interplay between psychological or internal ontology and the social or external ontology is the core issue for Prosser. He does not see that adequately reflected within the Butlerian model, however it is a central aspect of my understanding of the complex interplay between sex and gender. Nevertheless Prosser understands the value of recognizing gender as a construct but still wants there to be space for people to fully be a man or a woman. This is particularly the case where that sex differs from the label assigned at birth. The desire to just *be* one's sex without any need to 'signify subversive gender performativity' is frequently a core aspect of transsexuality.[133] Prosser emphasizes that 'there are transsexuals who seek very pointedly to be nonperformative, to be constative, quite simply to *be*'.[134] Seeking to be either a man or a woman is antithetical to queer's rejection of the gender binary. Yet Prosser emphasizes that gender and sex, no matter how incomprehensible to a cisnormative gaze, need not be treated as radical or deconstructive. They do, however, warrant full recognition, especially through bodies and the stories we tell of them (and ourselves).

131. Prosser, *Second Skins*, 67.
132. Prosser, *Second Skins*, 27.
133. Prosser, *Second Skins*, 32.
134. Prosser, *Second Skins*, 32.

Prosser then showcases how trans participants have fought and struggled for the recognition that cis people receive without question. He draws from autobiographies and he uses the voices of those authors to elaborate a richness and depth to trans embodiment. In particular, his use of these autobiographical accounts of transness confronts what he calls 'theory's cynicism over identity's embodiment'.[135] In turn, his analysis enables us to understand better the importance of actively working towards bringing our bodies to better reflect our own knowledge of our sexed and gendered selves, i.e. to facilitate and support bodily transitions. He contrasts a Butlerian approach with his own. 'In Butler's reading transgender demotes gender from narrative to performance. That is, gender appears not as the end of narrative becoming but as performative moments along a process: repetitious, recursive, disordered, incessant, above all, unpredictable, and necessarily incomplete'.[136] He then emphasizes the significance of the body in trans autobiography: 'the transsexual does not approach the body as an immaterial provisional surround but, on the contrary, as the very "seat" of the self. For if the body were but a costume, consider: why the life quest to alter its contours?'[137] Prosser's exasperation with those who seek to diminish the significance of embodiment and 'the *narrative* of becoming a biological man or biological woman (as opposed to the performative of effecting one)' is palpable.[138] He emphasizes the 'transsexual's struggle towards sexed embodiment' at all levels of the self.[139] He continues by referencing Simone de Beauvoir's famous epigram when he adds, 'One is not born a woman, but *nevertheless* may become one – given substantial medical intervention, personal tenacity, economic security, social support, and so on: becoming woman, in spite of not being born one, may be seen as a crucial goal'. For him, queer approaches threaten the understanding of transsexuality as an authentic way to be sexed. They exclude the potential to fully become a man or a woman, but instead offer the option to merely perform as one. This is one of the key differences between queer's theoretical approach to gender and trans insights into the same experience. Yet, just as Prosser cautions against an overreliance on (queer) gender theory, he also challenges his readers not to consider *only* embodiment as he moves further into his discussion of narratives.

The narratives Prosser analyses are written to raise awareness about trans experience. Yet the narratives also need to be recognized as both authoritative and authorised: they must be recognizably authentic in the account of their trans experience. Prosser notes that the autobiographies followed a formula which reflected the medical narrative of being trapped in the wrong body that proved to be both a trope and a recognizable leitmotif.[140] The shared style and language

---

135. Prosser, *Second Skins*, 67.
136. Prosser, *Second Skins*, 29–30.
137. Prosser, *Second Skins*, 67.
138. Prosser, *Second Skins*, 32. Emphasis original.
139. Prosser, *Second Skins*, 33.
140. Prosser, *Second Skins*, 69.

ensures that there is a recognizable consistency between authors. However, this does not do justice to the fullness and diversity of trans lives, although Prosser recognizes the complexity that comes with not always adhering to the established pattern. His description of his own challenge in writing is evocative, and contrasts markedly with Halberstam's account of the portrayal of gender nonconforming characters written by third parties. Prosser writes,

> autobiography brings into relief the split of the transsexual life; transsexual history brings into gendered relief the split of the difference present in all autobiography between the subject of enunciation and the subject enunciating. I was a woman, I write as a man. How do I join the split? How do I create a coherent subject. Precisely through narrative. Over the course of the recounting, the narrative continuity, the trajectory of autobiography (tracing the story of a single self), promises, like the transition itself, to rejoin this split into a single, connected life.[141]

In written form the 'conventions of transsexuality are thoroughly entangled with those of autobiography, this body thoroughly enabled by narrative'.[142] Both elements gain prominence in Prosser's account, emphasizing the importance of bodies within narratives, even beyond autobiography. Prosser uses the term 'body narrative' to describe 'the ways in which body and narrative work together in the production of transsexual subjectivity'.[143] Bodies reveal subjectivity, in distinction from the cis-oriented narratives Halberstam describes which seek to constrain trans and gender nonconforming characters, or to seek to shape them into more cisnormative moulds through stabilization or rationalization. For Prosser, the body really does open up narrative experiences so that the richness and nuance allow agency, autonomy and, most importantly, subjectivity. It allows for full personhood to emerge, especially when the experiences recounted do not conform to expectation.

Through Prosser's use of the somatic themes in trans autobiography he seeks to move beyond a voyeuristic and objectifying interest in othering bodies that do not conform to a fixed, narrow gender binary. There are the psychological and psychosomatic aspects of gender and sex that can, and do, reveal a very physical cost to living with gender dysphoria. Prosser's opening case studies are heavily medical, partly reflecting the enduring reliance on medico-juridical recognition of the truth of someone's transness.[144] As gatekeepers to legal recognition and access to medical support (including surgery and/or hormones), Prosser presents the physician as the first authorizing editor and 'reader' of trans narratives. The clear allusion to autobiography highlights the importance of the stories we tell of

---

141. Prosser, *Second Skins*, 102.
142. Prosser, *Second Skins*, 103.
143. Prosser, *Second Skins*, 105.
144. Prosser, *Second Skins*, 99–134.

ourselves and the recognition – and affirmation – those stories elicit. We, like Prosser's authors, add our stories to those already shared, including those from religious and folk traditions as well as those presented as life-writing. They contribute to our understanding of what it means to be human, and core to that being is our gender and sex. Those narratives attest to individual experiences that are no doubt more complex than these authorized versions indicate.

Prosser brings attention to themes of bodily experience and the stories we tell of ourselves in his concept of the 'body narrative'. This reflects 'the ways in which body and narrative work together in the production of transsexual subjectivity'.[145] He continues to outline how he understands trans narrative to work:

> Narrative is diachronic, not instantaneous but an organised recounting of episodes of time over time. Second, narrative ... is ... bound up with realization; in the development of its own plot, in the progression of its episodes, narrative crucially seeks its own *telos*. Finally, ... narrative suggests an interlocution between author and reader, a dialogics of interpretation. The meaning of narrative is arrived at in a textual exchange.[146]

Prosser's observations about the function and purpose of narrative, particularly trans autobiography, are insightful. We gain an understanding of the trajectory and progression of the life narrated – all as part of the journey towards the narrative's telos. This occurs even though we lose a sense of the immediacy of the actions themselves as the events are now firmly in the past. In his recognition of the interrelationship between reader and author, past and present, he also indicates a need to search for an understanding of the story, and one that comes from locating characters in their broader contexts.

Prosser's emphasis on sex and embodiment are essential correctives to queer's downplaying of the significance of the body. However his criticism of gender as a synonym for performativity also underplays the importance of gender in shaping identity. While queer has not adequately served the needs of trans lives Prosser is not in a position to conceptualize an alternative framework to complement heteronormativity. His work predates that of Serano and the naming of cisness. Prosser's desire to make apparent the array of trans experience and to highlight how that cannot adequately be addressed by queer theory or heteronormativity remains clear. Even in this project, over twenty years after *Second Skins* was first published, cisnormativity remains under-theorized and under-recognized. Yet that makes it all the more important to begin the process of addressing its presence now. For that to happen insights into the limitations of heteronormativity, such as Prosser's are invaluable. Alongside Prosser's observations, though, there continues to be a need to recognize the diversity of genders as well as sexualities. Returning to Prosser's condemnation of a queer commitment to deconstruction, my aim here

---

145. Prosser, *Second Skins*, 105.
146. Prosser, *Second Skins*, 105.

is to better punctuate a genderscape so we can all construct, assert, and recognize myriad genders and sexes of which man and woman are just two.

We now return to matters of context and build on Prosser's insights by turning to Viviane Namaste. Namaste rejects the idea that it is possible to decontextualise a person's sex. Instead she argues that whole-life contexts are essential in understanding trans experience. This is a necessary counterpoint to the erasure of trans experience. She describes this as 'the very act of nullifying transsexuality – a process wherein transsexuality is rendered impossible'.[147] She continues to explain,

> These three meanings of erasure support and sustain one another: the reduction of transsexual to the figural dimensions of discourse pre-empts the possibility of transsexuality [sic] subjectivity; the exclusion of transsexuals from the institutional world reinforces a conception that the world that presupposes the existence of only nontranssexual men and nontranssexual women; and the act of invalidating that very possibility of transsexuality bolsters rhetorical institutional practices that do not consider the needs of transsexual and transgendered people. In this manner, a reduction of transsexuals to rhetorical figures, institutional procedures that make transsexuals disappear, and the literal annulment of transsexual bodies all constitute a general social relation in which [transsexual/transgender] people are situated.[148]

Namaste's articulation of trans erasure is a useful accompaniment to Prosser's commitment to recognize trans experience. She offers a rationale for why that recognition is so hard to achieve. *Invisible Lives: The Erasure of Transsexual and Transgendered People* (2000), like Prosser's *Second Skins*, was published before cis language had gained prominence. Yet the image of erasure Namaste presents adds to my understanding of cisnormativity. She then continues to address ways to respond to that erasure.

'Undoing Theory: The "Transgender Question" and the Epistemic Violence of Anglo-American Feminist Theory', published in 2009, offers helpful guidance and caution when researching trans lives to prevent erasure.[149] Namaste calls out those who treat transness for theoretical posturing without engaging with trans perspectives.[150] Queer and feminist scholarship are subject to her ire as she considers the disciplines and their staunchest advocates complicit in epistemic violence. Like Prosser, Namaste is keen to emphasize that being trans is about everyday, mundane, run of the mill gendered and sexed life, which is rarely acknowledged. She argues that there needs to be greater engagement 'with the nitty-gritty realities of our lives, our bodies, and our experiences of the everyday world'.[151] However she sees

---

147. Namaste, *Invisible Lives*, 52.
148. Namaste, Invisible Lives, 52.
149. Namaste, 'Undoing Theory'.
150. Namaste, *Invisible Lives*, 9–23.
151. Namaste, *Invisible Lives*, 1.

exoticisation of transness for the personal and professional benefit of theorists who sit at a distance from the lives (so thoughtlessly) included in their work. This results in dehumanization as she sees trans people become the objects of research and theorising without any subjectivity or integration into those projects or their outputs.[152] She posits an alternative that champions trans perspectives *and* requires those undertaking such research to integrate themselves and their locations in the project. Such emphasis on what she calls 'indigenous perspectives' in 'Undoing Theory' recognizes that trans and gender nonconforming perspectives 'are produced in different institutional, social, economic and historical settings'.[153] She persuasively argues that to move beyond objectification requires attention to such broader contexts.

Recognizing the importance of those broader social contexts is as important to Namaste as bodies are to Prosser. Namaste writes: 'an approach that focuses on the social aspect of gendered identities, meaning, and relations allows scholars and activists to articulate a nuanced understanding of gender as a social construct. This perspective has obvious advantages over that of queer theory since it begins its investigation in the everyday world and its findings can be applied therein'.[154] Namaste's insight into the need to uphold indigenous perspectives, especially when they struggle for recognition is essential. Her understanding of (cis) gender norms as a colonising influence brings some clarity about why that is such a challenge. This insight builds on her earlier recognition of erasure, and once again contributes to my image of cisnormativity. Cisnormativity serves as a form of colonisation. Those voices most attuned to speak to that colonisation are essential to the cispicious endeavour, even though – or especially though – they contrast with long-held assumptions. Drawing from Namaste, I consider our starting point to come through the recognition that we are all located within a cisnormative context. Whether we are oblivious to it or recognize its impact on our lives requires us to be reflexive in our research practice.

To undertake such work well also requires a willingness to locate ourselves in the project, in part to acknowledge points of resonance and similarity, no matter how we understand our own gender. Namaste advocates for an inclusion of empiricism in gender studies, where insight is most effectively gained from those

---

152. Namaste, *Invisible Lives*, 1; 'Undoing Theory'.

153. Namaste, *Invisible Lives*, 21. For further discussion of the impact this has on identificatory and disidentificatory performance, as well as identity, see Muñoz, *Disidentification*. Muñoz describes disidentification as 'a strategy that works on and against dominant ideology. Instead of buckling under the pressures of dominant ideologies (identification, assimilation) or attempting to break free of its inescapable sphere (counteridentification, utopianism), this "working on and against" is a strategy that tries to transform a cultural logic from within, always laboring to enact permanent structural change while at the same time valuing the importance of local or everyday struggles of resistance' (11–12).

154. Namaste, *Invisible Lives*, 27.

who are the subjects of the research.[155] More specifically she argues that, in the case of trans studies, trans perspectives should be treated within the wider field of indigenous knowledge. Embedded within this is a commitment to respecting 'empiricism', in other words to respect the integrity and authority of experience without always needing to rely on theoretical underpinning for validity.[156] This enables recognition of 'the complex ways that colonialism has been enacted through knowledge-production'.[157] She makes an important acknowledgement of the way that 'both historically and today ... indigenous peoples have been subjugated through knowledge themselves.[158] The response is to develop knowledge-production initiatives and approaches through 'the articulation of meaningful social research, and therefore meaningful theory' which integrate 'relevance, equity in partnership, and ownership'.[159]

In this project those aspects of indigenous knowledge translate into a recognition of a richer genderscape in the lives of characters of the (Hebrew) Bible that reflects the relevance of each character's own context. It will also place into partnership the low theory-informed reading approach that elevates insights into the everyday aspects of trans and gender nonconforming lives, whilst also engaging with malestream and feminist scholarship. To do so is to recognize the equity in partnership that is core to an ideological approach such as this: it is most effective when it works with a close, detailed reading of the text in dialogue with both established voices in biblical scholarship *and* the insights from theorists and writers addressing trans experience, gender nonconformity, and cisnormativity. This further emphasises that gender diversity is an already present element of these familiar stories and need not serve any further ideological or political function beyond that of recognition. However, it is also important to remain attentive to our political and activist aim. Here those aims are to produce interpretations that resonate with trans and gender diverse readers and to confront the perception that characters in the Bible are ordinarily, only cisnormative.

An Emerging Cispicious Genderscape

The insights offered by Serano, Prosser and Namaste each emphasize why a queer approach to gender is not sufficient for addressing cisnormative presuppositions.

---

155. Namaste, 'Undoing Theory', 26–27.

156. Namaste, 'Undoing Theory', 22–23. Namaste acknowledges the limitations of empiricism alone when she writes, 'the challenge is not just to engage in empirical inquiry, but to think about different ways to achieve this. . . . If marginalized people like transsexuals and transvestites have been excluded from knowledge-production (including within feminist theory), how might we proceed otherwise? Attention to some of the central arguments of indigenous knowledge is helpful here' (23–24).

157. Namaste, 'Undoing Theory', 23–27, 24.

158. Namaste, 'Undoing Theory', 14.

159. Namaste, 'Undoing Theory', 24.

Althaus-Reid's caution about the temptation to treat liberation theologies as spaces for tourist-like sojourns is particularly pertinent here. She distinguishes between indigenous perspectives, even those with sufficient familiarity and engagement like her own, from those that are parachuted in and speak as outsiders. This is particularly common and problematic where such scholarship elevates marginalized perspectives such as in trans scholarship as well as liberation theologies. Namaste describes something similar when she writes of the exotic attraction of trans lives, especially when they are removed from their contexts. Her accusation of exoticism, along with Althaus-Reid's recognition of the need for a postcolonial indecent theology, emphasizes the value of indigenous perspectives. Such perspectives frequently emerge as challenges to hegemonic, colonising ideas such as those associated with cisnormativity, and its companion T-Theology. Namaste persuasively writes, 'if people are marginalised in and through the production of knowledge, then a truly transformative intellectual practice would collaborate with such individuals and communities to ensure that their political and intellectual priorities are addressed'.[160] Namaste's insights continue a trajectory of desubjugating knowledge as also advocated by Stryker. The whimsical, somewhat indecent approach advocated by Halberstam and Althaus-Reid is only possible through recognition of the whole lives of those whose stories are told.

There is a challenge when turning to the biblical narratives so central to this project. There is no autobiography or life writing directly akin to Prosser's body narratives in the Bible. Rather, there is value in treating the characters as representational figures through which to trace our lives in their stories. They exert their representative function as we as readers find glimpses of ourselves and our experiences in their stories. Something similar occurs in Prosser's account of the power of trans autobiography and life writing for him and other trans readers. His emphasis on the importance of narrative is a helpful contribution. The importance of trans insights into life, embodiment, and self-articulation add to the richness of the narrative and genderscapes. The imagined lives of biblical characters, particularly those in the ancestral narratives, hold appeal for the way their stories leave enough space to fill in details to enflesh each individual. In acknowledgement of Prosser's body narrative, I endeavour to find space for interpretations of somatic experiences that reflect cis and trans lives. They cannot come from theory alone, and will rely upon a whimsical and, at times, indecent disregard for inherited gender assumptions, yet must always return to an understanding that is rooted in experience and context.

Conclusion

Building on the theoretical foundations provided by Halberstam and Althaus-Reid, I have sought to identify relevant gender norms that affect recognition of

---

160. Namaste, 'Undoing Theory', 27.

gender diversity. The indecently whimsical approach embeds a playful irreverence for previous interpretations and presuppositions that opens a space for intriguing alternatives. To that I have taken from queer theory an acknowledgement of the limits of theoretical insights when not accompanied by due consideration of an individual's whole context. Central to that context is a recognition that cisnormativity informs our perception of gender norms, but that lives exist – and are marginalized – beyond its supposedly hallowed limits.

To read beyond the constraints of cisnormativity, Prosser outlines how narrative integrates trans perspectives into a broader genderscape. His attention to embodiment, especially through his description of a body narrative, emphasises the inextricable link between individuals and their stories. He advocates for an exchange of understanding of gender complexity between author and reader. I think this also applies between character and reader when the work is not (auto) biographical. Namaste's approach offers a fruitful contribution through an integration of first-hand experience and theory in combination with insights from trans theory and perspectives. Both Namaste and Prosser challenge the erasure or diminution of trans experience, something I also seek to counter through this project. It is then possible to make space for a broader genderscape, one that also acknowledges the frustrating influence of gender restrictive and constrictive gender frameworks. She also reminds readers that any conjecture must reflect every day, mundane, and unexceptional lived experiences of gender and sex. In arguing for the inclusion of indigenous perspectives, she makes a similar argument to those of Althaus-Reid who argues for the inclusion of marginalised perspectives and Halberstam whose low theory shares a similar aim: finding new, creative ways to elevate perspectives treated as anachronistic or implausible.

By recognizing the existence of cisnormativity and cis privilege through the work of Serano, I have undertaken the groundwork for a hermeneutical toolkit that responds to, and challenges, the dominance of such norms. The core components of such hermeneutics rely upon indecent whimsy, drawing on Halberstam and Althaus-Reid. Such indecent whimsy requires a willingness to explore the implausible, draw on underrepresented and marginalized perspectives, and challenge dominant ideology. An understanding that gender diversity is a matter of everyday embodied living, not exceptionalism, is also needed. Otherwise we risk perpetuating the problematic tropes Halberstam, Althaus-Reid and Namaste describe. The biblical texts, such as the ancestral narratives which Althaus-Reid briefly alludes to, hold much potential for such interrogation as they are well-known and well-loved representative texts. Her encouragement to find traces of our lives in the stories of our biblical counterparts enables us to read and respond to the texts as we most readily encounter them. These are received tales of cultural icons and their stories come with a wealth of commentary and interpretation that adds to their richness. In approaching the characters afresh, we must draw on the insights proffered by those most able to speak about gender diversity and transness and bring them into dialogue with the received traditions of those biblical narratives. A hermeneutics of cispicion must be aware of how these stories can be a body narrative, looking for the significance of the somatic in gender and sex. It must be willing and able to integrate indigenous perspectives and enable reflexive engagement. A cispicious approach must be open to finding inconsistencies and incongruities as well as clear indications of change and transition when arguing for transness. Finally, it must work with a model of sex and gender that understands the multiple components that contribute to an overall sense of gender or sex – and the potential for diversity or inconsistency amongst those different strands. In summary, the hermeneutics of cispicion must work playfully with a complex, contextual understanding of gender and sex that acknowledges that insights are grounded in the everyday experiences of readers and characters alike.

Chapter 2

FROM HERMENEUTICS OF
HETERO-SUSPICION TO CISPICION

The Bible has long been a source of exploration for those seeking rich, diverse genderscapes. It has not always been a place of welcome, though. Sandy Stone, for example, recognizes that Adam and Eve are the idiomatic figures at the of heart a clearly demarcated gender binary. Their status as seemingly universal ancestors contributes to the erasure and censure of gender nonconformity.[1] Another example is Leslie Feinberg, who condemns the prohibition on cross-dressing in Deuteronomy 22:5 as an early legal ban on transness.[2] Their shared recognition that the Bible can create 'divinising normativities' of gender is significant.[3] These examples highlight

---

1. Sandy Stone, 'The *Empire* Strikes Back: A Posttranssexual Manifesto', in *The Transgender Studies Reader*, ed. Susan Stryker and Stephen Whittle (New York: Routledge, 2006 [1987]), 221–235, 230. Stone's manifesto is a response to Janice Raymond's *The Transsexual Empire: The Making of the She-Male* (1979). Raymond's monograph is based on her PhD supervised by feminist theologian Mary Daly. In Raymond's diatribe against trans women, she attacks Stone personally for destroying the sanctity of (cis-only) women-only spaces. Stone's response, published informally some eight years later, gained significant attention and is considered one of the foundational documents of what has now become trans theory. Stone's discussion of theological and biblical themes is an important recognition of the power of such motifs in the enculturation of transphobia.

Note: I intentionally do not draw directly from, nor cite, either Raymond or Daly's scholarship in recognition of their contribution to transphobic discourses. Their work is counter to the aims of my research and needs no further amplification. In this decision I follow Sara Ahmed's model for citational practice that reflects the politics of the project undertaken. Here that translates to a refusal to cite writers whose work actively contributes to transphobia or cissexism. See Sara Ahmed, *Living a Feminist Life* (Durham, NC: Duke University Press, 2017), 15–16.

2. Feinberg, *Transgender Warriors*, 49–52.

3. See Johannes N. Vorster, 'The Queering of Biblical Discourse', *Scriptura* 111, 3 (2012), 602–620. Vorster provides an insightful analysis of how certain models of gender and sexuality become associated with God and Christianity. This then validates only those models, something Vorster calls 'divinised normativities'. See also Stone, 'Bibles That Matter'; Yannik [Annika] Thiem, 'The Art of Queer Rejections: The Everyday Life of Biblical Discourse', *Neotestamentica* 48, 1 (2014), 33–56.

why a new hermeneutics of suspicion is needed. A well-formulated cispicious reading strategy offers the space to posit alternative interpretations. And central to those new interpretations is a tacit recognition of the presence of cisnormativity. Meanwhile indigenous voices that challenge gender norms in biblical interpretation speak with only a limited ability to gain recognition. This relates back to trans erasure, negative tropes, and the endemic problem of cisnormativity, as outlined in the previous chapter.

Despite, or even perhaps due to, these observations, indigenous voices do confront the perception that there is no gender diversity in the Bible. Among them, Sally Gross traces routes through rabbinic traditions and biblical narratives to identify intersex forebears[4] and Victoria Kolakowski finds resonance in the stories of the many eunuchs that chimes with her transness.[5] Justin Sabia-Tanis sees the pastoral value in allegorical gospel figures.[6] Meanwhile, Virginia Ramey Mollenkott recognises 'omnigender' in both God and other characters throughout the Bible.[7] Such perspectives inform the diverse genderscape on view in *The Queer Bible Commentary*, an influential edited collection published in 2006 that shows the place such gender nonconforming perspectives,[8] like those of Kolakowski and Tanis,[9] have found within the wider sphere of queer interpretations.

However, both Prosser and Namaste persuasively argue that gender diversity cannot solely be addressed from a queer vantage point. The previous chapter elucidates the limits of queer approaches and a focus on heteronormativity. Yet it remains necessary to recognize the enduring influence of queer approaches to gender within biblical studies. The need to create space to differentiate between queer and trans approaches remains, informed by a recognition of transphobia and its causes. It is in creating this space that a cispicious strategy has something valuable to offer, with its central acknowledgement of how cisnormativity still unconsciously informs much work. The need for this space to remain open is one

---

4. Sally Gross, 'Intersexuality and Scripture', *Theology and Sexuality* 11 (1999), 65–74.

5. Victoria Kolakowski, 'The Concubine and the Eunuch: Queering up the Breeder's Bible', in *Our Families, Our Values: Snapshots of Queer Kinship*, ed. Robert E. Shore-Goss [Goss] and Amy Adams Squire Strongheart (Binghamton, NY: Harrington Park, 1997), 35–49; 'Toward a Christian Ethical Response to Transsexual Persons', *Theology and Sexuality* 1997b, 6 (1997), 10–31; 'Throwing a Party: Patriarchy, Gender, and the Death of Jezebel', in *Take Back the Word: A Queer Reading of the Bible*, ed. Robert E. Shore-Goss [Goss] and Mona West (Cleveland, OH: Pilgrim Press, 2000), 103–114.

6. Justin Sabia-Tanis [Tanis], 'Eating the Crumbs That Fall from the Table: Trusting the Abundance of God', in *Take Back the Word: A Queer Reading of the Bible*, ed. Robert E. Shore-Goss [Goss] and Mona West (Cleveland, OH: Pilgrim Press, 2000), 43–54; *Trans-Gender: Theology, Ministry and Communities of Faith* (Eugene, OR: Wipf & Stock, 2018 [2003]).

7. Virginia Ramey Mollenkott, *Omnigender: A Trans-religious Approach*, Revised and Expanded ed. (Cleveland, OH: Pilgrim Press, 2007).

8. Deryn Guest et al., eds., *The Queer Bible Commentary* (London: SCM Press, 2006).

reason why this project addresses at length the theoretical shift a hermeneutics of cispicion requires.

Since late 2015, there have been a number of new trans perspectives bringing insight to biblical interpretation and religious scholarship more broadly. Teresa Hornsby and Deryn Guest set the trajectory when they published *Transgender, Intersex, and Biblical Interpretation* in 2016.[10] J. E. Sumerau, Ryan Mathers and Lain Cragun then explored the authorizing power of religious imagery in 'cisgendering reality'.[11] That work coincided with Katherine Apostolacus's review of (Christian) trans hermeneutics, in which she argues for further development of the field.[12] Soon after came Joy Ladin's influential monograph, *The Soul of the Stranger: Reading God and Torah from A Transgender Perspective* (2019), and special editions of the *Journal of Feminist Studies in Religion* (2018), *Transgender Studies Quarterly* (2019), and *Journal of Interdisciplinary Biblical Studies* (2020).[13] Meanwhile public-focused and pastoral volumes also emerged identifying biblical characters whose experiences are akin to today's trans lives.[14] More recently, important works by

---

9. Kolakowski's earliest work is found in Robert E. Shore-Goss [Goss] and Amy Adams Squire Strongheart, eds., *Our Families, Our Values: Snapshots of Queer Kinship* (Binghamton, NY: Harrington Park, 1997). She and Sabia-Tanis both feature in Robert E. Shore-Goss [Goss] and Mona West, eds., *Take Back the Word: A Queer Reading of the Bible* (Cleveland, OH: Pilgrim Press, 2000).

10. Teresa J. Hornsby and Deryn Guest, eds., *Transgender, Intersex and Biblical Interpretation* (Atlanta, GA: SBL Press, 2016).

11. Sumerau, Cragun and Mathers, 'Cisgendering of Reality'.

12. Katherine Apostolacus, 'The Bible and The Transgender Christian: Mapping Transgender Hermeneutics in the 21st Century', *Journal of the Bible and its Reception* 5, 1 (2018), 1–29.

13. Joy Ladin, *The Soul of the Stranger: Reading God and Torah from a Transgender Perspective* (Waltham, MA: Brandeis University Press, 2019); 'Special Issue: Transing and Queering Feminist Studies and Practices of Religion', *Journal of Feminist Studies in Religion* 34, 1 (2018); 'Trans*/Religion', *Transgender Studies Quarterly (TSQ)* 6, 3 (2019); 'The Bible: Transgender and Genderqueer Perspectives', *Journal for Interdisciplinary Biblical Studies* 1, 2 (2020); Georgia Day, 'Trans-formed by the Spirit: How the Doctrine of Miraculous Conception Reveals Jesus to be an Intersex Trans Man' *Feminist Theology* 31, 2 (2023); and Holly Thompson, 'The Reception of Esther: A Genderqueer/Non-Binary Reading of the Ancient Texts and in Modern Scholarship', (DPhil, University of Oxford, 2021), https://ora.ox.ac.uk/objects/uuid:f263f6cd-ff25-4497-9a28-1c04c2113578.

14. Linda Tatro Herzer, *The Bible and the Transgender Experience: How Scripture Supports Gender Variance*, Kindle ed. (Cleveland, OH: Pilgrim Press, 2016); Samuel Neff, 'Transfigurations: Transgressing Gender in the Bible', (Barclay Press, Inc, March 2017). http://www.barclaypressbookstore.com/transfigurations; Austen Hartke, *Transforming: The Bible and the Lives of Transgender Christians* (Louisville, KY: Westminster John Knox Press, 2018). Neff's 'Transfigurations' is a pay-to-view film written by and starring Peterson Toscano, based on his well-received stage show of the same name. Toscano also released

Max Strassfeld and Alicia Spencer-Hall and Blake Gutt add to the wider field of religion scholarship and its rhetorical engagement with trans interrogations of past lives and texts.[15] These important and productive discussions all recognise these questions are not new, but still require critically engaged, rigorous study. And yet, I do not find a strong critique of cisnormativity in this work, so the challenge remains to determine how best to embed cispicion at the heart of any such endeavour.

Cisnormativity is not entirely absent, of course. Sumerau, Cragun and Mathers explain how scriptural motifs, in combination with religious teaching, make the links between transphobia and cisnormativity inescapable.[16] They show how the appearances of exclusively cisgender figures – including in mnemohistory – ensure that gender diversity is deemed impossible. Such cisgendered realities do not exist only outside the academy: Max Strassfeld makes inescapably clear the importance of acknowledging transphobia in religious scholarship.[17] They explain how cisnormativity impacts our perception of the relationship between transness and religion.

> Must religion be cisgendered? If we accept the underlying assumption that religion and trans bodies are some way mutually incompatible, we inherit a deeply impoverished discipline and collude with the same logics that govern the regulation of trans bodies; the creation of publics as white, able-bodied, and sex-segregated spaces; and cosmologies that write trans people out of existence. We collude with the logistics of transmisogyny that render transwomen [sic] monsters, or jokes, and always something less than human.[18]

Judith Plaskow builds on Strassfeld's argument, reflects briefly on the importance of biblical motifs, and even ponders how transphobic environments would impact

---

a study guide to accompany the film: Peterson Toscano, 'Transfigurations Study Guide', PetersonToscano.com, updated 13 April, 2018, https://petersontoscano.com/portfolio/transfigurations/.

15. Max Strassfeld, *Trans Talmud: Androgynes and Eunuchs in Rabbinic Literature*, University of California Press, (2022); Alicia Spencer-Hall and Blake Gutt. *Trans and Genderqueer Subjects in Medieval Hagiography,* (Amsterdam: Amsterdam University Press, 2021).

16. Sumerau, Cragun and Mathers, 'Cntemporary Religion'.

17. Max Strassfeld, 'Transing Religious Studies', *Journal of Feminist Studies in Religion* 34, 1 (2018), 37–53. Strassfeld addresses the hugely difficult transmisogynistic theology of Daly and Raymond and its legacy. They argue that religious studies and theology need to take responsibility for the abusive impact of such work. While their critique does not directly address biblical texts, their concluding commission applies to this project too. They write, 'My hope is that this analysis has been in service of the field collectively taking responsibility for our legacy of transmisogyny and transphobia and in making room in religious studies (and beyond) for new trans visions and analyses' (52).

18. Strassfeld, 'Transing Religious Studies', 52–53.

someone like David.[19] Her query exposes the invisible but nevertheless present impact of gender diversity within the Bible's genderscape. Plaskow argues for a more overt integration of trans theory in biblical interpretation, even though she does not explore it further in that short article.

Melissa Wilcox also responds to Strassfeld, noting that cisnormativity remains ubiquitous, and fosters anti-trans and anti-genderqueer ideas.[20] She compels others to acknowledge our 'obligation to fill the vacuum [created by blithely cisnormative voices] so that even a whisper can be heard'.[21] In order to respond accordingly, I aim for a cispicious approach to draw a subtle but nonetheless clear distinction between gender diversity in a trans-informed paradigm, and that which emerges through queer(er) rubrics. In other words, I want to enable scholarship that is attuned to the tacit presence of cisnormativity to enable greater recognition of the un(der)acknowledged gender diversity already present within biblical narratives.

Even though these recent trans perspectives bring a greater recognition of transphobia, they do not amount to substantial engagement with the overarching structural problem: cisnormativity. In order to articulate how the hermeneutics of cispicion will accomplish this, it is most helpful to explore what I consider to be the model closest to what I envisage. That model lies in the work of Deryn Guest. Guest develops a hermeneutics of suspicion for their lesbian-identified and gender-attentive scholarship. They name this a hermeneutics of hetero-suspicion. Their sustained commitment to dismantling heteronormativity, maintained through their lesbian-identified approach to trans scholarship, including in *Transgender, Intersex and Biblical Interpretation,* provides a roadmap for my project that simultaneously reveals some of the limitations that emerge in an overtly heteronormative model.

Deryn Guest: A Brief Scholarly History

Guest's work stands in a lineage of queer scholarship that intertwines gender and sexuality. In the intervening twenty years since *Take Back the Word* (2000) showcased work by Kolakowski and Sabia-Tanis, gender diversity has gained greater public and scholarly recognition in biblical studies. This attention has come primarily through queer scholarship – something that has perpetuated an underlying focus on both sexuality and heteronormativity.

19. Judith Plaskow, 'Transing and Gendering Religious Studies', *Journal of Feminist Studies in Religion* 34, 1 (2018), 75–80: 78.

20. Melissa M. Wilcox, 'Religion is Already Transed; Religious Studies is Not (Yet) Listening', *Journal of Feminist Studies in Religion* 34, 1 (2018), 84–88: 88. Wilcox's critique is directed at the American Academy of Religion (AAR), but is equally applicable to biblical scholarship.

21. Wilcox, 'Religion is Already Transed', 88.

Ken Stone's collection *Queer Commentary and the Hebrew Bible* (2001) exemplifies this well. In his introduction, Stone writes that 'queer theory's attempts to problematize normative approaches to *sexuality*. These translate into critical analysis of such dichotomies as "homosexual/heterosexual" and "male/female".'[22] He recognizes the need to hold transness within a queer paradigm, but remains focussed on its impact on sexuality.[23] Homoeroticism predominates in many other explorations of gender nonconformity in biblical studies following Stone, with male gaze and attraction featuring heavily, whilst lesbian-inspired motifs also appear with some frequency.[24]

Guest's work is a quintessential example of the lesbian scholarship arising from these earlier influences. They embed butch identity and female masculinities in their lesbian-hermeneutic from the outset.[25] Although in Guest's case, as they continue to refine their approach, gender nonconformity takes on an ever-increasing prominence. In fact, it becomes the predominant feature of their

---

22. Ken Stone, 'Queer Commentary and Biblical Interpretation: An Introduction', in *Queer Commentary and the Hebrew Bible*, ed. Ken Stone (London: Sheffield Academic Press, 2001), 11–34, 27. See also Roland Boer, *Knockin' on Heaven's Door: The Bible and Popular Culture* (London: Routledge, 1999), 14–15.

23. Stone, 'Queer Commentary', 24–25. 'Further complexities are introduced into static notions of queer identity by the inclusion of "transgendered" persons and practices into the queer rubric. The concepts of "heterosexuality", "homosexuality", and even to some extent "bisexuality" are built on the idea that each one of us has, or should have, a clear biological sex and a coherent sense of one's gender, for decisions about whether one is "heterosexual", "homosexual", or "bisexual" depend on assumptions about one's own sex and gender as well as the sex and gender of one's preferred sexual partners.' While he continues to include an array of trans and intersex experiences within his conceptualization of '"transgendered" phenomena', it is seen through the lens of sexuality. See also Stone, 'Garden of Eden'.

24. Male homosexuality drives the exploration of gender nonconformity in Theodore W. Jennings Jr., *Jacob's Wound: Homoerotic Narrative in the Literature of the Ancient Israel* (New York: Continuum, 2005). Jennings includes a brief introduction and two chapters directed towards the exploration of 'transgendering' through consideration of Israel [Jacob] as constructed in the prophetic literature ('Transgendered Israel', 131–176) and the gender diversity of Joseph ('Joseph as Sissy Boy', 177–196). Despite this, his focus throughout remains on redressing the lack of attention to homoeroticism. See also Greenberg, *Wrestling with God*, 11–14. Meanwhile male gaze on men's bodies and its links to attraction feature heavily in Philip L. Culbertson, 'Designing Men: Reading the Male Body as Text', in *Men and Masculinities in Christianity and Judaism: A Critical Reader*, ed. Björn Krondorfer (London: SCM Press, 2008), 115–124; Stuart Macwilliam, 'Ideologies of Male Beauty and the Hebrew Bible', *Biblical Interpretation* 17, 3 (2009), 265–287. Meanwhile, lesbian motifs feature heavily in Guest, *When Deborah Met Jael*; 'Looking Lesbian'; Caralie Focht, 'Butch-Femme Dynamics in Exodus 2–6 and 14: A Lesbian-Focused Character Study', *Theology & Sexuality* 25, 3 (2019), 188–204.

25. Guest, *When Deborah met Jael*.

scholarship and something they seek to address in myriad ways. Still, a persistent motif throughout is Guest's commitments to both queer praxis and to addressing heteronormativity.

Over the course of eleven years Guest addresses biblical gender nonconformity from lesbian, queer, genderqueer, 'gender critical' and trans perspectives.[26] Throughout they make clear the importance of addressing the overarching problem that means such voices are missing in the first place. When embarking on their lesbian-identified projects they emphasise their gratitude to feminist approaches which respond to patriarchy and androcentrism.[27] Whilst doing so they also acknowledge how blithely heteronormative such modes of interpretation are. In response, they then argue for a more nuanced, specifically lesbian approach. Then, as their recognition of butchness as a particular facet of their lesbian identity comes to the fore, they shift emphasis again. First, they move to deploy a genderfuck reading to provocatively play with gendered preconceptions.[28] This is intentionally, overtly queer in approach – and described as lesbian by Guest – but is primed to address genderqueerness or nonbinariness specifically.[29] Throughout these projects they have deployed the hermeneutics of hetero-suspicion. Here we see how the attention to the overarching system of norms informs their approach, at least in the name. It is more than just in name though. Guest persuasively recognizes the interplay between preconceptions and interpretations. Opposition to heteronormativity shapes Guest's approach strongly, and that becomes most apparent in their most recent publications, including their trans scholarship.

In 2012 Guest published *Beyond Feminist Biblical Studies* as a call for more gender-attentive interpretations. Despite initially appearing to move away from their predominantly queer practice, their 'gender critical' scholarship also works from a hetero-suspicious vantage point.[30] Marco Derks identifies the shared ground and ideology between queer and 'gender critical' scholarship: 'Although at prima facie queer criticism seems to focus on (non-normative) sexualities and gender criticism on constructions of gender, both approaches are strongly related, and preferring to work under either of these two rubrics does not seem to be a

---

26. Here, as throughout Guest's work, gender critical refers to an academic discipline informed by feminist, queer, trans and critical studies of masculinity. Guest's approach is clearly differentiated from the use of the same term by a movement associated with scepticism of and hostility towards trans people which has gained significantly in prominence in the UK during the preparation of this project. For further discussion of the term, see the Glossary (p. 201).

27. Guest, *When Deborah Met Jael*; 'Looking Lesbian'.

28. Guest, 'From Gender Reversal'.

29. Guest's is a specifically lesbian model but is inspired by Erin Runions. See Runions, 'Zion is Burning', 93–114.

30. Deryn Guest, *Beyond Feminist Biblical Studies*, Bible in the Modern World, (Sheffield: Sheffield Phoenix Press, 2012).

matter of strong ideological difference.'[31] Derks's observation gets to the heart of the limitation in such 'gender critical' approaches if they also seek to credibly address trans specificities. This is what turns out to the be the case in *Transgender, Intersex, and Biblical Interpretation*. When Guest eventually turns to trans-oriented scholarship it is the hetero-suspicious framework that guides their interpretations.

Guest continues to use their reliable motifs of butchness and masculinity to shape their trans biblical scholarship. Informed by Jack Halberstam's work on female masculinity and trans gaze, in particular, Guest identifies new gender nonconforming masculine figures. Even though their hetero-suspicious hermeneutic does not feature by name, their recognition of transphobia relates only to the influence of heteronormativity. Sexuality features to contextualize their study, establishing in readers a recognition that this may be a trans-informed project – but it remains a largely queer endeavour. There is no acknowledgment of cisnormativity but that does not stop *Transgender, Intersex, and Biblical Interpretation* offering a valuable contribution to my cispicious project.

Guest's scholarship has traversed a gamut of masculine gender nonconformity within a heteronormative paradigm. It is a valuable collection and one that reveals possibilities for a carefully designed suspicious hermeneutic. Their concerted attention to a specific overlying problem – in their case, heteronormativity – provides an exemplar for how to construct a similar model. They also show the value in recognising the limits of a given approach. For Guest, neither feminist approaches nor their queer counterparts (as broadly constructed) can adequately address the specificities of lesbian lives. By extension I argue that queer and Guestian-style 'gender critical' approaches, with their focus on heteronormativity, cannot sufficiently serve trans and gender nonconforming experience. That is not to say that each does not (at least partially) aid interpretation. But there is something notable, specific, albeit frequently so subtle it is barely recognizable, that warrants a shift in approach. That shift need only be incremental but, as Halberstam argues, there is untold value in the micro and inconsequential.

Given the importance of the hermeneutic of hetero-suspicion in shaping my cispicious approach, I now conduct a detailed analysis of Guest's gender attentive scholarship. In this overview I focus on the way gender nonconformity is conceptualized, especially its relation to butchness and female masculinity. I also investigate how a focus on heteronormativity aids and, in the end, limits Guest's

---

31. Marco Derks, '"If I Be Shaven, Then My Strength Will Go From Me": A Queer Reading of the Samson Narrative', *Biblical Interpretation* 23, 4–5 (2015), 553–573: 554. Derks specifically highlights Deryn Guest and Ken Stone for working across both fields interchangeably. See also Nicole J. Ruane, 'When Women Aren't Enough: Gender Criticism in Feminist Bible Interpretation', in *Feminist Interpretation of the Hebrew Bible in Retrospect: III. Methods*, ed. Susanne Scholz, Recent Research in Biblical Studies (Sheffield: Sheffield Phoenix Press, 2016), 243–260. Derks, like Guest, does not use the term 'gender critical' to signal trans exclusion. Instead he refers to an engagement in an array of gender identities and expressions in an inclusive way.

scholarship. In doing so I ask how I can take the best of Guest's hetero-suspicious hermeneutic into a cispicious model. This also enables me to identify any key areas in which queer-informed approaches do not adequately serve gender nonconforming readers.

When Deborah Met Jael: Lesbian Biblical Hermeneutics

From the beginning of *When Deborah Met Jael: Lesbian Biblical Hermeneutics* (*WDMJ*), published in 2005, the dual themes of gender nonconformity and female mutuality including eroticism are immediately visible. Guest outlines the need for a lesbian-identified hermeneutic by tracing the history of lesbian identity and erasure. Once established, they then demonstrate the value of integrating personal experience and influences in biblical interpretation, particularly to facilitate an engagement with problematic presuppositions. They distinguish *WDMJ* from other queer works by making explicit the focus on lesbian-identified interpretations, largely found in female mutuality. The outworking of what constitutes female mutuality comprises much of Guest's discussion but is of less relevance for this work. Rather my interest is in how Guest engages with gender nonconformity through their particular lesbian model.

In setting the context for *WDMJ*, Guest highlights the way masculine gender nonconformity has long been understood to signal lesbianism.[32] At least since the late nineteenth century both lesbianism and female masculinity have been associated with attraction to women *and* male attire and presentation (cross-dressing, short hair, masculine demeanour), performing male social roles, and undertaking hobbies or employment traditionally associated with men.[33] This historical context is essential to understand Guest and their approach. Guest finds parallels between their own experience and identity and the models of gender nonconformity that continue to be used to signify lesbianism. The two are treated as if synonymous, which Guest, like Halberstam, traces back to the sexological movement of the late nineteenth and early twentieth centuries. This movement, largely based in Europe and North America, categorized women as inverts through reference to masculine attire, expression and physicality.[34] Congenital inverts were

---

32. Guest, *When Deborah Met Jael*, 3. Here Guest's attention to historical models of lesbianism parallels Halberstam's in *Female Masculinity* (see Chapter 1 and Halberstam, *Female Masculinity*, 45–139, 152). Both trace the roots of lesbianism and butchness through historical accounts of gender nonconformity amongst people AFAB.

33. Guest, *When Deborah Met Jael*, 11–12. 'Physically, the lesbian was variously described as possessing well-developed muscles, a masculine type of larynx, and although some (Havelock Ellis, 1936) dismissed such claims, thought to be in possession of a lengthy clitoris. Behaviourally, she was likely to prefer the clothing and work/leisure activities traditionally associated with men, and enjoy "masculine" habits such as cigar smoking.'

34. Guest, *When Deborah Met Jael*, 3, 11–14. Cf. Halberstam, *Female Masculinity*, 75–109.

perceived to be attracted to people of the same sex as themselves, although they also performed a different – sometimes considered the opposite – gender. There are, however, risks in drawing parallels between these categories and today's diversely labelled genders and sexualities as we cannot accurately infer enough of each individual's context or their own understanding of themselves to know which would fit best.[35] Guest finds it striking that inverts were *not* conforming to expectations of gender *or* sexuality and they are worthy forebears of today's lesbians. They draw out the way that the enduring perception is that congenital inverts were 'born biologically female but possessing the emotions, desires, and preferences traditionally the preserve of the male'.[36] This ensured that lesbianism could be understood as a 'visibly marked condition', something that Guest implies holds today.[37] The lesbianism that Guest's biblical interpretation seeks to identify is thus inherently gender-nonconforming.

The inferred correlation between inversion and lesbianism presents two immediate problems. The first is in the omission of the experiences of the partners of inverts, many of whom were (sufficiently) gender conforming and did not warrant the same scrutiny as their lovers.[38] The second is acknowledging that the masculinity of people AFAB is not always tied to sexuality. Based on the description of masculine emotions, desires, and habits, Prosser argues that inverts are better understood as the forebears of trans men today than lesbians.[39] As the most well-known case studies chronicle the lives of AFAB inverts who took female lovers, both understandings remain relevant and resonant. Indeed, the shared histories and points of overlap enable points of solidarity. Recognition of this complexity is essential, even at such an early stage as it shows how established and enduring are the parallels between female masculinity and lesbian identity when engaging with Guest's writing.

Once Guest establishes the working assumption that female masculinity and lesbian identification can happen in parallel, they turn their attention to heteronormativity. In addressing the foundations of heteronormativity, Guest demonstrates the significance of the Bible in the construction and maintenance of compulsory heterosexuality. They particularly highlight 'the way in which religious

---

35. Lester, *Trans Like Me*, 163–176.
36. Guest, *When Deborah Met Jael*, 11.
37. Guest, *When Deborah Met Jael*, 11.
38. Joan Nestle, 'The Femme Question', in *The Persistent Desire: A Femme-Butch Reader*, ed. Joan Nestle et al. (Boston, MA: Alyson Publications, 1992), 138–146, 144. Nestle discusses the problems that erasure of femme (and non-masculine) lesbian perspectives causes. She writes, 'historically, we have been left disinherited, seen neither as true inverts nor as grown women'. Thus, the more feminine partners of masculine inverts were considered failed inverts.
39. Prosser, *Second Skins*. He argues that the emphasis on physical, emotional, and social markers of masculinity amongst those assigned female at birth corresponds closely with accounts from trans masculine autobiography.

institutional discourse draws on selected texts to enforce a hetero-homosexual binary that appears to be ordained by God'.[40] The focus on the hetero-homosexual binary predominates in *WDMJ*. Guest adopts Robert Corber and Stephen Valocchi's definition of heteronormativity to underpin the work on hetero-suspicion and lesbian-identified hermeneutics: 'the set of norms that make heterosexuality seem natural or right and that organize homosexuality as its binary opposite'.[41] By treating female masculinity as an intrinsic part of lesbian identity, Guest does not need to use a definition that makes explicit the link between gender and sex here. It remains implied. In Corber and Valocchi's definition heteronormativity becomes identifiable as a system of norms that inform our expectations. By drawing on Adrienne Rich, Monique Wittig, and Judith Butler's work on compulsory heterosexuality, Guest makes explicit the need to address the relationship between gender and sexuality.[42] A bifurcated gender model, where gender *and* sex are understood to be fixed and binary, underpins the expectation that different – indeed opposite – sex partners form the only valid sexual relationships within heteronormativity. Such relationships are treated as the only natural and normal form of sexuality which, in turn, reflects back on to gender and sex. To perform otherwise is to defy heteronormativity, so male femininity, female masculinity and homoeroticism are all problematic.

Where the focus on heteronormativity comes into its own in *WDMJ* – and throughout Guest's canon – is in their articulation of a hermeneutic of hetero-suspicion. Guest enables a suspicious reading of biblical texts with particular regard for the way heterosexuality is embedded in both text and interpretation. They position four 'guiding principles for lesbian-identified hermeneutics'. First, 'resistance' is a 'commitment to a hermeneutic of hetero-suspicion'.[43] Second, 'rupture' commits 'to the disruption of sex-gender binaries'.[44] 'Reclamation' is third, and advocates for a 'commitment to strategies of appropriation'.[45] Finally

---

40. Guest, *When Deborah Met Jael*, 5. See also Ken Stone's powerful articulation of the heterosexual contract in Genesis 1–3 in 'Garden of Eden'. Stone concludes his article by reflecting that a queer understanding of gender, sex, and sexuality in the Garden of Eden is particularly helpful for gay male readers, although his insights are particularly pertinent for interpreting greater gender diversity (which may or may not relate to queer sexualities).

41. Robert J. Corber and Stephen Valocchi, 'Introduction', in *Queer Studies: An Interdisciplinary Reader*, ed. Robert J. Corber and Stephen Valocchi (Oxford: Blackwell, 2003), 1–20, 4. Cited in Guest, *When Deborah Met Jael*, 25 n. 11. The broader text from which Guest's quote is taken also offers no specific comment on gender diversity, but rather focuses on homosexuality (in contrast to heterosexuality) and on lesbian and gay identities (4–5).

42. Monique Wittig, 'The Straight Mind', in *The Straight Mind: And Other Essays* (Boston, MA: Beacon Press, 1992), 21–32; Rich, 'Compulsory Heterosexuality and Lesbian Existence'; Butler, *Gender Trouble*; Guest, *When Deborah Met Jael*, 23–38.

43. Guest, *When Deborah Met Jael*, 111–156.

44. Guest, *When Deborah Met Jael*, 157–194.

45. Guest, *When Deborah Met Jael*, 195–230.

're-engagement' requires a 'commitment to making a difference'.[46] These four elements are essential for Guest's approach and shape this project as I share the same commitments. These can be easily remodelled to address cisnormativity with only resistance and rupture requiring minor reconfigurations. In their adaptation of a hermeneutic of suspicion Guest aligns their work with that of their feminist forebears in searching for 'liberation readings of scripture'.[47] Such a practice 'calls to attention not only the fact that texts are permeated by ideological perspectives and norms that distort their representations of the past, but that the history of reception has been similarly permeated with Eurocentric and androcentric philosophical and theological presuppositions and perspectives'.[48] They carefully outline how this translates into a lesbian-focussed hermeneutic of hetero-suspicion, something worth citing at length:

> A hermeneutic of *hetero*-suspicion is a specifically refined version of such feminist hermeneutic of suspicion. It draws critically upon the insights and principles that have already been established while appreciating the contribution that new lesbian critical studies can offer. But while it is grounded in a feminist framework, it necessarily challenges and broadens that framework just as womanist and *mujerista* insights continue to do. By exposing the way in which the hetero-patriarchal bias of both text and the history of interpretation has operated, a lesbian-identified approach demonstrates an area of neglect in existing research...
>
> Commitment to a hermeneutic of hetero-suspicion means that the researcher is resistant to the presentation of any storyworld where female homoerotic relations are virtually absent and seeks to problematize that apparent absence. And in those few cases where the possibility of female homoeroticism *is* raised, a hermeneutic is resistant to the portrayal of such relationships as unnatural, sinful, or 'other'.[49]

Guest's lesbian emphasis comes through clearly, but it relies on the alliance with – and shared foundations from – feminist scholarship.[50] The 'hetero-' prefix emphasizes their primary interest in sexuality without any reference to gender-(non)conformity.

---

46. Guest, *When Deborah Met Jael*, 231–268.
47. Guest, *When Deborah Met Jael*, 123. They name feminist, womanist, mujerista, and postcolonial modes of suspicious hermeneutics alongside 'any other engaged mode of interpretation' as akin to their hermeneutic of hetero-suspicion.
48. Guest, *When Deborah Met Jael*, 123.
49. Guest, *When Deborah Met Jael*, 124.
50. Schüssler Fiorenza, *Wisdom Ways*, 165–190. Schüssler Fiorenza describes seven 'hermeneutical moves and turns' as a synopsis of her theorization of feminist hermeneutics to this point. These strands: 'experience', 'domination and social location', 'suspicion', 'critical evaluation', 'creative imagination', 're-membering and reconstruction', and 'transformative action for change' all feature in recontextualized form in Guest's model, which continues through into this cispicious work.

Guest's emphasis on female perspectives only indicates that their hermeneutics of hetero-suspicion uniquely serves women (and thus lesbians). Here there is just an implicit suggestion that the hermeneutics of hetero-suspicion could be used in other anti-heteronormative contexts, but that remains a distant, secondary focus.

Despite the limitations placed on Guest's hetero-suspicious hermeneutic for a lesbian audience, their interpretations come to life through integrating their personal insights. This is most apparent in their principle of re-engagement. Guest's personal reflections do not stand alone, they have consistently engaged with critical theory and biblical scholarship to refine the hermeneutics of suspicion. By reflecting on the importance of lesbian specificities informed by first-hand experience they are able to make their hetero-suspicious approach accessible for lesbian readers and those who can critically engage as such. Guest's vantage point enables them to clearly articulate the need for something specifically attuned to the needs of lesbian readers. Their own location and its representation in *WDMJ* remains informed by their specifically *butch* lesbian identity. However, Guest's feminist and queer influences shine through clearly.

The lesbian-identified hermeneutic brings these strands together, and Guest's political commitment to each cause represents their point of intersection. Guest reflects on each strand through their personal experiences, using them as a gateway to biblical interpretation. This makes an engaging demonstration of the interplay between the individual and theoretical when it comes to interpreting biblical texts. They recognize the importance of making explicit the norms and presuppositions that lead to marginalization. I find this a compelling aspect of Guest's approach and it encourages me to direct my attention to cisnormativity.

Guest confidently advocates any willing reader to take on the interpretative mantle of lesbianism. They encourage readers to read texts creatively and playfully; to journey on thought experiments from a lesbian-identified starting point even if that is not a familiar location for the reader in question. This is particularly evident in their principle of reclamation. Two strands cohere: we are invited to take on the mantle of the lesbian perspective *and* we are encouraged to draw from creative, imaginative engagements with our source material beyond our primary discipline(s). We need not be writing directly from a lesbian perspective, in part because they acknowledge the problems of narrow definitions or conceptualizations of what it means to be a lesbian. We can, however, draw from the experiences of others in shaping their interpretation. Here Guest enables readers to imaginatively engage with the text beyond the assumption that there are no lesbians in the Bible. Rather relationships between women can be explored differently, acknowledging that there may well be examples of female mutuality within the text, such as in the story of Ruth and Naomi (Ruth 1–4).[51] Guest also uses non-biblical and non-

---

51. Celena M. Duncan, 'The Book of Ruth: On Boundaries, Love, and Truth', in *Take Back the Word: A Queer Reading of the Bible*, ed. Robert E. Shore-Goss [Goss] and Mona West (Cleveland, OH: Pilgrim Press, 2000), 99–102; Mona West, 'The Book of Ruth: An Example of Procreative Strategies for Queers', in *Our Families, Our values: Snapshots of*

scholarly works as points of provocation to reconsider characters, such as their engagement with Sara Maitland's retelling of the story of Deborah and Jael (Judges 4–5).[52] Maitland's fiction imagines the meeting between Deborah and Jael, where the biblical source material proffers no such encounter. Despite its brief inclusion within *WDMJ*, Guest is clear about the contribution of this short story (not least through the title to the volume):

> In her fictional retelling of their intertwined lives, one senses that they have known each other for many years. Maitland effectively disrupts the scriptural story to the extent where their (shared) victory cannot be so easily accommodated, where their friendship is a thing of fear and unnerving disquiet for their male peers. Here, the Song of Deborah never becomes one that men can share.... The song, like the women it celebrates, disturbs the status quo, upsets the norms, and destabilizes even further for the already upset order of things. This is what makes Maitland's reading such a valuable resource for the lesbian-identified critic.[53]

Inspired by Maitland, Guest imagines a storyworld free of its heteronormative erasure of lesbianism. They affirm Deborah and Jael's interaction by treating Maitland's writing as revelatory midrash to fill in narrative gaps. While Guest acknowledges that the text is silent about any meeting between these characters, the imaginative, perhaps slightly indecent, retelling offers a lesbian glimpse. In this example, it is Maitland's creative interpretation alongside Guest's self-reflections that provide a gateway, or an access point, for the lesbian perspective to shine through. By taking on the interpretative location of a lesbian, and at least temporarily becoming lesbian-identified, the method Guest offers is accessible and adaptable. This insight, then, is rather the culmination of Guest's argument for lesbian biblical interpretation and a (broadly) female-oriented hermeneutic of hetero-suspicion. In turn, Guest's creativity in facilitating a broader engagement with their approach is helpful preparation for my own. We share a commitment to enabling readers to undertake thought experiments, informed by relevant first-hand perspectives – perhaps those that emerge through Halberstam's low theory – to embark on new interpretative adventures. In my case those adventures are explorations of the genderscape, a terrain familiar to those approaching the text and its characters with sexuality as their primary focus, but one which is also marked by subtle and powerful differences too.

Queer Kinship, ed. Robert E. Shore-Goss [Goss] and Amy Adams Squire Stronghart (Binghamton, NY: Harrington Park Press, 1997), 51–60. Cited in Guest, *When Deborah Met Jael*, 139–141. See also West's subsequent commentary to Ruth in *The Queer Bible Commentary*: Mona West, 'Ruth', in *The Queer Bible Commentary*, ed. Deryn Guest et al. (London: SCM Press, 2006), 190–194.

52. Guest, *When Deborah Met Jael*, 154.

53. Guest, *When Deborah Met Jael*, 154–155. Guest cites Sara Maitland, *Telling Tales*, London: Journeyman Press.

WDMJ is an evocative plea for hermeneutics that directly attend to areas persistently overlooked in existing modes of scholarship. Our individual insights, with critical and theoretical material pertaining to those areas of omission, can generate new hermeneutical strategies for biblical interpretation. Guest's WDMJ provides a blueprint and encourages me to undertake the development of the hermeneutics of cispicion. The four central strands – resistance, rupture, reclamation and re-engagement – provide a framework for other projects with similar aims, most notably this one. Guest's insights into gender are contextualised through the lens of lesbianism, specifically butchness, and attend to heteronormativity. Guest's WDMJ shows how intertwined these themes are but how, ultimately, one facet is likely to predominate discussions. Here it is lesbianism that becomes the strongest theme of Guest's approach, despite repeated focus on butchness as a synonym for both gender diversity and lesbian identity. By contrast, I propose a cispicious lens that allows for space to respond to gender nonconformity. This allows me to conceptualize broader models of gender-nonconforming women even where there is no other hint of lesbian-identification.

In continuing to engage with Guest's use of the hetero-suspicious hermeneutic I am interested in how butchness shapes their exploration. Which models of butchness does Guest use and how do they relate to lesbian identity? How does Guest's personal identity and location in parallel with their engagement with theory aid interpretation, particularly when dealing with difficult texts? I will also explore how a subtle shift in emphasis can reveal new aspects of marginalisation that warrant greater recognition.

Looking Lesbian at the Bathing Bathsheba

Guest positions 'Looking Lesbian at the Bathing Bathsheba' ('LLBB', 2008) as a follow up to *WDMJ* and offers a gentle recontextualization of their lesbian-identified hermeneutic.[54] They reiterate their concern that lesbian scholarship remains invisible within the field of feminist biblical criticism, and at times warrants disagreement with assumptions made within feminist scholarship. The opening section highlights differences between the lesbians of whom Guest writes and the women associated with feminist scholarship – both authors and subjects. Guest's lesbian subjects are in marked contrast with their feminist but heteronormative counterparts. In feminist interpretations attraction to women (or female mutuality) is absent, while female masculinity is dismissed. As in *WDMJ* this differentiation emphasises the importance of gender-nonconformity overtly in Guest's argument.

Using discussions of artistic representations of Bathsheba bathing (2 Samuel 11:2) as example, Guest contrasts their lesbian approach from that of feminist interpreters.

---

54. Guest, 'Looking Lesbian'.

> From a feminist perspective, I understood only too well the necessity of keeping a critical distance from the scene, and appreciated the need to expose the androcentric interests implicit in such a representation. Yet I simultaneously found this painting attractive and pleasurable; therein lay the jarring. Perhaps this explains one of the major reasons why lesbian perspectives have not been forthcoming within feminist Biblical Studies: they transgress a feminist taboo that women should not themselves objectify another woman.[55]

Here it is sexual desire that Guest highlights as the differentiating factor between feminist and lesbian-identified perspectives. What endures is their recognition of the limits of an interpretative model that does not adequately address a given context. This is particularly evident when Guest reflects that lesbian scholarship may not readily find its home 'among women and feminist Biblical Studies'.[56] They continue:

> Indeed this is an assumption made in my recent attempt to define a lesbian biblical hermeneutic. However, I did not adequately address the fact that some key lesbian studies expose a very problematic, if not averse, relationship to the category 'woman'. Perhaps lesbian perspectives have not been readily found within feminist biblical criticism because their 'home' lies elsewhere, in lesbian/gay or in queer studies.[57]

Guest makes a noteworthy shift in their discussion of the disconnection between lesbian and feminist hermeneutics. In the earlier example Guest recognized their attraction to Bathsheba, an expression of desire that marked their perspective as different from their feminist counterparts. Here, however, it is an aversion to inclusion within the category of 'woman'.

The complex relationship between lesbian and woman features strongly in Guest's later discussions where they turn from a feminist to a lesbian interpretation of the bathing scene. Guest returns to discussion of the sexological movements that featured in the early portions of *WDMJ*. Here the sexological insights are interpreted through Cheshire Calhoun's reflections. From Guest's perspective, Calhoun 'suggests that [the sexological movement] created a category by which lesbians stood "*outside* of the sex/gender categories 'woman' and 'man'" and she reads them as constituting the lesbian not in terms of mannishness but "by her externality to binary sex/gender categories" (2000: 69)'.[58] The challenge to address gender diversity *and* sexuality comes through strongly with a return of Guest's butch figure. They emphasise that butch is differentiated from the category of woman. The resultant disconnection from feminist scholarship comes through

---

55. Guest, 'Looking Lesbian', 231.
56. Guest, 'Looking Lesbian', 233.
57. Guest, 'Looking Lesbian', 233.
58. Guest, 'Looking Lesbian', 239.

more strongly than in *WDMJ*.⁵⁹ Butchness appears a contested realm, where such female masculinity is maligned. Instead, Guest argues that from a butch perspective the relationship between femininity/masculinity and maleness/femaleness leads to a desire for a home free from the binaries. Here misogyny and sexism are accompanied by hostility from certain feminist quarters, highlighting butches are affected by problems from both androcentric and feminist norms. It is butchness, as a specific aspect of lesbianism, that comes to the fore strongly in this reading.

While Guest persuasively argues for the hermeneutic of hetero-suspicion, their emphasis remains on a butch lesbian perspective. They offer only a brief recognition of wider modes of lesbianism and no reflection on non-lesbian examples of female masculinity or butchness. They note that 'femme lesbians often (rightly) complain that they are invisible in lesbian discourse and history. Due to their presentation of "feminine" attributes, femme lesbians have been largely indistinguishable from heterosexual feminine women. It has only been when they are paired with butch partners that their sexuality becomes visibly evident'.⁶⁰ Guest's succinct discussion of feminine lesbian womanhood emphasises again their more dominant interest in butchness and female masculinity. There is no discussion about whether such femininity conforms to or diverges from gender norms, as in the case of butches.⁶¹ In addition, Guest does not offer any reflection on a combination of butchness or female masculinity and an attraction to men. While understandable given Guest's location as butch and lesbian, I am reminded again of the need to recognize the working assumptions in explorations of gender nonconformity and lesbian identity.⁶² Guest acknowledges, in a parenthetical remark, that '"lesbian" is not always a stable category: one can "do" lesbian in a variety of contestable ways and lesbians themselves do not always agree definitions'.⁶³ This is an important recognition of both the value of a lesbian-identified hermeneutic and its limitations: 'in a lesbian-identified hermeneutic there must be space to explore site-specific oppression, knowing that our choices bring additional burdens'.⁶⁴ Guest acknowledges that the decisions about

59. Guest, 'Looking Lesbian', 239–243.

60. Guest, 'Looking Lesbian', 243–244.

61. Cf. Nestle, 'Femme Question'. Nestle argues that femmes are also gender nonconforming, through a heightened performance of femininity. In butch-femme partnerships, the femme partner's performance frequently provides validation of, and security for, the butch partner.

62. Guest, 'Looking Lesbian', 250. Describing themself, Guest writes, 'Not-woman I may be, but *for*-woman, *pro*-woman I certainly am in a way that an androcentric, patriarchal narrative would never be'.

63. Guest, 'Looking Lesbian', 244.

64. Guest, 'Looking Lesbian', 250. One such recognition is in Guest's suggestion that a femme reading could offer insights into Bathsheba's perspective but they imply that they do not feel suited to offer such reflection: 'This paper has a butch lesbian take on the bathing scene, but this could be combined with a femme perspective that more ably provides a voice for Bathsheba – or rather provides a space for Bathsheba the femme to speak to us'.

which perspectives to amplify have implications for subsequent readers. Their articulation of the significance of butchness in their own location is powerful, but it comes at the cost of other forms of lesbian identity. It remains important to consider how a hermeneutic can build on Guest's foundation to move beyond only butch lesbian locations.

'LLBB' moves on significantly from *WDMJ* with regard to gender nonconformity. Guest foregrounds butchness here while putting themselves into the potentially problematic location of the voyeuristic observer of Bathsheba's beauty. They find a queer rupture through which to distance themselves from the original voyeur, David's abuse within the text and feminist scholarship's revulsion in the face of sexual desire. Here Guest clearly shows the difference between their lesbian-identified insights and the feminist approaches that predominate in sympathetic scholarship of Bathsheba. Desire, attraction and the sensuality of sexuality come to the fore, but the clearer image of Guest's lesbian gaze shines through the more confidently as they assert their neither male nor female masculinity. Clearly, for Guest these themes are inextricable, but I find that interplay to be limiting. In the relationship between feminist and queer approaches, between Guest's observer and Bathsheba's observee, there is a chasm that cannot entirely be addressed by a lesbian gaze. Nor can I see that solely being served by a cispicious interpretation. Here both hetero-suspicious and cispicious approaches find some value but it is only through Guest's distinctively butch lesbian perspective that the gender nonconformity aspect of Bathsheba's story becomes visible. Still, Guest acknowledges that a lesbian Bathsheba may have a very different insight. I value the articulation of gender nonconformity as part of a lesbian identity, but think the interpretation reaches beyond merely a lesbian-identified perspective. An engagement with cisnormativity would help here to consolidate this argument and clarify points of overlap and dissonance between gender nonconforming and lesbian identities.

Leaving 'LLBB', I want to see how biblical accounts of gender diversity are understood when approached with the creativity and critical aptitude demonstrated by Guest so far. I examine whether there is a deeper engagement with gender nonconformity, even if it is not always accompanied by lesbian desire and relationships. Whether this is contextualised in relation to heteronormativity is now of secondary interest since Guest's articulation of gender diversity is coming to the fore. With that in mind, I am interested in how such gender diversity is positioned *vis à vis* feminism, queer scholarship (broadly conceived), and Guest's particular models of lesbian-identified and hetero-suspicious hermeneutics. Fortunately, such attention follows in 'From Gender Reversal to Genderfuck: Reading Jael Through a Lesbian Lens'.

From Gender Reversal to Genderfuck: Reading Jael Through a Lesbian Lens

Continuing the application of lesbian-identified hermeneutics, 2011's 'From Gender Reversal to Genderfuck: Reading Jael Through a Lesbian Lens' ('FGRG') takes the exploration of gender diversity far further than 'LLBB'.⁶⁵ It is the first of Guest's works where gender (nonconformity) is the preeminent theme. With that shift comes a more assertive, indeed defiant, approach which facilitates a genderqueering interpretation. It is, however, still contextualized through a lesbian lens.⁶⁶ The shift in focus is evident through the opening discussion of genderfuck and its relation to queer theory:

> Genderfuck: a stark, startling word with which to commence a paper. It's an edgy word, capable of offense, especially with that harsh third syllable sitting so indecently within the respectable – decent – domain of biblical studies.... Genderfuck ... is the language and business of queer theory. Consistent with its aims of political activism, the confrontational, uncompromising stance of queer theory is one of resistance to such binaries: subverting, undoing, deconstructing the normalcy of sex/gender regimes, cracking them open, focusing on the fissures that expose their constructedness. If the word puts one on edge, then it accomplishes its purpose.⁶⁷

While a clarification of the lesbian contribution follows shortly, these introductory remarks establish a focus on gender, moving beyond the binary, that is edgy. There is a playfulness in Guest's articulation, especially through allusion to Althaus-Reid's indecency, that ensures a genderfuck reading is overtly, intentionally queer.

The central emphasis on queerness is a marked contrast with Guest's earlier lesbian-identified hermeneutic. Despite shifting focus in this interpretation, Guest's commitment to lesbian readings even here is striking. They reaffirm the need to keep a lesbian approach distinct from the wider queer discipline as 'it runs the risk of being assimilated all too soon, especially within the domain of biblical interpretation, where it is hardly established at all'.⁶⁸ They justify this with reference to an interdisciplinary foundation of their project and its inherent complexity through 'the overlapping yet simultaneous distinctions between butch-lesbian, transgender and transsexual communities [which] come to the fore in unexpected and complex ways' in this project.⁶⁹ The description 'butch-lesbian' now identifies clearly the specific hyphenated gender-nonconforming lesbian with whom we have journeyed throughout *WDMJ* and 'LLBB'. Guest now highlights the value of their work for a broader audience than just their lesbian readers. 'Transgender' here recalls Halberstam's *Female Masculinity* and his continuum of masculinity.⁷⁰ It also references the models of gender nonconformity associated with Leslie

---

65. Guest, 'From Gender Reversal'.
66. Guest, 'From Gender Reversal', 9.
67. Guest, 'From Gender Reversal', 9.
68. Guest, 'From Gender Reversal', 11–12.
69. Guest, 'From Gender Reversal', 11.
70. Halberstam, *Female Masculinity*. For further discussion, see Chapter 1.

Feinberg's gender warriors, Kate Bornstein's gender outlaws, and Riki Wilchins's sexual subversives who reflect a desire to destroy gender and live beyond the familiar and oppressive binary.[71] Meanwhile Guest's use of 'transsexual' specifically includes those trans people who have transitioned from one sex to another, generally through hormonal and surgical intervention.[72] These are subgroups gathered under the umbrella term trans in this project (and in the most recent of Guest's publications featured here), but they are best understood in their specific contextual forms in 'FGRG'.

Use of these three categories leads me, cautiously, to suggest that a lesbian lens – as Guest describes it – may be something of a misleading designation. Despite a discernible shift in focus, Guest argues for the continuing influence of a (their?) lesbian perspective that 'brings with it the influence of feminist theory, lesbian and gay studies, queer theory, transgender studies and queer film criticism, breaking upon the traditional and cherished norms of historical-critical exegesis with all the force of sexual gate-crashers at a party from which they have been excluded'.[73] The clarity that comes with an approach that 'consciously and deliberately interrogates

---

71. Feinberg, *Transgender Warriors*; Riki A. Wilchins, *Read My Lips: Sexual Subversion and the End of Gender* (Ithaca, NY: Firebrand Books, 1997); Kate Bornstein, *Gender Outlaw: On Men, Women, and the Rest of Us*, Revised & Updated ed. (New York: Vintage, 2016). See also Carol Queen and Lawrence Schimel, eds, *Pomosexuals: Challenging Assumptions About Gender and Sexuality* (San Francisco, CA: Cleis Press, 2001).

In their 2016 updated edition of *Gender Outlaw*, Bornstein acknowledges the problems caused by a destruction of the gender binary, especially to binary trans people (xi-xx). Acknowledging their shift in perspective, they write 'I understand today that for many people, cis and trans alike, it's a good deal more comforting to work with gender as a binary – but the either/or of it was never a comfort to me. All I knew to express, all those years ago, was in today's language:
 BINARY GENDER = BAD
 NONBINARY GENDER= GOOD
Of course that is not true. It's a binary notion that's been targeted by critics of my ideas of gender. In this edition, I've done my best to break that binary with a more nuanced analysis', Bornstein, *Gender Outlaw*, xvii-xviii, emphasis original. I also try to reflect that more nuanced engagement in this cispicious endeavour. They later add, evocatively, 'we need to do away with any system of gender that pressures us into believing that we are imperfectly gendered' (xviii).

72. Prosser, *Second Skins*; Namaste, *Invisible Lives*; 'Undoing Theory'. Prosser and Namaste both recognize the intersection between queer and trans identities amongst those who argue for a destruction of the gender binary. They critique high profile figures – such as Bornstein, Feinberg and Wilchins – for erasing or negating the experiences of trans people who find their identity bolstered by their identification within that same binary. For further discussion see Chapter 1.

73. Guest, 'From Gender Reversal', 10.

that with its own agenda' and 'is disobedient in its employment of a hermeneutic of (hetero-)suspicion' shines through with confidence. Such interdisciplinarity is not unique to lesbian approaches. In the subsequent close reading of Jael's story in Judges 4–5 Guest demonstrates an approach more aptly described as an interdisciplinary genderqueer approach.

The emphasis on a lesbian approach helpfully signals attention to a character who is traditionally understood as female and a woman, and who has previously been encountered through a differently focussed lesbian lens.[74] Now Guest offers a powerful and compelling argument to understand Jael as a genderqueer character, freed from the constraints of binary gender norms. Again, Guest introduces feminist insights into the character, highlighting the limitations of such readings. In particular they identify an inescapable perception of Jael as a woman, albeit with a recognition that *she* does not always conform to or cohere within traditional heteronormative expectations. Guest flags the use of pronouns by commentators as signifying the enduring perception of Jael as woman. They note this is particularly striking where otherwise Jael's gender is presented as liminal or performed in a reversed form. With regard to Gale Yee's exploration of Jael's liminal gender, Guest argues

> the use of 'liminal' is problematic since it could be read as stabilizing the two-sex paradigm. Liminality, insofar as it is suggestive of a third term, does not sufficiently do the work of disrupting or subverting, creating rather a space 'between', one that contains elements of both – stable – sex/gender categories.[75]

Contextualized as 'more closely resembling the lesbian questions and concerns' Guest's reflection on Yee's commentary emphasises an interest in queer's deconstruction of binaries.[76] By contrast with their feminist forebears, Guest uses their desire to consider gender(queerness) beyond the binary when closely reading the biblical text. Beginning with a recognition that all gender is performed, after Butler, Guest analyses Jael without relying on the assumption that the character is female or a woman. After rejecting the assignation of female pronouns for the character – either in the biblical text or in commentary – Guest reintroduces Jael. We now encounter someone with a masculine name accompanied by a recognition of their masculinity.[77] Jael briefly appears the perfect simulacra of the 'seductive tent-dwelling woman' before proceeding to rape and murder Sisera in what Guest calls 'a moment of genderfuck, for here is an unintelligible gender – a "female-with-a-penis"'.[78] Guest uses this striking term to emphasize gender-nonconformity

---

74. Guest, *When Deborah Met Jael*, 152–155. As discussed above, the engagement with Jael in *WDMJ* is brief and primarily undertaken through the lens of Maitland's short story.
75. Guest, 'From Gender Reversal', 16.
76. Guest, 'From Gender Reversal', 16.
77. Guest, 'From Gender Reversal', 21.
78. Guest, 'From Gender Reversal', 23, 26.

through the euphemistic connotations of the use of the terms 'hand' and 'peg' in Jael's murder of Sisera (Judg 5:26).[79] Equally Jael has long been understood as a *femme fatale*, leading Guest to consider parallels between the film character shockingly revealed to be trans through the 'totally unexpected exposure of the "woman's" penis'.[80] Guest rejects the suggestion that such revelation warrants captivation, titillation, horror or delight by emphasizing that 'penis possession is not necessarily an indicator of maleness'.[81] Rather they suggest Jael's story contributes to an emerging understanding of intersex or trans journeys whilst also serving to undermine 'the two-sex paradigm'.[82] This is particularly apparent when Guest concludes the section:

> Speaking of Jael as a woman warrior is thus insufficient. Jael is not a *woman* warrior and equally Jael is not a *male* rapist. The narrator has conjured a figure who carries a resonance he could probably never have anticipated for readers in the early twenty-first century. Jael is a figure who unsettles and destabilizes, whose performativity provides one of those unintelligible genders that give the lie to ideas of sex as abiding substance.[83]

No matter how much Guest focuses on Jael's genderfuckery and suggests that penises do not *necessarily* signify maleness, it is that very signifier Guest highlights. Indeed, they emphasize the phallic violence – rape – to consolidate Jael's unintelligible gender. This portrayal of Jael by Guest is a contentious one, no matter how welcome the emphasis on gender nonconformity – nor how much the focus remains on revealing Jael's masculinity and maleness.

One flaw is the persistent desire to explore Jael's rejection of femininity for fear that recognition of any femininity whatsoever will undermine Guest's argument. They seem unable to envisage that someone who is genderqueer, especially AFAB and who is not a woman, might embrace femininity and apparent femaleness for more than a moment. Reading Jael as 'a recognisable figure for those lesbians who organize their gender presentation as butch-ish' leads Guest to balk at the character who then appears almost the epitome of the womanly woman.[84] The fear that Jael's genderqueerness is lost through this return to femininity is palpable:

---

79. Guest, 'From Gender Reversal', 25. Guest traces the use of the euphemistic use of the term *yad* for penis in Isa 57:8; Song 5:4 and more questionably in Jer 5.31; 50:15. They cite Danna Nolan Fewell and David Gunn's identification of the phallic connotations of 'peg' in Aristophanes and the Anthologia Gaeca. See Danna Nolan Fewell and David M. Gunn, 'Controlling Perspectives: Women, Men and the Authority of Violence in Judges 4 and 5.' *Journal of the American Academy of Religion*, 58, 3 (1990), 389–411: 394 n.13.

80. Guest, 'From Gender Reversal', 25. Cf. Halberstam, *In a Queer Time*; Serano, *Whipping Girl*, 36–45.

81. Guest, 'From Gender Reversal', 26.

82. Guest, 'From Gender Reversal', 26. Emphasis original.

83. Guest, 'From Gender Reversal', 26.

84. Guest, 'From Gender Reversal', 23–24.

there are so few instances where such genderqueerness comes so clearly to the surface that it is important not to relapse readily into the simultaneous imaging of Jael as seductive tent-dwelling woman, *especially* when that female gender is allowed to overcome something that is thereby reduced to a momentary 'figuration'.[85]

This anxiety, and its contextualization through reference to the butch-ish lesbians 'who are not "men" or "wannabe men" yet are not comfortable with the category of "woman" either' is helpful for two reasons.[86] First, pausing in this moment is important. Second, Guest's mode of genderqueerness – which rejects the categories of both man and woman – provides *one* model for a genderqueer Jael,[87] whereas my cispicious framework offers a multiplicity of options. Cispicion allows me to see here someone as willing to play the woman as they will be to play the man later in the same story. Working from the assumption that nonbinary genders exist and come in many nebulous forms, Jael is rendered no less genderqueer or nonbinary for a momentary jaunt into the world of the woman – or, for that matter, that of the man. Within my purview, such behaviour by Jael contributes to, rather than detracts from, gender nonconformity.

While Guest's use of the language of a lesbian approach endures, there is a subtle shift in the language of their suspicious hermeneutic. What was a hyphenated term between *WDMJ* and 'LLBB' has become parenthetical here in its sole reference: (hetero)suspicion.[88] While there may be no substantive difference intended, I find this shift noteworthy. The parenthesis suggests less confidence in the mode of suspicion being deployed. Guest uses a queer deconstruction of gender binaries, informed by lesbian, queer and trans studies specifically, to address gender; sexuality features so minimally in this project. Rather it is an emphasis on butchness, again, that marks this as a lesbian reading. There is no space here for non-butch lesbian readings or for other models of genderqueerness than masculinity-driven ones to guide the interpretation. 'FGRG' offers a tantalizing and highly persuasive glimpse of a genderqueer reading strategy. This article offers one of, if not the most, compelling example of the potential engaging with gender diversity. Guest evocatively shows how to understand a character when their gender – as expressed through language including naming and pronouns, social roles and physical acts – is not assumed without question.

---

85. Guest, 'From Gender Reversal', 23.

86. Guest, 'From Gender Reversal', 24.

87. See Aysha Winstanley Musa, 'Jael Is Non-Binary; Jael Is Not A Woman', *Journal for Interdisciplinary Biblical Studies* 1, 2 (2020), 97–120; Aysha Winstanley Musa, 'Jael's Gender Ambiguity in Judges 4 and 5' (PhD University of Sheffield, 2020), http://etheses.whiterose.ac.uk/27692/. Musa contrasts her reading with Guest's arguing that through her interpretation Jael more definitively emerges as a nonbinary figure who cannot be constrained by the gender binary.

88. Guest, 'From Gender Reversal', 10.

In their own reflections, Guest notes the importance of ensuring the focus remains on genderqueering in projects such as 'FGRG':

> Genderqueer readers, especially those for whom the Bible remains a significant and/or sacred text, might find Jael's occupation of a not-man-not-woman ground not only of interest but a joyous and unexpected treasure within a canon of texts that are often used to provide ammunition against their choices. Given that Jael's liminality is celebrated, and that this is a powerful performance, Jael seems to provide an unforeseen biblical character for those butch lesbians who desire to wear their genderqueerness with pride. *For this to occur, the genderqueerness of Jael needs to remain uppermost in this interpretation.*[89]

Guest's enduring focus on application of the lesbian lens underplays, and perhaps even slightly undermines, the impact of this work for scholarship seeking to diversify biblical genderscapes due to the persistent spectre of sexuality. Guest pre-empts these challenges, addressing the importance of borders: 'Having been critical of feminist biblical studies for suppressing, unconsciously or otherwise, the voice of lesbian feminists, lesbian interpretation should not render invisible the specifics of transgender and transsexual histories, communities, and acts of interpretation.'[90] I value Guest's recognition of the limits of their own work in 'FGRG'. However, their continued focus on heteronormativity creates an unintended border, to use Guest's term. Given the critiques of queer approaches levied by Serano, Prosser and Namaste, Guest's genderfuck reading risks 'suppressing, unconsciously or otherwise' the trans readers they seek. Where heteronormativity offers us one opportunity to interrogate gender, it frequently remains inescapable from sexuality. In turn, that adds to the risk that lesbian or other modes of queer scholarship 'suppress, unconsciously or otherwise,' trans hermeneutics and those that facilitate an engagement with the strong current of cisnormativity. In response, I argue for a hermeneutics of cispicion that continues to engage with genderqueerness, but does so through locating it in a wider, trans-informed genderscape. The creation of such a genderscape is, in turn, an outworking of my commitment to treat cisnormativity with suspicion. My approach will act as a complement to Guest's lesbian hermeneutic and other queer models that work towards a diverse understanding of cisnormativity.

'FGRG' showcases both the potential for and value of an engagement with gender beyond cisnormative presuppositions. Where Guest's use of the lesbian-identified approach in the earlier works reveals something powerful about the understanding of queer women and heteronormativity, here the approach does not sit as easily. 'FGRG' brings into focus the importance of a subtle difference between their approach to butchness and Halberstam's. For me, Halberstam's interrogation of butchness is centred around the concept of AFAB masculinities. While butch identity does perpetually intersect with lesbianness, lesbian identification is less

---

89. Guest, 'From Gender Reversal', 31. Emphasis added.
90. Guest, 'From Gender Reversal', 32.

important than the revelation of non-male masculinities in Halberstam's *Female Masculinity*. By contrast, butch and lesbian are *almost* used interchangeably by Guest. The lesbian component of butchness is at least as integral to Guest's conceptualisation as is masculinity. This might appear a matter of nuance, but low theory argues attention to such small details really does matter. They profoundly impact Guest's presentation of genderqueerness. To be genderqueer here, at least, is to conform neither to heteronormative expectations of gender *nor* sexuality at the same time. Genderqueerness is so much of a focus in Guest's work that it almost obscures the lesbian specificities so important in *WDMJ* and 'LLBB'. Guest provides no exploration of the female mutuality that was so important earlier. Nor do they succeed in freeing gender nonconformity from its tie to sexual identities, i.e., lesbianism. 'FGRG' reveals more effectively than any of Guest's previous works the complexity of exploring gender nonconformity when the frame of reference is inescapably wedded to heteronormativity. In response, I acknowledge the interplay between gender and sexuality, but see possibilities for a more targeted and focussed exploration of gender. It is this commitment that leads me to build the hermeneutics of cispicion on the foundations of Guest's work, especially 'FGRG'.

Looking towards *Beyond Feminist Biblical Studies* I am interested in how distinctions and specificities associated with gender diversity feature in discussion with sexuality as the two themes more visibly jostle. By shifting their attention to gender scholarship more broadly conceived than feminist, queer, or critical studies of masculinity, Guest acknowledges that there are limitations in those approaches. Moreover, they implicitly recognise the importance of boundaries between these disciplines when seeking to elevate some interpretative insights over others. Given the importance of heteronormativity in shaping Guest's approaches, I continue to explore how that impacts their portrayal of gender nonconformity.

Beyond Feminist Biblical Studies

Beyond Feminist Biblical Studies (*BFBS*, 2012), Guest's second monograph, provides an excellent follow up to 'FGRG' and takes further their exploration of gender nonconformity. Here butchness takes a back seat as diversifying the understandings of gender predominates Guest's argument; butchness is implicitly just one part of that richer genderscape. This project consolidates Guest's critiques of feminist biblical scholarship which are significant contributions from (and to) their earlier works. A persistent theme in Guest's lesbian and genderqueer work is that of the shortcomings of feminist scholarship when faced with heteronormativity. *BFBS*, therefore, offers a robust engagement with the limitations of feminism through scholarship that calls into question the validity of heteronormativity in addition to androcentrism and patriarchy, namely 'gender critical' scholarship.[91]

---

91. While 'gender criticism' is the preferred name for the approach advocated by Guest in *BFBS*, it remains important to differentiate their inclusive approach from its trans-exclusionary

BFBS is a denouement for Guest's engagement with feminist scholarship and offers a clear articulation of possible ways forwards. It is an exciting and well-constructed argument that shows diversity of gender and sexuality to be complex and in profound need of more (nuanced) critical engagement. Guest argues for a more explicit engagement beyond heteronorms, not limited to women perceived to be (only) heterosexual. An array of men, non-gendernormative women, and genderqueer characters identifiable amongst the Bible's characters also warrant overt attention.

Guest locates 'gender criticism' in the legacy of Butler's work, specifically referencing compulsory heterosexuality, which serves as a foundation for socially constructed basis to gender and sex. They write:

> informed by the broad trends of [Butler's] work, though not always in agreement with it, the gender critic does not take sexed categories as givens, but interrogates the way in which sex, gender, and sexualities are constructed, naturalized, and policed. Critically, gender criticism also explores ways in which the regularizing and naturalizing compunctions can be subverted, for herein lies its capacity for a transforming politics.[92]

Once again, we encounter the continuing commitment to a political engagement with the outworkings of heteronormativity. In distinction from their earlier projects gender diversity features explicitly alongside explorations of sexuality. Even the subtle change to the language of sexual*ities* in their plural emphasizes the shift from the earlier lesbian hermeneutic. By contrast, sex and gender still appear in their singular forms. Despite that inconsistency, Guest goes on to stress that 'gender criticism' is interested in revealing richness of detail:

> As for the topics of interest, these include the significance that is attached to sex and gender in various texts, and the positive or negative or ambiguous valuing of these performativities. Gender criticism is interested in the differentiation *within* those categories (the many and various ways of doing 'man', for instance) and the indeterminate spaces between them (places where male/female, masculinity/femininity/ [sic] hetero-erotic/homoerotic are fluid and therefore call into question those very binaries). It explores cases of gender performance where one does 'woman' particularly badly, or well, or with unexpected flair, or fails to convince entirely.... Of key interest are cases of disruption.[93]

counterpart. Guest is not applying a methodology that seeks to challenging the validity of trans experience; quite the opposite. The use of 'gender criticism' for the type of research represented by *BFBS* has been superseded by those promoting a political and social agenda that privileges natal sex as the only authoritative basis for gender. This is not Guest's aim and is antithetical to the aims of this project.

92. Guest, *Beyond Feminist Biblical Studies*, 18.
93. Guest, *Beyond Feminist Biblical Studies*, 18.

This outline emphasizes how strongly gender diversity features in this project, in contrast with the earlier works where it is largely subsumed into lesbian readings. Both lesbian identity and butchness are less visible, although still discernibly inform Guest's approach. The difference in focus is clearest when Guest engages explicitly with transness and intersex: '[Gender criticism] actively explores intersex and transgender bodies and the myriad ways of doing sex and gender that do not map onto any existing categories; those that flit between categories as well as the abject category that falls through the cracks, i.e., non-category, those for which we have no adequate language'.[94] This explicit attention to gender and sex is welcome. I do, however, question the extent to which Guest foregrounds those perspectives, rather than merely acknowledges them. Recalling Guest's earlier comments about the limited lip-service paid to lesbian perspectives in both feminist and queer scholarship, I see a need for a more specific hermeneutic to address gender diversity, namely this cispicious one, alongside other trans-oriented hermeneutics.

Guest makes a compelling case for (trans inclusive) 'gender criticism's' contribution to textual interpretation:

> Gender criticism is interested in how the author of the text, consciously or unconsciously, applies heteronormative expectations on to the characters, whether to legitimise or ostracize, and in doing so grants them a solidity of sorts. The reader is lulled into a compliance that it is 'men' or 'women' one is reading about, even when those 'men' or 'women' do not maintain gender expectations terribly well.[95]

Guest importantly recognizes that there is a relationship between reader, author and all who have shaped the text and its interpretation. The original meaning contributes to a reader's understanding, but we are not solely reliant on it. There are unintended, occluded or otherwise different understandings of the same text that also warrant attention. More important still is Guest's recognition that we, the readers, are complicit in reproducing fixed, binary presuppositions drawn from dominant gender norms; this is not something we *have* to keep doing. They persuasively argue that 'gender critical' biblical interpretation holds the potential to diversify the genderscape in a way similar to the one I advocate for, but with one key difference: heteronormativity remains the primary frame of reference.[96] This is clear, specific, and helpful in preparing the way for a cispicious approach. Indeed, the focus on heteronormativity marks out 'gender criticism's' distinct contribution.[97] *BFBS* consolidates Guest's work to this point and highlights how far an overt focus on heteronormativity can take biblical scholarship. There still remains more to be done when it comes to gender and cisnormativity.

---

94. Guest, *Beyond Feminist Biblical Studies*, 19–20.
95. Guest, *Beyond Feminist Biblical Studies*, 20.
96. Guest, *Beyond Feminist Biblical Studies*, 30.
97. Guest, *Beyond Feminist Biblical Studies*, 40. 'Gender criticism is not, in reality, any less contentious than feminist criticism. When utilized to its full potential to unseat

In *BFBS* Guest returns to explore heteronormativity once again. Drawn from the same edited collection as the model used in *WDMJ*, here Guest opts for a more extended exploration, this time selecting Lauren Berlant and Michael Warner's conceptualization:

> Heteronormativity refers to 'the institutions, structures of understanding, and practical orientations that make heterosexuality not only coherent, that is, organized as a sexuality – but also privileged … It consists less of notions that could be summarized as a body of doctrine than of a sense of rightness produced in contradictory manifestations – often unconscious, immanent to practice or institutions' (Berlant and Warner 2003: 179–180 n.2). Berlant and Warner additionally describe heteronormativity as 'more than ideology or prejudice, or phobia against gays and lesbians; it is produced in almost every aspect of the forms and arrangements of social life: nationality, the state, and the law; commerce; medicine; and education; as well as in the conventions and affects of narrativity, romance, and other protected spaces of culture.' It is that 'sense of rightness' which can appear as if it is 'hardwired into personhood' (2003: 173).[98]

Even within this more nuanced definition gender diversity remains, at best, an implicit component of heteronormativity. Guest mitigates this, to some extent, by referring to '*hetero*gender' and includes this within the specific remit of 'gender

---

heteronormativity and categories of sex, gender and sexuality it will be seen to have its own radical agenda, though it does need to make more evident the transformative consequences of its theorizing'. See also Derks, '"If I Be Shaven"', 554.

98. Lauren Berlant and Michael Warner, 'Sex in Public', in *Queer Studies: An Interdisciplinary Reader*, ed. Robert J Corber and Stephen Valocchi (Oxford: Blackwell, 2003), 170–183. Cited in Guest, *Beyond Feminist Biblical Studies*, 57 n.18. This is in contrast with the definition from Corber and Valocchi's introductory chapter to the same edited collection and cited by Guest in *WDMJ*, see n.41 above.

In the original journal publication of the same work, the inclusion of gender norms is more explicit, but that emphasis has been lost *en route*. Berlant and Warner include reference to the contribution of gender and sex within the framework of heteronormativity: 'Gay and lesbian theory, especially in the humanities, frequently emphasizes psychoanalytic or psychoanalytic-style models of subject-formation, the differences among which are significant and yet all of which tend to elide the difference between the categories male/female and the process and project of heteronormativity. Three propositional paradigms are relevant here: those that propose that human identity itself is fundamentally organized by gender identifications that are hardwired into infants; those that equate the clarities of gender identity with the domination of a relatively coherent and vertically stable "straight" ideology; and those that focus on a phallocentric Symbolic order that produces gendered subjects who live out the destiny of their position'. Lauren Berlant and Michael Warner, 'Sex in Public', *Critical Inquiry* 24, 2: Intimacy (1998), 547–566: 552 n.11.

critical' scholarship.⁹⁹ They take into *BFBS* Chrys Ingraham's conceptualisation of the term: 'Gender, or what I would call "heterogenders", is the asymmetrical stratification of the sexes in relation to the historically varying institutions of patriarchal heterosexuality'.¹⁰⁰ From this foundation, Guest sees the value of heterogender 'making visible the connection of gender norms with heterosexuality that is often being analysed'.¹⁰¹ This is a helpful conceptualization as it clearly, inescapably allies the gender being interrogated with the normative framework for hetero*sexuality*; both are considered socially constructed *and* naturally given.¹⁰² Guest adapts Ingraham's insights for the hermeneutics of hetero-suspicion and genderqueer criticism.¹⁰³ Questions of sexuality still clearly persist here. Guest argues that perhaps '*genderqueer*' criticism is 'a more useful and accurate term, bringing together, as it does, the connection of gender and sexuality in a rich field of analysis'.¹⁰⁴ In their earlier works, gender nonconformity was the ever-present undercurrent to ostensibly sexuality-oriented works. Here the reverse is true: the topic of sexuality is inescapable although the focus on gender diversity is preeminent.

Guest does acknowledge some of the problems faced when trying to clearly differentiate queerness of gender from that of sexuality. They acknowledge that the majority of gender studies – including within 'gender criticism' – work from assumptions I would call cisnormative. Reflecting Guest's use of the term heterogender, the adoption of genderqueer criticism makes sense as a response to

99. As with all uses of the term 'gender critical' I refer back to Guest's own application. This has no link with, or sympathy for, trans exclusionary activism, gender scholarship, or politics.

100. Chrys Ingraham, 'The Heterosexual Imaginary: Feminist Sociology and Theories of Gender', *Sociological Theory* 12, 2 (1994), 203–219: 204.

101. Guest, *Beyond Feminist Biblical Studies*, 42–43.

102. Guest, *Beyond Feminist Biblical Studies*, 82. 'Heterogender is preferable because it makes clear the complicitness of gender in the institution of heterosexuality. It points to the cultural construction of both terms – gender (which is usually taken to be culturally constructed) and heterosexuality (which is not)'.

103. Guest, *Beyond Feminist Biblical Studies*, 82. Guest quotes Ingraham: 'Reframing gender as heterogender foregrounds the relation between heterosexuality and gender. Heterogender confronts the equation of heterosexuality with *the natural* and of gender with the cultural, and suggests that both are socially constructed, open to other configurations (not only opposites and binary), and open to change. As a materialist feminist concept, heterogender de-naturalizes the "sexual" as the starting point for understanding heterosexuality, and connects institutional heterosexuality with the gender division of labor and the patriarchal relations of production'. Ingraham, 'Heterosexual Imaginary', 204. While Ingraham and, by extension, Guest see the benefit in focusing on the 'hetero' part of heterosexuality to shift scholarship, I maintain that the frame of reference still continues to be on sexuality. The two strands are not disentangled successfully enough for the aims of this project.

104. Guest, *Beyond Feminist Biblical Studies*, 43. Emphasis original.

heteronormativity – and as a continuation of their (hetero)suspicious approach. Both evocatively capture queerness and the rejection of all that is 'hetero'.[105] Guest makes the multifaceted benefits of this term clear: 'it bespeaks queer theory's impact upon studies of gender, it implies that gender is not always to be understood in binary heterocentric terms but can be performed in alternative, queer ways, and the addition of "queer" indicates an interest in the sexual as well as the realm of gender'.[106] This shows how far Guest's work has come since *WDMJ* – gender nonconformity is now central and is conceptualized in myriad queer forms. Nonetheless, this queer-oriented approach also indicates something of a chasm between their gender-oriented framework and mine.

While the theoretical shifts that underpin *BFBS* are invaluable, it is Guest's application of their hermeneutic that truly shows its value. With the enduring emphasis on diversity of gender *and* sexuality Guest's choice to trial their genderqueer critical hermeneutic on the pornoprophetic debate makes sense.[107] They draw out the way the stories are already understood as sexual – problematically so. Guest focusses on the portrayal of the metaphorical figure of Woman/Zion, rather than on close readings of specific texts. They contrast their genderqueer reading with their earlier feminist one which addressed the pornographic portrayal of Woman/Zion in Lamentations.[108] At the heart of the metaphor is the city of Jerusalem (Zion) imagined as a woman. She is a lascivious figure who is unfaithful to her spouse, God.[109] Her infidelity is portrayed pornographically, as is the violent punishment by her husband. This leads to the designation of such texts as pornoprophetic.[110] Rape imagery and extremely graphic sexual abuse is endemic

---

105. Guest, *Beyond Feminist Biblical Studies*, 67. Guest describes the use of the term 'genderqueer criticism' as 'felicitous' for their current project, drawing from usage of the term. See Joan Nestle, Clare Howell, and Riki A. Wilchins, eds, *GenderQueer: Voices From Beyond the Binary* (Los Angeles, CA: Alyson Books, 2002). Guest cites Wilchins who 'speaks of bringing "back together those two things that have been wrongly separated: gender and gayness" (27)'.

106. Guest, *Beyond Feminist Biblical Studies*, 67.

107. Guest, *Beyond Feminist Biblical Studies*, 87–117.

108. Deryn Guest, 'Hiding Behind the Naked Women in Lamentations: A Recriminative Response', *Biblical Interpretation* 7, 4 (1999), 413–448.

109. Kathleen M. O'Connor, 'Lamentations', in *Women's Bible Commentary*, ed. Carol A. Newsom, Sharon H. Ringe, and Jacqueline E. Lapsley (Louisville, KY: Westminster John Knox Press, 2012), 278–282, 280. '[Zion] is God's beloved daughter. She an eloquent spokeswoman for the people's grief, and like many speakers in the psalms, she expresses her sorrow with language of intense feeling (1:16, 20; 2:11). Ultimately she discards the role of victim (Lam. 1) to become God's adversary, challenging divine mistreatment of herself and her people (2:20–22).'

110. This term finds its root in T. Drorah Setel, 'Prophets and Pornography: Female Sexual Imagery in Hosea', ed. Letty M. Russell, *Feminist Interpretation of the Bible* (Philadelphia, PA: Westminster Press, 1985), http://www.womencanbepriests.org/classic/

in the stories which are found in Jeremiah, Lamentations, Hosea, Ezekiel and Isaiah.[111]

Feminist scholarship has long addressed the sexual and sexualixed abuse directed at a female anthropomorphized figure by a male deity. It treats the pornographic motifs as inherently problematic, whilst queer approaches do not see such sexual motifs as a problem. Queer scholarship has explored the sexualized relationship between male prophet and deity. Guest, meanwhile, indicates that nobody has looked particularly at the outworking of gender (nonconformity) beyond these frameworks. They respond with an account that foregrounds genderqueerness. They emphasise how the sexual economy is used to underpin the marriage metaphor, central to the pornoprophetic texts.[112] This leads them to consider different connotations of male and female homoeroticism; and address the complexities of masculinity. They identify masculinity in the portrayal of God, the prophets, and in Zion. This case study shows how the themes of sexual economy, homoeroticism and gender nonconformity all become visible through Guest's genderqueer reading. Guest argues that there is no other equivalent methodology so attentive to all those elements; I agree. I find it a powerful and persuasive reading, highlighting the potential for identification of gender diversity amongst the Bible's characters. Sexuality serves as something of a launching pad for those genderqueer aspects of the interrogations. Here sexuality is so significant that the characters who feature in the narrative are introduced only after the designation 'pornoprophetic' is discussed. I query how the reading strategy can be adapted to a given character who may appear to conform to many of the heterocentric expectations placed upon them but, through a cispicious lens, might appear differently. Whether they can and do appear differently will be matters for the close readings offered in Chapters 3 and 4. Neither case study proffers a character for whom diversity of sexuality is considered a defining attribute: Esau and Sarah rarely come to mind as characters to read as if they are gay.[113] Rather,

---

russ_cnt.asp. See also Athalya Brenner-Idan [Brenner], ed., *A Feminist Companion to The Latter Prophets* (Sheffield: Sheffield Academic Press, 1995). Brenner-Idan dedicates a section of her edited collection to address pornoprophetic motifs specifically (244–353).

111. While Ezekiel 16 and 23 are amongst the most notorious, the motif is clearly present in Isaiah 3: 'The Lord said: Because the daughters of Zion are haughty and walk with outstretched necks, glancing wantonly with their eyes, mincing along as they go, tinkling with their feet; the Lord will afflict with scabs the heads of the daughters of Zion, and the LORD will lay bare their secret parts (16–17).

112. Guest, *Beyond Feminist Biblical Studies*, 105–116.

113. While Sarah and Esau are rarely subject to analysis of their (non-straight) sexuality, there are a small number of queer readings of each. Gil Rosenberg, for example, foregrounds a relationship between Sarah and Hagar, see *Ancentral Queerness: The Normal and the Deviant in the Abraham and Sarah Narratives*, Hebrew Bible Monographs, (Sheffield: Sheffield Phoenix Press, 2019). See also Michael Carden's contribution to *The Queer Bible Commentary*: 'Genesis/Bereshit', in *The Queer Bible Commentary*, ed. Deryn Guest et al. (London: SCM Press, 2006), 21–60.

their relationships are just one component of the broader context which Namaste and Prosser argue is so essential to any credible analysis of gender nonconforming experience.

At the conclusion of *BFBS*, Guest clarifies that their explicitly genderqueer methodology consolidates earlier (trans-inclusive) 'gender critical' approaches. They suggest it can be adopted by anyone willing to deploy such a technique. Like the lesbian-identified hermeneutic, this approach requires a willingness to 'put their energies into the critical examination of the heterosexual imaginary, rather than the "others" that keep it stable'.[114] Guest's genderqueer criticism is a thought-provoking development that takes biblical gender scholarship forwards enormously – for that it can and should be commended. Still, we differ in the significance we each put on sexuality in understanding diverse genderscapes. That said, Guest's articulation of the need for a broader-reaching engagement that overtly recognises diversity within, beyond and between established categories – man, woman, both, neither – is particularly helpful. Their reduced focus on butchness as the primary lens of interpretation is welcome too since it shows the value in engaging with a wider genderscape than is visible through Guest's earlier works. Their theoretical insights provided by this text make it a welcome development. When read closely alongside 'FGRG' the potential for genderqueer readings emerges most clearly. In combination there are both close readings and comparisons between feminist, queer and genderqueer, allowing for differences between each to emerge clearly. Guest's publications from 2011 and 2012 provide a helpful foundation for both their subsequent trans scholarship and my own cispicious project, whilst also emphasizing the need for further refinements.

While I want to commend the importance of recognizing heteronormativity in biblical interpretation, I remain convinced of the need explicitly to address cisnormativity. Guest has enabled a shift in the understanding of heteronormativity to increase attention to gender and I am keen to build on this foundation. I interrogate *Transgender, Intersex, and Biblical Interpretation* for any recognition of the contribution that cisnormativity can make to the understanding of transness today and in our approaches to biblical interpretation. The focus on transgender *and* intersex biblical interpretation suggests it would be an optimum place to address the differences between cisnormative influences and those of heteronormativity.

Transgender, Intersex and Biblical Interpretation

The final, and most recent, of Guest's works to feature in this project is their collaboration with Hornsby published in 2016: *Transgender, Intersex and Biblical Interpretation* (*TIBI*).[115] Each author contributes individual chapters, so Guest's are

---

114. Guest, *Beyond Feminist Biblical Studies*, 162.
115. Hornsby and Guest, *Transgender, Intersex and Biblical Interpretation*.

treated as stand-alone – although they are interpreted with reference to the introduction written by Hornsby.[116] Guest's chapters, 'Troubling the Waters: תהום, Transgender, and Reading Genesis Backwards' and 'Modeling the Transgender Gaze: Performances of Masculinity in 2 Kings 9–10', provide close readings of texts from the Hebrew Bible.[117] The authors continue to respond solely to heteronormativity even though it is trans and intersex interpretation that falls within their purview. Butchness figures as a key part of the interpretative lens for both authors and I show that this directs attention once again towards performances of masculinity.

Transness predominates in the volume, with intersex receiving little attention beyond inclusion in the title. Hornsby and Guest focus on heteronormativity immediately. Much of Hornsby's 'Introduction: The Body as Decoy' and 'Gender Dualism, or The Big Lie' address the interplay between transness, gender diversity and heteronormativity, while outlining how the authors shape their interpretations.[118] While not words attributed to Guest, these opening chapters direct both the reader and authors moving forward and are worth pausing for a moment to explore.[119] Hornsby provides a substantial discussion of ways heteronormativity shapes contemporary understanding, and underpins how difficult it remains to look beyond the supposed naturalness of that understanding:

> The bottom line is this: the complexity of bodies and their social destinies are all entangled within (and produced by) heteronormativity: the dominant belief system that relies on fixed and binary genders and the certainty that heterosexuality is the norm that occurs naturally, that is, apart from cultural influences. All other sexual relationships are deemed culturally produced (unnatural), and are regulated and defined in relation to heterosexuality, and thus are devalued. In this system, females and males (whose bodies are produced *naturally*) are assumed to be the only appropriate sexual partners. Heterosexism, then, is a systematic social bias that stems from heteronormativity in which society rewards heterosexuals (in the form of economic benefits and civil rights) and punishes all other sexualities.[120]

116. Hornsby, 'Introduction'.

117. Deryn Guest, 'Troubling the Waters: מוהת, Transgender, and Reading Genesis Backwards', in *Transgender, Intersex, and Biblical Interpretation*, ed. Teresa J. Hornsby and Deryn Guest (Atlanta, GA: SBL Press, 2016a), 21–44; 'Modeling the Transgender Gaze: Performances of Masculinity in 2 Kings 9–10', in *Transgender, Intersex, and Biblical Interpretation*, ed. Teresa J. Hornsby and Deryn Guest (Atlanta, GA: SBL Press, 2016b), 45–80.

118. Teresa J. Hornsby, 'Introduction'; 'Gender Dualism, or The Big Lie', in *Transgender, Intersex and Biblical Studies*, ed. Teresa J. Hornsby and Deryn Guest (Atlanta, GA: SBL Press, 2016), 13–20.

119. Hornsby returns to these words and themes explicitly in a later chapter, Teresa J. Hornsby, 'The Dance of Gender: David, Jesus, and Paul', in *Transgender, Intersex, and Biblical Interpretation*, ed. Teresa J. Hornsby and Deryn Guest (Atlanta, GA: SBL Press, 2016), 82–93, 84–85.

120. Hornsby, 'Introduction'.

Hornsby effectively highlights the link between sexualities and the privileged, 'natural' binary form model for gender and sex that heterosexuality produces and in which it is entangled. Even here Hornsby's clear focus on sexuality as the primary reference point remains clear. There is no recognition throughout the volume that heteronormativity is not the only influential belief system that produces hard to escape norms that profoundly shape trans and intersex lives. Hornsby's contextualisation draws briefly from Serano's exploration of cis privilege and assumption. Cisnormativity itself is notably absent. Instead, Hornsby uses Serano's insights to consolidate the way transness relates primarily to heteronormativity:

> [C]issexuals experience some social privilege that trans people may not. As with *heterosexism* (and racism, classism, and sexism), privilege is invisible to the dominant group, and basic privileges are denied to the 'lesser' group – in this case, noncissexuals (transsexual/transgendered persons). Since Western social arrangements depend upon *heteronormativity* (there being two, and only two, sexes that occur naturally), cissexuals' privilege tends to occur on a more personal level (in addition to institutional biases).[121]

Hornsby's acknowledgement of heterosexism, which results directly from heteronormativity, is a pertinent observation. It is a particularly striking juxtaposition with cissexism, as Hornsby does not posit a distinct and structural system of gender norms from which cissexism emerges. Rather, Hornsby continues to link heteronormativity and transness, even while acknowledging that it is not (always) an obvious fit.[122]

Guest and Hornsby's attention to the interplay between cissexist violence and Christianized gender norms is helpful. They explore stories that feature frequently in the Christian imaginary and which contribute to cissexism. In particular, I think here of Guest's chapter exploring *Tehom* as a genderqueer disruptor in creation (especially in Genesis 1) and Hornsby's chapter addressing David, Jesus and Paul and gender nonconformity.[123] Given Guest's base in the UK and Hornsby's in the USA, acknowledging the way Christianity has a socio-cultural capital in the creation and maintenance of gender norms is invaluable.[124] It emphasizes the

---

121. Hornsby, 'Introduction', 9. Emphasis added to highlight *heterosexism*.

122. Hornsby, 'Introduction', 3. 'Though at first glance it may seem that heteronormativity and its subsequent heterosexism are not explicitly bound to trans issues, on the contrary, heteronormativity with its dependence upon an artificial framework of only two, naturally occurring sexes (as determined by genitalia) is the linchpin that holds together all of the justification of the violence and discrimination that is placed on trans bodies'.

123. Guest, 'Troubling the Waters'; Hornsby, 'Dance of Gender'.

124. Hornsby, 'Introduction', 3. 'Like sexism, racism, or classism, heterosexism depends on the assumption that there is a "normal" (thus superior) way of being (divinely ordained and/or "natural"). Those who view themselves as in the "better" of any of the previously

significance of the hallowed texts even where an individual may have little direct involvement with the religion. Equally, when we are more immersed in a religious tradition, those authorising texts take on a more significant role in establishing our presuppositions about gender and sex.[125] *TIBI* serves as an explicit, necessary and welcome corrective to the (mis)perception that gender diversity cannot be encountered in the Bible.

'Troubling the Waters: תהום, Transgender, and Reading Genesis Backwards'

The first of Guest's chapters, 'Troubling the Waters: תהום, Transgender, and Reading Genesis Backwards' ('TtW') offers the first glimpse into Guest's explicitly trans-oriented scholarship. Continuing on the trajectory set by 'FGRG', Guest provides a genderqueer interpretation of *Tehom* (תהום), the chaotic deep introduced in the creation account of Genesis 1. They creatively present *Tehom* as an anthropomorphized character akin to the more established figures of Woman Zion and Lady Wisdom. Recognising *Tehom* as a marginalized figure, who is othered in the text, Guest sees *Tehom* as genderqueer or nonbinary, and proffers the honorific 'Mx' (short for Mixter).[126] Guest's nonbinary *Mx Tehom* represents a radical reconceptualization of binaries established in the creation narratives of Genesis 1 and 2, of which gender and sex are just two.[127] Guest powerfully locates gender diversity right at the beginning of the world and embeds someone intrinsically 'queer'. Their interpretation uses a three-stage process: first is the creation of *Tehom* as an anthropomorphism; second comes the recognition of their genderqueerness; and finally the exploration of abjection. They describe their endeavour as a reading backwards that 'allows us to re-collect what has been lost or marginalized and to see the mechanics of a text that creates an atmosphere in which heteronormativity can live and breathe, but where gender/sex transgression is banished to the abject'.[128]

---

mentioned binaries usually do not see the privilege society grants them – they may assume that those in the lesser binary do not deserve the same rights and privileges (this seems most evident in racism and in heterosexism), or they are ignorant (or in denial) of their own privilege'.

125. For example, Sumerau, Cragun and Mathers, 'Cisgendering of Reality'. Sumerau, Cragun and Mathers undertook an ethnographic study amongst young Mormon adults and explored their beliefs about cisnormative expectations. Published at a similar time to *TIBI*, it is noteworthy that Sumerau, Cragun and Mathers focus their interrogation on cisnormativity rather than its heteronormative counterpart, as favoured by Hornsby and Guest. They concluded that religious authorities, especially texts and their grand narratives of creation and our place within that, instil a sense of a fixed and binary gender. This they call the 'cisgendering of reality'.

126. Guest, 'Troubling the Waters', 25.

127. For discussions of these binaries and the biblical foundations of heteronormativity in Genesis 1–3, see Stone, 'Garden of Eden', 15; Hornsby, 'Introduction'.

128. Guest, 'Troubling the Waters', 43.

Guest's queer reading recalls their hermeneutic of hetero-suspicion, although *TIBI* does not feature explicit reference to it. It is a theory-driven interpretation where Guest's own reflexive engagement with the text does not come through as strongly as it does in their later chapter (or as in *WDMJ*, or 'LLBB'). Rather Guest focuses on abjection, following Julia Kristeva, and monstrosity after Margrit Shildrick.[129] It may be the third of their stages, but it is certainly dominant. That said, the strands soon become intertwined leaving the reader to try and hold all three elements together. Guest seeks to reclaim the way that *Tehom* is maligned and presented as monstrous in ways that find parallels for trans and queer readers.[130] They aim to use the parallels between othering and abjection, faced by many gender nonconforming people, to find a monstrous biblical being that can be celebrated and in whose experience we can find resonances. I do not find this to be fully successful as Guest is forced to try to establish *Tehom*'s personhood whilst also calling that very personhood into question.

Tehom's abjection is key to Guest's argument, leading them to treat *Tehom* as a monster.[131] Guest picks *Tehom* precisely because they can be seen as an abjected figure. Only then does Guest try to make them human. In other words, Guest creates them as monster for the purpose of reclaiming monstrosity.[132] Unless they can offer cause for celebration, reading *Tehom* as a trans or nonbinary character seriously risks perpetuating rather than undermining Bible-based transphobia. Moreover, Guest's endeavour strikes me as one that is far more heavily weighted to queer motifs than recognizing the importance of trans influences.

I recall Strassfeld's caution about the way monstrosity perpetuates transmisogyny and transphobia.[133] Monstrosity has long been used to dehumanize trans people, so

129. Guest, 'Troubling the Waters', 22–23.
130. See, for example, Guest, 'Troubling the Waters', 39.
131. Guest, 'Troubling the Waters', 39. Guest follows Shildrick in this regard, and writes: 'While I do not want to homogenize the experiences of trans people who engage in different types of body modification, it is important to recognize, as Shildrick does, that the "normal" body is "always an achievement" requiring constant maintenance and/or modification to hold off the ever-present threat of disruption: extra digits are excised at birth, tongues are shortened in Down's Syndrome disease [sic], noses are reshaped, warts removed, prosthetic limbs fitted, "healthy" diets commended, and hormone replacement therapy is prescribed. In such cases, it is the unmodified body that is seen as unnatural in need of "corrective" interventions (Shildrick 2002, 55)'. See Margrit Shildrick, *Embodying the Monster: Encounters with the Vulnerable Self* (London: Sage, 2002).
132. Jeffrey Jerome Cohen, 'Monster Culture (Seven Theses)', in *Monster Theory: Reading Culture*, ed. Jeffrey Jerome Cohen (Minneapolis, MN: University of Minnesota Press, 1996), 3–25. Cohen writes that monsters are always meaningful and provides a way to read the cultures from which they emerged, but that does not mean that all monsters nor all monstrosity function the same way. Guest's conflation of modes of monstrosity risks undermining the efficacy of their argument.
133. Strassfeld, 'Transing Religious Studies', 53. Strassfeld allies the perpetuation of trans women as monstrous with the trans exclusionary feminist theologies of Daly and

Guest's reclamation effort is far from simple.[134] In fact, Guest addresses those links explicitly in the following chapter, but here they remain unacknowledged.[135] *Tehom* cannot sufficiently function as an all-purpose monster and convey Guest's intended meaning for trans liberation. Closer attention to the complexities in the relationship between transness would be beneficial.[136] While Guest's aim is laudable, I am left with the sense that they attempt too much. Ultimately, they cannot see, or show, a fully realized person through their portrayal of *Tehom*. Given the significance of embodiment in Guest's argument, I find it notable that the *Tehom* who emerges is more of a conceptual character than an embodied one. Primarily, then, *Tehom* must be successfully anthropomorphized and thus recognizable as a human-esque figure. They must also remain someone with an abjected, monstrous, othered body – with all the overlaid connotations that accompany such designations. Then, and only then, can Guest see them as liberational and representational figures. In the end, this is too much for one figure to hold. I remain unconvinced that *Tehom* can escape their abjection to be recognizable as human.[137]

Raymond. They argue that treating trans women, in particular, as monstrous figures reproduces this rather than offers a reclamation. For Strassfeld it is particularly problematic to do so in religious contexts as it perpetuates religious and theological abuse.

134. Anson Koch-Rein, 'Monster', *Transgender Studies Quarterly (TSQ)* 1, 1–2 (2014), 134–135. 'In a world where the monster is circulating as metaphoric violence against trans* people, reclaiming such a figure faces the difficulty of formulating resistance in the same metaphorical language as the transphobic attack. Moreover, as a figure of difference, the monster appears in racist, ableist, homophobic, and sexist discourses, making its use especially fraught' (134–135).

135. Guest, 'Modeling the Transgender Gaze', 54. Guest clearly state their desire to provide correctives to the abusive and dehumanizing portrayal of transness as less than human, and thus abject and monstrous. They highlight feminists who 'continue denouncing transsexuals as dupes of gender'. They expand by adding, 'historically, this position was taken by Janice Raymond (1979), Mary Daly (1978), Germaine Greer (1999), and Sheila Jeffreys (2003), who criticized transsexuality as a damaging fantasy that could never match experiential knowledge that comes from being born as, and positioned as, "woman" within a patriarchal society' (54–55 n.11).

136. See, for example, Susan Stryker, 'My Words to Victor Frankenstein Above the Village of Chamounix: Performing Transgender Rage', *GLQ: A Journal of Lesbian and Gay Studies* 1, 3 (1994), 237–254. Stryker's articulation of her rage is also helpful in showing the costs and benefits of aligning transness with monstrosity: 'Like the monster, I am too often perceived as less than fully human due to the means of my embodiment; like the monster's as well, my exclusion from human community fuels a deep and abiding rage in me that I, like the monster, direct against the conditions in which I must struggle to exist' (238). In the end she argues that monstrosity can be reclaimed but, as Koch-Rein shows, it must be done with extreme care. Koch-Rein, 'Monster'.

137. Ebony Elizabeth Thomas, *The Dark Fantastic: Race and the Imagination from Harry Potter to the Hunger Games*, Kindle ed. (New York: New York University Press, 2019),

There are, perhaps, too many components for Guest to successfully achieve their aims in this chapter. Finding trans representation, especially in the Bible's creation stories, is enormously valuable, but must be handled with care. Accounts of biblical monstrosity and dehumanized bodies must also be addressed in order to see what those monsters signify, but there is a plenitude of such bodies. Endeavours that serve to (re)create monstrous bodies must be treated with caution. Guest's confidence in drawing the personal and experiential together with the theoretical in order to make their creative interpretations of biblical stories accessible is a highlight of their earlier works. They implicitly embrace a Halberstamian approach to low theory and a more explicitly Althaus-Reid-like approach to indecency – but both remain intertwined throughout Guest's carefully constructed interpretative approach. Here, however, the approach feels more tentative, and the theoretical components drive Guest's reading of *Tehom* to the cost of its overall effectiveness.

Mx Tehom falls short of the aims of Guest's chapter and threatens to drag all those with whom Guest draws parallels into the realm of the unhuman monster: trans, genderqueer and disabled readers. I am left wanting to know more about how this interpretation meets Guest's commitment to taking responsibility for the ethics of their interpretations. I see Mx Tehom emerge as a dehumanised anthropomorphism who has been intentionally made abject, something I find to be deeply problematic.[138]

'The Curious Case of Bonnie Bennett'. Thomas acknowledges that certain forms of monstrosity can become desirable and, indeed, celebrated. The valorised subjects of her case study are vampires, well-known for their monstrous nature ('The Vampire Diaries' television show, 2009–17). She pertinently observes that such reclamation can only happen when it is only that one aspect of their identity – their monstrosity as vampires, say – that makes them an outsider, or othered. However when that monstrosity is combined with other marginalized statuses, such as gender or race, none of that character's monstrosity can be redeemed. Indeed, they are more likely to face increased marginalization and abjection as a result. The abjected figure she analyses is a young, black witch, Bonnie Bennett, in a storyworld that celebrates vampiric monstrosity. Her status as witch marks her as a less desirable monstrous figure, but it is her status as the only black character in the central narratives that truly marks her as irredeemably other. I see parallels between the multiple aspects of Thomas's contradictory monstrosity and that of *Tehom*. *Tehom*'s initial status as a non-human figure, in combination with Guest's creation of a monstrous body, ensures the *Tehom* can never truly escape their abjected state.

138. Guest, 'Troubling the Waters', 22. 'Reading backwards permits me to undo creation, to resist the assumptions and desires of the biblical narrator, and to find in that primordial mix a surprisingly fruitful way of reconsidering our relationship with it, one that might allow chaos a voice. This rationale for doing so lies in the need to take ethical responsibility for biblical interpretation, to question texts that make some lives unspeakable – that is, lives that are not routinely permitted to speak for themselves in theological discussions and unspeakable in the sense that those lives are often plunged into the abject'.

'Modeling the Transgender Gaze: Performances of Masculinity in 2 Kings 9-10'

Guest's second chapter 'Modeling the Transgender Gaze: Performances of Masculinity in 2 Kings 9-10' ('MTG') offers a more open and engaging exploration of Guest's gender nonconformity in combination with theoretical and textual details. In 'MTG' Guest draws on Halberstam's work on masculinity and transgender gaze to explore the presentation of Jehu and Jezebel in 2 Kings 9-10. They embed themselves and their perspective on gender in a cautious, nuanced and enormously powerful way which adds to the confidence and richness of the interpretation. This is by far the strongest of their works on gender diversity, in part because of Guest's openness with their audience about the complexity of taking on such work. Guest acknowledges that the boundaries between butch lesbian and trans identities are fluid and have points of overlap.[139] It is from that location, and through use of an adapted form of Halberstam's transgender gaze, that Guest undertakes a close reading of Jehu and Jezebel's masculinity. In each case, Guest asserts that this masculinity has been learned and is performed in ways that resonate with trans masculine readers today.

Both Jehu and Jezebel present different aspects of nonconforming masculinities: Jezebel continues Guest's interest in female masculinity, while Jehu appears through Guest's interpretation as a trans masculine figure whose learned masculinity is performed to excess. Jehu is the first of the two figures subject to Guest's analysis, and they immediately use him to show how his story is a case study for the construction of masculinity when glimpsed through a trans lens.[140] Jehu's male character is constructed through distinct facets of masculinity: the man's man; accoutred masculinity; his violent ruthlessness, as the wordsmith; madness; and phallic masculinity. Each of these points is elaborated through a close reading of the text, drawing attention to features that emphasise how Jehu renders the construction of masculinity visible. The first and most striking example is where Guest highlights Jehu's 'double male heritage' as unusual (2 Kgs 9:2, 14) – it is recorded in two generations and made explicit in the text twice.[141] Similarly Jehu's violence is so excessive that Guest notes that 'Jehu's actions are so extraordinary that commentators have often pulled themselves out of the narrative'

---

139. Guest, 'Modeling the Transgender Gaze', 53. 'Within this debate, I find myself an unhappy straddle: I have self-tagged as butch lesbian in most of my writing to date but I have FtM affinity and regularly ponder surgery and transitioning. It is an uncomfortable place to be; and at the time of writing, I use *transgender* in its encompassing capacity and have empathy with Hale's view that "borders between gender categories ... are zones of overlap, not lines" (323)'. Guest cites C. Jacob Hale, 'Consuming the Living, Dis(re)membering the Dead in the Butch/FtM Borderlands', *GLQ: A Journal of Lesbian and Gay Studies* 4, 2 (1998), 311-348. Guest's discussion also recalls Halberstam's continuum of masculinity or butchness evocatively here.
140. Guest, 'Modeling the Transgender Gaze', 57-67.
141. Guest, 'Modeling the Transgender Gaze', 58-59.

to remark on the ethics: it is far from the usual levels of violence!¹⁴² These excesses are combined with indicators of conformity to masculine expectations, such as the inclusion of reference to Jehu's chariot, bow, and arrow (v. 24) ensuring that he is 'a man carefully surrounded with the correct accessories'.¹⁴³ Together these components lead Guest to conclude that Jehu is an example of someone whose masculinity has not been assumed from birth. They argue that the transgender gaze enables the reader to 'observe keenly how masculinity is performed but inevitably stands at a distance from it, but ultimately there is that gap, that remoteness of not having being [sic] hailed in one's "maleness" from birth.'¹⁴⁴

Guest then turns their attention to Jezebel. In keeping with Guest's reading of Jael in 'FGRG', it is Jezebel's masculinity that is of primary interest. When Guest reflects on the feminization of Jezebel, they see it is in part to emasculate this masculine woman. Attention to makeup in the run up to Jezebel's death and the abuse of her body afterwards all contribute to the image of a woman whose femininity is created, or even exaggerated, in an attempt to ensure that she is fully destroyed (vv. 30–37). This is, for Guest, part of the punishment for being gender nonconforming, especially for someone assigned female at birth but who rejects femininity. Together Jehu and Jezebel represent hugely resonant figures for someone approaching the text with an interest in performances of masculinity encountered through a trans gaze. This they summarise by writing that their interpretation 'demonstrates how the interpreter, hailed originally as "woman" but choosing to occupy territory associated with "man", does masculinity with a different set of experiences'.¹⁴⁵

In discussing what their trans-informed, masculinity-attuned approach achieves, they write that they (and their approach) 'has to deal with the potential for disdaining the feminine.'¹⁴⁶ Guest also acknowledges that they find 'it difficult myself to associate with words like *woman, feminine*.'¹⁴⁷ While they do not intentionally show disdain for the feminine, there is little space for femininity in the lives of the characters Guest explores. Even though Guest writes that they 'would be unwilling to encourage any cultural understanding of masculinity as a ring-fenced zone, *uncontaminated* from women or the feminine', their language is telling.¹⁴⁸ Femininity risks contaminating Guest's masculine figure! While this makes sense within Guest's carefully situated model of interpretation, something

---

142. Guest, 'Modeling the Transgender Gaze', 61.
143. Guest, 'Modeling the Transgender Gaze', 59. Guest contextualises this when they write 'The narrator thus presents again a feminine-avoidant form of masculinity, for no one would have associated Jehu with distaff and spindle: this is a man carefully surrounded by the right correct things'.
144. Guest, 'Modeling the Transgender Gaze', 66.
145. Guest, 'Modeling the Transgender Gaze', 79.
146. Guest, 'Modeling the Transgender Gaze', 79.
147. Guest, 'Modeling the Transgender Gaze', 77. Emphasis original.
148. Guest, 'Modeling the Transgender Gaze', 77. Emphasis added.

attuned to the perspectives of trans men and trans masculinity, it also underplays the value of both/and models of gender rather than either/or. Guest's recognition of their own disregard for femininity shows the limits of their masculinity-attuned interpretations. When Jezebel's femininity is contextualised as emasculation, Guest's interpretation forecloses potential readings where femininity and masculinity are not treated as oppositional. While Guest acknowledges the importance of interpretative choices and owning our own location, 'MTG' reveals how much their masculinity frames their work.

'MtG' is the closest of Guest's interpretations to the one I envisage emerging through hermeneutics of cispicion. What makes their work so striking and relevant for my own is how they clearly and succinctly outline how they intend to adapt and apply Halberstam's work to biblical texts. Essential to this endeavour is Guest's articulation of the aims they share with Halberstam – aims to which I also subscribe:

> The transgender gaze bears certain hallmarks. It holds up an alternative vision for the reader, one fragile yet resilient, one that needs the confirmation of the others against the prevailing norms that would discount it, one where expectations of sex and gender are criticized or destabilized and narrative paradigms are shifted. It is that gaze that fights against abjection and erasure for the survival of its different imagining, and it is a gaze embodied in the transgendered [sic] person.[149]

Guest continues to advocate for the need to criticize or destabilize prevailing norms, again something core to this endeavour. The paradigm shift Guest seeks is served well by their tweaks to Halberstam's trans gaze, although Halberstam's plural masculinities remain more enticing than Guest's. They move the emphasis from a gaze that becomes visible *through* a trans character, such as in Halberstam's film analysis, to one that looks into the text from outside. In making this shift Guest enables identification of transness and gender nonconformity where none has previously been seen. Importantly, they acknowledge that such a shift will 'inevitably produce different emphases and observations, but ... there are strong commonalities between the two approaches' before outlining the key elements of a trans gaze for biblical interpretation.[150] A transgender gaze into biblical texts will:

1. 'locate the transgender gaze in trans experience';
2. 'expose the constructedness of gender (noting how sex/gender stability is maintained and how disruptions to it are suppressed)';
3. confront 'heteronormativity with alternative visions of gender that may be fragile but are resilient and capable of shifting paradigms of existing thought';
4. require 'political and religious engagement, challenging the (negative) effects of biblical interpretations for trans people'.[151]

149. Guest, 'Modeling the Transgender Gaze', 50.
150. Guest, 'Modeling the Transgender Gaze', 50.
151. Guest, 'Modeling the Transgender Gaze', 50–51.

Guest's transgender gaze demonstrates many commonalities with my cispicious approach and definitely privileges things essential to my project. They emphasize the importance of foregrounding transness and the insights that brings. Those insights must be combined with recognition of the religious and political interplay that comes with biblical interpretation. Their attention to the constructedness of gender – especially how it is stabilized and disrupted – is particularly helpful. They also demonstrate a powerful recognition of the complexity of identifying and challenging such norms especially in textual interpretation. The spectre of heteronormativity warrants recontextualization for my purposes; cisnormativity can easily be substituted. Transness/cisness and gender diversity then remain in clearest focus and cissexism can be best addressed.

Guest's carefully crafted methodology for a trans gaze provides an invaluable opportunity to take a moment to gaze back across their work to this point. Of particular resonance at this stage is Guest's adoption of Halberstamian influences. One aspect is especially striking, and it remains unacknowledged in Guest's scholarship. Halberstam draws attention to the different and competing motivations in the representation of trans life.[152] This is important for ensuring the characters we encounter have sufficient agency, identity and depth for them to be recognizably human. Halberstam identifies the problems of stabilization, rationalization and trivialization (see pages 26–27 above). 'Stabilization' occurs when a character or their gender nonconformity is presented as abnormal, pathological, or otherwise indicative of wrongness. 'Rationalization' is where gender nonconformity is seen as the result of external factors; once the individual is freed from those external influences the gender nonconformity will subside. 'Trivialization' occurs where trans people are presented as 'nonrepresentative and inconsequential', rendering such people as perpetual outsiders. While none of Guest's subjects are particularly affected by rationalization, both stabilization and trivialization feature within Guest's transgender and intersex biblical interpretations.

Guest notes that there is a necessary shift from Halberstam's approach to theirs, moving from inside the narrative to outside, one must address which characters are subject to a trans gaze. Jehu and Jezebel are fascinating characters, and they both reflect Guest's assertion that they can be read as demonstrating learned, acquired, and at times excess masculinity that becomes visible through trans-tinted glasses. They represent quintessential examples of Guest's search for nonconforming performances of masculinity.

And yet, Jehu and Jezebel are relatively marginal and unfamiliar biblical characters. Neither the narrative itself nor the named characters themselves are particularly prominent – even within the wider stories in which they are located. This position marks them as notably different from those figures who feature in my case studies. Looking back over all the characters Guest makes the focus of their gender-attentive readings (genderfuck, genderqueer and now trans), Jael, *Tehom*, Jezebel and Jehu are all relatively minor characters even in their own

---

152. Halberstam, *In a Queer Time*, 54–55.

stories. Guest acknowledges that the relevance of trans biblical hermeneutics will always be subject to extra scrutiny, which is why it is so important that our new modes of interpretation do not fall into the traps identified by Halberstam.[153] Therefore, Guest's suggestion that the trans gaze is 'fragile and needs to be immensely defiant and resilient in staking its claim to alternative knowledge' must be combined with a similarly defiant rejection of the problematic tropes that Halberstam identifies.[154] There is an inherent value in applying the trans gaze (and other hermeneutical tools that place cisnormativity under scrutiny) to characters who are more narratively prominent and even privileged to counter the risk of trivialization; to a wider selection of characters than just those who appear abject or monstrous to avoid stabilization (such as with *Tehom*); and to avoid justification for the identification of gender diversity based on external factors. These are challenges, but given Guest's success in demonstrating the value of transgender gaze for biblical interpretation, these additional components would strengthen their methodology further.

Guest's chapters in *TIBI*, and the volume as a whole, show the important potential and value of placing biblical interpretation in dialogue with trans theory and experience. Their continuing, explicit emphasis on heteronormativity becomes stretched to the point that the need for an approach more discretely directed at cisnormativity emerges clearly. Moreover, the characters subjected to analysis by Guest are all of interest for their nonbinaryness or masculinity; femininity does not feature significantly in either of their chapters. Both authors demonstrate the contributions of adapting queer theory to a more distinctively trans endeavour but, in doing so, they reveal some of the problems that come when conflating different facets of otherness. Guest's reading of *Tehom* in 'TtW' makes this particularly clear. There are new troubles caused by putting too much weight on the creation of *Tehom* as a monstrous, trans-adjacent anthropomorphism. Here the contrasting desires to find a representative nonbinary figure; to celebrate monstrosity/reclaim the abject; *and* to confront the 'heteronormativity' associated with creation jostle for supremacy, never quite cohering. Guest's *Tehom* risks falling into the realm of a character whose gender diversity switches between stabilization and justification, both tropes that eventually dehumanise the character in question. Meanwhile their application of the trans gaze is hugely effective in highlighting the presence of gender diversity in the stories of Jehu and Jezebel, but it does so at the cost of reproducing the problem of trivialization. These minor characters become more recognisable through their gender nonconformity and their constructed performances of masculinity become visible through Guest's trans gaze. Here Guest's toolkit provides a great basis for future

153. Guest, 'Modeling the Transgender Gaze', 68. 'A transgender hermeneutic will always be on the back foot, because it has to assert itself in the face of the overwhelming strength of heteronormative assumptions. It will always be vulnerable to appeals to "common sense".'

154. Guest, 'Modeling the Transgender Gaze', 68.

trans-identified readings of biblical stories. There remains an unaddressed need to address wider examples of gender diversity – notably femininity and plural identities – and to interrogate the stories of more narratively privileged characters.

Conclusion

Guest has published a wealth of resources to develop and refine an engagement with heteronormativity within biblical scholarship. These publications parallel shifts in their own self-understanding, and of the competing priorities of feminist, lesbian, queer, 'gender critical' and trans readers (and the corresponding norms that push each towards the margins).[155] While butchness and heteronormativity most significantly inform Guest's critical attention, they show the power of recognizing the dominant norms at each stage. Guest pays close attention to idiosyncrasies in characterization to reveal new insights into potential lives for the individuals whose stories they interpret. Guest puts themself into the controversial role of Bathsheba's observer. In so doing they shift attention away from King David, the emblematic patriarchal tour de force whom feminists see as the villain. Instead Guest's lesbian observer reveals themself anew as a highly underrepresented feminist and anti-patriarchal queer figure. When reading Guest's interpretation, I see significant distance between David and this new observer, while also recognizing a shared interest in Bathsheba. Similarly, Guest's reading of Jael as a genderqueer figure provides ways to engage with the complexity of a character who does not conform to binary-gendered expectations. Their recognition of the contribution of discontinuities alongside the social role of the character adds to the richness of their presentation of a gender diverse character. Similarly, the reading of *Tehom* demonstrates the important possibilities for reimagining biblical anthropomorphisms as nonbinary beings, especially within the creation stories. It is in applying a trans gaze to Jehu and Jezebel that Guest's work demonstrates the greatest significance as a foundation for hermeneutics of cispicion. They show how to adapt Halberstam's work to the Bible and offer a roadmap for treating trans-informed perspectives as authoritative in interpreting the lives of biblical characters. Amidst this a new problem emerges: Guest treats both Jael and Jezebel's femininity as a potential 'contamination' of each character's transness. This is something I wish to explore further in my own cispicious readings, to ensure there is space for femininity as well as masculinity alongside aspects of gender that are harder to interpret.

---

155. Once again, this use of the term 'gender critical' refers to the holistic critical engagement with gender and sexuality, as favoured by Guest. Guest argues for a wide-reaching engagement with gender that recognises an array of diversity that extends across gender identities and expressions. 'Gender criticism', as used by Guest, is antithetical to the trans-critical scholarship and activism that now carries the same name.

What I find so powerful in Guest's writing is that we, the readers, have accompanied them on their own gender journey through their scholarship. They have adapted and refined their suspicious hermeneutics in line with their changing self-understanding. This gives me confidence to bring my own voice – and my own uncertainties – into dialogue with biblical texts and theorists alike. I feel encouraged to follow my own whims and hunches, to be intellectually playful, and to trust in the authority (and authenticity) of my own complex, uncertain knowledge. Guest demonstrates the value of trusting in our own first-hand knowledge to recognise the limitations and benefits of current suspicious hermeneutics. By emphasizing Guest's enduring interest in butchness and masculinity, I have shown that explorations of gender nonconformity in their work primarily reflects these two themes. In 'FGRG' this is evident when Guest worries that Jael's potential femininity threatens their genderqueerness, something with which I disagree. Guest's personal insights facilitate further exploration of the limitations of one person's vantage point, even when it forms the basis of such careful engagement with dominant and oppressive norms. Their highly personal approach also compels me to consider further how and where different constellations of gendered being cohere across the Bible's genderscape.

In conclusion, Guest's collected works demonstrate the importance of a theory-rich, critically engaged mode of biblical interpretation that privileges the contribution of voices not usually recognized within biblical scholarship. Through focusing on butchness for so much of their work, Guest has taken the hermeneutic of hetero-suspicion from its lesbian foundations into the realm of trans scholarship. In taking it further, amplifying a wider and more diversely gendered range of voices is essential to place cisnormativity under scrutiny. Drawing from Guest's use of queer theory it will, at times, be creative, attending to unfamiliar and low theoretical perspectives even if they appear contradictory or challenging to established interpretations. It will also take responsibility for the outcomes such hermeneutics produce. Recognition that the approach does not work or causes more problems than it solves is important here. For my purposes, and to confront the risk of trivialization I directed at Guest's work, I focus on characters with a greater narrative prominence and/or cultural familiarity. Core to my model, and in distinction from all Guest's work, I centre cisnormative presuppositions in order to ask how they impact biblical interpretation. The success, or otherwise, of such an approach will become clear when tested through my own case studies.

Chapter 3

SARAI AND THE PROBLEM OF CISNORMATIVE EXPECTATIONS[1]

Sarai/h (Genesis 11:27–23:2) is a tantalizing prospect for cispicious interpretation as their life unfurls in three distinct phases that confront assumptions of cisnormative femaleness.[2] In this case study we approach Sarai/h from a cispicious vantage point, testing my hermeneutic for the first time. By treating their story as a single narrative, I am able to interrogate the literary effects of reading the text in its final form which, in turn, affects how Sarai/h is encountered today. It is central for this work to attend to gender diversity and the presence of common tropes affecting gender nonconforming individuals. Of particular interest will be how a cispicious hermeneutic aids interpretation of Sarai/h's experience in significantly different ways to that of its queer and feminist counterparts.

We encounter Sarai for the first time when they arrive with no fanfare and little context in the final verses of Genesis 11 (vv. 29–31). They soon come into clearer view through accounts of their beauty proffered by their spouse and unnamed Egyptian officials alike in Genesis 12:10–20. This first phase provides an opportunity to gender Sarai/h, recalling Serano's description of the almost instinctive, immediate process of assigning gender when first encountering someone new.[3] Here, at the beginning of Sarai's story, femininity and femaleness emerge most clearly, but by engaging with Halberstam's low theory and trans gaze I argue that the picture is one that warrants

---

1. For an abridged version of this chapter see Jo Henderson-Merrygold, 'Gendering Sarai: Reading Beyond Cisnormativity in Genesis 11:29–12:20 and 20:1–18', *Open Theology* 6, 1 (2020), 496–509.

2. Throughout this chapter I refer to Sarai/h using gender-neutral pronouns, 'they/them/their'. This is an intentional decision to emphasize the complexity and plurality of gender that does not conform to cisnormative expectations. Where feminine pronouns are applied, I do so deliberately to emphasize significant features within Sarai/h's story. Use of the 'they/them/their' schema is not intended to degender Sarai/h, but rather to challenge the dominance of feminine pronouns and to avoid the presumption that gendering either as male *or* female is authoritative. I do, however, note the limit of pronouns, especially as they are primarily assigned to an individual by third parties.

3. Serano, *Whipping Girl*, 162–164.

further scrutiny. The micro details that indicate potential space for whimsical exploration emerge almost immediately, when Sarai appears the visual focus of the story even if they are not actively present.[4] Textual clues, including marital status, context and lineage, and childbearing status jostle with third person accounts of their identity – especially *her* beauty – in providing a basis from which to make judgements about Sarai's conformity to cisnormative gender expectations. Sarai's femaleness appears successfully constructed in these opening passages, despite the presence of niggling doubts – but then they disappear from view until Genesis 16.

Sarai/h then reappears to come into the sharpest focus of their entire story arc, while Halberstam's reflections on the challenge facing gender nonconforming characters to hold the gaze of a cisnormative viewer come to mind. In this second phase of Sarai/h's narrative, they emerge in a markedly different way to that found in the accounts of Genesis 11 and 12. In Genesis 16–18, Sarai/h's masculinity comes to the fore, while they also become a character with agency, identity, power and authority for the first time. Here both gender capaciousness and nonconformity become apparent at once in a way that stands in contrast with their presentation earlier in the narrative. Both their womanhood and their masculinity are now visible, so much so that they successfully meet David Clines's template for masculinity. This enables Sarai/h to be recognized as a biblical man akin to Moses or Aaron (Exod 32–34), or even David (1 Sam 16–1 Kgs 2).[5] Clines's recognition of the interplay between today's masculinities and those of the biblical world is instructive in this appraisal of Sarai/h. He is particularly interested in the interplay between the norms apparent for biblical men and their impact on the perception of men and masculinity today.[6] He outlines a number of social markers of masculinity for each context which contribute to the construction of what it means to be a man.[7] Today's men in Clines's North Atlantic context are expected to be successful, aggressive, sexual and self-reliant.[8] Their biblical counterparts, meanwhile, are required to be fighters, persuasive, beautiful, socially adept (with other men), avoidant of female company, musical and not averse to conflict.[9] But

4. Halberstam, *Queer Art of Failure*, 21.

5. David J. A. Clines, *Interested Parties: The Ideology of Writers and Readers of the Hebrew Bible*, Journal for the Study of the Old Testament Supplement Series, (Sheffield: Sheffield Academic Press, 1995), 212–243; 'Dancing and Shining at Sinai: Playing the Man in Exodus 32–34', in *Men and Masculinity in the Hebrew Bible and Beyond*, ed. Ovidiu Creangă, The Bible in the Modern World (Sheffield: Sheffield Phoenix Press, 2010), 54–63.

6. Clines, *Interested Parties*, 212. His underlying questions are: '1. What does it mean to be a man in our own culture? What roles are available for young men to grow into, what images are there for young men to imitate, what criteria exist from defining manliness? 2. And what was it like in the world of the Bible? Was it different, or much the same? 3. How do our answers to the first set of questions determine or influence our answers to the second set? How have our images of biblical men been shaped by our own cultural norms?'

7. Clines, *Interested Parties*, 214–215.

8. Clines, *Interested Parties*, 213–214.

9. Clines, *Interested Parties*, 214–233.

according to Clines there remains 'the primary rule' for manhood in both contexts: 'don't be female'.[10] This statement ensures that Clines's interrogations of masculinity only locate it within the stories of men, and narratively privileged ones at that. Even in his tacit acknowledgement of a potential plurality to masculinities, he emphasizes that all his subjects will be 'males'.[11] He explains that

> the fact that not all males, in whatever culture, conform with the social norms. The norms may privilege young, heterosexual, strong and physical men, for example, and those who cannot be characterized will be deviants from socially acceptable maleness. *But they will still be male.* We can expect, then, to find in our texts, as well as in our own society, representations of conflicting masculinities.[12]

Clines's recognition of the importance of recognizing multiple representations and constructions of masculinity is persuasive.[13] However his focus on only those perceived as male leaves much to be explored, not least that found in the central phase of Sarai/h's life. Indeed, his work has rightly been criticized for its isolation from feminist and queer scholarship.[14] In turn, this serves as an effective foundation from which to argue that more nuanced gender theories are needed to respond to the problem of cisnormativity. Nevertheless, Clines's model continues to shape and

---

10. Clines, *Interested Parties*, 213.

11. Clines, *Interested Parties*, 215. Clines's study is contemporaneous with Connell's paradigm-shifting recognition of multiple masculinities, see Connell, *Masculinities*. Clines writes, 'And we had better be open to the possibility of a plurality of masculinities. Perhaps the society legitimated more than one way of being a man – though perhaps not, since social pressures tend toward uniformity rather than diversity'. Connell's study consolidates Clines's observations and gives clear insight into the privileged forms of masculinity (i.e., hegemonic) and their lower status counterparts (66–80).

12. Clines, *Interested Parties*, 215. Emphasis added.

13. Cf. Roland Boer, 'Of Fine Wine, Incense and Spices: The Unstable Masculine Hegemony of the Books of Chronicles'. In *Men and Masculinity in the Hebrew Bible and Beyond*, edited by Ovidiu Creangă. The Bible in the Modern World, 20–33. (Sheffield: Sheffield Phoenix Press, 2010), 21. 'Masculinities may be constructed discursively, socially or economically, they may be constituted through performance, they may be fluid and constantly shifting, the multiplicity of masculinities is a feature of any historical period, and masculinities change over time, are created, die and are recreated again and again.'

14. For a sustained discussion of such criticism, see Brian Charles DiPalma, *Masculinities in the Court Tales of Daniel: Advancing Gender Studies in the Hebrew Bible*, Routledge Studies in the Biblical World, (London: Routledge, 2018), 13–15. DiPalma's question, after Cheryl Exum, about who is served by such readings is a pertinent question for this analysis. My response would be to emphasise the extent to which the cispicious endeavour is also aimed at addressing and recognising that very question. As such, the application of Clines' 'masculist' approach can be a useful tool to draw attention to agendas and power dynamics of gender theories disconnected from their wider contexts (cf. DiPalma, 15).

inform many studies of masculinity in the Bible.[15] And here, his foundational framework provides a way to recognize and affirm a model of masculinity that should, according to cisnormative expectations, not be found in Sarai/h. For much of this portion of Sarai/h's story, their masculinity faces no condemnation or censure within the narrative. They do not face trivialization, rationalization or stabilization and appear, at least initially, to be a stable gender-nonconforming character.[16] Only after they are renamed by God (Sarai to Sarah, Gen 17:15), and are promised children of their own do we get the first inkling that their masculinity may be less acceptable than it first appeared. Nevertheless, Sarai/h's confident masculinity rings through most clearly in this phase of their story.

The third and final portion of their story, found in Genesis 20 and 21, functions as a retcon – a retrospective continuity. Details from earlier in the story are tweaked or edited to transform the way the narrative develops going forward. Drawing on Halberstam's low theory, I explore what it means for Genesis 20 to (re)create a context that was lacking in Genesis 11 and 12 in order to (re)assert a more cisnormative model of womanhood for Sarah. Occurring immediately before the miraculous birth of Isaac, Sarah's son to (the renamed) Abraham, the use of the same narrative found in Genesis 12 recalls Sarah's femininity. Now, in Genesis 20, the sister-wife motif is subtly different and the construction of Sarah's gender is changed from the earlier version. Sarah's womanhood is directly referred to by man and God alike in what appears to be an attempt to remove any last vestiges of doubt about their gender conformity (especially Gen 20:3). Sarah also finds their spouse attempting to fill in the gaps of their origin story: Abraham provides details of their heritage lacking earlier in the narrative. Sarah appears as a rationalized character, whose gender nonconformity is explained away as (only) a temporary aberration that can be overlooked given their revered status as mother. Such gender nonconformity is rarely left unacknowledged. It must be mitigated – rationalized – in order to facilitate a character's return to the cisnormative world.[17] In Sarah's case, I treat Genesis 20:1–20 as a rationalization and a retcon. The retcon changes something previously established in Sarah's characterization, in this case to remove the instability caused by the lack of context in Genesis 11:29–31; with it comes a recontextualization of Sarah's gender. While this seeks to provide clarity and close the ruptures in the text, it makes them more obvious and open to reinterpretation. Only after Sarah is made (a) mother in Genesis 21:1–3 do they appear to perform expected femininity, although this image cannot be sustained. Sarah's final action is to expel Hagar, the woman they had forced into surrogacy,

---

15. Clines's voice is a constant and enduring presence throughout Peter-Ben Smit's substantial literature review of studies of masculinity. He recognises the emerging voices that are more dialectical and, perhaps, even intersectional, yet the Clines's influence and endurance in the field cannot be overstated. See Peter-Ben Smit, *Masculinity and the Bible: Survey, Models, and Perspectives*. Brill Research Perspectives. (Leiden: Brill, 2017).

16. Cf. Halberstam, *In a Queer Time*.

17. Halberstam, *In A Queer Time*, 55.

and her son Ishmael (Gen 21:10). Sarah promptly disappears from view – this time with permanent effect. They are neither heard nor seen again. Even at key moments in their son Isaac's development they are absent. Eventually their death is reported in 23:2.

Sarai/h emerges as a valorized *and* abusive figure who appears at times to typify femininity and then reject it in the next moment. Their bullish, masculine authoritative voice is counterpointed by the persistent spectre of motherhood, something that both confirms and withholds recognition of them as a cisnormative woman. They need not *necessarily* conform to cisnormative expectations at all times – though that is what commentators habitually see. Showcasing both masculinities and femininities together differentiates my approach from Guest's butch-centred, hermeneutic of hetero-suspicion. Any recognition of Sarai/h's masculinity or nonbinariness similarly distances this reading from feminist hermeneutics of suspicion. Instead, this interpretation is grounded in a critical engagement with cisnormative presuppositions. Reading the story cispiciously brings into sharp relief the juxtaposition between the portrayal of Sarai/h by onlookers, even within the narrative, and the case they make for themself. Through the accounts of the Egyptian onlookers and Abra(ha)m and the interjections by God and Abimelech, Sarai/h is a one-dimensional but quintessentially womanly woman. When they are allowed their own voice and actions, to offer powerful insights to their personhood, they demonstrate a complex gender beyond cisnormative expectations.

Introducing Sarai's Femininity – Genesis 11:29–12:20

From their first appearance (Gen 11:29–31), Sarai sets a challenge for reader and fellow character alike to discern their gender and identity. Without uttering a word, they arrive in a story in which they will become a prominent figure, yet in these introductory verses they lack key elements of a recognisable and desirable introductory contextualization. They are a *tabula rasa*, free from details that indicate a wider sense of 'being, relation, reproduction, and ideology' sufficient to establish lineage, class, and ethnic or racial heritage.[18] They bear only their name, status as Abram's wife, and carry the portentous knowledge that Sarai 'was barren; she had no child' (v. 30). No more is known of them at this introductory stage. It is precisely because Sarai is missing such significant details of their background that they become such a tantalising character in this exploration of gender. Their silence and lack of context indicate ruptures in the anticipated reproductive continuity of the narrative. This creates a space for queer and trans interpretation.[19] Halberstam suggests the details provide reassurance the character conforms to enduring expectations of gender and sexuality: reliable consistency comes when a

---

18. Halberstam, *Queer Art of Failure*, 42.
19. Halberstam, *Queer Art of Failure*; *In a Queer Time*.

character is in continuity with their (heteronormative) parents and, in due course, will bear their own offspring to continue the line.[20] Even the smallest cracks then make space for indecently whimsical rejections of norms: silence indicates a rejection of the need to self-articulate and locate ourselves as anticipated; lack of connection to family and lineage represents a breakaway from normative gendered and reproductive expectations. The dual themes – lack of context and lack of speech – set the scene for Sarai's arrival in the Genesis text.

Cispiciously Encountering Sarai

> Abram and Nahor took wives; the name of Abram's wife was Sarai, and the name of Nahor's wife was Milcah. She was the daughter of Haran the father of Milcah and Iscah. Now Sarai was barren; she had no child. Terah took his son Abram and his grandson Lot of Haran, and his daughter-in-law Sarai, his son Abram's wife, and they went out together from Ur of the Chaldeans to go into the land of Canaan; but when they came to Haran they settled there.
>
> Genesis 11:29–31

A cispicious vantage point gives us justification to pause at Sarai's introduction and to consider the extent to which context is (not) provided. Even when Sarai is first introduced, it is without ceremony or substantial detail. Curt and to the point, Sarai is listed as a member of Terah's family, through their status as Abram's wife, and described as childless (Gen 11:27–31). They are immediately contrasted with Milcah, wife of Abram's brother Nahor, who is provided with the familial context Sarai lacks. Milcah is the daughter of Haran, who also fathered Lot and Iscah (v. 29).[21] The inclusion of Milcah's lineage will turn out to be of great value as the story progresses since she is the forebear of both Rebekah, wife of Sarai's son Isaac, as well as Rachel and her sister Leah, wives to Isaac's son Jacob.[22] Endogamous marriage, which secures both maternity *and* paternity, is essential for Abram's

---

20. Halberstam, *Queer Art of Failure*, 42–43.

21. Tammi J. Schneider, *Sarah: Mother of Nations* (New York: Continuum, 2004), 15–17. Schneider argues that the context proffered for Milcah makes her appear the more significant character at point of introduction.

22. Rebekah and her heritage – including her status as a descendant of Milcah – are introduced through a genealogy found in Genesis 22:20–23 before her suitability as an endogamous wife is made irrefutable in Genesis 24. Rebekah's genealogy names Milcah, reintroducing her for the first time since Genesis 11:29: 'Now after these things it was told Abraham, "Milcah also has borne children, to your brother Nahor: Uz the firstborn, Bus his brother, Kemuel the father of Aram, Chesed, Hazo, Pildash, Jidlaph, and Bethuel". Bethuel became the father of Rebekah. These eight Milcah bore to Nahor, Abraham's brother' (Genesis 22:20–23). Rebekah's context is further consolidated through the repeated acknowledgement of her lineage (Genesis 24:15, 24, 47). Her status as daughter of Bethuel

favoured descendants. It is so significant that even at this point in the story Milcah's propriety must be guaranteed. Milcah and the future matriarchs are each provided the name of their father to consolidate their status as daughter – and not just anyone's daughter but a specific named person on each occasion. This grants each woman an introduction that authoritatively offers reassurance that they are and always have been who they purport themselves to be. No such context is proffered for Sarai. This really is a moment to stop, pause and reflect. If it is so important for Milcah, why are the same details lacking for Sarai? It is Sarai who is the narratively significant character, who embarks with their spouse on the journey of faith. The introductory text offers no such reassurance of their status as a (cis)normative character.[23]

The lack of context takes on new meaning in this cispicious reading, but Sarai's quirky introduction has been noted within malestream commentary.[24] Claus Westermann notes that 'Sarah's childlessness … is a threat, because it breaks the continuity of the generations'.[25] Bill Arnold pays close attention to the rhetorical function of the parallel terms of Genesis 11:30: 'Now Sarai was barren; she had no child'. The repetition for dramatic effect emphasizes that Sarai's situation is the most important information in the family tree and 'nothing like this has happened in Genesis before'.[26] Arnold continues to discuss the word translated as 'child': 'The root of that rare term, the "child" (wālād) that Sarai lacks, is the same root as tôlĕdôt, "descendants," and môledet, "birth place." The abrupt news that Sarai has no "child" brings the reader up short'.[27] Arnold's analysis of the Hebrew indicates that Sarai's childlessness also emphasizes their lack of location as they have neither

son of Milcah and Nahor is included on each occasion. Rachel's introduction similarly provides the desired context as she is described as the daughter of Laban son of Nahor before the reader or her future husband have even caught a glance of her (Genesis 29:5–6).

23. For further queer exploration of Sarai's story, see Rosenberg, *Ancentral Queerness: The Normal and the Deviant in the Abraham and Sarah Narratives*. Rosenberg argues that while there is no indication that Sarai or Abram 'ever had sex with someone of the same gender or that they identified with a gender that did not match their biology', they present a valuable case study for queer sociality (25–27).

24. Gerhard von Rad, *Genesis: A Commentary*. Revised ed., Old Testament Library, (London: SCM Press, 1972), 158. Von Rad acknowledges that it is 'strange that Milcah's father is named but not the father of the far more important Sarai!' See also E. A. Speiser, *Genesis*, The Anchor Bible Commentary, (Garden City, NY: Doubleday, 1964), 78. Speiser similarly notes that the omission of Sarai's lineage is interesting.

25. Claus Westermann, *Genesis 12–36*, trans. John J. Scullion, A Continental Commentary, (London: SPCK, 1985), 138.

26. Bill T. Arnold, *Genesis*, Google Play ed., The New Cambridge Bible Commentary, (New York: Cambridge University Press, 2009), 'Comments on 11:27–12:9'. Cf. von Rad, *Genesis: A Commentary*, 158. Von Rad does not recognise the comments as so significant, rather declaring the description of Sarai's childlessness to be 'mentioned only in passing'.

27. Arnold, *Genesis*, 'Comments on 11:27–12:9'.

birthplace nor descendants either; they stand alone in a narrative where such isolation is far from typical. This lack of context becomes a moment of silence that provides a small gap into which my cispicious approach can begin to find leverage. A provocative 'what if . . . ?' provides a flickering glimpse of a character whose lack of context opens the possibility of identifying gender differently within their own story.

> Now there was a famine in the land. So Abram went down to Egypt to reside there as an alien, for the famine was severe in the land. When he was about to enter Egypt, he said to his wife Sarai, 'I know well that you are a woman beautiful in appearance; and when the Egyptians see you, they will say, "This is his wife"; then they will kill me, but they will let you live. Say you are my sister, so that it may go well with me because of you, and that my life may be spared on your account.' When Abram entered Egypt the Egyptians saw that the woman was very beautiful. When the officials of Pharaoh saw her, they praised her to Pharaoh. And the woman was taken into Pharaoh's house. And for her sake he dealt well with Abram; and he had sheep, oxen, male donkeys, male and female slaves, female donkeys, and camels.
>
> But the LORD afflicted Pharaoh and his house with great plagues because of Sarai, Abram's wife. So Pharaoh called Abram, and said, 'What is this you have done to me? Why did you not tell me that she was your wife? Why did you say, "She is my sister", so that I took her for my wife? Now then, here is your wife; take her, and be gone.' And Pharaoh gave his men orders concerning him; and they set him on the way, with his wife and all that he had.
>
> Genesis 12:10–20

Sarai is such a significant female character within the ancestral narratives that mitigating any nagging doubt is essential, but they remain barely present within the text. In Genesis 12 Sarai really begins to come into focus, even if holding them in that gaze remains challenging. Narratologically, Sarai is only present through inclusion of their name as one of Abram's party when they embark on the journey that takes them to Canaan (Gen 12:5).[28] They are named alongside Lot, Abram's nephew, and the unspecified possessions and unnamed 'persons they had acquired in Haran' (v. 5). They are brought into sharper focus once they arrive in Egypt (v. 10), but it is through the words of the omniscient narrator that Sarai comes into clearer view. From Genesis 12:10–20 Sarai piques interest while remaining present, just, to hold the viewers' gaze long enough to gender them.

---

28. See Bal, 'Introduction', 17. I follow Bal's narratological approach. She argues that through paying close attention to who speaks, who is named, and who acts, we can identify who holds power. She points out that women rarely appear as orators, subjects, or agents and lack authority and presence within the narrative. In this case Sarai is granted the status neither of orator nor of agent.

Viewing Sarai's arrival in Egypt (Gen 12:10–20) through a trans-informed gaze reveals the construction of their sex and gender. Their name and the feminine pronouns applied to them are familiar but now the reader is invited to share in Abram's appraisal of his wife. Abram appears as a reliable commentator as he is provided with the lineage that is withheld from Sarai (Gen 11:26–32).[29] Receipt of personalized divine messages and his construction of an altar (v. 7–8) show he is favoured by God (Gen 12:1–3, 7). Abram's status also emerges through reference to his possessions and the size of his (largely enslaved) party (v. 5). Abram, the orator, can speak confidently and authoritatively of Sarai:

'I know well that you are a *woman* beautiful in appearance; and when the Egyptians see you, they will say, "This is his *wife*"; then they will kill me, but they will let you live. Say that you are my *sister*, so that it may go well with me because of you, and that my life may be spared on your account.'

vv. 11–13, emphasis added

It is not only what he says, but how he says it, that becomes important in creating a clear enough image of Sarai to contribute to gendering them. Often a comforting reassurance comes when a character is gendered in a way that conforms to expectation. So a cisnormative reading needs to recognize how language – including translational choices – signals gender. A character must meet presuppositions but not so excessively that the authenticity of the gender assignment is bought into question.[30] Therefore the word 'woman' alongside the designation that Sarai is

---

29. Abram's genealogy is traced through his father, Terah, back to Shem and from Shem to Noah (Gen 10:32; 11:10–32).

30. For examples of using a transgender gaze to reveal excess gender performance in biblical characters, see Guest, 'Modeling the Transgender Gaze', (discussed in Chapter 2); Samuel Ross, 'A Transgender Gaze at Genesis 38', *Journal for Interdisciplinary Biblical Studies* 1, 2 (2020), 25–39. Ross applies Guest's trans gaze to the character of Tamar who is generally understood to be female and who undertakes sex work to secure a future. His article contributes a welcome interrogation of a female-identified character from the ancestral narratives in Genesis, however like Guest's chosen characters Tamar is a marginal figure. As Ross draws directly on Guest's reformulation he does not trace the genealogy of the trans gaze back to Halberstam's *In A Queer Time and Place*. The result is that some of the shortcomings I identify – notably the perpetuation of the problem of trivialization – remains present. Where his article excels, however, is in identifying the parallels between today's experiences of trans sex workers and Tamar's story. He demonstrates that integrating trans insights adds to the understanding of Tamar's motivations. Ross's attentions to the risks and benefits for both Tamar and today's trans sex workers attests to the impact of cisnormativity in their lives. However, as he draws so heavily on Guest's work – and the wider *Transgender, Intersex, and Biblical Interpretation* co-edited with Teresa Hornsby – Ross's focus remains on the influence of heteronormativity. His article powerfully demonstrates the possible applications not only of Guest's trans gaze but other hermeneutical tools that address trans experience and gender diversity, notably a cispicious approach such as this one.

beautiful becomes somewhat clanging.[31] Abram's words to and about Sarai are clearly, repeatedly gendered and the description of sexed beauty further feminises *her*, so why the need to make her womanhood so explicit? 'Beautiful' gives the merest glimpse of Sarai as embodied, but no further detail is provided at this stage. When combined with Abram's use of the terms 'woman', 'wife', and 'sister' there is a rather overwhelming insistence on the femaleness and femininity of Sarai. It is not only the gaze of Abram and the narrator who present their appraisal of Sarai; the text shares an account of the gaze of unnamed Egyptians who report to Pharaoh of Sarai as Abram predicts.

When Sarai and Abram enter Egypt, the narrator tells us

> the Egyptians saw that *the woman* was very beautiful. When the officials of Pharaoh saw *her*, they praised *her* to Pharaoh. And *the woman* was taken into Pharaoh's house. And for *her* sake he dealt well with Abram; and he had sheep, oxen, male donkeys, male and female slaves, female donkeys, and camels.'
>
> Gen 12:14–16, emphasis added

For now, Sarai has lost their name making the gendered language used to describe them all the more visible and powerful. *She* is no longer *a* beautiful woman, but now appears as *the* (only) woman. Clearly there is only one woman of note! Given that Sarai is the only woman visible, we can infer that, like us, the Egyptians are trying to find ways to facilitate their own gendering. They cling to the beauty as Abram has previously described, but here the multiple unnamed voices confirm Abram's appraisal of Sarai. As a result, this beautiful femininity ensures that *she* is taken into Pharaoh's household. Only in verse 17, when Abram's deception unravels, is Sarai given back their name. Pharaoh and Abram jostle while Sarai disappears from view only to be referred to in the third person through use of pronouns (she/her) and relational gendered terms (wife/sister) (vv. 18–19). Even on their departure from Egypt, Sarai remains beyond the gaze of the reader, hidden once again behind the nameless designation 'wife' (v. 20).

Fixing a Trans Gaze on Sarai's Beauty?

In these fleeting glimpses of Sarai, apparently pertinent details emerge to facilitate the gendering process, but their value is yet to be established. From a cispicious perspective, it becomes possible to focus anew on Sarai and their portrayal in the narrative. Halberstam positioned a transgender gaze as a tool for analysing

---

31. Fokkelien van Dijk-Hemmes, 'Sarai's Exile: A Gender-Motivated Reading of Genesis 12.10–13.2', in *A Feminist Companion to Genesis*, ed. Athalya Brenner-Idan [Brenner], The Feminist Companion to the Bible (Sheffield: Sheffield Academic Press, 1993), 222–234, 226. Van Dijk-Hemmes also finds this problematic in her feminist reading of the text. She finds discomfort in the male-centred view of Sarai's beauty and the absence of Sarai's own perspective as she is the subject of sustained male gaze.

the 'visual representations of gender ambiguity' in film.[32] In translating Halberstam's approach for biblical interpretation, I focus on his observation that gender ambiguous characters struggle to hold the gaze of the viewer over a sustained period of time.[33] Sarai fades in and out of focus, slipping beyond the attention of reader and narrator alike for a sustained period which is common in gender nonconforming characters portrayed for a largely cisgender (or cisnormative) audience. Where gender is unstable or chimerical, it exists beyond the comprehension of the reader and it must fade into the background so as not to cause disquiet – and with it goes the character whose gender is under scrutiny. It is that lack of comprehensibility that marks Sarai's gender as nonconforming. Halberstam argues it is a dangerous for such nonconforming characters to remain visible, so they 'disappear in order to remain viable'.[34] This then means 'the transgender gaze becomes difficult to track because it depends on complex relations in time and space between seeing and not seeing, appearing and disappearing, knowing and not knowing'.[35] These complexities become apparent for Sarai; even when they are in view they easily become lost behind highly gendered, but depersonalised, language (Gen 12:10–20).

In order to assess whether Sarai's story parallels accounts of gender diversity, we must engage carefully with the gaze of those who see them most clearly *in* the text. We lack Sarai's own perspective at this stage, so we must rely on those around them to examine if their views of Sarai contribute to a cisnormative perception of the character. Abram's privileged status within the narrative ensures his account of his spouse carries most weight (Gen 12:11–13). It is when his voice joins with those of the Egyptian officials (vv. 14–15) that the significance of their shared contribution to a cisnormative reading becomes clearest. The Egyptian officials are independent – or even potentially hostile – viewers, so they present Sarai without undue favour and represent the perspective of a casual, non-partisan observer. So, Sarai's beauty is not only subjectively praised by Abram but can be understood as universally recognisable. The Egyptian officials and the Pharaoh symbolize a significant hegemonic political power in the region, so their perspectives are particularly powerful in endowing Sarai with sex and gender. Here beauty is aligned consistently with hegemonic womanhood and femininity. The combination of these observations and the frequency of the gendered language applied to Sarai ensures that *she* is presented as an inescapably female beauty. Such beauty is also far from neutral, leading Shirley Anne Tate, who works at the intersection of Black, feminist, decolonial and diaspora studies, to describe beauty itself as 'the fetishized outcome of the work of fantasy'.[36] Sarai's fantastical beauty has something of Goldilocks' porridge to it – it is neither too excessive to be believed nor sufficiently lacking to

---

32. Halberstam, *In a Queer Time*, 76. For further discussion, see Chapter 1.
33. Halberstam, *In a Queer Time*, 76–96.
34. Halberstam, *In a Queer Time*, 78.
35. Halberstam, *In a Queer Time*, 78.
36. Shirley Anne Tate, *Black Beauty: Aesthetics, Stylization, Politics* (London: Routledge, 2009), 17.

be unremarkable: once again it needs to be just right. In being so carefully judged it allows Sarai to be perceived as the quintessential embodiment of feminine beauty.

Looking at Sarai's beauty through this cispicious, trans-informed lens, brings into sharp focus a question about what it means to be a just-right level of beauty. How can Sarai's beauty – something that is acknowledged to be culturally-constructed and changing – be recognized by both Abram and the Egyptians alike? The plural voices that serve to affirm the integrity and authenticity of Sarai's beauty are essential. Indeed, the attention to Sarai's beauty in the Genesis Apocryphon contributes to that polyphony, even if it is a later and non-canonical addition. Sarai is described to the king as the perfect embodiment of desirable femininity: 'she is fairer than all other women. Truly, her beauty is greater than theirs' (1QapGen XX).[37] So many diversely gendered people, especially trans women and femme people, face persistent accusations of fakeness, so recognition of Sarai's beauty is powerful. Serano considers such accusations as a core component of transmisogyny, where trans women are treated as duplicitous and pitiable.[38] Where an interest in beauty or bodily aesthetics is praised in a cisnormative woman, it is too often seen as an inauthentic affectation or mimicry in others.[39] The advantage of the third-party accounts in Sarai's story are that they remove the potential for us to see their beauty as an ersatz affectation. Rather the eye-witness accounts instil a sense of something that appears authentic and thus it confers Sarai with a cisnormative feminine beauty – something all the more evident through use of the definite article when referring to Sarai as *the* woman. She is, by implication, the most womanly woman there is – but it comes at the cost of her subjectivity.[40]

---

37. '... and beautiful is her face! How ... fine are the hairs of her head! How lovely are her eyes! How desirable her nose and all the radiance of her countenance ... How fair are her breasts and *how beautiful all her whiteness*! How pleasing are her arms and how perfect her hands, and how [desirable] all the appearance of her hands! How fair are her palms and how long and slender are her fingers! How comely are her feet, how perfect her thighs! No virgin or bride led into the marriage chamber is more beautiful than she; she is fairer than all other women. Truly, her beauty is greater than theirs. Yet together with all this grace she possesses abundant wisdom, so that whatever she does is perfect (?).'

Emphasis added, particularly to draw attention to Sarai's whiteness within the conceptualization of their beauty (cf. Tate); Geza Vermes, *The Dead Sea Scrolls in English*, (Sheffield: JSOT Press, 1987), 254.

38. Serano, *Whipping Girl*, 35–52.

39. Serano, *Whipping Girl*, 41. 'It's telling that TV, film, and news producers tend not to be satisfied with merely showing trans women wearing feminine clothes and makeup. Rather, it is their intention to capture trans women *in the act* of putting on lipstick, dresses, and high heels, thereby giving the audience the impression that the trans woman's femaleness is an artificial mask or costume'.

40. Joseph McDonald, *Searching for Sarah in the Second Temple Era: Images in the Hebrew Bible, the Septuagint, the Genesis Apocryphon, and the Antiquities.* Scriptural Traces:

The account of Sarai's sojourn in Egypt provides invaluable information to allow the reader to gender them. The language and description of beauty contributes to an apparently inscrutable image of Sarai as woman as it alludes to both sex and gender. Even though they remain a narrative object, yet to speak and act for themselves, a key detail from the introductory remarks in Genesis 11:29–31 remains unresolved. Sarai's childlessness, if it becomes the focus, has the power to destabilize the effects of the gendering made possible through Genesis 12:10–20.

A Pregnant Pause

The one clear thing that we learn about Sarai in Genesis 11:29–31 is that they are childless. Otherwise, they are understood through their relationship to Abram as his wife. The childlessness is something attributed to them, and not shared with their spouse; it becomes a core part of their characterization: 'Sarai was barren; she had no child'.[41] The significance of the description makes the designation of childlessness inescapable but with it comes further connotations for gendering them. Candida Moss and Joel Baden argue that 'womanhood continues to be most associated with motherhood, and with the assumption that motherhood is the highest state of womanhood'.[42] For trans women, in particular, this is all the more problematic as 'a common assumption for dismissing trans women is tied to reproductive assumptions – because they cannot give birth, trans women are not "real" women'.[43] Given that cisnormative womanhood is synonymous with motherhood the emphasis on Sarai's childlessness in this introductory, gendering portion of their story cannot be overlooked. Here the gendered language and emphasis on beauty serve as the necessary juxtaposition to facilitate a cisnormative reading of Sarai.

However, focussing on the childless Sarai who finds herself in Egypt, I return to the question of a potential pregnancy or lack thereof – despite the contribution of the beauty motif. Their beauty ensures that *she* is *the* woman taken into Pharaoh's harem, but with that welcome recognition come new risks. Those risks are both to the patriarchal requirements placed on Sarai and the parallel cisnormative expectations. These strands coalesce around Abram's need for descendants.

Critical Perspectives on the Reception and Influence of the Hebrew Bible. (London: T&T Clark, 2021), 139. 'Sarai's objectification – by Abram, Pharaoh, and God – coincides precisely with the disappearance of her subjectivity. After her timely words save Abram's life, Sarai is virtually drained of humanity, and her role from that point onward could as easily be played by a lovely treasure chest, locked up tight'.

41. Schneider, *Sarah*; Renita J. Weems, *Just A Sister Away: A Womanist Vision of Women's Relationships in the Bible*, Kindle ed. (San Diego, CA: LuraMedia, 2005), 'A Maid, A Mistress, and No Mercy'.

42. Candida R. Moss and Joel S. Baden, *Reconceiving Infertility: Biblical Perspectives on Procreation and Childlessness* (Princeton, NJ: Princeton University Press, 2015), 7.

43. Katy E. Valentine, 'Examining Scripture in Light of Trans Women's Voices', in *The Oxford Handbook of Feminist Approaches to the Hebrew Bible*, ed. Susanne Scholz, Oxford Handbooks (New York: Oxford University Press, 2021), 509–524.

During the Lord's appearance to Abram prior to the exile to Egypt, Abram is promised offspring who will be heirs to Canaan (Gen 12:7). Feminist biblical scholar Cheryl Exum notes that Sarai is invisible during the receipt of this promise; they have faded from the gaze entirely.[44] Sarai has not conceived, and perhaps cannot conceive, the promised children at this stage. So, as the entourage arrive in Egypt, there are significant potential risks and opportunities for pregnancy. Pimping his *wife* out on arrival seems a counterintuitive move for Abram when trying to bring a child of his own into the world. Exum acknowledges that while Abram fears for his own life, he displays no such worries for Sarai. Rather, she suggests that the biggest concern is 'the possibility that [Sarai] might have sexual relations with a man other than the patriarch, which can be regarded as a threat to the purity of the line'.[45] This is a major threat to what Exum sees as the primary function of the matriarch: mother to the heir to the ancestral dynasty. Here in Genesis 12 specifically, she notes that there is no explicit confirmation that Sarai did not have sex with Pharaoh.[46] Having described the use of this motif as 'curious' and 'peculiar' Exum concedes that the accounts 'are so unusual and unconventional, and traditional interpretations of them are so unsatisfying'.[47]

In her own non-traditional interpretation of Sarai's story, Exum makes clear that Abram must have considered there to be no substantial risk for Sarai to play the role of concubine.[48] She offers a particularly pertinent observation: 'If the patriarch does not suppose that the matriarch is in danger, neither is there any evidence that the *matriarch* thinks she is in danger'.[49] While Exum argues this is primarily the result of androcentric texts that keep the matriarchs beyond the consideration of the story, I offer an alternative explanation. By rejecting the presupposition that potential for (biological) motherhood conveys womanhood (and vice versa), new possibilities emerge. Perhaps Abram and Sarai are well acquainted – and indeed comfortable – with the knowledge that there are biological and/or anatomical reasons why Sarai cannot have children, at least not without a miracle! This would explain why neither Sarai, Abram, *nor* the narrator feel the need to claim that Sarai did not have sex during their stay in the harem.

There is, perhaps, one motivation for Abram, and to a lesser extent Sarai, to commit to this course of action which recognizes that Genesis 12 contributes so significantly to the gendering of Sarai. Abram's actions provide an opportunity to resolve Sarai's apparent lack of context and their childlessness, each of which

---

44. J. Cheryl Exum, *Fragmented Women. Feminist (Sub)Versions of Biblical Narratives*, Second ed., Cornerstones, (London: Bloomsbury, 2016), 77.
45. Exum, *Fragmented Women*, 85.
46. Exum, *Fragmented Women*, 86. Exum contrasts the way the narrative is more explicit in clarifying that the matriarch remains untouched by Abimelech in Genesis 20 and Genesis 26, where the motif is repeated.
47. Exum, *Fragmented Women*, 86.
48. Exum, *Fragmented Women*, 117–118.
49. Exum, *Fragmented Women*, 118.

undermine a cisnormative assumption, all in one go. Perhaps he is trying to add a layer of decency over the potentially indecent character by providing a narrative where they appear reliably feminine despite their childlessness.[50] Even with limited view of Sarai to this point there are already questions about the extent to which they fit neatly within cisnormative expectations for their sex and gender. By making Sarai the object of such sustained and diverse gaze – a gaze that has the power to ascribe womanhood – Abram puts his spouse in the spotlight. In doing so he presents them as the subject of a cisnormative male gaze that centres on Sarai's beauty and femininity. At the same time, the focus on Sarai's feminine womanhood distracts from the questions and instabilities that still feature in the account of their gender (non)conformity. It is clear that beauty is one major hook on to which to attach a cisnormative reading, but there remain alternative possibilities for understanding Sarai's gender even beyond the competing themes of beauty and childlessness.

Sarai's lack of historical or familial context offers no reassuring confirmation that they are reliably cisgender. If the information is withheld by a third party, perhaps by the narrator, questions emerge about what is being hidden and why. What features of Sarai's context are sufficiently worrisome that they cannot be shared? Alternatively, if Sarai takes ownership of the gaps in the story, their narrative silence can be understood as an act of defiance. In the end, it matters little whether or not their omission is an act of patriarchal silencing: Sarai symbolizes a rejection of the need to speak, to self-locate, and to confirm the expectations placed on their identity.[51] Their lack of speech then brings an additional perspective to their narrative, even if it makes it more of a challenge for the interpreter. Sarai fades in and out of focus in parallel with the representation of gender nonconforming characters who appear incomprehensible. At this stage it is clear that Sarai increasingly does not fully or neatly fit into the cisnormative mould; rather they sit at a slight angle to those norms. Even while Abram's actions try to shout over Sarai's silence it becomes possible to imagine space for cispicious readings to step in and fill the gap.

Sarai's childlessness, in combination with their lack of context, represents a rejection of the cisnormative ideals associated with success, health, and perfection that are wedded to reproduction.[52] It provides just enough of a rupture through which to glimpse a different view of Sarai. Seeing Sarai as a woman, but one who does not fully fit within a cisnormative reading, is hugely powerful. One such example is Sally Gross's readings, where she emphasizes the parallels between Sarai's story and intersex experience.[53] For Gross, Sarai is someone who experiences

---

50. See Althaus-Reid, *Indecent Theology; Queer God*. Here I recall Marcella Althaus-Reid's conceptualizations of (in)decency, especially signified through disidentification with gender and reproductive norms. For further discussion see Chapter 1.
51. Halberstam, *Queer Art of Failure*, 42–43.
52. Halberstam, *Queer Art of Failure*, 120.
53. Gross, 'Intersexuality and Scripture'.

diversity of sexual development beyond the narrow limits of normative maleness or femaleness, meaning that they would today be recognized as an intersex person. Gross highlights the way that the rabbinic tradition makes space for those who do not easily fit into the categories of male and female. She then draws on Rabbi Nahman's identification of Sarai as an *'aylonith*, 'a woman without a womb'.[54] While Gross acknowledges that the Talmudic Rabbis offer glosses that are perhaps 'a trifle far-fetched and quaint', she celebrates them for the equanimity with which they explored 'the possibility that leading and revered scriptural characters were intersexed'.[55] The problem emerges today when intersex lives continue to be overlooked by cisnormative models of gender. Virginia Mollenkott and Michael Carden, for example, highlight Gross's interpretation for its value in reading for greater gender diversity in the Bible.[56] These interpretations do not preclude the miracle of Isaac's birth to Sarai in Genesis 21:1 but offer a different foundation from which God intervenes. Nevertheless, that remains some way into Sarai's future for now. Gross's intersex interpretation of Sarai adds to the details I identify through use of Serano and Halberstam's insights. A picture is emerging of someone who is not intelligible by cisnormative standards, irrespective of how much those around them seek to direct how they are understood. They will not easily be gatekept by overly simplified litmus tests of cisnormative femininity that relate primarily to procreative capacity.[57] Nor will they easily fit into what an androcentric, cisnormative gaze tells us – sometimes quite determinately – is a femininity demanded for womankind.

Showcasing Masculinity – Genesis 16; 18

Now Sarai, Abram's wife, bore him no children. She had an Egyptian slave-girl whose name was Hagar, and Sarai said to Abram, 'You see that the LORD has prevented me from bearing children; go in to my slave-girl; it may be that I shall obtain children by her.' And Abram listened to the voice of Sarai. So, after Abram had lived for ten years in the land of Canaan, Sarai, Abram's wife, took Hagar the Egyptian, her slave-girl, and gave her to her husband Abram as a wife. He went in to Hagar, and she conceived; and when she saw that she had conceived, she looked with contempt on her mistress. Then Sarai said to Abram, 'May the wrong done to me be on you! I gave my slave-girl to your embrace, and when she saw that she had conceived, she looked on me with contempt. May the Lord judge between you and me!' But Abram said to Sarai, 'Your slave-girl is in your

---

54. Gross, 'Intersexuality and Scripture', 72. Gross draws heavily on rabbinic commentary on Isa 51:1–2, which Rabbi Nahman uses as an intertext to reach the conclusion that Sarai was without a womb.

55. Gross, 'Intersexuality and Scripture', 73.

56. Mollenkott, *Omnigender*; Carden, 'Genesis/Bereshit'.

57. Valentine, 'Examining Scripture', 511–512.

power; do to her as you please.' Then Sarai dealt harshly with her, and she ran away from her.

The angel of the LORD found her by a spring of water in the wilderness, the spring on the way to Shur. And he said, 'Hagar, slave-girl of Sarai, where have you come from and where are you going?' She said, 'I am running away from my mistress Sarai.' The angel of the LORD said to her, 'Return to your mistress, and submit to her.

Gen 16:1-9

In this new phase of Sarai's story, a different figure comes to the fore: one now able to speak, act, and to demonstrate personhood for the first time. Sarai's first spoken act is to instruct their spouse to impregnate Hagar (Gen 16:1-3). Contrasting Sarai's introduction, Hagar is given a geographic and ethnic home – Egypt – and a class and gender status, that of an enslaved woman. This introduction is hardly rich in detail, but it is at least on a par with that of Milcah in Genesis 12. Hagar is not an equal to Abram nor suitable for endogamous marriage, but that is made explicit in the text.[58] Meanwhile Abram accepts Sarai's authority and does as they tell him (v. 4), something that leads to the breakdown of any pleasantries between Hagar and Sarai (v. 5). Abram absents himself of any responsibility or culpability, declaring that the power resides with Sarai (v. 6). Sarai invokes God's approval for their actions, in contrast with their spouse's, then exercises significant power by dealing harshly with Hagar, leading the younger woman to run away. The anachronism at the core of this relationship, notably Sarai's authority over Hagar, is noted by Gordon Wenham who writes '"slave girls" [such as Hagar] usually seem to be answerable to a master as opposed to a mistress'.[59] This is a difficult text as the abuse of Hagar is so egregious, and the passage contributes to a wider text of terror for Hagar (Gen 16:1-16; 21:9-21).[60] While Exum notes the trope of rival, hostile women that features heavily in the ancestral narratives, designed to serve patriarchal aims, use of a cispicious strategy offers an alternative view.[61] Exum argues that

---

58. Weems, *Just A Sister Away*, 'A Mistress, A Maid, and No Mercy'. Weems describes the underlying context when she writes, 'Like our own situation, the story of the Egyptian Hagar and the Hebrew Sarai encompasses more than ethnic prejudice. Theirs is a story of ethnic prejudice exacerbated by economic and sexual exploitation'.

59. Gordon J. Wenham, *Genesis 16-50*, Google Play ed., Word Biblical Commentary, (Dallas, TX: Word Books, 2000).

60. Phyllis Trible, *Texts of Terror*, SCM Classics, (London: SCM Press, 2002), 5-24. For Trible, Hagar's terror occurs in two phases: 'the plot of the first story is circular, moving from bondage to flight to bondage, whilst the action of the second is linear, proceeding from bondage to expulsion to homelessness' (6). The abuse central to this terror lies largely in the hands of Sarai/h.

61. Exum, *Fragmented Women*, 69-114. Exum argues that the creation of tension between two women, especially rivals for a single man, is a quintessential part of the patriarchal construction of (a lack of) community between women.

hostility between women in close social and familial contact, such as co-wives, serves patriarchal interests by keeping women as rivals rather than peers. Such tension, including the perception of another woman as a threat, ensures that the patriarch's (and patriarchy's) power remains unchallenged. Cispicion, alternatively, enables the gendered differences between each character to gain greater prominence.[62] Sarai's masculinity, typified by their authority over their spouse and implied status as de facto head of the household, remains largely unacknowledged both in feminist readings like Exum's and in malestream commentaries. Yet that masculinity drives the story and contributes to the emergence of Sarai as a character with narrative presence and a lasting influence. Therefore, I do not regard the relationship between Sarai and Hagar as one of rival femininities, albeit one exacerbated by class, race, and reproductive capacity. Instead, I explore how Sarai's masculinity comes to the fore and how they deploy that forcefully.

Sarai the Emerging Patriarch?

With the nascent recognition that Sarai's masculinity features within their narrative, it is worth pausing to consider how their masculinity is signalled for readers and fellow characters alike. Howard Eilberg-Schwartz argues that biblical masculinities require recognition and validation by others in the narrative as well as the reader.[63] Masculinity is asserted, challenged and reinforced, with human performances forced to compete against the masculinity of God. The human characters are then stuck in a mimetic cycle where each tries to assert their own masculine dominance over other male characters whilst also remaining subordinate to God. While Eilberg-Schwartz shows the complexity and competition inherent to masculinity, David Clines's

---

62. Hagar's gender warrants further consideration, especially from a cispicious perspective; however that is not possible within the remit of this project. Given that she is ethnically othered within the text and is a secondary character, there is far less detail on which to build a gendered reading akin to that of Sarai in this chapter. See, for example, Weems, *Just A Sister Away*; Anna Fisk, 'Sisterhood in the Wilderness: Biblical Paradigms and Feminist Identity Politics in Readings of Hagar and Sarah', in *Looking Through a Glass Bible: Postdisciplinary Biblical Interpretations from the Glasgow School*, ed. A. K. M. Adam and Samuel Tongue, Biblical Interpretation Series (Leiden: Brill, 2014), 113–137; Yvonne Sherwood, 'Hagar and Ishmael: The Reception of Explusion', *Interpretation: A Journal of Bible and Theology* 68, 3 (2014), 286–304; Nyasha Junior, *Reimagining Hagar: Blackness and Bible* (New York: Oxford University Press, 2019). It will be pertinent to explore the implication of the relationship between race and gender, as explored in Hortense J. Spillers, 'Mama's Baby, Papa's Maybe: An American Grammar Book', *Diacritics* 17, 2 (1987), 64–81; C. Riley Snorton, *Black on Both Sides: A Racial History of Trans Identity* (Minneapolis, MN: University of Minnesota Press, 2017).

63. Howard Eilberg-Schwartz, *God's Phallus and Other Problems for Men and Monotheism* (Boston, MA: Beacon Press, 1994), 139–140.

signifiers of masculinity are particularly pertinent here.[64] Sarai is not usually considered an archetypal male – or even masculine – character who must compete for divine favour, even in the ways their spouse faces, but that does not stop them from performing noteworthy masculinity. In Genesis 16, Sarai demonstrates a masculinity that maps directly on to Clines's schema: they are persuasive in speech – especially when conversing with (other) men and God; they are strong; they make life-and-death decisions over another; and they protect the needs of the wider family.

The story builds and so does Sarai's masculinity, especially through their status as Hagar's master.[65] In Genesis 16:1-6, Sarai's persuasiveness comes to the fore in their demonstration of (masculine) authority over their household.[66] Abram is subservient and subordinate to Sarai, who expresses their strength and authority over both spouse and Hagar alike.[67] This is a model performance of masculine dominance over those around them and they are not chastised in or by the narrative for their actions at this stage. They do not need to hide or repress this masculinity in any way, but their successful performance brings into sharp relief Abram's secondary status to his spouse at this point in the story. Abram's masculinity has previously been demonstrated through his interactions with God (Gen 12; 15) and throughout Genesis 14, especially in his interactions with Melchizedek (Gen 14:17–24). Now, however, his masculinity is ceded to Sarai in these opening verses of Genesis 16. Here he is far from the authority who can influence Pharaohs and vanquish enemies, such as in Genesis 12 and 14; neither is he the rich and secure settler of Canaan found in Genesis 13. Deborah Sawyer suggests that Abram's masculinity is, at times, lacking confidence and power, but I do not see that to be clearly visible prior to Genesis 16.[68] Eilberg-Schwartz suggests

---

64. The model of masculinity used here draws from 'David the Man: The Construction of Masculinity in the Hebrew Bible', Clines, *Interested Parties*, 212–243 ('DTM'); 'Dancing and Shining at Sinai', ('DSS'). Across the two works four themes appear consistent across both sets of Clines's case studies, Aaron and Moses (Exod 32; 34) and David (1 Sam 16 – 1 Kgs 2). He calls these themes: 'The Warrior Male' ('DTM', 216–219; 'DSS', 55–56); 'The Persuasive Male' ('DTM', 219–221; 'DSS', 56–57); 'The Beautiful Male' ('DTM', 221–223; 'DSS', 59–62); and 'The Womanless Male' ('DTM', 225–227; 'DSS', 57–59). In 'DTM', he also includes 'The Bonding Male' (223–225) and 'A Conflict of Masculinities' (228–231) which are also relevant for Sarai's masculinity.

65. Cf. Wenham, *Genesis 16–50*. Given the power of gendered language in this story, Wenham's description of Hagar's relationship with their master, not mistress, is particularly notable.

66. Wenham, *Genesis 16–50*. Wenham describes this as a scene 'dominated by Sarai'. He continues to add that 'obeying one's wife [is] an action automatically suspect in the patriarchal society of ancient Israel'.

67. Wenham, *Genesis 16–50*. 'In consummating the marriage, Abram and Hagar are simply instruments of Sarai'.

68. Deborah F. Sawyer, 'Biblical Gender Strategies: the Case of Abraham's Masculinity', in *Gender, Religion and Diversity: Cross-Cultural Perspectives*, ed. Ursula King and Tina Beattie (London: Continuum, 2004), 162–171.

there is a need for men to subordinate themselves to God (the example of ultimate masculinity), which results in uncertain performances of masculinity in those lauded by God such as Abram.[69] Yet each of these readings overlooks the importance of Sarai's own masculinity, especially when contrasted with that of their spouse.[70] It is Sarai who sets the standard, with God intervening to return Hagar to her abusive mistress (vv. 7–14). Hagar is told to submit, validating Sarai's authority and status (v. 9).

The relationship between Sarai and Hagar can also be understood differently once Sarai's masculinity is acknowledged. Exum suggests tension between the women occurs due to the patriarchal need to keep the women as enemies. Yet, by reflecting on Clines's understanding of masculinity there is a further facet of the story that supports a cispicious interpretation of Sarai. He argues that quintessential biblical masculinity requires a 'womanless male', someone who does not socialize with women, nor embark upon womanly roles.[71] There is no discernible relationship between Sarai and Hagar; the former never speaks directly to the latter, leaving Abram to serve as intermediary (Gen 16:1-3). Once Hagar conceives, Abram and Sarai converse again, this time driven by Sarai's anger. In this exchange Sarai clearly declares themself to be a direct peer to Abram: 'May the LORD judge between you and me!' (v. 5), emphasising their status as *his* equal before God. The outcome is Sarai's abuse of Hagar, leading the pregnant woman to run away. While it is Abram who has vanquished enemies external to the family, Sarai effectively demonstrates their power to do so within the family by their treatment of Hagar. Wenham considers Sarai's description of Hagar's pride to be sufficient justification for such vicious retaliation.[72] In so doing, Sarai continues to demonstrate further aspects of Clines's schema for masculinity: willingness to respond with violence when their family is under threat.

By changing how we understand the relationship between Hagar and Sarai, the one between Sarai and Abram must also be reconsidered. If the antagonism between Hagar and Sarai is exacerbated by the distance needed between ostensibly male and female figures, how does that impact Abram as the subordinate(d) man? Here two further strands of Clines's model appear and jostle for primacy at different points in the story. First is the idea of 'The Bonding Male', where male characters

---

69. Eilberg-Schwartz, *God's Phallus*, 161–162. See also Susan E. Haddox, '"The Lord is With You, You Mighty Warrior": The Question of Gideon's Masculinity', *Proceedings of the East Great Lakes and Midwest Biblical Societies* 30 (2010a), 70–87: 86.

70. Eilberg-Schwartz, *God's Phallus*, 137–138. Eilberg-Schwartz describes the masculinity of the patriarchs as 'uncertain' due to the relationship with God, which 'required their unmanning' through its reification of compulsory heterosexuality.

71. Clines, *Interested Parties*, 225–227; 'Dancing and Shining at Sinai', 56–59.

72. Wenham, *Genesis 16–50*. '[Sarai's] anger comes through not only in ascribing her troubles to Abram but in calling Hagar's new-found pride "violence" (חמס), a term used elsewhere in Genesis to describe the sins that prompted the flood (6:11, 13) and the vicious retaliation wreaked by Simeon and Levi (49:5; cf. 34:25)'.

socialize and dialogue primarily with other masculine characters.[73] Even before Sarai exclaims that they and Abram are peers, it is clear in the interactions at the start of the chapter (vv. 1–2). Abram and Sarai are each the other's sole interlocutor in this chapter, so there is equality of status, and each seems comfortable with that parity. When Abram first defers to Sarai (v. 2), he is willing and able to accept their status as an authority over him, both reinforcing his recognition of a masculine peer and his subordination to Sarai. When the dispute between Sarai and Abram emerges later in the chapter, his acquiescence appears less willing and more antagonistic (v. 6). It is here that the next strand of Clines's model comes into focus: a conflict of masculinities.[74] For the first time since Sarai's masculinity has become visible, there is discernible tension between them and Abram. In the shared desire to *not* deal with Hagar, each seeks to absent themselves from the responsibility of dealing with the only feminine figure (vv. 5–6).[75] Were this an anticipated interaction between a masculine figure and their feminine counterpart, Sarai's demand for justice should be met by Abram protecting his woman and exerting his authority rather than doing all that he can to absent himself from such responsibility.[76] This is not a condemnation of Sarai's masculinity (or Abram's), but rather two individuals manning off against each other; neither clearly wins. Abram gets the last word, but it is Sarai's violence that ends this stage of the story. The tension between spouses consolidates Sarai's masculinity rather than undermining it even as the bonding phase makes way for conflict.

After the spoken dispute between Abram and Sarai ends, 'Sarai dealt harshly with [Hagar], and she ran away' (Gen 16:6). Here the warrior strand of Clines's schema, associated with violence and protection of the family comes into focus most clearly. The extent of the violence to Hagar remains undisclosed but is nevertheless significant. Arnold notes the similarities between the language used to describe Sarai's harsh dealings with Hagar and the Egyptian oppression of Israel.[77] Sarai clearly senses a threat to their family and acts, swiftly, decisively – and abusively. It is so notable that the exiled Hagar is met by an angel of the Lord, to

73. Clines, *Interested Parties*, 223–225.
74. Clines, *Interested Parties*, 228–231.
75. Wenham, *Genesis 16–50*. While Wenham suggests initially that Abram's words are a 'soft answer' designed to mollify Sarai and turn away their wrath, he later recognizes that Abram 'rather weakly, abjures any responsibility for the one whom he has recently made his wife and encourages Sarai to take out her feelings on Hagar'. I see Abram's comments as further inflaming the antagonism with something of a 'fuck you!' response to Sarai who, in turn, reacts violently.
76. Westermann, *Genesis 12–36*, 240–241. Westermann considers Sarai's actions as a formal legal case directed to Abram. Given Westermann's recognition of Abram as *the* masculine figure, 'he alone has the judicial authority that can effect a change' as demanded by Sarai.
77. Arnold, *Genesis*.

whom she says, 'I am running away from my mistress Sarai' (v. 8). This admission is met by a command that Hagar must not only return but also submit to Sarai (v. 9). While Sarai is Hagar's enslaver, the utterance by the angel also confirms that Sarai has authority and a status that is recognized – and affirmed – by God. Sarai may be called 'mistress' by the angel, but clearly functions as Hagar's master, recalling Wenham's comments. Sarai suffers no direct ill treatment or condemnation for their violence, even though it is Hagar who receives a divine blessing. They do, however, fade from focus for the remainder of the chapter.

There is one final strand of Clines's model of masculinity that applies to Sarai, even though it does not feature directly in Genesis 16. Rather it is necessary to return, briefly, to the main theme that emerged in Genesis 12. For Clines, quintessential biblical masculinity also requires beauty.[78] While he acknowledges that 'beautiful people in the Bible are both male and female', his recognition of the significance of beauty for masculine characters is nevertheless significant.[79] In Clines's case study of David, beauty is a core component of his masculinity and his divinely authorized status:

> Beauty is not generally a state to which a man who does not have it can aspire, but obviously it is very desirable, in the world of David's story, for a man to be beautiful. Beauty is to be seen, at the least, in bodily shape, in the eyes, in the skin colour, and in the height. The language used here is not of some diffused notion of 'good looks', but reflects some quite precise and analytical thought about what makes a man beautiful. . . . [W]e learn that beauty is not regarded by men in Israel as a mere accident of birth that is for the most part to be shrugged off as the way the cookie crumbles. Rather, it is an aspect of 'real manhood' for which the man can expect praise and admiration.[80]

Clines's insights bring a new perspective into the praise heaped on Sarai for their appearance. What initially appeared to be a clear signifier of Sarai's femininity is now less authoritative in bestowing gender or sex upon them.[81] Rather, the affirmation of Sarai's beauty can, and perhaps should, bolster their demonstration of 'real manhood'. Their beauty further contributes to a recognizable form of

---

78. Clines, *Interested Parties*, 221–225.

79. Clines, *Interested Parties*, 221.

80. Clines, *Interested Parties*, 222–223. Clines contrasts his beautiful figures with 'the servant of Isaiah 53, who because of his disfigurement has no "form" (תאר) or "splendour" (הדר) that "we" should gaze upon (ראה) him, and no "appearance" (מראה) that "we" should desire (חמד) him (53:2); it is implied that ordinarily one would expect a high-ranking "servant of Yahweh" to be beautiful in form and face, and to be sexually attractive (חמד) to "us" (? Males)' (222).

81. Macwilliam, 'Ideologies of Male Beauty', 267–271. Macwilliam notes that beauty does not reliably convey gender in the Hebrew Bible.

masculinity, in keeping with other significant male biblical figures such as Clines's exemplars.

This Sarai, who speaks and acts, is a far more masculine counterpart to the one whose beauty and marital status have predominated the earlier portions of the narrative. Even at this early stage in witness and listening to Sarai's perspective, it is possible to add richness and detail to the recognition that they do not conform to cisnormative expectations. Going forward a significant aspect of the exploration of their masculinity will be the extent to which it accompanies or confronts their supposed femininity. In continuity with Guest's interest in female masculinity discussed in Chapter 2, I have identified a character whose masculinity is overlooked when *she* is considered to be a (cisnormative) woman. My approach differs to Guest's in a few distinct ways. First, I hold the presence of substantial elements of both masculinity and femininity within a given individual to indicate discontinuity with cisnormativity. *Contra* Guest's readings of Jael and Jezebel, identifying aspects of femininity in a character does not *necessarily* signify a diminution of (female) masculinity, let alone emasculation.[82] Sarai performs masculinity, to the point that they typify Clines's schema, but their performance is not to excess – except that it is not expected in a character perceived as female. Given the extent to which Sarai fits within the parameters of Clines's model of masculinity, they appear to conform to expectations of manhood. There is little or no sense that this is a performance that differs substantively from that of Abram, ensuring that Sarai's masculinity can be understood to be just as innate, just as learned, and just as performed as that of their spouse. Yet it is precisely because they are perceived to be a woman that this performance of masculinity is overlooked. Even in setting out his argument Clines suggests that his model enables men and women to see 'how *men* should "play the man"'.[83] Sarai's masculinity, however, is remarkable and offers a fascinating insight into the complexity of gender in their story. Yet, like many complexly gendered characters, there remains a pressure to hold the gaze for a sustained period and this feature returns once again to Sarai's narrative. When Sarai fades from view again before Ishmael's birth (Gen 16:15), it is a much more masculine figure that we have heard and witnessed. Sarai becomes all the more recognisably nonconforming ensuring that they have to disappear once again, destined to fade perpetually in and out of focus and coherence.

82. Guest, 'From Gender Reversal'; 'Modeling the Transgender Gaze'. See discussion of Jael and Jezebel in Chapter 2, where Guest's butch interpretations present recognition of female masculinity as a necessary diminution of the feminine *or* see femininity as a form of emasculation.

83. Clines, 'Dancing and Shining at Sinai', 54. Emphasis added.

Reaching the Limits of Masculinity?

> They said to him, 'Where is your wife Sarah?' And he said, 'There, in the tent.' Then one said, 'I will surely return to you in due season, and your wife Sarah shall have a son.' And Sarah was listening at the tent entrance behind him. Now Abraham and Sarah were old, advanced in age; it had ceased to be with Sarah after the manner of women. So Sarah laughed to herself, saying, 'After I have grown old, and my husband is old, shall I have pleasure?' The LORD said to Abraham, 'Why did Sarah laugh, and say, "Shall I indeed bear a child, now that I am old?" Is anything too wonderful for the LORD? At the set time I will return to you, in due season, and Sarah shall have a son.' But Sarah denied, saying, 'I did not laugh'; for she was afraid. He said, 'Oh yes, you did laugh.'
>
> Gen 18:9–15

Sarai remains beyond the view of the narrator for much of Genesis 17, although during that time they are the unknowing recipient of a divine covenant which comes with a change of name and promise of children (17:15–22). As in Halberstam's examples, Sarai cannot sustain the gaze of a cisnormative audience and must disappear to remain viable.[84] Rather it is their spouse and God who move into clearest view. The newly renamed Abraham laughs as God promises that the also renamed Sarah will 'bear you a son and you shall name him Isaac' (v. 19). While Sarah is presented with their new name, the remainder of this information is clearly not passed from one spouse to the other. Sarah reappears briefly in chapter 18 to overhear the same announcement again, something that on this occasion leads them into trouble. Abraham's laugh at the suggestion of their impending joint parenthood receives no censure in the way that Sarah's does, so I am interested in how the reception of gendered behaviour may impact the different responses.

While their shared masculinity makes space for bonding, as in Genesis 16:1–2, it is also a cause of hostility (vv. 5–6). Sarah re-enters the narrative in Genesis 18 and it is the first time both parties come into focus since the antagonistic encounter where each tried to outman the other. While Sarah disappeared from view, however, a different pair became recentred in the narrative: God and Abraham. When Sarah reappears, they must jostle against the more prominent characters for recognition. Unlike in Genesis 16, this story is not about Sarah – but their perspective, or what can be gleaned of it, still matters. The first recognition of their presence occurs in Genesis 18:6 when, after welcoming divine guests, Abraham runs in and demands Sarah prepare food. Here Abraham's authority over Sarah is implied, but that is all. Whether Sarah completes the preparations is left unaddressed, but the food duties do not particularly imply anything significant about gender for either party. This is apparent when Abraham also continues to prepare food, which he serves directly to the guests (v. 8).[85] Sarah's absence from

---

84. Halberstam, *In a Queer Time*, 78.

85. By way of contrast, the later preparation of food by Jacob is treated as a more feminine behaviour but that follows comment that Jacob spent his time living in (the

the meal, however, conveys a sense that they are intentionally side-lined (v. 9). Perhaps this exclusion comes as a result of Abraham's masculinity overriding Sarah's meaning that they must step aside; their spouse outmans them. When asked where Sarah is, his reply seems brusque and offhand – 'There, in the tent' – as if to dismiss any suggestion they might have had a right to be there at all! Equally, their omission from the party functions as a tacit reminder that gender nonconformity is not always treated favourably. Sarah lost the battle of (masculine) wills and must face the consequences, of both their newly subordinate(d) masculinity *and* their gender nonconformity.[86] Yet this apparent chastisement is a new feature within Genesis 18, something in marked contrast with Sarah's earlier expressions in chapter 16.

Sarah's voice is eventually recorded in the narrative, when they 'laughed to herself, saying, "after I have grown old and my husband is old, shall I have pleasure?"' (Gen 18:12). This only occurs once the inescapable feature of their apparently failed femininity, indicated by *her* status as a post-menopausal childless woman, is interjected by the narrator (v. 11). Its location at this point serves to emphasise Sarah's womanhood immediately prior to an action that will, very shortly, cause them and their masculinity to be censured. Sarah's laughter, then, can only occur once the narrator interrupts the story to say, effectively, 'she is *definitely* a woman, and this is a pertinent piece of information right now'. By contrast, Abraham's (acceptable) laughter (17:17) differs from Sarah's in that it is part of a conversation between God and Abraham. In Abraham's case, each is active and present in the dialogue, showing Abraham's masculine power and authority, especially in the presence of God. Meanwhile, Sarah's is a response to overhearing a conversation, but the omniscient God still knows what they are thinking and how they have responded (18:12–13). This is not a two-way dialogue, but otherwise there is little noticeable difference between the two. Yet Sarah's behaviour appears to irk God (18:13–15). Is the difference in response because Abraham is perceived to be a man and Sarah a woman? I do not think that is solely the reason, but rather I see Sarah's action as a continuing demonstration of masculinity akin to that performed by their spouse. It is a shared behaviour that consolidates the idea that Sarah and Abraham are peers in continuity with Genesis 16:5. While Abraham's conversation makes space for his laughter, Sarah is forced

---

women's) tents (Gen 25:27, 29–34). Meanwhile the contentious way food is prepared in Gen 27:5–29, by both Esau and Jacob, emphasises that cookery fell within the remit of the masculine figure. For further discussion of Esau and Jacob, see Chapter 4. A longer discussion of Jacob's femininity can be found in Jo Henderson-Merrygold, 'Reading Biblical Embodiment Cispiciously', in *Embodying Religion, Gender and Sexuality*, ed. Katy Pilcher and Sarah-Jane Page, Gendering the Study of Religion in the Social Sciences (London: Routledge, 2021), 129–144.

86. Connell, *Masculinities*, 78. Masculinities that are subordinated are frequently the ones that attract social vilification and cultural stigmatization. Connell is keen to point out that subordination of masculinities is also far more than stigmatization alone.

to interject theirs as they are not given any opportunity for dialogue. Despite the silencing and chastisement that accompany their behaviour, Sarah's actions continue to add to the richness of their masculinity – even if that masculinity is no longer treated as favourably as it once was.

Here Sarah is silenced and the reader glimpses for the first time a reminder that they are a woman; such masculinity is not expected of them. But through a cispicious lens, their bite back and audible laughter indicate once more that they will not be denied expression of their masculinity. Revisiting Clines's model of masculinity, I wish to explore the idea of the womanless male again. The initial indication of relevance of the womanless male figure emerged in the interrelationship (or lack thereof) between Hagar and Sarah. Here, though, a further detail is added: sex. Clines argues that the biblical masculine figure treats coitus as perfunctory,[87] as has already been seen earlier in Sarah's story when their spouse 'went in to Hagar, and she conceived' (Gen 16:4). From a cispicious perspective, Sarah's wry laughter in Genesis 18:12 shows just the disinterest Clines describes when they refer to the prospect of sexual fulfilment with Abraham. It is unlikely to be either pleasurable or perfunctory, so why would they bother?! The narrator's interjection about their age and post-menopausal status further implies that Sarai is neither desirable nor desiring of sex: the picture is of a wizened, desexualised old hag. Yet even while Sarai deigns to reassert the very masculinity that was affirmed in Genesis 16, there is something else hanging over them. Impending motherhood is an inescapable spectre hovering over them and threatening the acceptance of Sarai's gender. There is now an increasing need to identify femininity in this *woman* ahead of *her* impending motherhood because it is now not just Abraham who has been promised offspring of his own, but Sarah has too (Gen 17:16).

---

87. Clines, *Interested Parties*, 225–226. Clines argues that in David's story there is 'on the whole, no sexual desire, no love stories, no romances, no wooing, no daring deeds for the sake of the beloved. This is not a world in which men long for women. . . . There is sex in the story, of course, but it is perfunctory and usually politically motivated'. In Sarai/h's story, there is similarly no sense of sensuality or romance between husband and wife, even though their partnership endures for a long period of time and Abraham mourns the death of his wife (Gen 23:1–20). There is no sexual encounter recorded between Abraham and Sarah, even in the conception of Isaac (20:1). This is in contrast with Abraham's (perfunctory) encounter with Hagar (16:4). Their descendants will, in turn, express some of the sexuality that they (and Abraham) are missing: Isaac is witnessed 'fondling' his wife by Abimelech in the third and final sister-wife story (Gen 26:8). Jacob's desire for Rachel, his primary wife, is clearly and repeatedly articulated from the point of her introduction in Genesis 29: 'Then Jacob kissed Rachel, and wept aloud' (v. 11); 'Rachel was graceful and beautiful. Jacob loved Rachel; so he said "I will serve you seven years for your younger daughter Rachel. . . . So Jacob served seven years for Rachel, and they seemed to him but a few days because of the love he had for her."' (vv. 17–18, 20).

While the earlier expressions of masculinity have been overlooked to ensure Sarah's femininity comes to the fore, it is important to acknowledge how significant their masculinity is, especially in this central portion of their story. Yet, in Genesis 17 and 18 they are being taunted by the prospect of motherhood, whether they want it or not. It becomes increasingly important to find further clues in the narrative that serve to shoehorn Sarah (back) into the expectations of a cisnormative woman. Sarah's involvement in Genesis 18 comes to an end so any perception that they are considered a (masculine) peer with Abraham and God is necessarily reined back. The expression of fear – 'she was afraid' (v. 15) – that ends Sarah's involvement in this chapter correlates with the risks of not conforming to dominant gender expectations, something far too often met with violence. God's voice closes the verse and it is clear that the final say on what is, or is not acceptable, lies with the divine being: Sarah is firmly and inescapably put in *her* place. In YHWH's judgement, *she* is a woman, thus *she* must accept that, and the child that accompanies normative femininity. This complex woman, whose masculinity is confident, assertive and clearly recognisable must fade away in fear as their nonconformity overshadows their potential for inclusion in the narrative. Once again Sarah's appearance cannot be sustained, but this time their departure is portentous and foreshadowing. In the meantime, the challenge remains for reader and character alike: can Sarah's masculinity withhold the onslaught of the cisnormative expectations placed on them as the arrival of their child becomes imminent?

Retconning Sarah's Gender – Genesis 20–21

Genesis 17 and 18 taunt Sarah with the prospect that motherhood is a necessity for them. It is inescapable and, following the promise of the angelic visitors in 18:10, the clock is ticking. In the meantime, Sarah is once again hidden from view. While the discussions between Abraham and God, then the destruction of Sodom and Gomorrah, held the focus for the remainder of Genesis 18 (16–33) and 19, the threatened (or promised) arrival of a son rapidly approaches. Yet Sarah themselves remains the most substantial challenge to this outcome as they have been far from the cisnormative feminine woman expected. The temptation to try to find enough of a consistent picture of Sarah to facilitate a cisnormalized reading of their gender still remains; that is to force Sarah to conform to cisnormative preconceptions, especially in the face of substantial challenges to such an interpretation. Sarah still does not quite fit the hallowed expectations of cisnormativity, but rather emerges as a masculine figure. The character encountered in Genesis 20 consolidates the nascent sense that Sarah is a gender nonconforming character in continuity with the picture that first emerged in Genesis 11. Yet ahead of the birth of Isaac (Gen 21:1–3) it is Genesis 12 that is recalled through a second sister-wife story. Given the repetition of the motif, in Genesis 20, I consider this as an attempt to undermine the earlier discontinuities. In other words, it functions as a 'retcon': a retroactive continuity, where changes are made to 'already-established facts and canonical material'.[88] Mark Wolf describes it as an opportunity to 'reinterpret past events or make use of holes or audience assumptions to recontextualize events'.[89]

If Genesis 20 functions as a retcon, its contribution is to actively try to change the earlier context in order to rationalize and stabilize Sarah's feminine gender. This is the necessary preparation for Sarah's femininity to emerge in their postnatal world and for it to appear with any credibility such as in Genesis 21. For the retcon to be successful, Sarah has to be kept just out of focus once again, leaving the reader to become reliant on apparently authoritative third person perspectives. Genesis 20 presents another story in which Sarah is far from an active participant, so the challenge remains to try and fix a (trans) gaze on them once again whilst those surrounding them try to control how they are understood. Whether or not the retcon is successful will be tested in Genesis 21, where Sarah returns once again to the role of active participant. If the retcon is successful, Sarah will appear a more confident woman with a consistent display of femininity and the masculinity that featured so heavily in their earlier speech and actions will have dissipated. However, even after an attempt to reconstruct the character and their gender, Sarah's masculinity still remains clearly discernible. Ultimately the retcon brings into clearer view the disconnection between the way Sarah is portrayed by others and how they present themselves. Only third parties seem unduly concerned that *she* is understood as feminine, but ultimately Sarah's own words and actions are far more authoritative accounts of their own gender.

(Re)Creating the Feminine Woman

> From there Abraham journeyed towards the region of the Negeb, and settled between Kadesh and Shur. While residing in Gerar as an alien, Abraham said of his *wife* Sarah, '*She* is my *sister*'. And King Abimelech of Gerar sent and took Sarah. But God came to Abimelech in a dream by night, and said to him, 'You are about to die because of *the woman* you have taken; for *she* is a *married woman*'. Now Abimelech had not approached *her*; so he said, 'LORD, will you destroy an innocent people? Did he not himself say to me, "*She* is my *sister*"? And *she herself* said, "He is my brother". I did this in the integrity of my heart and the innocence of my hands.' Then God said to him in the dream, 'Yes, I know that you did this in the integrity of your heart; furthermore it was I who kept you from sinning against me. Therefore I did not let you touch *her*. Now then, return the man's *wife*; for he is a prophet, and he will pray for you and you shall live. But if you do not restore *her*, know that you shall surely die, you and all that are yours'.
>
> Gen 20:1-7, emphasis added

---

88. Mark J. P. Wolf, *Building Imaginary Worlds: The Theory and History of Subcreation* (New York: Routledge, 2012), 212–213.

89. Wolf, *Building Imaginary Worlds*, 213.

Recalling the first sister-wife story of Genesis 12, the juxtaposition between the overt attention to Sarai's beauty and the covert theme of their childlessness emerge as a feature unique to the Egypt story (Gen 12:10–20). When the sister-wife storyline reappears in Genesis 20 Sarah's beauty is left unremarked. Sarah and Abraham find themselves exiled to Gerar, and their fate lies in the hands of King Abimelech rather than the unnamed Pharaoh in the earlier incident (Gen 20:1–2). While decades have passed since the previous deception, Sarah is still welcomed into Abimelech's court with an expectation that concubinage is in their immediate future – 'And King Abimelech of Gerar sent and took Sarah' (v. 2) On this occasion God intervenes via a dream to ensure that Abimelech does not have sex with – and potentially impregnate – Sarah (vv. 3–7). Their beauty is implied only through reference to Abimelech's implied (albeit unactioned) desire for Sarah indicated by taking her. Sarah's only interjection into this narrative is reported second hand. Abimelech cites Sarah's own words – 'And she herself said, "He is my brother"' (v. 5) – to justify his behaviour before God, leaving Sarah to appear unreliable. They are hardly presented as someone asserting their own identity and personhood even in this brief citation! Instead, the narrative uses other means of centring Sarah's femininity, this time through attention to reproductive capacity and to the power of gendered language to create that which it names: Sarah, *the woman*.

Like Genesis 12, the text is rich in gendered language that clearly instils a sense of Sarah's femaleness throughout. There is one interjection that is more significant and far more powerful than any of the gendered utterances about Sarah up to this point. God does not refer to Sarah by name at any point, but directly refers to her as 'the woman' (v. 3). A divine locutionary act designates Sarah inescapably as woman; God has made her so! Womanhood is bestowed upon *her*, yet again without any active involvement or even presence from Sarah. God alone has the power to confer sex and gender irrespective of the identity or desires of the individual on whom it is bestowed. No longer is the discussion of Sarah's gender a mere matter of speculation as God appears to offer an irrefutable account. Yet there remains a significant question: does the divine intervention impact the perception of Sarah as someone who conforms to, or at least is clearly recognizable within, cisgender norms or not? If it is not so, does that mean that it becomes possible to see divine affirmation of non-cisnormative expressions of womanhood – as I hope? Genesis 21 will offer further insight, but for now Sarah is both woman *and*, despite repeated interventions to try and overlay femininity, persistently masculine. Nevertheless, God's interjection provides the most significant component of the retcon.

> So Abimelech rose early in the morning, and called all his servants and told them all these things; and the men were very much afraid. Then Abimelech called Abraham, and said to him, 'What have you done to us? How have I sinned against you, that you have brought such great guilt on me and my kingdom? You have done things to me that ought not to be done.' And Abimelech said to Abraham, 'What were you thinking of, that you did this thing?' Abraham said, 'I did it because I thought, There is no fear of God at all in this place, and they will

kill me because of my wife. Besides, she is indeed my sister, the daughter of my father but not the daughter of my mother; and she became my wife. And when God caused me to wander from my father's house, I said to her, "This is the kindness you must do me: at every place to which we come, say of me, He is my brother."' Then Abimelech took sheep and oxen, and male and female slaves, and gave them to Abraham, and restored his wife Sarah to him. Abimelech said, 'My land is before you; settle where it pleases you.' To Sarah he said, 'Look, I have given your brother a thousand pieces of silver; it is your exoneration before all who are with you; you are completely vindicated.' Then Abraham prayed to God; and God healed Abimelech, and also healed his wife and female slaves so that they bore children. For the LORD had closed fast all the wombs of the house of Abimelech because of Sarah, Abraham's wife.

Genesis 20:8–18

This passage adds momentum to the sense that Genesis 20 is part of an attempt to retcon Sarah in order to facilitate a cisnormalized reading of them. Context is added where it had been left open earlier in Sarah's story (Gen 20:10–13; cf. 11:29–31). When confronted by Abimelech over the deception, Abraham justifies himself by speaking of Sarah's history in a way that differs significantly from any earlier accounts of his spouse. He says, 'Besides, she is indeed my sister, the daughter of my father but not the daughter of my mother; and she became my wife' (Gen 20:12). This directly contrasts the notable lack of detail offered in Genesis 11:29–31. If these details matter so greatly, why were they not present at Sarah's introduction? More importantly, why is adding that context so important now? The answer to both questions relates directly to the need to rationalize and reclaim Sarah's status as a cisnormative woman in order to facilitate their impending motherhood. The lack of context or lineage that so effectively opens the possibility for Halberstamian queer and trans readings is foreclosed here to prevent them at the point where lineage matters most. Even as Abraham layers on this context for Sarah, the extent to which he does so is also noteworthy. His response is rich in detail, ensuring he has given a good account of his own scrupulousness by explaining Sarah's status *and* ensuring *she* is understood as sister, daughter, *and* wife: '"Besides, she is my *sister*, the *daughter* of my father but not the *daughter* of my mother; and she became my *wife*"' (Gen 20:12, emphasis added). He even adds a comment about the supposed cordiality between spouses (which also justifies the repeated use of the ruse): 'And when God caused me to wander from my father's house, I said to her, "This is the kindness you must do me: at every place to which we come, say of me, He is my brother"' (v. 13). The importance of inscrutable paternity becomes clearer as the stay in Gerar ends: only as Sarah, Abraham and their inflated entourage leave does God reopen the wombs of the house of Abimelech (at Abraham's request), having earlier closed them 'because of Sarah, Abraham's wife' (Gen 20:17–18). When they prepare to leave Abimelech seeks Sarah explicitly to make amends for mistreating them in an act that emphasizes their status as a desirably feminine woman (v. 16). Sarah is clearly not acknowledged as a potential peer of Abimelech's, in contrast with their relationship with Abraham.

They are spoken at, not with; this is no two-way conversation. Their status is restored through the gifts to Sarah's spouse. Rather than making any reparation to Sarah, Abimelech focuses on the man in their life to further emphasise their femaleness and to heighten the contrast with Sarah's earlier masculinity.[90]

While Sarah's child is yet to make his appearance and any pregnancy is still to be either discovered or disclosed, (in)fertility haunts Genesis 20. The brief acknowledgement that God closed the wombs of Abimelech's 'wife and female slaves' (Gen 20:17–18) ensures that there are no other pregnancies to remark on or to threaten the sanctity of Abraham's lineage.[91] This serves to foreground fecundity more overtly in the narrative, even though it is a lack of conception that warrants comment. Genesis 20 is the first time Sarah features in the story after they have become aware of God's promise that they will bear a child (Gen 18:1–14). Sarah has already laughingly recognized that this will not be possible without divine intervention (vv. 11, 14). While that does follow in due course (Gen 21:1), there is a nascent recognition that pregnancy might be possible for the first time. The promise – or threat – was made explicit during Sarah's most sustained performance of masculinity (Gen 16; 18). There is yet to be any suggestion that Sarah actively wants the child they are having imposed on them. Yet there remains a persistent and enduring expectation that motherhood and womanhood are almost synonymous![92] Childbearing still connotes womanhood even though the correlation is increasingly being critiqued.[93] It is significant that the attention to procreation in Genesis 20 occurs alongside a largely silent (perhaps silenced) Sarah as they are unable to speak to the situation directly.

---

90. To Sarah he said, "Look, I have given your brother a thousand pieces of silver; it is your exoneration before all who are with you; you are completely vindicated" (Gen 20:16).

91. Once again there is a reminder that slaves, whether categorized as male or female, belong to the master – here, Abimelech. It continues to recall Sarah's anomalous status as master over Hagar.

92. Moss and Baden, *Reconceiving Infertility*, 7. They add, 'Womanhood continues to be associated with motherhood, and with the assumption that motherhood is the highest state of womanhood'.

93. For discussions of the Bible and infertility, see Moss and Baden, *Reconceiving Infertility*. For discussion of the limits of pronatalism, see Dawn Llewellyn, 'Maternal Silences: Motherhood and Voluntary Childlessness in Contemporary Christianity', *Religion and Gender* 6, 1 (2016), 64–79. For research that challenges the correlation between womanhood, motherhood and pregnancy, see Ruth Pearce and Francis Ray White, 'Beyond the Pregnant Man: Representing Trans Pregnancy in *A Deal With The Universe*', *Feminist Media Studies* 19, 5 (2019), 764–767; Damien W. Riggs et al., 'Men, Trans/Masculine, and Non-binary People Negotiating Conception: Normative Resistance and Inventive Pragmatism', *International Journal of Transgender Health* (2020), 1–13. For the gatekeeping effects of pregnancy and fertility for cis and trans women, see Valentine, 'Examining Scripture'.

Given their earlier masculinity, it seems all more pertinent that allowing Sarah space to speak about their own impending motherhood is delayed for as long as possible. At the conclusion of the chapter, Sarah's missing context is interjected in a story that seeks to recall the earlier explicit accounts of their beauty and femininity. In case those details are too subtle, God directly confirms *her* gender and sex through a locutionary act that directly bequeaths womanhood on Sarah. Meanwhile it is divine intervention rather than spousal disregard or lack of risk that prevents an unplanned pregnancy in Gerar, *contra* Egypt (Gen 12:10–20). Abimelech is stopped in his tracks by God. Only now the time, place, and planning must be cohering for the much-anticipated pregnancy to finally enter the story, and with it comes Sarah's reaction.

Motherhood

> The Lord dealt with Sarah as he had said, and the Lord did for Sarah as he had promised. Sarah conceived and bore Abraham a son in his old age, at the time of which God had spoken to him. Abraham gave the name Isaac to his son whom Sarah bore him. And Abraham circumcised his son Isaac when he was eight days old, as God had commanded him. Abraham was a hundred years old when his son Isaac was born to him. Now Sarah said, 'God has brought laughter for me; everyone who hears will laugh with me.' And she said, 'Who would ever have said to Abraham that Sarah would nurse children? Yet I have borne him a son in his old age.'
>
> The child grew, and was weaned; and Abraham made a great feast on the day that Isaac was weaned. But Sarah saw the son of Hagar the Egyptian, whom she had borne to Abraham, playing with her son Isaac. So she said to Abraham, 'Cast out this slave woman with her son; for the son of this slave woman shall not inherit along with my son Isaac.' The matter was very distressing to Abraham on account of his son. But God said to Abraham, 'Do not be distressed because of the boy and because of your slave woman; whatever Sarah says to you, do as she tells you, for it is through Isaac that offspring shall be named after you. As for the son of the slave woman, I will make a nation of him also, because he is your offspring.' So Abraham rose early in the morning, and took bread and a skin of water, and gave it to Hagar, putting it on her shoulder, along with the child, and sent her away. And she departed, and wandered about in the wilderness of Beer-sheba.
>
> Gen 21:1–14

After all the foreshadowing, taunting, and overt emphasis on fecundity, in the end the creation of Sarah's pregnancy is both understated and anomalous. If Genesis 21 began with an image reminiscent of 'Abraham took Sarah and went in to her and she conceived', to echo the language of Genesis 16:3–4, it would go a long way to set aside the persistent, niggling discontinuities in Sarah's story. That is not what happens. None of the frequent euphemisms for coitus are to be seen: there is no taking, no going in to, no fucking of any variety – or at least, not by Abraham. Genesis 21:1–2 tells a very different story: 'The Lord dealt with Sarah as he had said, and the Lord did for Sarah as he had promised. Sarah conceived and bore Abraham a son at his old age, at the time of which God had spoken to me'. Abraham is not even present at the conception; it is a moment of *deus ex* (or even *in*) *machina*. The impossible becomes possible through the divine intervention and a sleight of hand that still ensures that there will be a child to uphold the covenants with Abraham and Sarah, but without all the mess of common human reproduction. Here the features of the retcon, and the broader (re)contextualization offered by Genesis 20 come to the fore. Sarah's pregnancy, following divine intervention, is not inherently more remarkable than God closing and opening the wombs of Abimelech's household (Gen 20:17–18). In fact, the closing verse of chapter 20 leads directly into the details of Isaac's conception, preparing the way directly for the opening of Sarah's own womb. It almost succeeds in making the remarkable unremarkable – but not quite. Ever since the narratorial remark that apparently disclosed Sarah's post-menopausal state in 18:11, some form of divine intervention has been needed, but to remove Abraham from the process could hardly have been foreseen. It is, in the end, Abraham's absence that prevents Sarah's conception and the birth of Isaac forcing them back into a preconceived notion of cisnormative womanhood.

This portion of Sarah's story contributes heavily to Gross's intersex reading. She treats this as an indication that preconceived notions of reproductive capacity (or lack thereof), do not foreclose childbearing if God wills it to be so in Genesis.[94] This enables her to argue for an interpretation that affirms and validates intersex women, bolstering the idea that childbearing capacity does not undo or undermine womanhood. This is a valuable reading since reproductive capacity still defines the womanhood, especially cis womanhood. Katy Valentine highlights the way a biological potential for childbearing – even if never used – is still seen as a 'common litmus test in general for femininity amongst trans and cis women'.[95] She also, importantly, recognizes that 'the womanhood of a cis woman who has a hysterectomy is rarely questioned in the same way as that of a trans woman'.[96] Sarah's significance as a character for whom childbearing could not occur without a miracle is powerful. Valentine argues that trans women find it a challenge to locate characters with whom they can identify, especially given the frequency with which biblical women are described as mothers.[97] Here is someone who, even if considered a mother, has not arrived at that status through conventional methods. These details address just one half of the paradoxical impact of bearing a child: womanhood need not be synonymous with motherhood, but does bringing a child into the world convey gender on the gestational parent?[98]

---

94. Gross, 'Intersexuality and Scripture', 71–73. Gross also creatively draws on Isaiah as an intertext to indicate bolster her interpretation of Sarah as someone who needs divine intervention to secure her pregnancy.

95. Valentine, 'Examining Scripture', 511.

96. Valentine, 'Examining Scripture', 511.

97. Valentine, 'Examining Scripture', 512.

98. At the time of writing, the (case) law of England and Wales says that a gestational parent must be recorded as a child's mother on birth certificates, see Robert Booth,

Isaac's birth presents interesting challenges for considering how his parents understand their roles. They do not speak to one another, and each acts in apparent isolation: it is Abraham who names and circumcises the baby (Gen 21:4), but it is Sarah who speaks (vv. 6–7). Through her words and actions emerges a sense of motherhood. Sarah's laughter returns, something that features in Isaac's name, but now it is not problematic. It is no longer seen as a symbol of their masculinity, shared with Abraham, but rather signifies their status as a joyful mother. Like motherhood itself, this is seen as a core component of the idealized feminine, cisnormative model of womanhood.[99] Sarah articulates this in an audibly smoother and more feminine expression than we have previously encountered. The softness is accompanied by a reflection on the embodied experience of breastfeeding (nursing) the child too: 'Now Sarah said, "God has brought laughter for me; everyone who hears me will laugh with me." And she said, "Who would ever have said to Abraham that Sarah would nurse children? Yet I have borne him a son in his old age"' (Gen 21:6–7). For the first time we encounter a Sarah who seems to fit comfortably in the idealized model of femininity associated with both motherhood and cisnormative womanhood. There is a sense of joviality and femininity in these words, in marked contrast with the brusqueness of their speech in chapter 16 or her hidden, diffident voice in chapter 18. Yet these are Sarah's only words on parenting, and one should not take them in isolation to assert that Sarah definitively conforms to cisnormative expectation. Neither do the words undermine the importance of their earlier masculinity. If it were the end of the

---

'Transgender Man Loses Appeal Court Battle to be Registered as Father', *The Guardian*, 29 April 2020, https://amp.theguardian.com/society/2020/apr/29/transgender-man-loses-appeal-court-battle-registered-father-freddy-mcconnell. Freddy McConnell brought the case and is seeking leave to challenge this decision in his attempt to be recognized as his child's father from birth, not mother. The earlier High Court judgement has caused consternation as it ruled that 'mother' is not a gendered term but rather indicates a biological role in reproduction; see Patrick Strudwick, 'A Trans Dad Will Now Go To The Supreme Court To Be Named The Father On His Child's Birth Certificate', *Buzzfeed*, 29 April 2020, https://www.buzzfeed.com/patrickstrudwick/trans-dad-supreme-court-named-father; Patrick Strudwick, 'A High Court Judge Has Ruled that "Mother" No Longer Means "Woman"', *Buzzfeed*, 10 October 2019, https://www.buzzfeed.com/patrickstrudwick/mother-no-longer-means-woman-judge-rules. The decision has been condemned for its biological essentialism, de-gendering parental roles, and unacknowledged implications for adoptive parents, LGBT+ parents, surrogacy and fertility services, amongst others. While motherhood does not currently convey gender, following the High Court and Court of Appeal rulings, I follow McConnell's argument that status as a gestational parent does not necessarily confer a specific gender or status as mother. In other words, an individual's gender is not changed through pregnancy and childbirth.

99. Moss and Baden, *Reconceiving Infertility*, 8. Moss and Baden argue that even today women who fail to meet the social expectations of motherhood, willingly, 'are subject to additional scrutiny' and vilification.

story, perhaps it would add to the significance of this brief moment, but it is not. Even though Sarah's embodied femininity is once again asserted by the narrator, masculinity soon returns. The effect is to add to Sarah's fluid, inconsistent and whimsical expressions of gender.

The phrase 'The child grew, and was weaned; and Abraham made a great feast on the day that Isaac was weaned' (Gen 21:8) initially appears innocuous. This is another narratorial interjection that subtly brings Sarah's sexed body to mind once again. It is all about breastfeeding, something Sarah apparently did for a sustained period of time.[100] The repetition of 'weaned' following Sarah's own acknowledgement of nursing their child brings into sharp focus the significance of their embodied capacity to nurture their child. This is a detail unique to Sarah's childbearing in Genesis; it is not found with Hagar and Ishmael nor in the accounts of the children born further down Sarah's family line. Cynthia Chapman finds reference to Sarah's nursing an unusual inclusion. She suggests the more usual option would be to have a wet nurse, a role that would be common for Hagar.[101] Chapman's rationale for such behaviour is Sarah's enduring commitment to endogamous reproduction: lineage and kinship continue to be transferred through breastmilk.[102] Here Chapman's argument shows how the physical actions of feeding and the socio-political importance of the act combine to reinforce the expectations of (cisnormative) womanhood. So successful is this brief excursus on Sarah's femininity and motherhood, that Susan Schept considers Sarah to be, above all, a mother – and a happy, willing one at that.[103] For Schept, Sarah demonstrates what it means 'to be a "mothering person"' [which] is to hold "care" of one's children above all else, above faith'.[104] This image of Sarah as not only a mother, but the quintessential mothering figure, should imply that *she* has finally slid into cisnormative expectations. Even now, if this were the end of *her* story, the retcon would have been successful. Yet this visible femininity precedes the strongest affirmation of Sarah's masculinity by a third party – God.

The apparently successful period of femininity (Gen 21:1–8) is followed by the equally clear demonstration of Sarah's masculinity when Hagar once again becomes subject to their abusive ire (vv. 9–20). After Isaac is weaned, Sarah takes issue with Hagar and Ishmael, demanding that Abraham 'cast out this slave woman

---

100. Cynthia R. Chapman, *The House of the Mother: The Social Roles of Maternal Kin in Biblical Hebrew Narrative and Poetry*, The Anchor Yale Bible Reference Library (New Haven, CT: Yale University Press, 2016), 139. Chapman suggests that weaning usually occurred when the infant was about three years old.

101. Chapman, *House of the Mother*, 138.

102. Chapman, *House of the Mother*, 139.

103. Susan Schept, 'Hesed: Feminist Ethics in Jewish Tradition (Genesis 12, 24)', in *Reading Genesis: Beginnings*, ed. Beth Kissileff (London: Bloomsbury T&T Clark, 2016), 83–91, 86.

104. Schept, 'Hesed', 86.

with her son' (v. 10). This continues and concludes Hagar's text of terror.[105] Initially the interaction between Abraham, God and Sarah appears to conform to the expected masculine hierarchy, where Sarah defers to their spouse for the final say. By contrast, Abraham remains silent and does not engage, even though the narrator suggests he was troubled (v. 11). Phyllis Trible argues that while Abraham's silence signifies his resistance, Sarah speaks less than she did in Genesis 16 but accomplishes more.[106] This demonstrates Sarah possesses greater power and authority at this point. God then intervenes once again, and the effect is to bolster Sarah in her claim (v. 12). In doing so, God treats Sarah as a peer and equal in a very different way to Genesis 18:13–15 where their laughter was condemned. It is these acts and words that mark Sarah's final active involvement in the narrative. They are a heightened demonstration of their masculinity that violently excises Hagar and Ishmael from the family in an attempt to kill them both. Clines's models of masculinity hold forth once again, with violence returning to the fore. The threat to Hagar that was overruled by God in Genesis 16 now comes to fruition here; this time Hagar does not return. Sarah's power to make life and death decisions – to orchestrate the deaths of woman and (young) man alike – in combination with a persuasiveness that convinces God to side with them, are no small performances of masculinity. Sarah is now influencing the divine (masculine) being and has ascended to the lofty heights of a masculine performance validated by God. Abraham is unambiguously instructed to follow 'whatever Sarah says to you, do as she tells you' (v. 12): Sarah is given dominion over Abraham and, by extension, Hagar, and Ishmael. Sarah is second only to God in the hierarchy of masculinity at this point. They really are the patriarch and master of the family! While the rationale proffered in the text is that Abraham's covenant will continue through Isaac, Sarah's child rather than Hagar's, it continues to signpost aspects of Sarah's gender that are unconventional.

Despite having successfully ensured that Hagar and Ishmael are unceremoniously dumped in the wilderness, Sarah cannot and does not remain in view. Two things need to happen to resolve the complicated gender dynamics here. The first is for the story to provide a conclusion for Sarah. Sarah can *either* be the feminine mother *or* the masculine authority now, not both. The result is that they are unintelligible, nonconforming and hard to quantify, so they must be carefully excised from the text just as Halberstam predicts. It is not possible to achieve an enduring gaze on gender nonconformity in the face of the overwhelming pressure of cisnormative expectation. Sarah disappears, even at the most tumultuous period of Isaac's life during which time Abraham conspires to murder their son (Gen 22). The second resolution, meanwhile, offers Hagar some consolation. Facing impending death from starvation and dehydration, Hagar once again encounters an angel of God who 'opens her eyes' so she could find water (21:15-19). At the

---

105. Trible, *Texts of Terror*, 5–24. Trible describes Sarah's treatment of Hagar throughout Genesis 16 and 21 as a text of terror.

106. Trible, *Texts of Terror*, 15.

conclusion of her story, her son is thriving, he has discovered an aptitude with the bow, and Hagar has found a wife for Ishmael from her homeland (vv. 19–20). Hagar then disappears from view, her narrative arc complete and the loose ends tied up neatly. Sarah's story is not nearly so tidy. Only once more do we return to Sarah, and then for the account of their death. At the age of 127, they die in Canaan and are mourned by Abraham (Gen 23:1–2). The machinations required to secure a decent burial make up the rest of the chapter (vv. 3–20), but Sarah features no further.

Conclusion

Sarah, and their quirky, chimerical, ever-changing gender leaves the reader to make sense of the story of their life. From the moment they join the narrative, there is just enough space to whimsically explore Sarah's story from a cispicious vantage point. Using Halberstam's insights into the portrayal of complex, gender nonconforming characters, details of Sarah's life that have previously been identified as anomalous or quirky find new meaning. Genesis 12 provides the opportunity to consider how Serano's insights into gendering apply to biblical characters. The presentation of Sarah provides a glimpse of an apparently female character who just might remain credible and coherent within cisnormative presuppositions about gender and sex. Yet even as Sarah's femininity appears through the glances of observers within the narrative, the spectre of the instability in the opening verses remains a persistent niggle. Halberstam's recognition of the gift of subversion possible through a character without context comes to the fore in Sarah's story.

The opening lack of historical and familial context highlights the rupture – the space – available for alternative readings. In so doing they reveal the anachronisms already present in the story. Through reading the text with a close attention to the micro details, alongside trans theories of gender such as those of Halberstam and Serano, the processes by which a reader actively constructs a character's gender become clear. When the construction itself becomes visible, it is possible to view components in distinction from each other rather than always in continuity. Sarah becomes centred in the narrative just as their masculinity comes to the fore. Throughout the central portion of the narrative, a rounded masculine character emerges. Persuasiveness, bonding and conflicts, authority and violence combine to bring depth to Sarah's personhood. Through Clines's model of masculinity, even the beauty that so effectively contributed to the perception of femininity in the initial phase of their story, now contributes to the image of Sarah successfully playing the man. This masculine Sarah is initially validated by God in Genesis 16:5–9, before becoming subject to censure in Genesis 18:15. In the interim, God has promised a child to Sarah (as well as Abraham), and the threat of childbearing hangs over the next stage of their story.

The final portion of Sarah's story presents the most concrete example of femininity (Gen 21:1–8), which follows a reconfiguration of *her* context and womanhood (Gen 20:1–18). Through the words of God, Abraham and the narrator, Sarah's womanhood is made explicit and the missing context is added to provide the lineage necessary to secure endogamous reproduction. Sarah appears, albeit briefly, to settle into the status of subordinate woman and happy, willing mother. Features such as the overt and sustained emphasis on breastfeeding in combination with joyful laughter from Sarah present an archetypal feminine motherhood. This is juxtaposed with a conception that could not have occurred without God but definitely did happen despite Abraham. Even though Sarah's woman-making motherhood appears through their words and actions, the story does not end with the glorious display of femininity. Rather Sarah returns to their more familiar and comfortable masculinity when they expel Hagar and gain recognition in their authority over Abraham.

It remains perpetually difficult to fix a gaze on Sarah because they remain so frequently beyond the focus of the narrative or relegated to locations where they are not an active participant. Sarah's gender is complex, meaning that they cannot sustain that gaze and must frequently disappear to secure their future. In the end the narrative cannot sustain the portrayal of this complexly gendered character which necessitates a pre-emptive departure for Sarah. Their own perspective and self-expression are notably absent at key points in the life of the family, particularly after the birth of Isaac. These gaps and discontinuities represent the silent defiance of a woman who will not slide willingly into either androcentric or cisnormative expectations and thus cannot hold our gaze. Despite Sarah's frequent silence, there are still powerful if fleeting glimpses of this paradoxical character. These glimpses emphasise that there is more to Sarah – and their gender – than is regularly acknowledged. The power of cisnormative presuppositions ensures that Sarah's masculinity is overlooked. Rather, Sarah's assumed femininity becomes the template for not only the later matriarchs, but for the very perception of so-called biblical womanhood.[107]

What this chapter demonstrates is that Sarah cannot be easily constrained within the simplified tropes of beautiful wife, potential mother or even matriarch. Sarah's relationship to the category of woman is up for further discussion following this cispicious interpretation. This reading facilitates a way of engaging with characters' gender that recognizes instability, discontinuity, and diversity in order to place them in discussion with today's changing understandings of gender and sex. Reading Sarah with a cispicious scepticism towards gender expectations ultimately identifies a rich and diversely gendered character open to further queer and trans interpretation.

---

107. For further discussion of Sarah's significance as proto-matriarch and role model, see, Schneider, *Sarah*; Schept, 'Hesed'; Katie Jayne Woolstenhulme, 'The Role and Status of the Biblical Matriarchs in Genesis Rabbah' (PhD Durham University, 2017), 118–119, http://etheses.dur.ac.uk/12197/.

Chapter 4

ESAU: MORE THAN JUST A BODY THAT FAILS

Esau is a very different character to subject to cispicious analysis from his grandparent, Sarah. His maleness is clearly asserted from birth. Allusions to his embodied and phallic masculinity dominate the story of the firstborn son and heir-apparent to the patriarchal covenant given to Abraham in Genesis 17:2. Esau is not, however, the only child vying for their share of the patriarchal lineage: his status is threatened by his younger twin, Jacob. Each twin is presented as the antithesis of the other; Esau's story is inextricable from that of his sibling. Esau appears in Genesis as the embodiment of hegemonic masculinity, to the extent that his body both defines and constrains his identity.[1] With his sexed body come expectations about the man he should become. Those demands are placed upon him by family members and narrator alike, who set him up to fail more effectively than they prepare him for success. From his birth in Genesis 25:25, Esau's idealized male body is typified by presence of a phallus, ruddy complexion and hirsuteness. These physical attributes instil an inescapable image of the successful embodiment of all that hegemonic masculinity entails. Yet Esau seems neither to want such masculinity nor to be able to gain recognition of his own identity within such narrow perceptions of maleness. Jacob, meanwhile, is free from such sexed and gendered expectations and appears as a far more gender-fluid character.[2] The younger twin is given space and freedom to develop a gendered identity free from the narrative construction of a (male) body and its accompanying links to idealised masculinity.[3] Jacob can, and does, play with gender expectations in a way that Esau

---

1. Connell, *Masculinities*, 66–80. 'Hegemonic masculinity can be defined as the configuration of gender practice which *embodies* the currently accepted answer to the accepted problem of the legitimacy of patriarchy, which guarantees (or is taken to guarantee) the dominant position of men and the subordination of women' (77, emphasis added).

2. Henderson-Merrygold, 'Reading Biblical Embodiment Cispiciously'; 'Jacob – A (Drag) King Amongst Patriarchs', in *Texts, Contexts and Intertexts of Women and Gender in the Bible*, ed. Zanne Domoney-Lyttle and Sarah Nicholson (Sheffield: Sheffield Phoenix Press, 2021), 125–140.

3. Connell, *Masculinities*, 56. Connell acknowledges that the body 'is inescapable in the construction of masculinity, but what is inescapable is not fixed. The bodily process,

cannot. Esau must uphold the expectations placed upon him, otherwise he will be a failure of masculinity. Yet he cannot and does not succeed. He fails as a hunter, unable to satisfy his own need for sustenance so he trades his birthright with Jacob for the food he desperately needs. He marries undesirable women, who offend Rebekah his mother's sensibility. Then, Jacob performs a drag version of Esau in order to steal the paternal blessing from Isaac, ensuring Esau's fate is sealed. Esau is a failure of masculinity. The failure allows for his firstborn status and 'patriarchal dividend' to pass to Jacob instead.[4] Nonetheless, Esau is, at least occasionally, able to demonstrate an agency and identity beyond the constraints placed upon him due to his embodiment. His perspective parallels in the indecent knowledge of one's self privileged by Namaste and Althaus-Reid, which they show frequently struggles for recognition.[5]

In this reading, I juxtapose the persistent reliance on images of Esau's embodiment with the accounts of failure that surround him. Following Halberstam, I treat these examples of failure as indications of discontinuity with cisnormative expectations.[6] The discontinuities that emerge create a space for Esau to reveal the more diverse, nonconforming aspects of his gender. Such indications of nonconformity become apparent on his body as much as they are evident in his behaviour. Prosser reminds us that bodies do matter and our relationships with those around us are based in an embodied experience.[7] Esau quickly moves from the potentially lauded heir-apparent to *persona non grata*. In parallel, he and his body become less comprehensible and more animalistic. Esau speaks into his own narrative (Gen 25:30) and immediately narrator and fellow characters alike judge his words by reflecting back to his body. When he does speak, he is treated as a less reliable narrator than those around him – even when speaking of himself – since his voice does not always cohere with the gendered expectations placed upon him. His words appear inarticulate and fail the demand for successful men to be gifted communicators, leading to wide-ranging judgements that he is a failure of masculinity. Moreover, the nascent glimpses of his femininity – his emotion, kindness and subservience – are overlooked entirely or used to build further pictures of failure.[8] The narratorial response is to punish him for his transgressions,

---

entering into the social process, becomes part of history (both personal and collective) and a possible object of politics. They have various forms of recalcitrance to social symbolism and control'.

4. Connell, *Masculinities*, 79. Connell defines the patriarchal dividend as 'the advantage men in general gain from the overall subordination of women'. She acknowledges that the patriarchal dividend is beneficial to all men, and this is reliant on male complicity in the perpetuation of hegemonic masculinity.

5. For further discussion, see Chapter 1.

6. Halberstam, *Queer Art of Failure*.

7. Prosser, *Second Skins*.

8. Sarra Lev, 'Esau's Gender Crossing: *Parashat Toldot* (Genesis 25:19–28:9)', in *Torah Queeries: Weekly Commentaries on the Hebrew Bible*, ed. Gregg Drinkwater, Joshua Lesser and David Shneer (New York: New York University Press, 2009), 38–42, 38. Lev argues that

and that takes place through primary reference to his body, the main source of those sexed and gendered preconceptions. In the face of such violence, Esau appears to acquiesce in the demands placed upon him before he is temporarily excised from the narrative. When he eventually reappears several chapters later (in Genesis 33), he is, for the first time, treated more compassionately, notably without any reference to the body that so defined him and constrained him earlier in the narrative.

Esau's troublesome experiences provide insight into the problems of being defined by bodily features and unable to escape the gendered expectations those attributes cultivate. His failures mount up, and he appears less coherent and less desirably masculine. The failures combine with his inarticulate speech to render Esau an incomprehensible figure, who struggles to hold the gaze of narrator and reader alike. Like Sarah and other gender diverse characters, Esau faces erasure from his own narrative. He experiences the 'struggles of the dispossessed', all while he has to compete with Jacob, who comes to represent success and perfection.[9] Yet his small acts of defiance, along with the apparent peace and calm that appear once third parties cease to overlay their gendered and sexed preconceptions on Esau equally offer hope in living beyond the constraints of cisnormative expectations.

Encountering Esau('s Body) – Genesis 25:19–34

Esau's story is tough to pin down. He appears most frequently through the image created by the narrator, without being given space to speak or act on his own volition. Rather, the image created from birth onwards is that of a body to be objectified. On entering the ancestral narrative, Esau's body is vividly described as red and hairy (Gen 25.25). Even before he is given a name, this striking image confronts the reader, and sets the course of Esau's story (and his name), all before his younger twin emerges from Rebekah's womb. The birth story is a rare inclusion and one of only two detailed birth stories in the ancestral narratives. Attention to Esau's body here is a unique feature of this narrative as neither Jacob here nor

---

the perception of Esau as the more masculine twin is 'only half the story, for the hairy hunter is also characterized as a stereotypically feminine character: emotional, kindly, subservient. This feminine Esau continually approaches life with innocence, only to be shoved aside in favor of his more savvy, cool, and street-smart little brother.'

9. Halberstam, *Queer Art of Failure*, 120. 'Queer fairy tales are often organized around heroes who are in some way "different" and whose differences is offensive to some larger community: Shrek is an ogre forced to live far away from judgmental visitors; Babe is an orphaned pig who thinks he is a sheepdog; Nemo is a motherless fish with a deformed fin. Each "disabled" hero has to fight off or compete with a counterpart who represents wealth, health, success, and perfection. While these narratives of difference could easily serve to deliver a tidy moral lesson about learning to accept yourself, each links the struggle of the rejected individual to larger struggles of the dispossessed.'

Perez and Zerah in the later birth story (Gen 28:24–30) face such similar scrutiny. There must be something distinctive about Esau that warrants such detailed discussion of his physique. The picture emerges of a child who is inescapably male, through use of gendered terms to discuss his physicality and even a euphemistic allusion to his penis. Esau is definitely assigned male – this occurs at birth – and until he is granted his own voice he cannot speak of his image as created by the narrator to either confirm or challenge that assignation (Gen 25:25–26). The only perspectives offered in this initial portion of Esau's life come from his parents who make their preference for one twin over the other clear (vv. 27–28). Here Isaac's preference for Esau continues to be tied to the gendered role Esau fulfils and the resultant performance that accompanies it: Esau is an adept hunter.

An Auspicious Arrival – Genesis 25:19-26

> These are the descendants of Isaac, Abraham's son: Abraham was the father of Isaac, and Isaac was forty years old when he married Rebekah, daughter of Bethuel the Aramean of Paddan-aram, sister of Laban the Aramean. Isaac prayed to the LORD for this wife, because she was barren; and the LORD granted his prayer, and his wife Rebekah conceived. The children struggled within her; and she said, 'If it is to be this way, why do I live?' So she went to enquire of the LORD. And the LORD said to her,
>
> 'Two nations are in your womb,
>   and the two peoples born of you shall be divided;
> the one shall be stronger than the other,
>   the elder shall serve the younger.
>
> When her time to give birth was at hand, there were twins in her womb. The first came out red, all his body was like a hairy mantle; so they named him Esau. Afterward his brother came out, with his hand gripping Esau's heel; so he was named Jacob. Isaac was sixty years old when she bore them.
>
> Gen 25:19–26

Esau is set up to fail even from the point of his birth in Genesis 25:25. It is an auspicious introduction. Reference to his dual lineage (maternal and paternal) is accompanied by a divine oracle into the tempestuous nature of the sibling's relationships (Gen 25:19–23).[10] Details of the twins' lineage are comprehensive and leave no gaps unfilled, unlike in the initial appearance of their grandparent, Sarah. Similarly, when Esau is born the details focussed on his body instil an

---

10. Like Sarah, Rebekah's heritage is as significant as Isaac's even though it is the birth even more than his life that is the matter of the narrative. Both are within the endogamous community that finds a shared root in Abraham's father Terah (Gen 11:26–30; 24:15) which marks them as potential holders of Abraham's legacy.

inescapable image of his gender and sex (Gen 25:25–26). Meanwhile the account of Jacob's birth lacks the equivalent details, which further highlights the importance of Esau's male body by their absence. Clearly Esau's body matters, and it is placed on full show to the reader in order to bolster the emerging perception of Esau as *the* striking male figure. And who would not want to be the embodiment of cisnormative masculinity?

Before the reader is told Esau's name, the narrator announces that Esau 'came out red, all his body like a hairy mantle', a description used to explain the elder twin's name (Gen 25:25). These details are multifaceted and multifunctional. The description serves an aetiological function as Esau is the antecedent of Israel's great rival, the Edomites, whose name shares a common root with the red colour ascribed to Esau.[11] It also provides a prolepsis for the later stew incident where Jacob contentiously acquires the first of Esau's patriarchal dividends (Gen 25:29–34).[12] It also conveys a maleness on the child as the descriptions of ruddiness associated with the redness of tone, and hirsuteness are celebrated elsewhere in the Hebrew Bible. So affirming is this description that Esau appears to typify the male body associated with hegemonic masculinity in the Hebrew Bible.

Ruddiness is an attribute Esau shares with David (1 Sam 16:12; 17:42), while his hairiness is shared with Absalom (2 Sam 14:26) and Samson (Judg 16:17). These designations are specifically male, embodied, and, elsewhere at least, signify praiseworthy masculinity.[13] When referring to the ruddiness of David in 1 Samuel, David Clines argues that 'whatever exactly that means, it obviously refers to some

---

11. Claus Westermann, *Genesis*, trans. David E. Green (Edinburgh: T&T Clark, 1987), 183. Westermann argues that Esau is 'a name that has nothing to do with either description' – of redness/ruddiness or hairiness. He also notes that 'the explanation may be that 25:26 required the etymology of the name here; and, the etymology of "Esau" being unknown, two suggestions were introduced: the familiar identification of Esau with Edom and Seir in the land of Edom. Both suggestions would then have originated elsewhere' (137).

12. Benno Jacob, *The First Book of the Bible: Genesis* (New York: KTAV Publishing House Inc, 1974), 167. Jacob links Esau's name to a later portion of the story, 'Plainly an allusion to the red pottage in verse 30', before addressing the links with Edom, blood and 'Esau's savageness'.

13. Victor P. Hamilton, *The Book of Genesis: Chapters 18-50*, NICOT (Grand Rapids, MI: Eerdmans, 1995), 183. Hamilton draws on Cyrus Gordon when he asserts that 'men (but never women) are coloured red or reddish brown when they assume heroic or ceremonial purposes'. Gordon draws on evidence from across the Ancient Near East, indicating a preference for red amongst men and yellow for women. He specifically cites Esau, along with David as 'two of the most heroic men of the Old Testament' before noting that their natural redness showed 'that they were born to be heroes'. Cyrus H. Gordon, *Before the Bible: The Common Background of Greek and Hebrew Civilisations* (London: Collins, 1962), 230–231.

aspect of physical beauty'.[14] Johanna Stiebert highlights the allusions to an 'attractive and heathy hue of the skin (Song. 5.10; Lam. 4.7; 1 Sam. 16.12; 17.42)'.[15] For Bradford Anderson and Susan Niditch these descriptions indicate Esau's potential as a credible patriarch in the legacy of Abraham and Isaac.[16] Being both hirsute *and* ruddy seems to warrant a problematic embodiment of masculinity, at least for Esau. Indeed, Raewyn Connell argues that it is rarely (if ever) possible for one person to be the embodiment of hegemonic masculinity. It is an aspirational, idealised image.[17] Instead those whose lives most closely represent the patriarchal dividend that accompanies hegemonic masculinity also demonstrate a more nuanced and complex masculinity than its idealised form suggests as possible.[18] Esau, then, is endowed with a double dose of male physicality which lacks any such nuance and leads commentators to question Esau's apparent fit within conventional, binary-gendered identities.[19] The accounts of his hairiness *and*

---

14. Clines, *Interested Parties*, 212. The discussion of David's ruddiness forms part of Clines's contention that beauty, including ruddiness, is a desirable attribute for maleness and masculinity in the Hebrew Bible.

15. Johanna Stiebert, 'The Maligned Prophet: Prophetic Ideology and the "Bad Press" of Esau', in *Sense and Sensitivity: Essays on Reading the Bible in Memory of Robert Carroll*, ed. Alastair G. Hunter and Philip R. Davies, The Library of Hebrew Bible/Old Testament Studies (Sheffield: Sheffield Academic Press, 2002), 33–48, 34 n.1, n.2. Stiebert also notes the potential negative associations of redness, where the root occasionally refers to inflammations of the skin (Lev 13:19, 24, 42–43) but concludes that 'this does not seem to be at issue in Gen 25.25' (n.1).

16. Bradford A. Anderson, *Brotherhood and Inheritance: A Canonical Reading of the Esau and Edom Traditions*, Library of Biblical Studies (London: T&T Clark, 2011), 4; Susan Niditch, 'Genesis', in *Women's Bible Commentary: Revised and Updated*, ed. Carol A. Newsom, Sharon H. Ringe and Jacqueline E. Lapsley (Louisville, KY: Westminster John Knox Press, 2012), 27–45, 38.

17. As Brian Charles DiPalma emphasizes, Connell's model does not address the political component of masculinity even where someone otherwise appears the hegemonic ideal. While this is certainly the case for Esau, who remains subordinate to Jacob's political power, Connell's attention to complex, relational masculinities remains apposite. For further discussion of the limits and benefits of applying Connell's work to the Bible, see DiPalma, *Masculinities in the Court Tales*, 24.

18. Connell, *Masculinities*, 77. 'The most visible bearers of hegemonic masculinity are not always the most powerful people. They may be exemplars, such as film actors, or even fantasy figures, such as film characters.... Nevertheless, hegemony is likely to be established only if there is some correspondence between cultural ideal and institutional power, collective if not individual'. Connell later adds, 'Normative definitions of masculinity … face the problem that not many men actually meet the normative standards. The number of men practising the hegemonic pattern in its entirety may be quite small. Yet the majority of men gain from its hegemony, since they benefit from the patriarchal dividend' (79).

19. See, for example, Speiser, *Genesis*, 196; Westermann, *Genesis 12–36*, 414; *Genesis*, 183; Hamilton, *Genesis 18–50*, 178.

ruddiness are over the top ensuring that Esau moves from the realm of desirable masculinity to an excessive form. Gerhard von Rad considers the narrative to favour neither twin strongly, before asserting that Esau should be considered unfavourably based on the physical descriptions where 'comic and ridiculous characteristics are emphasised'.[20] Rather than seeing it as a story that establishes overly valorised images of national ancestors, he repeatedly emphasises the comedic, joking, parodic elements of the story. Meanwhile he also commends the story for its sober and realistic portrayal of the twins, even though baby Esau was 'so hairy that he seemed to have been a fur coat by nature'.[21] Esau is not just masculine, but hypermasculine – not in an entirely recognizable way – and his apparent excess calls masculinity itself into question.

Esau's hirsute hypermale body becomes more recognizable in the Mesopotamian wild-man figure Enkidu than his biblical counterpart Samson.[22] Enkidu is the hairy wildman created from clay and contrasted with the 'renowned king' and eponymous hero in the Mesopotamian *The Epic of Gilgamesh*.[23] Enkidu's physicality is in marked difference from that of Gilgamesh, who is created by the Gods with perfect body and perfect beauty. Meanwhile Enkidu is a clay facsimile: 'His body was rough, he had long hair like a woman's; it waved like the hair of Nisaba, the goddess of corn. His body was covered with matted hair like Samuqan's, the god of cattle.'[24] Enkidu is also described as 'the savage man' who eats grass alongside the gazelles, and who is initially unfamiliar with human experience or expectation.[25] Here the animalistic aspect of Enkidu's character comes across more clearly than

---

20. von Rad, *Genesis: A Commentary*, 265.

21. von Rad, *Genesis: A Commentary*, 265. Von Rad emphasizes how much he sees Esau as an 'other', inferior figure, albeit his picture of 'the dark-skinned Esau' is an orientalist image par excellence. Cf. Edward Said, *Orientalism* (New York: Pantheon, 1978), 40. Said makes the important observation that 'the Oriental is irrational, depraved (fallen), childlike, "different"'.

22. Westermann, *Genesis 12–36*, 414. Westermann notes only the physical similarities of 'being "hairy," like a wild man"'. He also highlights the consistency between Esau and Ousōos, a character who features in the writings of Philo of Byblos. Westermann notes that since F. Delitzsch the parallels between Esau and Ousōos are apparent as each is 'one of a pair of brothers and has clothes of animals skins' (Westermann cites G. Grottanelli, Or Ant 1 1 [1972] 46–63). For further discussion of wild men in the Bible and antiquity, see Gregory Mobley, 'The Wild Man in the Bible and the Ancient Near East', *Journal of Biblical Literature* 116, 2 (1997), 217–233.

23. N. K. Sandars, *The Epic of Gilgamesh*, Revised ed., Penguin Classics, (Harmondsworth, Middlesex: Penguin 1972), 7; Robert Alter, *The Art of Biblical Narrative* (London: George Allen & Unwin, 1981), 43.

24. Sandars, *Epic of Gilgamesh*, 61–63.

25. Sandars, *Epic of Gilgamesh*, 64–69.

is ever made explicit in Esau's story. Enkidu's affinity for the animals and his wild-man life see him set up to be seduced by a sex worker, so that he may be humanized.[26] So extreme are his animalistic tendencies that he (and they) can only be tamed by sex with Shamhat for six days and seven nights, after which the animals who were formerly his companions no longer recognize him.[27] Prior to being broken by Shamhat, Enkidu is 'the primitive man', but afterwards he is clean and able to '[know] his own mind' for the first time.[28] Enkidu *can* be made a man, but it is not possible for him to be a wild-man, akin to Esau, at the same time. The parallels between Enkidu and Esau rely on the perception of the former as a less-than-human wildman, a neanderthal-like hypermale figure. Esau is presented in the same way. Unlike Enkidu, Esau does not have a Shamhat figure to break his wild spirit. He, therefore, gets stuck as a hypermasculine and animalistic individual for whom personhood is something that needs to be acquired. Yet Esau is not, at least in infancy, given any space to act, or speak, or even (just) be, but the gendered script is written for him. Treating Esau as an Enkidu-like figure emphasizes the cost of an excessively male body, unrecognizably human, and these parallels 'insinuate a bias against [Esau] from the beginning'.[29]

The problem that emerges following the allusion to Enkidu is that the image of Esau's male physique is not yet complete. There remain further elements to add to this excessively gendered hypermasculine body. The dual components, hirsuteness and ruddiness, have already instilled an image of a body that is an excessive, almost comedic, facsimile of maleness, and yet there remains one further element to add. In the story of Jacob's birth it is *Esau's* physicality that warrants narration: Jacob's defining act is to grasp Esau's heel. Even so, von Rad finds this 'scarcely more, to begin with, than a touch of popular joking!'[30] While Esau's name is attributed to his body's colour, Jacob's is linked to the term for heel.[31] Yet it is Esau's heel, not Jacob's,

---

26. Stephanie Dalley, *Myths from Mesopotamia: Creation, The Flood, Gilgamesh, and Others*, Oxford World Classics, (Oxford: Oxford University Press, 1989), 53–59. Dalley notes that 'Shamhat is used as a personal name here, it means "voluptuous woman, prostitute", in particular as a type of cultic devotee of Ishtar in Uruk' (126 n.4). See also Mobley, 'Wild Man in the Bible', 221. Mobley also notes that Enkidu needs conversion from his animal-like ways and his humanisation comes through coitus with Shamhat.

27. Dalley, *Myths from Mesopotamia*, 55–56.

28. Dalley, *Myths from Mesopotamia*, 56.

29. Bruce Vawter, *On Genesis: A New Reading* (London: Geoffrey Chapman, 1977), 288.

30. von Rad, *Genesis: A Commentary*, 265.

31. The linguistic similarities between the roots for 'heel' and 'one who supplants' or 'fraud' are frequently as given reasons for Jacob's name, see J. P. Fokkelman, 'Genesis', in *The Literary Guide to the Bible*, ed. Robert Alter and Frank Kermode (Cambridge, MA: Harvard University Press, 1987), 36–55, 46; Eilberg-Schwartz, *God's Phallus*, 153. Cf. Westermann, *Genesis*, 183. Westermann notes that the Hebrew root is common between Jacob and heel although he also suggests that the name 'was originally a theophorous name meaning "May God protect"'. See also von Rad, *Genesis: A Commentary*, 265.

that provides the basis for the younger sibling's name. Jacob's embodiment warrants no comment: perhaps it was not noteworthy enough to remark upon. In other words, Jacob is sufficiently (cis)normal.[32] If so, this emphasizes all the more clearly that Esau's physique should *not* be understood as normal and is thus remarkable. Still, that remarkable heel itself warrants further consideration.

While it is an attractive image to imagine Jacob grasping the back of Esau's foot, it is equally credible that the younger sibling grabbed the elder by his dick. Heels, like many terms associated with feet in the Hebrew Bible, function both literally and euphemistically. For Howard Eilberg-Schwartz, feet terms, including heels, are well-established, and at times are 'obvious reference to genitals'.[33] His observations correspond with Roland Boer's recognition that the ancestral narratives are rich in euphemisms. Boer argues that the repeated allusion to Jacob's name connoting 'heel' cannot be overlooked for its multifaceted meaning.[34] The reference to the grasped heel provides an overtly phallic component to Esau's natal embodiment that parallels the birth announcements that a boy is born based on the observation of his penis. S. H. Smith even sees the euphemism as an essential component of the narrative, given that it symbolizes so aptly Jacob's desire to assume Esau's status. Here Esau's genitals are the symbolic marker both of God's promise to Abraham and of Esau's own 'procreative power'.[35] Yet Stiebert suggests euphemistic terms both create *and* muddle gender.[36] Esau's dick may well be apparent, but it remains only as visible as the euphemism that both hides and reveals it. Stiebert's

---

32. For an alternative reading, where the lack of detail is treated as narrative silence about Jacob's embodiment, see Henderson-Merrygold, 'Reading Biblical Embodiment Cispiciously'. I argue that the lack of an explicit embodied maleness for Jacob, akin to that provided for Esau, leaves space to consider the younger twin as a trans masculine figure, assigned female at birth.

33. Eilberg-Schwartz, *God's Phallus*, 153. Eilberg-Schwartz identifies this case as 'consistent with the use of the foot more generally as a euphemism (Judg. 3.24, 1 Sam. 24.5, Isa. 6.2, 7.20, 47.2)'.

34. Roland Boer, 'The Patriarch's Nuts: Concerning the Testicular Logic of Biblical Hebrew', *Journal of Men, Masculinities and Spirituality* 5, 2 (2011), 41–52.

35. S. H. Smith, '"Heel" and "Thigh": the Concept of Sexuality in the Jacob-Esau Narratives', *Vetus Testamentum* 40, 4 (1990), 464–473: 465. 'I venture to suggest that the spirit of the narrative is more generally adhered to if 'qb is taken in this instance as a euphemism for genitals. Since the ancient Hebrew thought the sexual organs were regarded as the seat of a man's procreative power, the suggestion that in the story Jacob is gripping Esau not by the heel but by the genitals would aptly prefigure the narrative plot as a whole: by any means at his disposal Jacob wants to appropriate his brother's power for himself, thereby inheriting God's promise to Abraham of countless descendants. Jacob's act of gripping his brother's genitals is symbolic of his desire to assume procreative power.'

36. Johanna Stiebert, *First-Degree Incest and the Hebrew Bible: Sex in the Family*, The Library of Hebrew Bible/Old Testament Studies, (London: Bloomsbury T&T Clark, 2016), 122 n. 81.

observations about euphemism add a further nuance: euphemisms, she argues, can serve as precursors to sexual assault.[37] Thus the inclusion of the detail of Jacob grasping Esau's 'heel' establishes a threat of sexual violence between the twins. The result is a dangerous, ominous narrative.

However the euphemism functions, it is a third distinct signifier of Esau's maleness, taking his already excessive masculinity into new realms. Esau's physicality is clearly and inescapably drawn for him at birth – long before he speaks or acts – while Jacob's is a blank slate.

Familial Gender Roles – Genesis 25:27-28

> When the boys grew up, Esau was a skilful hunter, a man of the field, while Jacob was a quiet man, living in tents. Isaac loved Esau, because he was fond of game; but Rebekah loved Jacob.
>
> Gen 25:27–28

These two concluding verses provide the only insight into wider family dynamics during the twins' development (Gen 25:27–28). It continues in the narrator's observational style without giving voice to any of the participants. These verses offer an invaluable bridge to take the twins from their natal images to the gendered roles within their family. It also, importantly, introduces another proleptic detail, that of parental favour seen through a lens of social role: Esau the hunter is contrasted with Jacob, who stays at home in the tents. These roles have so little in common that Victor Hamilton suggests that 'wordplay might be the author's way of saying that about all Jacob and Esau have in common is the acoustical similarity between the sounds of their activities'.[38] There remain clear gendered delineations between the roles each twin fulfils within the family. This brings mixed blessings for Esau: hunting may well be a quintessentially masculine role, but whether that is more akin to an uncivilized, animalistic Enkidu or a confident, commendable warrior may be a matter for debate.[39] Meanwhile, Jacob is

---

37. Stiebert, *First-Degree Incest*, 34 n.3. In this specific example Stiebert outlines the links between heel in its literal and euphemistic terms, especially in 'prelude[s] to rape,' where '"feet" is a circumlocution for genitals (e.g. Judg. 3.24; 1 Sam. 24.3),' before concluding that 'it could be that "heel" is here euphemistic'.

38. Hamilton, *Genesis 18–50*, 182. Hamilton explains the similarities are primarily audible: 'Jacob: *zûd/zîd* [from *zîd*, "prepare"]; Esau: *ṣûd* [from *ṣayid*, "hunter"]'.

39. Von Rad, *Genesis: A Commentary*, 265. Von Rad, for example, sees Esau's hunting as a sign that he is more primitive and less evolved than Jacob. Meanwhile Harry Hoffner identifies Esau as a specific example of the virile manhood symbolised by the bow and arrow (referenced later in Gen 27:3) and contrasts him with Jacob who 'is portrayed as somewhat less than a true man, because he confines his activities to the flocks and tents'. Harry A. Hoffner Jr, 'Symbols of Masculinity and Femininity: Their Use in Ancient near Eastern Sympathetic Magic Rituals', *Journal of Biblical Literature* 85, 3 (1966), 326-334: 329.

quiet and lives in tents, a role associated with female (or at least feminine) members of the community.⁴⁰ While von Rad does not attend to these gendered differences, he confidently asserts that 'as they grew up, the boys lived completely separated from each other'.⁴¹ These social roles consolidate the earlier comments on Esau's sexed embodiment: Esau's masculinity continues to be asserted, now appearing alongside Jacob's femininity. Jacob is granted space to explore a richness and diversity to gender through this role, while Esau's identity as masculine hunter continues to be the only model for his gendered being. It remains notable that neither twin comments on their role in this drama. Rather, the first reflections lie with their parents and their preferences. Jacob, the grasping, potentially deceptive child, found in the tents, is loved by Rebekah for no discernible reason beyond that of a mother for her child. Esau, however, is the favoured – indeed loved – child of Isaac, but this love relies upon Esau's hunting ability and thus his performance of masculinity. Given Isaac's favour for Esau, here (at least) he seems to be making a success of the role he finds himself in.

Both Isaac and Esau fare ill through this dependent and contingent love. Isaac, like his favoured son, is shown as having physical desires – his desire for, and appreciation of, game is fateful. It is Isaac's love of game that proves to be the basis of Jacob's later deception of the patriarch in Genesis 27. While the deception serves to abuse Esau, Isaac does not emerge positively as his interest in Esau is shaped almost solely around the desire for game. Von Rad considers Isaac's stated love for Esau to be worth considering 'only from the humorous viewpoint',⁴² whereas Michael Carden suggests that Isaac's love is based on a perception of Esau as a representative of 'hegemonic masculinity, the patriarchal ideal' who is 'the man Isaac can never be no matter how hard he tries'.⁴³ It appears a sad indictment of Isaac in particular, but the account presented is that of the omniscient narrator

---

40. Ellen Frankel, *The Five Books of Miriam: A Woman's Commentary on the Torah* (San Francisco, CA: HarperSanFrancisco, 1998), 50; Susan E. Haddox, 'Favoured Sons and Subordinate Masculinities', in *Men and Masculinity in the Hebrew Bible and Beyond*, ed. Ovidiu Creangă, The Bible in the Modern World (Sheffield: Sheffield Phoenix Press, 2010b), 2–19, 11; Niditch, 'Genesis', 37–39. Frankel argues that Jacob was schooled in the ways of women and 'set up to play the women's role' while Niditch and Haddox both identify the tents as the women's domain. From a queer perspective, Michael Carden writes that 'in declaring Jacob to be a man living in tents, Genesis is questioning his masculinity – Jacob is effeminate'. Carden, 'Genesis/Bereshit', 47.

41. von Rad, *Genesis: A Commentary*, 265. Von Rad later adds that 'the roving and more uncultured hunter was a sinister person for the settled shepherd living in more cultivated conditions. The evaluation of both ways of life, however, is not unprejudiced in the text, but is given from the standpoint of the established farmer. Jacob is "orderly," "respectable"' (265). He uses this to justify his condemnation of Esau as well as the divine and narratorial preference for Jacob.

42. von Rad, *Genesis: A Commentary*, 266.

43. Carden, 'Genesis/Bereshit', 47.

without the active participation of any of the characters. It is into this silence that Sarra Lev offers an alternative option. She suggests that the narrator reports 'a description of a parent's own image and expectations of his firstborn son for gender conformity'.[44] They have not spoken or acted in these verses; we are still in the scene-setting phase of the story and the characters are on the cusp of action and dialogue. Those interactions have the power to challenge preconceptions about each character no matter how carefully constructed they have been until this point.

Failing to Perform and Performing to Fail – Genesis 25:29-34

> Once when Jacob was cooking a stew, Esau came in from the field, and he was famished. Esau said to Jacob, 'Let me eat some of that red stuff, for I am famished!' (Therefore he was called Edom.) Jacob said, 'First sell me your birthright.' Esau said, 'I am about to die; of what use is a birthright to me?' Jacob said, 'Swear to me first.' So he swore to him, and sold his birthright to Jacob. Then Jacob gave Esau bread and lentil stew, and he ate and drank, and rose and went his way. Thus Esau despised his birthright.
>
> Gen 25:29-34

After an unknown period, where the siblings are beyond view, the twins reappear. This is the first of two antagonistic interactions between Esau and Jacob, each of which ends with Jacob the victor and Esau the fool. It is a story of Esau's failure: he fails as a hunter, fails to communicate effectively and fails to retain his inherited birthright, one of the symbols of his firstborn male privilege. Some of these failures appear, at least initially, to be Esau's doing; however that risks oversimplifying to a binary where Esau = bad and Jacob = good. While the simple bifurcation represents the narratorial preferences and Jacob's eventual ascendency to become the patriarch, it overlooks the complex gender dynamics inherent in the story.

Meanwhile, the scene is also the first time either twin's words or actions are on show. Esau's words are regarded as failures by Jacob, who uses them for their own benefit, something that culminates in the trade of birthright for stew. In so doing, Jacob signals that Esau is justifiably the target of mockery and legitimately perceived as an Enkidu-like figure. However, Halberstam argues that failure – whether intentional or not – serves to rupture gender expectations. Halberstam's approach offers a new perspective on Esau's words and actions. In what follows, I

---

44. Lev, 'Esau's Gender Crossing', 38. She clarifies, 'It is unclear, however, whose mouth the text refers to in this verse. Isaac loved Esau because the hunt was in whose mouth? Is it Esau's mouth that desires the hunt? Is he the stereotypically masculine figure who longs to go out into the field and kill? Or is it his father, Isaac, whose taste for venison drives Esau into the fields to act the role of "the man of the house?"'.

show that there is a profound value in reading Esau's behaviour as intentional, retaining agency, to reveal that he rejects the constricting gender norms in which he finds himself. The unintelligibility of his words emphasizes his disruption of convention which his body communicates via his actions.

'Red Red' and a Life-Altering Hunger

The twins come clearly into view, with each undertaking their social and domestic roles; Jacob in the tents making stew, and Esau working outdoors, implicitly hunting for food (Gen 25:29). Esau is famished, something confirmed by both Esau and the narrator (vv. 29–30). For von Rad, 'if he takes no prey, he goes hungry', so Esau must have failed on that day's trip.[45] He is so hungry that his first words come out clumsily, failing to find the right words to express his hunger or desire. This is hardly the auspicious speech anticipated of the heroic figure whose textual equivalent of a baby photo suggests he is destined to become a great, noble, successful, eloquent figure.[46] Instead it is the image of someone whose outdoor life is really taking its toll and whose endeavour immediately prior to this scene has ended in failure.[47] Esau arrives harried and stressed. His hunt has clearly not provided him with sufficient sustenance to prevent the ravenous hunger with which he returns to Jacob's tent. The sense of Esau's failure comes through even more clearly when his words to Jacob are fumbled and inarticulate. He 'asks for the stew with a verb used for feeding animals … and, all inarticulate appetite, he cannot think of the word for stew but only points to it pantingly, calling it "this red red stuff"'.[48] The very loaded phrase conveys not only Esau's problems of communication and his animalistic tendencies, but it also recalls the meaning of his name, something the narrator is at pains to make clear. Once again, he is constricted by the expectations placed on him due to his (hyper)masculine embodiment. Here we begin to see the frustrations with that role and status emerging.

The use of the colour term is a clear and deliberate allusion to Esau's physicality and naming, introduced earlier in the birth narrative. The link to Edom (and, by extension, the Edomites) is made explicit, but Esau's desires are also tied to the

---

45. von Rad, *Genesis: A Commentary*, 266.

46. For discussion of persuasive speech as a feature of masculinity, see Chapter 3. See also Clines, *Interested Parties*, 212–243; 'Dancing and Shining at Sinai'.

47. Robert Davidson, *Genesis 12–50*, The Cambridge Bible Commentary on the New English Bible, (Cambridge: Cambridge University Press, 1979), 124; Arnold, *Genesis*, 233. Davidson writes, 'The harshness of the hunter's life is underlined. If he does not kill he returns home hungry and *exhausted*' (emphasis original). Arnold draws attention to Jacob's success, in contrast with Esau's failings, by emphasizing the quality of Jacob's cooking that tempts the elder twin.

48. Alter, *Art of Biblical Narrative*, 44.

features of his embodiment that bind him both to name and action.[49] The repeated colour term אָדֹם (*'adom*, red) is frequently glossed in translation into English to make Esau's desire for food more apparent.[50] It serves to instil a clearer sense of how Esau's linguistic shortcomings map back onto his embodiment: his request is 'uncouth and abrasive', which is as much a description of him as of his words.[51] He appears crude, uncivilized and even animalistic in his behaviour, with von Rad arguing that this is evidence that Esau is a less evolved figure than the more civilized Jacob.[52] To see Esau's words as flawed communication is to call into question the success of his performance of masculinity. Indeed, Westermann writes, 'Esau's words and actions are a deliberate caricature: he is uncouth, coarse, and stupid.'[53] Westermann's interpretation of Esau as stupid relies on the perception of the remark as inarticulate. In contrast, Athalya Brenner-Idan argues that the language is deliberate. The repetition is part of a passage rich in grammatical and syntactical complexities where Esau's utterance must be understood to convey 'the sense of urgency and the oblique, too-tired-to-care attitude'.[54] What Brenner-Idan's observation reveals is that Esau's words are incomprehensible rather than inarticulate: readers such as Westermann see fumble and bluster, in part because they cannot comprehend such a quintessentially masculine figure opting for the 'oblique, too-tired-to-care language' expected of him. Esau is expressing his frustration and failing to find an understanding in either Jacob or the narrator. It is a subtle but nevertheless

---

49. Aetiologically, Esau's descendants become the Edomites, residents of the region of Edom, to the south east of Israel. This link is apparent through the repeated motif of describing Esau as red – the word shares its root with Edom and the terms sound very similar. Edom itself goes on to become the representative type figure for all Israel's enemies, leading Bradford Anderson to note that 'arguably no other nation in the Hebrew Bible is spoken of in such harsh language, and held in such low esteem'. Anderson, *Brotherhood and Inheritance*, 1.

50. The majority of translations translate the second אָדֹם as 'stew' (ESV, NIV, NIRV, CEB), 'pottage' (ASV, RSV), 'broth' (REB), or 'stuff' (CSB, JPS, LEB, NAS, CEB, GNB). The repetition ('red, red') is preserved in CJB, DBY, GW, JB, NET, YLT.

51. Arnold, *Genesis*, 233. Arnold argues that the effect of the repetition 'combined with a rare word for "swallow," gives the impression of an uncouth and abrasive request: "let me chow-down some of that red – that red stuff there!"'

52. von Rad, *Genesis: A Commentary*, 265. See also John Skinner, *A Critical and Exegetical Commentary on Genesis*, The International Critical Commentary, (Edinburgh: T&T Clark, 1910), 361; Speiser, *Genesis*, 195; Alter, *Art of Biblical Narrative*, 44. Skinner argues Esau's language is 'a coarse expression suggesting bestial voracity'. Meanwhile, Speiser emphasizes the assertions of Esau's crudeness. He contrasts unfavourably Esau's 'swallowing, gulping down' with the more favourable (and 'civilized') language of 'eating, or the like'. Alter concurs and treats Esau's actions more clearly as animalistic.

53. Westermann, *Genesis*, 183.

54. Athalya Brenner-Idan [Brenner], *Colour Terms in the Old Testament*, Journal for the Study of the Old Testament Supplement Series, (Sheffield: JSOT Press, 1982), 60.

significant small detail to suggest Esau's rejection of the expectations placed on him as the man of the family. He is given no space to create an image of a desire for perhaps a more feminine activity, such as Jacob's cooking. What matters is the strength and determination of his frustrated incomprehensible exasperation. His meaning is successfully conveyed even if he does not care to follow linguistic and social convention. Yet his disregard for such expectation gives Jacob enough space to begin to punish Esau for his lack of (gender) conformity. This quirky, atypical expression of need is the first real indication of Esau's self-expression that we get and remains one that is poorly and unsympathetically understood.

Was Esau really so hungry that he could not form a phrase cogently, or was he overwhelmed by the vice of gluttony? His behaviour is met with disdain from commentators who are unwilling or unable to find any validity to his actions and are equally eager to treat the expression of hunger as an act of vulgar indecency.[55] Susan Brayford returns to Esau's physicality to justify her condemnation of his actions. She draws on the birth narrative to justify her incredulity at Esau's behaviour: 'Esau epitomizes a crude rube who discounts everything but his appetite. He claims he is close to death for lack of food, so the birthright has little importance. One wonders why this strong countryman could not just overpower his domesticated brother and take the food'.[56] She is clearly suspicious of Esau's decision and, given the persistent focus on his body, she deems it an undeployed weapon that Esau could easily and effectively use to protect his own interests. It is what is anticipated for the male archetype. She implies that the man she has previously described as 'big, bold, and somewhat wild' must also be devoid of the skills of social interaction or respect for a sibling or peer.[57] In addition, she does not hear his repeated cries about the extent to which he currently feels under threat and at risk of imminent danger (vv. 30, 32). Overlooking Esau's own perspective is the result of treating him as an unreliable voice even within his own narrative. Instead, third parties within and beyond the narrative place more authority in their own insights. That inevitably that means Esau's sexed body and gendered behaviour feature heavily, especially given the enduring incapacity to understand Esau's perspective.

Ilona Rashkow's perspective emerges as a rare and dissenting voice as she treats Esau's words as an intentional expression of his own agency. She notes Esau's

---

55. Jacob, *First Book of the Bible*, 168; Speiser, *Genesis*, 195. In his commentary Jacob dismisses the character for his 'vulgar language' and 'uncontrolled gluttony', while Speiser opts to declare Esau 'an uncouth glutton'. See also Bruce Vawter, *A Path Through Genesis* (London: Sheed & Ward, 1957), 188; Derek Kidner, *Genesis*, Tyndale Old Testament Commentaries, (London: Tyndale Press, 1967), 152. Vawter considers Esau's need temporary and his appetite vulgar, leading him to declare Esau 'feckless'. Kidner concurs with Vawter's assessment that Esau is feckless, pejoratively suggesting Esau's 'spluttering' request is frequently toned down in translation into English.

56. Susan Brayford, *Genesis*, Septuagint Commentary Series, (Leiden: Brill, 2007), 345.

57. Brayford, *Genesis*, 343.

plaintive declaration of hunger, including the phrase 'I am at the point of death' could apply to 'his perilous life as a hunter' or it could be limited to 'his present condition'.[58] Here she recognizes that the hunger that impedes Esau on the occasion recounted here may be a cumulative rather than singular effect. The immediacy of Esau's extreme hunger recognizes the life-impacting seriousness of his claim. Esau was in dire need, whatever the cause, so much so that the transaction – any transaction, perhaps – seems no bad outcome. Esau at the point of death is a powerful image, and Rashkow's insight encapsulates a scenario that is unlikely to be the result of one single activity out of doors. Rather it is the cumulative effect of a pattern of behaviour or mode of living that is slowly but surely placing Esau at risk of his life. Lev also identifies this pattern. She makes explicit that Esau's tiredness (v. 29) and disregard for his birthright (v. 32) comes from a deep emotional hunger that comes with exhaustion in 'performing his role as a male'.[59] It happens that the story in Genesis 25 recounts the occasion at which this persistent pressure finally leads Esau to cry out for that which nourishes him. Prosser recounts the stories of the very real physical outworkings and pain that comes with living with gender dysphoria.[60] Such experiences can be profoundly life-limiting in a way that finds resonance in Esau's pained cries. Prosser describes the ways such conflict can be all-encompassing: 'The conflict between inner and outer body is incarnated and the figure of authentic body seeking to break out of its outer body prison is dramatically enacted'.[61] This appears through the challenges Esau experiences in conveying his need, expressing his frustration, and ultimately only securing what is needed at huge personal cost. Lev suggest that 'if we step into Esau's shoes, this is the moment when he has finally managed to walk away from the expectations placed on him as the firstborn son, and he disdains those expectations'.[62] However the underlying problem emerges once again when even Rashkow returns to the gendered expectations written on Esau's natal body to contextualize her insight: 'Esau, the hungry, hairy hunter, swears to the sale and loses his inheritance to Jacob, a mama's boy with smooth skin who does not venture far from home'.[63] Through the contrast of each twin's physique, she conveys a sense

---

58. Ilona N. Rashkow, *Taboo or not Taboo: Sexuality in the Hebrew Bible* (Minneapolis, MN: Fortress Press, 2000), 124.

59. Lev, 'Esau's Gender Crossing', 39.

60. Prosser, *Second Skins*, 69–70. Prosser discusses at length Raymond Thompson's account of his body as a claustrophobic enclosure that provoked 'an intensely sensory, visceral experience'.

61. Prosser, *Second Skins*, 67–76. Prosser uses this description for Thompson's somatic experiences pre-transition, which include sickness, semi-paralysis and blistered, rupturing skin. He astutely writes that these psychosomatic experiences are 'not "made up" but somatized, the body's manifestation of, its bringing to the material surface deep psychic disturbances' (71).

62. Lev, 'Esau's Gender Crossing', 39.

63. Rashkow, Taboo or Not Taboo, 124.

that Esau's body inescapably shapes his identity. It is not just Esau's birthright that gets traded, though: aspects of his maleness – perhaps his virility – are handed over too.

Birthright for Life

If Esau's self-narration appears unreliable because he will not slide neatly into the model of male success written on his body, then Jacob's perspective gains greater prominence and authority. While Esau's engagements are guttural (literally), somatic and impassioned, Jacob appears calculating, aggressive, and emotionless, although the monikers used in commentary are more likely to highlight someone 'astute and farsighted', clever and ruthless.[64] Since Jacob's words are particularly authoritative, they warrant close attention:

> Jacob speaks with a clear perception of legal forms and future consequences, addressing his brother twice in the imperative – 'First sell ... swear to me first – without the differential particle of entreaty, *na*, that Esau used in his own initial words to his twin. When Jacob asks Esau to sell the birthright, he withholds the crucial 'to me' till the end of his proposal with cautious rhetorical calculation.[65]

Robert Alter's description highlights both the disregard of Jacob for Esau at the emotional and interpersonal level as well as the younger twin's direct and driven focus on the end goal. It is Jacob who is discourteous and abrupt. That matters not because Esau has already failed too greatly to be taken seriously. In the face of such egregious failures by Esau, Jacob has the power to make demands. Hamilton notes that the entreaty ascribed to Esau, 'give me some of that red stuff *please*', is not met by a similarly courteous response from Jacob. The younger sibling's utterance lacks any such entreaty: 'Jacob is the aggressive one, dictating the terms of the transaction. He speaks from a position of strength and will use that position to get his hands on his older brother's birthright'.[66] From the perpetual 'position of strength' all Jacob need do is name the birthright and it can, and must, be given by Esau in order for the elder twin to continue to live. One of the greatest narrative sleights of hand is to malign Esau for losing something that was at best meaningless and at worse severely detrimental to him without giving credence to any justification for his act. It is similarly impressive to imply that Jacob is sufficiently conforming to all the gendered and sexed expectations placed upon either twin, while ensuring that Esau remains perpetually under scrutiny. Both responses rely on the perception of Esau's acts as failures, and failures as irredeemable.

---

64. Kidner, *Genesis*, 152; Walter Brueggemann, *Genesis*, Interpretation: A Bible Commentary for Teaching and Preaching (Louisville, KY: Westminster John Knox Press, 1982), 217; Westermann, *Genesis*, 183.
65. Alter, *Art of Biblical Narrative*, 44.
66. Hamilton, *Genesis 18–50*, 183.

For Hamilton it is the final descriptor of Esau that contextualizes the whole narrative: 'the narrator does not hesitate to use a verb or phrase that shows his condemnation of Esau – "he spurned his birthright" – in this particular incident, but employs no corresponding verb that shows a negative evaluation of Jacob'.[67] Benno Jacob uses this concluding remark to justify Rebekah's preference for her younger child through an evocative reference to privilege: 'The attitude of Esau to his privilege explains *and excuses* the preference of the mother for Jacob'.[68] Sadly this is Esau's legacy: to be recalled as the failure who discarded his birthright needlessly. Esau's (hyper)male body is not matched with either the anticipated aptitude with the masculine tasks such as hunting, and his voice does carry persuasively or even coherently. As with so many cissexist and cisnormative tropes, Esau's voice is lost to those who assert authority for his life over him. In the midst of this story, though, Esau demonstrates his agency through words and actions that do not conform to that which is expected of him. In so doing he transforms the judgment of failure placed upon him into a personification of gendered nonconformity. His small acts of disobedience serve as a timely reminder that Esau's voice is one of discontinuity and present a nascent insight into a character more complex than merely the inarticulate oaf imagery would suggest.

A Rebellious Interjection – Genesis 26:34–35

> When Esau was forty years old, he married Judith daughter of Beeri the Hittite, and Basemath daughter of Elon the Hittite; and they made life bitter for Isaac and Rebekah.
>
> Gen 26:34–35

While Genesis 25 left a broken Esau, having spurned his birthright in the final verse (Gen 25:34), he makes a surprising appearance in the concluding verses of Genesis 26. All but the final two verses are focussed on the way his parents sought to deceive Abimelech as his grandparents did before them (Gen 26:1–33; cf. Gen 20:1–20). The interjection about Esau's behaviour in the final verses is an almost stand-alone comment and once again takes no interest in Esau's words. In what I see as an intentional rejection of the demands his parents place on his status as the family man, Esau marries outside the family line: neither Judith nor Basemath are from his extended family line on either maternal or paternal side.[69]

---

67. Hamilton, *Genesis 18–50*, 182.
68. Jacob, *First Book of the Bible*, 169. Emphasis added.
69. The names and lineages of Esau's wives in this story are not consistent with those featured in his genealogy in Genesis 36:2–3: 'Esau took his wives from the Canaanites: Adah daughter of Elon the Hittite, Oholibamah daughter of Anah son of Zibeon the Hivite, and Basemath, Ishmael's daughter, sister of Nebaioth.' The disregard for female characters, particularly incidental characters, is well established. See Davidson, *Genesis 12–50*, 133. According to Davidson inconsistencies are hardly a surprising feature of this story given the

He has already emerged as a failure and one who cannot sufficiently be understood by either his family or the narrator. In the act of embarking on an exogamous marriage he is committing to an act that intentionally and irrevocably locates him outside the lineage and expectations so heavily placed upon him. He cannot be the heir apparent if his own children do not conform to the endogamous demands. If Esau's words do not adequately convey his frustration at the perpetual demands of social and bodily gender norms, these actions show it irrefutably. Alter notes in his translation that the wives 'were a provocation to Isaac and Rebekah'.[70] He is showing his indecency and lack of conformity once again. While narrator and commentator may treat it with hostility, Esau intentionally undertakes an action he – and we – knows marks him out as a failure. His parents, the narrator, and reader alike, cannot dismiss the significance of Esau's earlier behaviour as misplaced youthful exuberance or adolescent rebellion. While the twins' age is not provided for the birthright exchange, Esau's adulthood and autonomy cannot be ignored here: at forty he is the same age as Isaac, his father, was when he married Rebekah (Gen 25:20). We do not hear his words; his actions are clear enough. This is inescapably the rebellion of a mature and self-aware adult.

This interjection may be short and appear in marked contrast with that which precedes it, yet as the prelude to Genesis 27 it is invaluable for Esau. His actions have been noticed, and he has placed himself beyond the models of success placed upon him. Yet what faces him next is the harshest and most violent of his familial experiences. The events of the next phase of the Esau cycle are done to him and he just has to take whatever his family and the narrator throw at him. The last thing he does before entering this horrific gauntlet is to assert his own agency, autonomy and identity, even if it is disregarded by those around him. Despite this overt demonstration of agency, importantly, he knows not of what is to come. His action seems portentous, even if he is unaware of that. With even a glimpse at what faces him in the next phase of his story, I am inclined to see Esau's choice of wives – and the antagonism it causes – as an intentional defiant 'fuck you' to the expectations that seek so desperately to constrain him. Such indecency and failure cannot remain unpunished, which Genesis 27 will show, but these two verses indicate Esau is not going down without a fight.

---

way it is passed between generations. While I agree it is unsurprising, I consider this to add to the picture of Esau as a disregarded character; the carelessness with which his wives are recalled is indicative of the narrator's ongoing dismissiveness of Esau.

70. Robert Alter, *Genesis: Translation and Commentary* (New York: Norton, 1996), 136. His justification is that 'the morphology of the word points to a more likely derivation from m-r-h, "to rebel" or "to defy," and thus an equivalent such as provocation is more precise'. In this succinct term, so frequently glossed in translation to remove the agency and intentionality of rebellion or defiance, we glimpse another fleeting example of Esau's self-expression.

In childhood, Esau was seen only as the sum of his physique, which declared him to be a hypermale heir apparent to the patriarchy. In adolescence this trajectory made way for a widely condemned act of apparent self-sabotage, leading Esau to lose his birthright. Respecting Esau's agency and self-expression throughout the birthright trade, he emerged as someone pained – perhaps even at risk of death – by the expectations placed on him. By demanding the birthright in response to a request for sustenance, Jacob provides Esau with an exit from this restrictive gender drama. While the birthright symbolizes security and hope in the future for Jacob, for Esau the associations are with the life-limiting and constraining expectations placed on him because of assumptions made about him based primarily on his gender and sex. He is more than the sum of his body parts and his somatic experiences matter to him even if they do not to anyone around him. His subsequent provocative choice of wives further alienates him from his family and emphasizes his rebelliousness and lack of willingness to descend quickly and quietly into the anticipated and preferred route through life. He would rather 'fail' on his terms than succeed in an environment that will not allow him to do so as himself. Besides he has clearly asserted that he is not going to be constrained by the preferences of narrator or family, and he will find ways to subvert those expectations, even if only fleetingly. The problem is that such misbehaviour cannot remain unacknowledged; rejection of norms will almost certainly lead to condemnation. This is a story of gender norms – particularly cisnorms – and any castigation is likely to correspond with established patterns of transphobia or cissexism. We return to Esau's story with trepidation, but in anticipation that a trans-informed reading can bring clarity and context to the story as it unfurls.

A Man Mocked: Family-based Cissexist violence in Genesis 27:1–46

Esau's story has appeared in fits and bursts, and he has been given space to speak on just two occasions (Gen 25:30, 32). Just as Sarah experienced before him, a gender nonconforming character will struggle to hold the reader's attention, and throughout Genesis 27 that is made most visible. It is Jacob's mocking portrayal of Esau that holds attention, even while Esau is granted the greatest opportunity to speak in his whole life. His words function primarily as a counterpoint to those of Jacob rather than enabling Esau to appear openly before the reader. Genesis 27 represents the most violent and abusive treatment of Esau through the way he is absent at key moments; his embodiment is parodied and mocked by Jacob. His resultant fury is treated then as excessive and unmanly. The key players are known, along with their allegiances. Jacob, newly crowned heir to the birthright, remains Rebekah's favoured child and doyenne of the tents. Meanwhile, Esau and his masculine fortitude (typified by his hunting skills) carry Isaac's pride and joy. These allegiances will be tested, and the one between Esau and Isaac will ultimately fall due to the machinations of Rebekah and Jacob. In addition to these players, though, there is the constant spectre of Esau's body, whether he himself is present or not. The hypermasculine body that initially appeared laudable, before becoming the source of threat or instability, now becomes the focus for the cissexist violence directed toward Esau.[71]

Preparation

> When Isaac was old and his eyes were dim so that he could not see, he called his elder son Esau and said to him, 'My son'; and he answered, 'Here I am.' He said, 'See, I am old; I do not know the day of my death. Now then, take your weapons, your quiver and your bow, and go out to the field, and hunt game for me. Then prepare for me savoury food, such as I like, and bring it to me to eat, so that I may bless you before I die.'
> Now Rebekah was listening when Isaac spoke to his son Esau. So when Esau went to the field to hunt for game and bring it, Rebekah said to her son Jacob, 'I heard your father say to your brother Esau, "Bring me game, and prepare for me savoury food to eat, that I may bless you before the Lord before I die." Now therefore, my son, obey my word as I command you. Go to the flock, and get me two choice kids, so that I may prepare from them savoury food for your father, such as he likes; and you shall take it to your father to eat, so that he may bless you before he dies.' But Jacob said to his mother Rebekah, 'Look, my brother Esau is a hairy man, and I am a man of smooth skin. Perhaps my father will feel me, and I shall seem to be mocking him, and bring a curse on myself and not a blessing.' His mother said to him, 'Let your curse be on me, my son; only obey my word, and go, get them for me.' So he went and got them and brought them to his mother; and his mother prepared savoury food, such as his father loved. Then Rebekah took the best garments of her elder son Esau, which were with her in the house, and put them on her younger son Jacob; and she put the skins of the kids on his hands and on the smooth part of his neck. Then she handed the savoury food, and the bread that she had prepared, to her son Jacob.
>
> Gen 27:1–17

An indeterminate period after Esau's marriages, we return to Isaac in the company of Esau.[72] Isaac is now 'old and his eyes [are] dim,' when he calls his 'elder son Esau' to him, requesting that Esau hunt game and prepare a hearty meal before what he perceives to be his imminent death (Gen 27:1–4). These opening verses not only reveal the task at hand but also recall the most important aspects of the earlier narrative for this story. Isaac, the patriarch, is now old and 'his eyes were dim so that he could not see' (Gen 27:1), establishing him as the show's stooge who has fallen from implied glory. His masculinity is just a shadow of what once was. There is no need to witness Isaac at his prime, but merely to know that such times have gone for him. Meanwhile Esau's accoutred phallic masculinity is alluded to

---

71. Aspects of the following discussion of Jacob's performance as Esau also feature in Henderson-Merrygold, 'Jacob – A (Drag) King'.
72. Judith and Basemath, Esau's wives, are notably absent throughout.

through reference to his quiver and bow (v. 3).⁷³ These phallic allusions ensure that the most visible features of Esau's masculinity are front and centre before Jacob enters to begin the drag show.⁷⁴ His dick is on show, albeit euphemistically, just as it was in the birth narrative when Jacob grasped on to his 'heel' (25:26): the very 'heel' that provided the basis for Jacob's name and the perception of the younger twin as deceptive usurper. These visually striking images ensure that Esau's 'masculinity has first [been] made visible and theatrical before it can be performed'.⁷⁵ Esau clearly continues to be an adept hunter, a necessary skill to retain Isaac's preferential love, but has added to those skills the more feminine attribute of cook. The paternal love – here presented through the patriarch's blessing – remains as contingent on Esau's performance as did the initial declaration of favour in Genesis 25:28. In requesting Esau to serve him on this occasion he also reaffirms Esau's phallic embodied maleness. Esau's quiver and bow typify the male accoutrements that symbolize 'virile manhood' and successful masculinity.⁷⁶ Amidst this call-to-action Esau remains silent and even when he obliges, he does so without speaking (v. 5). His perspective is clearly not necessary in setting this scene since the authority to narrate and direct his life has returned to his elders and betters. It is only as Jacob and Rebekah begin to craft the costume that other facets of Esau's physicality begin to feature.

While Esau silently undertakes his task, Rebekah and Jacob enter the scene. Rebekah, having overheard Isaac's request, embarks upon a deception that will see Jacob acquire Esau's promised blessing (vv. 5–17). In contrast with the one-sided interaction between Esau and Isaac, Rebekah and Jacob discuss together the practicalities of their plan. Their discussion reveals how both sibling and parent see Esau's body. As Jacob explains: 'Look, my brother is a hairy man, and I am a man of smooth skin. Perhaps my father will feel me, and I shall seem to be mocking him, and bring a curse upon myself not a blessing' (vv. 11–12). While this picture recalls the natal image of Esau, the red and hairy baby of Genesis 25:25, he now appears a fully grown man trapped in the same image. Apparently unmoved by any of the other possible ways in which Isaac may differentiate his children, Esau's physicality dominates when Rebekah prepares Jacob for this deception. Rebekah dresses Jacob in Esau's best garments and puts 'the skins of kids on his hands and on the smooth part of his neck' (v. 16). She begins a transformation that will see Jacob perform the role of drag king. Meanwhile the Enkidu-like imagery reappears

---

73. Hoffner, 'Symbols for Masculinity and Femininity', 329. Hoffner considers Esau an example of 'the ideal male, the true "man's man" of ancient Canaan, [who] was skilled with the bow' in order to 'procure game for his table'. Guest draws on Hoffner in asserting the same tools – bow and arrow – contribute to the image of Jehu's phallic and accoutred masculinity in 2 Kgs 9–10. Guest, 'Modeling the Transgender Gaze', 59, 65–67.

74. See Boer, 'Patriarch's Nuts'. Boer effectively argues that the Jacob cycle is rich in euphemistic language and phallic allusion.

75. Halberstam, *Female Masculinity*, 235.

76. Hoffner, 'Symbols for Masculinity and Femininity', 329.

in this portrayal of Esau's body as a poor, animal-like opposite to the 'smooth skin' of Jacob, the preferred child. It is a striking visual juxtaposition to imagine Jacob in Esau's finest clothes whilst covered in this freshly butchered animal skin. It is all the more extraordinary to imagine that disguise proving sufficient to deceive Isaac, which it eventually does.

While Esau's body is indecent, Jacob's warrants no such condemnation. Now, for the first time the younger twin comes into view, and provides a suitably contrasting image to Esau. Without a natal image, Jacob is free to create and present *him*self in any way *he* chooses. Jacob begins by asserting his manhood – 'I am a *man* of smooth skin' (Gen 27:11, emphasis added) – but he could not look more different from Esau. In uttering these words Jacob begins to show that he alone has authority over how he and his body are understood in this narrative. Esau is afforded no such privilege. Jacob then begins to build his own body narrative; he ensures that an inscrutable image of a man (albeit in drag) stands clearly before Rebekah and the reader alike.[77]

Isaac's stated desire is for Esau's hunted game, cooked by Esau, yet Rebekah prepares for him the meat of kids from their own flock (vv. 3–4; cf. vv. 9–10). This is remarkable for its understated switch in roles. In preparing the meat herself, Rebekah removes the last vestiges of Jacob's feminine role as cook, and in doing so bolsters the nascent image of her *son*. Meanwhile it is Esau's cooking that warrants the praise from Isaac. In the time that Esau has been hidden from view (between the birthright exchange and this incident), the incoherent figure who could not name the red stew has become an accomplished cook. Rebekah is clearly acquainted enough with her elder child's cooking to mimic it for her husband, emphasizing Esau's familiarity with the domestic, feminine spaces. So, it is Rebekah's cooking that Jacob delivers mid performance to secure the paternal blessing, all while Esau continues in his search for the treasured meal. Once again small details of family life emerge in unexpected ways. While Rebekah is clearly acquainted with Isaac's preferences, Jacob is not, emphasising the ongoing distance between father and younger child. Esau, meanwhile, is not only the accomplished hunter, but also a cook capable of servicing his father's desires. Here his femininity begins to emerge, at exactly the point that Jacob takes on the role of drag king.

Jacob's performance reveals the stark contrast between the freedom granted to the younger sibling and the strictures faced by Esau. Jacob's latent, more fluid, gender enables him to emerge as drag king all the more clearly. 'Fluidity ... seems to define many of these drag kings' relations to gender expression, and few of them articulate a sense of being definitely bound to a category or mode of expression.'[78] Here the clear assertion of maleness emerges directly through the phrase 'I am a man...' (v. 11). No matter what happens beyond this performance now, at least,

---

77. Halberstam, *Female Masculinity*, 259. Halberstam describes the theatrics of the drag king who 'constrains and becomes silently macho' and who 'learns to convey volumes in a shrug or a raised eyebrow' (259).

78. Halberstam, *Female Masculinity*, 263.

Jacob is playing the man. This linguistic construction of Jacob's manhood has an interesting effect on the presentation of gender. It is in such marked contrast with the overly embodied and euphemistic terms used to describe Esau. Jacob has to verbally assert that male persona in order to stabilise it, but alongside those words is a tacit acknowledgement that without such articulation Jacob's manhood remains (at least partially) intangible. Through *his* words, Jacob affirms not only a current maleness, but also renders their own gender and identity unrecognizable by appearing earnest and delivering a 'reluctant and withholding kind of performance' (Gen 27:23).[79]

The performance aspect of Jacob's act comes through most clearly in the explicit recognition that the display has the power of mockery (v. 12). It is not a case of merely impersonating Esau in order to present a credible likeness. 'Whereas the male impersonator attempts to produce a plausible performance of maleness as the whole of her act, the drag king performs masculinity (often parodically) and makes the exposure of the theatricality of masculinity into the mainstay of her act'.[80] Jacob recognizes the risks inherent in such an act, and expresses concern at being seen to mock Isaac, but it is only the paternal deception that causes consternation, not the effect any performance may have on Esau. Both Jacob and Rebekah clearly know that the ruse can only lead to the discovery of the deception: Esau will return unless he is even more of a failed hunter than anticipated. This emphasizes all the more clearly the shared understanding that Jacob's role is that of actor in a drama, and one that relies yet again on Esau's failures. Rebekah offers herself as mitigation of the risk, while Jacob also recognizes that kinging carries with it a core component of irreverent imitation and a mockery that is designed to have an impact beyond mere impersonation. The problem for Esau emerges more powerfully as the performance establishes. He is already trying to show a rejection of the idealized masculinity into which he has been forced since birth, but it is through Jacob's drag performance that the sham of such ideals is made most visible. The consequence is that Esau, who remains yet to speak or even hold the narrator's attention in Genesis 27, is treated as a secondary source for his own life. Rather Jacob's parodic kinging is the authoritative image of Esau's (gender) identity, relegating Esau further from the focus of the narrative.

Performance

> So he went in to his father, and said, 'My father'; and he said, 'Here I am; who are you, my son?' Jacob said to his father, 'I am Esau your firstborn. I have done as you told me; now sit up and eat of my game, so that you may bless me.' But Isaac said to his son, 'How is it that you have found it so quickly, my son?' He answered, 'Because the LORD your God granted me success.' Then Isaac said to Jacob, 'Come near, that I may feel you, my son, to know whether you are really my son Esau or not.' So Jacob went up to his father Isaac, who felt him and said, 'The

---

79. Halberstam, *Female Masculinity*, 239.

voice is Jacob's voice, but the hands are the hands of Esau.' He did not recognize him, because his hands were hairy like his brother Esau's hands; so he blessed him. He said, 'Are you really my son Esau?' He answered, 'I am.' Then he said, 'Bring it to me, that I may eat of my son's game and bless you.' So he brought it to him, and he ate; and he brought him wine, and he drank. Then his father Isaac said to him, 'Come near and kiss me, my son.' So he came near and kissed him; and he smelled the smell of his garments, and blessed him, and said,

'Ah, the smell of my son
  is like the smell of a field that the LORD has blessed.
May God give you of the dew of heaven,
  and of the fatness of the earth,
  and plenty of grain and wine.
Let peoples serve you,
  and nations bow down to you.
Be lord over your brothers,
  and may your mother's sons bow down to you.
Cursed be everyone who curses you,
  and blessed be everyone who blesses you!'

Gen 27:18–30

Jacob now embarks on a new level of performance before Isaac. Jacob, the drag king, has now created a different character to deploy in this next part of the show: faux-Esau. It is worth recalling here that Jacob's kinging did not start with receipt of the stew or when enrobed in the costume. Rather, it began when Jacob arrived and asserted a manhood to rival Esau's. This new aspect of the performance adds elements of layering and hyperbole to the kinging act. These reflect the drag king's skill in 'finding the exact form of masculine hyperbole' whilst enabling multiple gendered layers to peek through performing, especially as a recognizable figure such as Esau.[81] The risk increases exponentially; Isaac is the unwitting stooge in the drama, and Jacob's success relies on paternal recognition of an authentic enough Esau in the ersatz presentation before him. Jacob's carefully crafted kinging facilitates disbelief, especially through earnest, cautious and, at times, understated gesture, alongside carefully articulated words.

Jacob's opening words to Isaac are as carefully crafted and important as those uttered to Rebekah, but here they are far more succinct – at least initially. Von Rad observes that 'the narrator has described Jacob meeting with his father very sparingly'.[82] The initial address 'My father' is met by an uncertain but nevertheless

---

80. Halberstam, *Female Masculinity*, 232.

81. Halberstam, *Female Masculinity*, 259. 'When a drag king performs as a recognizable male persona (Sinatra, Elvis, Brando), she can choose to allow her femaleness to peek through, as some drag queens do in camp, or she can perform the role seamlessly'.

82. von Rad, *Genesis: A Commentary*, 277.

telling response from Isaac, 'who are you, my son?' (v. 18). Jacob's assertion invites Isaac's recognition of his *son*, a role that ordinarily Jacob has not readily been seen in. The expression of these roles and relationships is unambiguous at this point, even if the use of such terms by each is unfamiliar prior to this point. There is a clear differentiation between Rebekah and Jacob on the one hand, and Isaac and Esau on the other, that has been there since the twins' infancy. Jacob's life within the tents, amongst the women, was clearly separated from Esau's manly role as hunter (Gen 25:27-34). Even as Rebekah prepared the stew, she expressed her familiarity with Isaac's preferred food, something she held in common with her elder child, but apparently not shared with the younger one (Gen 27:9, 15, 31). It is a striking image of a parent and child unfamiliar with one another, but it is that unfamiliarity that initially leads Isaac to tentatively recognize Jacob as both faux-Esau and son. Jacob speaks immediately to both settle and disorient Isaac when he says: 'I am Esau your firstborn. I have done as you told me; now sit up and eat of my game, so that you may bless me' (v. 19). First, he confidently asserts his identity as (faux-)Esau, then invites Isaac to recall the request, before turning to focus on the goal: receipt of the paternal blessing after successful deception. Jacob displays a loquaciousness not directly matched by Esau, either earlier in Genesis or later when the elder sibling delivers his own food (Gen 27:19; cf. v. 31) yet it is sufficient to settle Isaac's concerns.[83] Jacob's confident performance assuages Isaac's concerns, even when he remarks on the speedy arrival of his meal and hearing the voice of Jacob (vv. 20, 22).

The image of Esau's body predominates Isaac's focus, even while the patriarch eats the food and talks to faux-Esau. He even remarks on the delightful recognizability of the odour of his favoured son, something that adds an unusual or awkward insight into Esau's embodiment (v. 27). This continues the repeated motif of adding an additional detail or layer to Esau's male physique to move it from the ordinary into the realm of the excessive. Here the odour is a strange addition, but it adds to the disquieting image of the elder twin's physique. It combines with Isaac's references to Esau's phallic maleness (via quiver and arrows) in Genesis 25:3, and the narrator's repeated interest in the hairiness of Esau's hands (vv. 22-23). Equally Isaac's disregard for *hearing* his younger child's voice, also something in marked difference from Esau's based on the patriarch's reaction, shows how little weight he puts in Esau's words. Again, the image appears of the man who fails to communicate successfully with those around him.

In order to perform as Esau (or at least his body), Jacob must also draw on other aspects of the drag king's arts. Jacob not only embodies the role of faux-Esau,

---

83. v. 19: 'Jacob said to his father, "I am Esau your firstborn. I have done as you told me; now sit up and eat of my game, so that you may bless me."' Cf. v. 31 'He also prepared savoury food, and brought it to his father. And he said to his father, "Let my father sit up and eat of his son's game, so that you may bless me"'. It is only when Isaac directly prompts Esau for response that he adds 'I am your firstborn son, Esau' (v. 32).

but also renders their own gender and identity unrecognizable by appearing uncharacteristically earnest (Gen 27:23).[84] Jacob's performance also requires careful use of gesture, whilst also ensuring he says enough to secure Isaac's engagement. The whole charade offers a creative portrayal of not only Esau, but also the hypocrisy inherent in Isaac's idealization of his elder child's (physical) masculinity.[85] Even though Isaac's eyes fail him (27:1), he will persist in relying on the image of Esau despite words and actions that indicate deception. Jacob, now the consummate artist, 'renders visible the mechanisms of privilege' that fuel the lascivious desire for that which Esau's masculinity symbolizes.[86] As if describing Jacob's show, 'the drag king performance, indeed, exposes the structure of dominant masculinity by making it theatrical and by rehearsing the repertoire of roles and types on which masculinity depends'.[87]

It is the idolization of Esau's masculinity in combination with an engaging theatrical show that enables the suspense of disbelief and offers a reason to those commentators who find the endeavour wholly incredible. Brayford observes that 'unable to distinguish between the hair of an animal and the hair of his older son, Isaac is deceived. His ears tell him that he's hearing Jacob's voice, but his hands tell him differently.... The scent of Esau's robes that Rebekah put around Jacob convinces Isaac that it is Esau he is blessing.'[88] Here Esau just does not matter enough for the performance to go unchallenged. The patriarch's obliviousness to Esau continues as he seems unaware of the birthright trade from Genesis 25.[89] Esau's character was fixed at the moment of his birth and nothing can create a way for Isaac to see his son beyond those initial, highly gendered, and sexed images (Gen 26:34–35). It is this interest in what Esau represents, not who Esau is that makes Jacob's portrayal of faux-Esau so successful. And it is what marks it so essentially as a drag performance. The most significant thing for Isaac in this story is the recognizability of Esau's body; we have been told as much since his birth and the narrative persists in reducing him to his body as established earlier in the story (Gen 25:29–34). Here Isaac does exactly the same once again: Esau is nothing more than his physical body. Jacob's faux-Esau, who symbolizes the hegemonic masculine ideal, is presented as no more than a young kid in human form, draped with finery. The story has not run its course: Esau remains unaware of what has befallen him in his absence, yet Jacob will not sit around and wait for the fall-out. It is now Jacob's turn to make the strategic exit.

---

84. Halberstam, *Female Masculinity*, 239.

85. Muñoz, *Disidentification*, 133. Muñoz argues that camp such as that on display in Jacob's performance 'imagines new realities' on the one hand whilst 'also lodg[ing], through auspices of humor, a pointed social critique', especially on gendered privilege.

86. Muñoz, *Disidentification*, 135.

87. Halberstam, *Female Masculinity*, 239.

88. Brayford, *Genesis*, 351.

89. Davidson, *Genesis 12–50*, 138.

Facing the Consequences

As soon as Isaac had finished blessing Jacob, when Jacob had scarcely gone out from the presence of his father Isaac, his brother Esau came in from his hunting. He also prepared savoury food, and brought it to his father. And he said to his father, 'Let my father sit up and eat of his son's game, so that you may bless me.' His father Isaac said to him, 'Who are you?' He answered, 'I am your firstborn son, Esau.' Then Isaac trembled violently, and said, 'Who was it then that hunted game and brought it to me, and I ate it all before you came, and I have blessed him? – yes, and blessed he shall be!' When Esau heard his father's words, he cried out with an exceedingly great and bitter cry, and said to his father, 'Bless me, me also, father!' But he said, 'Your brother came deceitfully, and he has taken away your blessing.' Esau said, 'Is he not rightly named Jacob? For he has supplanted me these two times. He took away my birthright; and look, now he has taken away my blessing.' Then he said, 'Have you not reserved a blessing for me?' Isaac answered Esau, 'I have already made him your lord, and I have given him all his brothers as servants, and with grain and wine I have sustained him. What then can I do for you, my son?' Esau said to his father, 'Have you only one blessing, father? Bless me, me also, father!' And Esau lifted up his voice and wept.

Then his father Isaac answered him:

'See, away from the fatness of the earth shall your home be,
  and away from the dew of heaven on high.
By your sword you shall live,
  and you shall serve your brother;
but when you break loose,
  you shall break his yoke from your neck.'

Now Esau hated Jacob because of the blessing with which his father had blessed him, and Esau said to himself, 'The days of mourning for my father are approaching; then I will kill my brother Jacob.' But the words of her elder son Esau were told to Rebekah; so she sent and called her younger son Jacob and said to him, 'Your brother Esau is consoling himself by planning to kill you. Now therefore, my son, obey my voice; flee at once to my brother Laban in Haran, and stay with him for a while, until your brother's fury turns away – until your brother's anger against you turns away, and he forgets what you have done to him; then I will send, and bring you back from there. Why should I lose both of you in one day?'

Then Rebekah said to Isaac, 'I am weary of my life because of the Hittite women. If Jacob marries one of the Hittite women such as these, one of the women of the land, what good will my life be to me?'

Gen 27:31–46

While Jacob is serving Isaac Rebekah's food, Esau is busy preparing his game as requested; he is as oblivious to the machinations of his mother and sibling as is his father who feasts elsewhere (vv. 31–32). It is only when he presents himself and his cooking before Isaac that either becomes aware of their statuses as stooge (Isaac) and victim (Esau) in the drama. 'Isaac trembled violently' in response to realising he has been deceived, which leads Esau to cry 'out with an exceedingly great and bitter cry' (vv. 33–34). The Esau who appears here is devoid of the references to his body that have punctuated his story until now – they have served their purpose. Jacob's performance as Esau was so outrageous yet successful that Esau's body is carefully excised from the text so that any recollection remains focussed on the image of the kidskin enrobed smooth and effeminate twin in drag. Here he appears angry but articulate; there is no misinterpreting his words on this occasion as he requests a paternal blessing, which Isaac declares that he cannot provide having given it to Jacob (vv. 34–35). Esau despairingly remarks 'is he not rightly named Jacob? For he supplanted me two times. He took away my birthright; and look, now he has taken away my blessing' (v. 36). On further rejection of his request, Esau 'lifted up his voice and wept'; this is met with a lesser blessing from Isaac, albeit after recognition that Jacob has been made lord over Esau (vv. 37–40). In this interaction Esau demonstrates an eloquence he has previously lacked, and his impassioned dialogue replaces the attention to his failed tasks. On this occasion his hunting is successful, as is his cooking, yet he is at last usurped. Jacob's actions, in combination with Rebekah's cooking, satiated Isaac so successfully that Esau's entire purpose in the family is rendered null and void. Even the love, first expressed in Genesis 25:28 appears at risk as it is no longer Esau alone who can provide Isaac with the game he so loves.

Esau leaves a broken man. Devoid of the favour of his father, he has lost more than just the status associated with either birthright or blessing. The loss of the former symbol of his patriarchal dividend was at least partially consensual, albeit under duress. The second is entirely against his will and leads directly to his hatred of Jacob, the thief and deceiver. The result is that he expresses his hatred by exclaiming a desire to kill Jacob (v. 41). Esau's anger is reported to Rebekah and she promptly returns to scheming with Jacob to secure the younger child's future to the cost of the elder (vv. 41–45). Esau is not allowed his understandable anger; like so many other examples of Esau's personhood it is treated as excessive in order to make it appear unnatural and unacceptable. The anger is all-consuming, visceral, almost animalistic, in keeping with the animalistic, visceral somatic desires of Genesis 25:29–34. Esau is once again presented as the embodiment of indecency. The final verse completes the chapter in such a way as to leave Esau silenced. Rebekah makes an argument to convince Isaac to dispatch Jacob to her brother, for the good of the family, so he does not become like Esau (v. 46). Rebekah is allowed to hate and scheme about Esau's wives – who form the justification for Jacob's commissioning (rather than exile), from the perspective of Isaac – but Esau cannot be trusted with his hatred of his family. That Isaac does not reject, or even challenge, this argument indicates that he is persuaded of the risk Esau presents. Esau is seen as an incomprehensibly volatile and unstable hypermale figure who, in the face of the violence perpetrated against him by parents and sibling alike, will shortly be excised from the text, leaving only the shadow of reported utterances and decisions made about, but not with, him.

Such presentation of Esau is not accidental in a narrative described as 'skilfully constructed'.[90] The most enduring theme for writers primarily attentive to Jacob's arc is the successful acquisition of Esau's blessing – even if it is through deception. This comes through perpetually refusing to see the validity of Esau's perspective. The story prior to Genesis 27 succeeds in creating him as an unreliable commentator even within his own life. The concluding exile faced by Jacob is considered 'a bitter harvest' that results from cheating and deception, but that usually remains the extent of any recognition of the consequences for either of the twins; Esau's perspective is noticeably absent.[91] The closest acknowledgement of the cost for Esau is found in Isaac's prayer of blessing. Isaac notes the hardships that will face Esau but acknowledges that his eldest son will (continue to) live (vv. 39–40). It is not a blessing for joy, happiness, wealth or success. There are no positive markers beyond the hope that Esau will persist in the endeavour of living, but he need not thrive in that life![92]

At the conclusion of the story Esau has been betrayed, not only in the loss of the paternal blessing, but in the abrupt lack of acceptance and recognition of his identity within the family. The loss of the blessing symbolises the catastrophic loss that Esau has just experienced. He expresses his anger and frustration on two occasions (Gen 27:33–34 and 27:41) and neither is heard as valid by those around him. In the first instance his great and bitter cry is 'not the macho response of biblical men who experience an injustice and respond with rage and revenge. Rather, it matches word for word the anguished cry of a biblical woman – Hagar – as she puts Ishmael down in the desert and walks away so as not to watch him die'.[93] On the second occasion his anger is treated as excess: how dare he be beyond consolation in response to the egregious act of violence perpetrated against him by his family! They cannot accept someone who persistently fails in the duties assigned to him due to the appearance of his body at birth. Esau utters his desire to literally kill the one who has taken relish in a performance to destroy him: Jacob. Jacob ensured that Esau's personhood could be denied by their parents, effectively rendering Esau dead. The reciprocal response from Esau – to kill Jacob – is taken literally and met with implicit condemnation within the narrative as Rebekah discerns Esau's plan through divine guidance. On this occasion, perhaps because they conform to the expectations placed on Esau due to his physique, stature and profession, the emotions are acknowledged. Maybe the reason is also the threat Esau's explosive comment holds for Jacob, but there is no suggestion that this is merely an impassioned cry of pain that will, in time, pass.[94]

---

90. Davidson, *Genesis 12–50*, 137.

91. Davidson, *Genesis 12–50*, 138.

92. Westermann, *Genesis*, 195. For Westermann 'you shall live' in v. 40 is crucial in understanding both Isaac's prayer and Esau's life: 'Esau is to have a hard life, but he will live'.

93. Lev, 'Esau's Gender Crossing', 40. Lev contrasts Esau's response with those reported in Gen 34:7, 13–26 and Judg 19–20.

94. Westermann, *Genesis*, 195. Amongst those taking the threat to Jacob literally include Westermann who explores the opportunities for fratricide and the potential optimum time.

A new problem then emerges through the reappearance of a character who has not made an appearance since Rebekah was pregnant: God intervenes to uphold Jacob on the one hand, and to invalidate or undermine Esau's anger. God's intervention implicitly justifies the dehumanisation of Esau through the reduction of individual to body devoid of emotion, identity, or self-expression. When later voices in the Hebrew Bible and New Testament assert that God hated Esau,[95] I consider their argument to be a justifiable claim. Not for the reasons they imply, but because within this narrative God authorizes the violence perpetrated against Esau.

A Nod Towards Decency? – Genesis 28:6–9

Now Esau saw that Isaac had blessed Jacob and sent him away to Paddan-aram to take a wife from there, and that as he blessed him he charged him, 'You shall not marry one of the Canaanite women', and that Jacob had obeyed his father and his mother and gone to Paddan-aram. So when Esau saw that the Canaanite women did not please his father Isaac, Esau went to Ishmael and took Mahalath daughter of Abraham's son Ishmael, and sister of Nebaioth, to be his wife in addition to the wives he had.

Gen 28:6–9

While Jacob may be the one exiled from the familial home at the end of Genesis 27, it is Esau who has to remain at home and deal with the consequences. The only insight offered by the narrator is another comment on a new marriage for Esau. Just as his marriages in Genesis 26:34–35 consolidated the earlier narrative, the same occurs here, albeit with one marked difference. Esau's actions are not those of autonomous, and perhaps isolated, defiance, but rather appear as an intentional act of failure to reject his parent's authority. In this storyline details of Esau's life are placed in the midst of a narrative focussed on Jacob. Jacob has just received spoken instructions from his father which say, in effect, 'do not be like Esau' (v. 6). The narrator consolidates this instruction by confirming that Jacob 'obeyed his father and mother' (v. 7), leaving Esau facing unspoken paternal disapproval relegating him even further to a position of silence on the outside (v. 8). Without speaking he embarks on a new, potentially more favourable, marriage (v. 9), before he fades from view (until Genesis 33) while Jacob takes primacy. Unlike his earlier marriages, his new wife is partially from a shared family line. Mahalath's maternal line is unknown, while her father Ishmael's comes from the line of Terah: it is insufficient. Esau's decision to marry a child of his uncle carries further problematic connotations. Ishmael, like his nephew, is the less favoured elder sibling who has

---

95. Jeremiah 49.8–10 refers to the calamity of Esau, akin to punishment. Malachi 2–3 ascribes the phrase 'I have hated Esau' to God, a reference recalled in Romans 9.13. Hebrews 12.16 describes Esau as 'an immoral and godless person'.

been overlooked for the sake of the younger child. Esau marries a woman whose legacy is tarnished by a similar perception of failure to his own. The result is that he is cast aside by the narrator which further emphasizes that he is condemned to fail, whether intentionally or not, and thus must fade out of view.

A Life Beyond Constraints of Family and Body – Genesis 33:1-17

Now Jacob looked up and saw Esau coming, and four hundred men with him. So he divided the children among Leah and Rachel and the two maids. He put the maids with their children in front, then Leah with her children, and Rachel and Joseph last of all. He himself went on ahead of them, bowing himself to the ground seven times, until he came near his brother.

But Esau ran to meet him, and embraced him, and fell on his neck and kissed him, and they wept. When Esau looked up and saw the women and children, he said, 'Who are these with you?' Jacob said, 'The children whom God has graciously given your servant.' Then the maids drew near, they and their children, and bowed down; Leah likewise and her children drew near and bowed down; and finally Joseph and Rachel drew near, and they bowed down. Esau said, 'What do you mean by all this company that I met?' Jacob answered, 'To find favour with my lord.' But Esau said, 'I have enough, my brother; keep what you have for yourself.' Jacob said, 'No, please; if I find favour with you, then accept my present from my hand; for truly to see your face is like seeing the face of God – since you have received me with such favour. Please accept my gift that is brought to you, because God has dealt graciously with me, and because I have everything I want.' So he urged him, and he took it.

Then Esau said, 'Let us journey on our way, and I will go alongside you.' But Jacob said to him, 'My lord knows that the children are frail and that the flocks and herds, which are nursing, are a care to me; and if they are overdriven for one day, all the flocks will die. Let my lord pass on ahead of his servant, and I will lead on slowly, according to the pace of the cattle that are before me and according to the pace of the children, until I come to my lord in Seir.'

So Esau said, 'Let me leave with you some of the people who are with me.' But he said, 'Why should my lord be so kind to me?' So Esau returned that day on his way to Seir. But Jacob journeyed to Succoth, and built himself a house, and made booths for his cattle; therefore the place is called Succoth.

Gen 33:1-17

Esau's final appearance in Genesis is in marked contrast with his portrayal in earlier accounts, and only appears after a sustained absence from the narrative. He is sidelined after failing to conform once again. Now, however, he appears a different person. Westermann, for example, sees here an authentic portrayal of man, in contrast with the earlier caricature found in Genesis 25:19-34.[96] He appears

---

96. Westermann, *Genesis 12-36*, 417; *Genesis*, 183-184.

a nuanced, rounded character, not that Jacob is aware of this apparent shift in Esau's demeanour. The younger twin prepares for this encounter with trepidation (vv. 1-4). The anticipated Esau is the one Jacob mocked in the drag show: the failure of a man whose animalistic tendencies accompany his incompetence, but whose anger has the power to emerge physically. Yet Jacob seems to have little awareness that this characterization has always been a fictive nonsense. Here, in this final encounter, the twins are free from the persistent reminders of Esau's sexed body or the machinations of their parents. For the first time Esau can provide an account of himself through his own words and actions, without the demand that he must also reveal his failures. He is even graced with markers of success: he travels with a party of four hundred men (32:6). Despite its ominous introduction in Genesis 32:1-22, the narrator provides an account of what Esau does that is not a reductive account of his body nor does it place the twins in conflict with each other.

Esau's emotional expression, communication and behaviour appear for the first time to fall within the normal and anticipated parameters for a biblical man. No longer is he the embodiment of excess, although his lack of proper decency still peeks through when he runs enthusiastically towards Jacob.[97] The interaction between siblings, particularly from Esau's perspective, is open, polite and engaging. Instead, it is Jacob who appears the exaggerated figure constructed through reference to natal attributes: Jacob is the manipulative deceiver once again. The display of humility and generosity performed by Jacob and family is sufficiently excessive that Esau, on this occasion, queries the intention (v. 8).[98] The ever-consummate actor begins by the exaggerated performance of humility found in the seven bows (v. 3) and Jacob's repeated use of the terms 'My lord' and Jacob as 'your servant' (vv. 6, 8, 13, 14, 15); as von Rad astutely writes, Jacob is 'completely subservient'.[99] There is no nuance or subtlety in Jacob's words or actions. Esau, meanwhile, refers to Jacob as 'my brother' (v. 9), greeting Jacob fondly without the 'hint of the murderous bitterness with which they parted (27:41-42)'.[100] All of Jacob's children and their mothers contribute to this act of apparent deference, yet Esau appears without wives or child (Gen 33:6-7; cf. 36:1-41). Despite Esau's warmth and openness, Jacob still treats the elder twin with disdain, lying to him and duplicitously heading in the opposite direction to the one stated to Esau (vv. 14-17). The response to Esau's apparent change in character is notable. Davidson's surprise is evident through his parenthetical remark: 'The tension is broken as

---

97. Claire Amos, *The Book of Genesis*, Epworth Commentaries, (Peterborough: Epworth, 2004), 206. 'The spontaneity of Esau's generous welcome still contrasts with Jacob's more formal response'. Whereas von Rad considers Esau's actions quite impulsive, 'in clear contrast with the deliberate Jacob'. von Rad, *Genesis: A Commentary*, 327.

98. Wenham, *Genesis 16-50*. Wenham notes his incredulity, albeit through problematic allusions, that 'even oriental courtesy would not lead to such extravagant humility toward a twin brother'.

99. von Rad, *Genesis: A Commentary*, 327.

100. Wenham, *Genesis 16-50*.

Esau, *who is depicted in a very favourable light*, warmly embraces his brother' (emphasis added).[101] Westermann strikingly describes Esau's behaviour towards Jacob as 'heartfelt and natural'.[102] Not all voices are so supportive; others treat Jacob's deception as (continued) evidence of Esau's inescapable failures. For Bruce Vawter, Jacob's deception reiterates the sense of a man easily deceived, while for John Skinner Esau's hostile intention 'cannot reasonably be doubted'.[103]

In this encounter Jacob remains in continuity with the assignations at birth: Jacob the deceiver. This image is persistently cultivated, with Jacob even securing economic and familial security through a duplicitous battle of wits with Laban (Gen 28-31). Esau and Isaac are not the only victims of Jacob's deception. This oily performance continues in the legacy of the earlier drag act: however on this stage it appears excessively calculated rather than understated or earnest. Instead, it is Esau who comes across as the unassuming figure, even if he still cannot perfectly gauge social convention and etiquette. His physical expression of love to Jacob disregards the expected male propriety and, perhaps, reveals another of his more feminine attributes. Esau appears changed, but with the enduring spectre of the failure brought on by his social ineptitude, the symbol of his gender nonconformity remains present. The biggest shift, however, is in the absolute disinterest in Esau's physicality and the assignations made at birth that have so confined him until this point. Here he is able to demonstrate his embodiment through the hug with Jacob, but it is a confident and intimate appearance. It is the only physical expression of love shared between the siblings in their entire story. It is not reliant on references to his phallic or accoutred masculinity, and attention to his ruddy hairiness is absent. Esau is *finally* allowed to be himself, free from the constraints of the sexed and gendered expectations placed upon him at birth. Halberstam reminds us that flourishing as a gender nonconforming character cannot be sustained. Especially now he appears happy, content and settled, Esau cannot sustain this gaze, which rejects someone who finds delight and identity in (gender) failure. It is the ultimate incoherence of Esau: having been defined through excessive attention to his body, it is not possible to recognize the man without that constantly narrated body. Esau can only truly be himself once that constraint is removed.

Esau, like Sarah before him, must disappear from view.[104] He appears just once more, very briefly, and without any inclusion of words or actions, or even attention to his body. On Isaac's death, Esau's attendance at the burial is acknowledged alongside that of Jacob (Gen 35:29).[105] Immediately thereafter the genealogy of

101. Davidson, *Genesis 12-50*, 189.

102. Westermann, *Genesis*, 232. In his extended commentary Westermann opts for '[Esau] greets him naturally and warmly', conveying once again the normal, comfortable and safe Esau who now appears in the narrative. Westermann, *Genesis 12-36*, 525.

103. Vawter, *On Genesis*, 353. 'For all his panoply of success and power, Esau is as easily gulled as he was so long ago'. See also Skinner, *Critical and Exegetical Commentary*, 412.

104. Halberstam, *In a Queer Time*. See also Chapter 3.

105. And Isaac breathed his last; he died and was gathered to his people, old and full of days; and his sons Esau and Jacob buried him.

Esau's descendants is recounted (Gen 36). These two details add further to the carefully curated image of a conforming, rather than failing, Esau. He has fathered the requisite progeny, and his descendants have done similarly. At the conclusion of Esau's story, he appears the dutiful son and father, who achieves the most important aspects of manhood, but that is only possible through disregarding the person himself. Esau cannot and does not appear again. Both his failures and his successes as a gender nonconforming man are overridden by the narratorial insistence that he is, ultimately, a successful although undesirable masculine figure.

Conclusion

Esau's experiences correspond closely with so many accounts of the constraining impact of the assignation of sex at birth that does not cohere with our own understanding of self or body. Throughout his life he struggles to escape from the bodily designations that convey gendered expectations upon him: his ruddiness, his hairiness, and his penis. These features map out a life for him, and demand he succeeds in the anticipated roles and duties – but he does not. Esau repeated fails to display the masculinity required, most frequently in subtle, minuscule ways. These are most striking in narratives where his success should be a foregone conclusion, but he fails, most notably in Genesis 25:29–34. Even when he attempts to complete actions or take on roles that appear successful at first glance, there is always that small, sometimes almost imperceptible, aspect of failure: completing the outdoors task – but failing to secure sufficient sustenance; asking for much-needed nourishment – but fumbling the words; marrying – but selecting insufficiently endogamous wives – on two occasions; greeting Jacob with a warm and gracious embrace – but not observing expected social decorum. He is the consummate embodiment of the artful failure Halberstam advocates.[106] The persistence of this failure, in combination with Esau's striking physique, gives Jacob and Rebekah sufficient impetus to deliver a performance that mocks him catastrophically. His maleness may be the vessel for that abuse, but Jacob's act makes a stooge of Isaac – father and (eldest) son are brought face to face with the consequences of privileging and failing in masculine expectations. Jacob emerges unscathed by these endeavours, while Esau faces condemnation from his own family and the narrator for what is done to him. Isaac's silent response to Esau's marriage to his niece says all that needs to be said about his ongoing love and

---

106. Halberstam, *Queer Art of Failure*, 147. 'I have made the case for stupidity, failure, and forgetfulness over knowing, mastering, and remembering in terms of contemporary knowledge formations. The social world we inhabit, as so many thinkers have reminded us, are not inevitable, they were not always bound to turn out this way, and what's more, in the process of producing *this* reality, many other realities, fields of knowledge and ways of being have been discarded'.

respect for his eldest child, who he formerly cherished so highly. Esau is usurped, and it is his failure to conform to gender expectations that is his undoing.

Amidst this story there are small signs of hope and life for Esau. His identity and agency may frequently be overlooked by his family, but it is recorded by the narrator. In these small ruptures his perspective brings essential knowledge and adds to the richness of a gendered life. Yet that complexly gendered life demonstrates a capaciousness beyond the markers found in a binary gender model. The difficulties he faces in conveying his perspective to those around him also corresponds with the challenge for recognition faced by gender-nonconforming individuals. It is his actions that become important as they do not require the same narration. His unwelcome acts show an intentionality that he is rarely afforded, and time and time again these acts move him from the realm of the decent (typified by the familial expectations), into the realm of the indecent. When he is encountered one last time in Genesis 33, free from the baggage laid upon him, he emerges as a confident, warm, articulate person. The image of Esau in this final appearance cannot be sustained, not least because it would call into question the validity of so many of the preconceptions nurtured in the text, so he must disappear. Esau's gender failures not only call into question narrow, binary gender expectations but also open up the possibility of a more diverse genderscape. In this story cispicion can, and does, reveal an embodiment of gender that is more diverse than merely vacillating between expectations of masculinity and femininity. Esau's story shows that whimsical indecency allows space for a gendered life that offers untold possibilities beyond our male/masculine, female/feminine expectations. Nevertheless, his story like Sarah's before him, makes clear that there is insufficient space within these ancestral narratives for an individual who wants to live beyond the gender norms. Sarah and Esau show that there is a rich thread of gender diversity hidden within the narratives, and this cispicious interpretation is one way of revealing it.

CONCLUSION

Throughout the course of this project, I have presented a new hermeneutical strategy, attentive to cisnormativity, that opens up the potential for a more diverse biblical genderscape. It continues in the established tradition of biblical hermeneutics of suspicion by naming and responding to a specific ideology. My cispicious endeavour has led me to flesh out what it means for biblical interpretation if we read with a commitment to challenge cisnormative presuppositions.

I began with an exploration of indecent whimsy, a playful approach that does not take too seriously the expectations of propriety, decency, success or intelligibility. Instead, like Jack Halberstam, I have been interested in small ruptures and inconsistencies that allow me to open up new possibilities for the characters whose lives I interpret. Informed by trans theory – notably that of Julia Serano, Jay Prosser and Viviane Namaste – my approach embeds a recognition of the disconnection between trans experiences and their cis counterparts. Here, I have resisted the tendency for the latter to be centred while the former are marginalized and explained away to keep them beyond either narrative centring or the perception of normality. I have integrated these insights into the established pattern of suspicious hermeneutics, which attend to specific areas of structural or systematic oppression. In doing so I have emphasized that cisnormativity is not inherent within the biblical texts, but has been and remains today prevalent in readers' presuppositions. The overwhelming majority of readers assume that biblical characters, like the people we encounter in everyday life, are ordinarily, perpetually fixed and binary in their sex and gender. Through the development and application of a hermeneutic of cispicion it becomes possible to see beyond those presumptions.

The approach employed here supports an innovative model for interpretation that develops Deryn Guest's paradigm-shifting hermeneutic of hetero-suspicion into the hermeneutic of cispicion. Guest's work has shown the need for, and potential value of, diversifying the genderscape. Indeed, they have embedded a commitment to gender nonconformity throughout their work. That work has remained largely intertwined with their lesbian-identified approach. Guest's scholarship carefully addresses heteronormativity, and in doing so attends to both gender *and* sexuality. That is also the limitation on their work. They predominantly address nonconforming masculinities and give little space for femininities of any form. Through refining and recontextualizing Guest's approach to address specifically cisnormative concerns, I have demonstrated the value in looking at a broader model of gender than their scholarship showcases. More work is needed in this area since my case studies also (re)present characters for whom masculinity is a large part of their identity, although both Esau and Sarai/h also demonstrate small but nevertheless discernible aspects of femininity. This emphasis on masculinity is, in no small part, due to biblical – especially the ancestral – narratives privileging (appropriately) masculine characters. Nevertheless, their perspectives are not the only ones that emerge from a cispicious reading of the text.

My initial focus was to develop from existing methods by reshaping them to focus more explicitly on challenging cis-assumption and cis-privilege in literary characters. Halberstam provided much of the framework. Three aspects of his insights into the portrayal of gender diversity, especially nonconformity, in text and media profoundly shape this endeavour. First, he recognises the diversity inherent within the category of masculinity. This diversity can be found in various ways among individuals AFAB as well as those for whom masculinity is treated as natural and normal (i.e., AMAB). Through this exploration, Halberstam encourages engaging with ways masculinity – and by implication femininity – appear in unexpected locations. That such locations can even be considered unexpected reveals how enduring is the assumption that women must be feminine, men must be masculine, and there is no space for any other ways of being. Yet Halberstam shows those categories are repeatedly, perpetually ruptured. He also acknowledges that within a cisnormative context, such discontinuities are punishable and mark that individual as a failure. Second, Halberstam demonstrates ways of using these very symbols of discontinuity to reveal gender diversity that is otherwise hidden or rendered as recognizably other, as through the tropes of stabilization, rationalization and trivialization. By using these tropes as indicators of gender nonconformity, opportunities arise for reclamation, celebration or imaginative recreation. In other words, Halberstam makes it possible to see apparent failures or enforced marginalization as a point of entry to identify diverse, nonconforming gender presentations. He consolidates this attentiveness in his low theory. It not only provides tools for revealing new knowledge and insights but also expresses why it is so important not to rely solely on traditional, established methods. Instead, the playful, whimsical approach that challenges hegemonic presumptions about the norms of gender, sex and sexuality he advocates brings to the fore provocative 'what if' questions that may seem idiosyncratic, inappropriate or implausible, but which create space for such unfamiliar and underrepresented perspectives.

Halberstam's approach does not, and cannot, exist in isolation. Recognizing familiar and, indeed, authorized perspectives is the first step to challenging and confronting the erasure caused by such dominant presuppositions. For Marcella Althaus-Reid, this includes being intentionally, overtly provocative in order to present alternatives free from the colonising imagery and effects of hegemonic North Atlantic, Christian influence. Gender falls within her remit for decolonisation, and she draws on indigenous perspectives both from her own Argentinian heritage and from the stories and experiences of queer and gender transgressive individuals. By classifying queer and gender nonconforming perspectives as indigenous voices, Althaus-Reid implements Namaste's encouragement to actively include indigenous knowledge in any scholarship that engages with trans lives. A foundational commitment for the hermeneutics of cispicion is to identify potentially trans voices in the Bible, and to treat them as authoritative perspectives that demand sustained attention.

Alongside Halberstam's low theory, the trans insights from Namaste, Prosser and Serano are essential. Each adds to the genderscape through their attention to what is missed when viewing transness as subordinate to cisness. Prosser highlights how the body is the point at which our stories really come alive. He describes the 'body-narrative' as central to both storytelling and to our experiences as gendered individuals. It is on the body that our dis/connection with cisnormative gender presuppositions becomes most apparent. He also shows evocatively how much of a struggle it is to make sense of ourselves and our bodies when they do not match either our own preconceptions or those of the wider society. It is those insights that make his work such a compelling inspiration to the hermeneutics of cispicion. Prosser's insights are crucial to reading Esau's story, where clarity arises through reference to his guidance to attend to gender nonconforming bodies and the failures of recognition that accompany them.

Meanwhile Serano's interest in revealing the impact of cisnorms on our preconceptions revolutionized my conceptualization of gender in the Bible. She shows so effectively how reliant we are on gendering one another, even in literature. We use even the smallest details to affirm our perception that the person we encounter is the gender we now see them to be – and that must always have been the case. Once again, we can easily – perhaps even willingly – be enticed into overlooking inconsistencies in order to see only what we expect. So often that instinct ensures the perpetuation of an apparently fixed, binary genderscape. That comes with high costs: there is a price to be paid for not conforming, and that price is invisibility, marginalization or vilification. Instead, attention needs to remain on the way that diverse genders struggle for recognition, acceptance, and validation. Serano, like Halberstam, shows there is already a greater diversity than such narrow preconceptions acknowledge. That reality must be met with a richer, more diverse, and representative genderscape – not only in culture today but also throughout our mnemohistory.

Cispicious Achievements

Through my case studies I have introduced a hermeneutical approach that can be effectively used to confront cisnormative presuppositions. My interpretations of Sarah and Esau's stories enable exploration of aspects of each character's gender that have long attracted intrigue or confusion. Reading the text closely, I have used the quirky and idiosyncratic details that are already within the narrative to open up new interpretations. My strategy works effectively with the text, even though much of the narrative is sparse in detail.[1] The indecent, whimsical reading strategy

---

1. See Erich Auerbach, 'Odysseus' Scar', in *Mimesis: the Representation of Reality in Western Literature* (Princeton, NJ: Princeton University Press, 2003), 3–23. Erich Auerbach contrasts the relative paucity in detail in the ancestral narratives of Genesis with the detail-rich stories of the Homerian epics.

hones in on small details to facilitate dialogue with established scholarship.[2] In Sarah's case, these are mostly from feminist interpretations; in Esau's case, the interlocutors are malestream interpretations of Esau's story. Such commentaries have also identified moments of discontinuity that struggle for explanation: Sarah's absences in narratives where she is a key figure and her striking excision during and after Abraham's attempted sacrifice of Isaac (Gen 22); Esau's excessively rugged image, his incomprehensible speech, and the disconnect between his antagonistic demeanour in Genesis 25 and 27 with his calmer, more eloquent behaviour in Genesis 33. In my cispicious reading, those details were not defined as discontinuous. Rather, eschewing a cisnormative presupposition, these details provided a fresh coherence that gets to the core of the characters.

The coherence that emerges through my readings comes through careful construction of an interdisciplinary framework, with low theory at its core. My adaptation of Halberstam's low theory enables interpretation that is whimsical and indecent but remains focussed on experiences that otherwise struggle for representation. Here I have maintained a clear, specific focus on gender diversity, but such low theory-informed insights need not always be tied to gender. My conceptualization of indecent whimsy provides an excellent vantage point from which to address multiple axes of poverty and oppression. Once again I follow Althaus-Reid in treating poverty as both cause and effect of marginalization; like her I also refrain from specifying named groups who fall into the remit of 'the poor'. Additionally, I strongly believe that where systemic and/or structural oppression is identifiable, a low-theory informed approach can offer an interpretative and liberational point of entry. In other words, I see this cispicious approach as a hermeneutical template for other facets of liberation-focussed scholarship.

The biblical case studies demonstrate more than just bringing new coherence through engaging with the widely recognised ruptures in Sarah and Esau's story. Each builds on Guest's model of interpretation and demonstrate the way the hermeneutics of cispicion makes space for exploring both femininity *and* masculinity. In Sarah's case this emerges through the apparent curation of their identity in order to make the proto-matriarch appear not only female but feminine. Rather, it is Sarah's masculinity that is most evident in their self-expression, although that masculinity frequently provokes censure and erasure from the narrative. The behaviour and treatment attributed to Sarah are in such marked contrast with that of their spouse, Abraham. It is Abraham who remains more

---

2. My nascent approach has already garnered a favourable response from Stiebert, who sees the value in a cispicious approach that 'rouse[s] questions concerning what indeed *is* appropriate for males and females and *who* decides this'. Stiebert, *First-Degree Incest*, 90 n.2, emphasis original. Paul Joyce similarly highlights my early work on cispicion as a notable addition to scholarship of gender and transness in Hebrew Bible Studies in the UK. Paul M. Joyce, 'The Way of the Future? Into Our Second Century', in *SOTS at 100: Centennial Essays of the Society for Old Testament Study*, ed. John Jarrick (London: Bloomsbury T&T Clark, 2017), 159–177.

privileged within the narrative. Meanwhile Hagar, who Sarah enslaves and forces into surrogacy, is treated egregiously but she still displays divine (and narratorial) favour. Abraham's favoured status is clearest when he is actively working to control the way Sarah is received by fellow characters. In parallel, the narrator keeps insisting that Sarah is incontrovertibly female *and* feminine – but they are not. For a character long perceived to be female, who bears a child, it is important to recognize that such social and biological roles of a mother are not the same as being a gestational parent. Sarah's experiences cannot be adequately, or solely, understood through a feminist lens as their masculinity and gender nonconformity are overlooked to make *her* conform. This repeats the treatment Sarah receives from Abraham and the narrator within their own narrative. In the face of motherhood, Sarah's disconnection from the solely feminine identity that is imposed upon *her* becomes a stretch to maintain. Eventually, Sarah disappears from the narrative. Just as Halberstam shows, a gender-nonconforming character like Sarah cannot hold the focus.

Esau's story, meanwhile, demonstrates a complexity within male identity revealed as he repeatedly and recognizably fails to conform to the expectations placed on him due to his excessively sexed body. Those almost immediately post-natal judgments constrain Esau, so much so that when he does not cohere to those expectations he appears unintelligible. The repeated implication is that if Esau, like any gender *conforming* character, would just behave appropriately, he would not face the censure and abuse that he does. Isaac's contingent expression of love for his eldest child highlights this: his affection relies on Esau's hunting skill rather than anything intrinsic to the child. Esau gains agency, so his failures become more visible and apparently intentional. Drawing once again on Halberstam, I see Esau's failures as a way to identify his disquiet with the gendered restrictions in which he finds himself. In combination with his lack of intelligibility, he appears as not only a failure of hegemonic masculinity but also an exemplar for gender nonconforming manhood. His story moves us beyond binary models of gender and encourages recognition of a more diverse genderscape, not tied primarily to masculinity and femininity.

When Jacob takes on the role of faux-Esau in order to fraudulently acquire Isaac's paternal blessing, the mockery and disdain for Esau's failing hypermasculinity comes to the fore. Jacob, a child given more space to explore and play with gender, sets aside infant and adolescent femininity to play the man through establishing a drag king persona. With Rebekah's help a new and apparently reliable masculine character emerges to usurp *his* elder twin and to undermine Esau's identity further in the process. Jacob's masculinity grows in confidence and acceptance ensuring Esau's feminine traits become visible. Where Jacob's playful approach to gender is accepted as part of the future patriarch's identity, Esau's is punished, and he is progressively dehumanised as the chapter progresses. Reading Esau's story cispiciously makes the abuse narrative akin to Trible's texts of terror, something that warrants further exploration beyond the remit of this project.[3] In the face of such catastrophic familial

3. Trible, *Texts of Terror*.

violence, exacerbated through mocking his gender identity, expression and embodiment, Esau's anger is denied the emotions that accompany such treatment. He is not allowed genuine self-expression. Rather, the narrative perpetually favours his younger sibling and forces Esau's actions to speak for him. Esau's own agency emerges when we read his repeated marriages as a 'fuck you' to parents and narrator alike, with their limited expectations for him. In the end, he breaks these constraints. In his last sustained appearance, Esau is different. His demeanour perplexes many commentators who struggle to reconcile this loving, benevolent, calm, and erudite figure with the sub-human, neanderthal-like figure they saw earlier. The Esau of Genesis 33 emerges free from the constriction of familial expectations placed on his highly gendered body and instead a softer, more feminine figure able to greet Jacob anew. This juxtaposition reveals both the cost of Esau's nonconformity to restrictive gendered presuppositions – his apparent incomprehensibility and animalistic presentation – and the liberation that comes with being given space and opportunity to live beyond such constraints. Esau's final appearance provides hope because it offers a powerful example of greater diversity within the biblical genderscape. Esau finds, at the end of his struggle, a space to be himself.

The ancestral narrative – in particular, through the stories of Sarah and Esau – includes a richer, more complex and nuanced genderscape than represented in the dominant, binary model of gender. Indeed, gender diversity is not only identifiable in Genesis, but is a common feature within the ancestral line. In both the case studies, my cispicious model for interpretation has used micro and apparently inconsequential aspects of each narrative to reveal that the cisnormative assumptions cannot hold. Reflecting Namaste and Althaus-Reid's emphasis on the colonising impact of hegemonic cisnormative gender expectations, Esau and Sarah emerge with their own perspectives intact. Each is able to demonstrate their own agency and personhood more clearly through this cispicious reading. I find their richly gendered stories to be in such revelatory contrast with earlier interpretations. So different does each character appear – but still closely aligned to the textual details – that to overlook these micro details is to recolonise them once again. Sarah and Esau do not fully meet cisnormative presuppositions, and so to force them to conform is to erase key details of their identity, especially those bits that make them so remarkably engaging in the first place. Each contributes to a richer picture of biblical gender than that identified prior to this project and these interpretations show there is ample opportunity to open up new vistas on to the biblical genderscape.

Growing Cispicion

Since this intentionally indecent, openly whimsical hermeneutic for close reading has identified and addressed so effectively the problem of cisnormativity when interpreting Genesis, the challenge – and opportunity – now is to continue to apply, refine, and develop this approach. There is still much that can be done to take the hermeneutics of cispicion further.

The cispicious genderscape that appears through my case studies demonstrates that there is surely no less gender diversity in the Bible than Guest points out. In fact it shows that there is *more* gender diversity in the Bible than Guest suggests, and it appears in rich, plural forms. In my analysis I critiqued two main aspects of Guest's scholarship and sought to extend their foundational work. First, amongst their gender nonconforming characters, masculinities shape their interpretations, and they acknowledge their reservations in discerning femininities. By contrast, I identify important glimpses of femininity in both Esau and Sarah's stories, although I do also recognize that masculinity remains prominent in each case study. This remains a challenge as masculinity and the experiences of characters AMAB predominate androcentric texts such as the Bible. Katy Valentine's attention to the limited representational possibilities for trans women, in particular, already highlights this problem. When so many apparently AFAB biblical figures are seen only as mothers – a proxy for conformity – or as discernibly atypical, marginal masculine figures, the genderscape remains far from representative. For the more feminine AMAB characters my cispicious approach opens new interpretative possibilities. While someone like David has long attracted the attention of queer scholarship, to be read as a pseudo-gay character, my approach creates space for more attention to his gender specifically. Further work on a character like David (1 Sam 16–1 Kgs 2) offers perhaps the clearest opportunity for exploring differences between Guest's hetero-suspicious approach and my cispicious one.

David is a tantalizing character for cispicious analysis because he has been subject of so much attention for his masculinity (as with David Clines) and as a proto-gay figure (such as for Thomas Horner, Anthony Heacock and James Harding, in particular).[4] He even features as one of Guest's subjects for their hetero-suspicious interrogation, although Guest displaces David for a more anonymized viewer of the bathing Bathsheba.[5] For Clines, David seems one of the most quintessential examples of laudable biblical masculinity – he is the character around whom Clines's masculinity schema is formulated. Yet, David also has feminine traits too. Like Esau, he is emotional, domesticated, and at times subservient. He is humiliated by his sons, yet he is also a brutal murderer and a

---

4. See, for example, Thomas M. Horner, *Jonathan Loved David: Homosexuality in Biblical Times* (Philadelphia, PA: Westminster, 1978); Greenberg, *Wrestling with God*, 59–65; Anthony Heacock, *Jonathan Loved David: Manly Love in the Bible and the Hermeneutics of Sex*, The Bible in the Modern World (Sheffield: Sheffield Phoenix Press, 2011); James E. Harding, *The Love of David and Jonathan: Ideology, Text, Reception* (Abingdon, Oxon: Routledge, 2014).

5. Guest, 'Looking Lesbian'. David also features briefly in Hornsby, 'Dance of Gender'. Hornsby does not provide a close reading in this chapter of *Transgender, Intersex, and Biblical Interpretation*. Rather, she explores the value of identifying trans-informed experiences in the imagined interplay between David, Jesus, and Paul, three of the most well-known 'men' in the Bible.

political tour de force – all while remaining a highly lauded and narratively privileged figure.

David as a character for future cispicious exploration highlights both a limit to my study and a further extension from Guest's. Both Esau and Sarah are narratively prominent, but they are not the most privileged, central characters in their story arcs. Meanwhile, Guest's figures are all marginal characters. Due to their subordinate status within their own narratives, they can only ever, at best, offer limited representation. Guest's figures each face a challenge to fight against the problem of trivialization. Is the diversity of gender that becomes apparent through Guest's exemplars a cause or effect of their marginalization? There is no definitive answer to that question, but until more prominent characters demonstrate a more complex, less recognizable, or nonconforming gender that risk remains. I intentionally picked more visible, higher profile characters, from the heart of the ancestral family, located prominently in the first book of the Bible. That status makes their gender nonconformity all the more noteworthy. Both Esau and Sarah are well known figures and have attracted sustained attention in commentary from malestream and feminist scholars. However, I do want to acknowledge that while my subjects are far more narratively prominent than Guest's, none is the most privileged even within their stories. With this in mind, it is clear there is more that can be done by exploring the central figures within the most well-known and influential narratives.

The distinction between narratively prominent and privileged is somewhat nuanced but, like so many of the nuances I highlight in this project, it remains important. Both Sarah and Esau fade in and out of focus with some regularity. Their gender nonconformity exacerbates this, but it has been so rarely challenged because Sarah's spouse and Esau's sibling each seize the narrator's attention. How would privileged characters such as Abraham and Jacob emerge through the hermeneutics of cispicion? I have already alluded to some of the opportunity Jacob provides given that Esau's younger sibling is recognisably feminine *and* central to the narrative.[6] Similarly, Joseph – adorned in a virginal princess dress and trafficked at the hands of his(?) elder brothers (Gen 37:2–36) – is an intriguing figure who displays masculinity and femininity. Joseph also struggles for acceptance and recognition within the natal family before and after migration to Egypt (see, in particular, Gen 42–45). Amidst this story Benjamin appears as another enthralling, albeit more marginal, character. Following a difficult labour Rachel dies in childbirth, only after being reassured that she can die easily knowing she has borne a son (35:16–20). The child's identity is then contested as her spouse, Jacob, renames him Benjamin over and against Rachel's choice of Ben-oni (v. 18). Afterwards Benjamin appears only through the accounts of his siblings and father, ensuring his identity is always curated. This leaves ample opportunity to creatively reimagine and reconstruct a character who is always just beyond focus.

6. See, for example, Henderson-Merrygold, 'Reading Biblical Embodiment Cispiciously'; 'Jacob – A (Drag) King'.

The cispicious model warrants further testing and application beyond the characters of the ancestral narratives. Moses, Miriam and Aaron appear particularly beguiling prospects later in the Torah. Howard Eilberg-Schwartz highlights Moses's gender indeterminacy, albeit through reference to a heteronormative marriage model. He writes that Moses is 'caught between genders – a man as leader of Israel, a woman as wife of God'.[7] Rhiannon Graybill also explores how much of Moses' story relates to his body, whether it appears abjected or beatific.[8] She later introduces the way Miriam is treated differently as a female prophet, in contrast with her male counterparts, notably her brother.[9] These concluding remarks from Graybill, in combination with Eilberg-Schwartz's observations, demonstrate the potential for two of the three siblings. My analysis of Esau alongside Jacob shows the value of the context added through attention to sibling dynamics, so I think this can be replicated with Moses' family. Beyond these figures, there is scope to apply cispicion to less family-driven narratives and to characters beyond the Torah.

Graybill, for example, argues for a move away from the successful male figures, such David and Samson (Judg 14:6–16:30), to explore the stranger prophets.[10] The former have garnered significant scholarship, while attention to the more complex and unstable masculinities of the less studied prophets warrants more attention. Graybill's queer interpretations still work from a queer but cisnormative paradigm addressing how the subjects of her study can be understood as nonconforming. She neither directly addresses the impact of cisnormativity on them nor countenances them as anything other than cis figures. Her language focusses on male bodies, albeit ones that are 'deficient or excessive, or perhaps even both at once'.[11] She notes that 'to read the prophetic narratives with close attention to the body is also to perceive a series of challenges to the norms of masculinity and masculine embodiment' but continues to see her subjects as solely (albeit queerly) male.[12] What she does effectively, however, is to show the value of critically engaging with the gender of prophetic figures – Moses, Hosea, Jeremiah and Ezekiel. She does not deploy low theory, or use an approach akin to my indecent whimsy; however, she does see the parallels between Ezekiel's struggle for intelligibility and Halberstam's *The Queer Art of Failure*.[13] This opens the door for further interrogation of particularly Ezekiel's gender performance, through dialogue between Graybill's approach and my own.

There is one further character who Graybill and I both share an interest in analysing with our respective approaches: Jonah. In addition, Jonah is Joy Ladin's

---

7. Eilberg-Schwartz, *God's Phallus*, 145.
8. Rhiannon Graybill, *Are We Not Men? Unstable Masculinity in the Hebrew Prophets* (New York: Oxford University Press, 2016), 22–47.
9. Graybill, *Are We Not Men?*, 134–136.
10. Graybill, *Are We Not Men?*, 1.
11. Graybill, *Are We Not Men?*, 1, 5.
12. Graybill, *Are We Not Men?*, 5.
13. Graybill, *Are We Not Men?*, 97–120, 147 n.6.

go-to example for a biblical character in whose life she sees trans experiences.[14] For Graybill he is 'a prophet of refusal', who she describes as unsuccessful. However, she sees 'neither gender nor embodiment ... explicitly addressed or thematized in the Jonah narrative'.[15] Through my approach the body is just one facet of a broader cispicious picture, and it is Jonah's overt commitment to failure that intrigues me.

Throughout Jonah 1 the scene is set by both Jonah's intentional failure and rejection of God, and the divine reprimand for his action. Jonah cries out to God from the belly of the fish allowing him space to speak of his own circumstances. I see in his prayer the indication of his failure to conform to divine commandment and expectation, rather than an outright rejection of all that God is, symbolised by the people of Nineveh and worshipping in false idols (Jonah 2). Even once Jonah establishes himself as a prophet, he does so reluctantly and is horrified by its success (Jonah 4). Through his dialogue with God he is able to express his anger and frustration at the divine being and to fail yet again to behave according to expectations. These clear insights into his agency and identity make him at odds with the expectations of a man, especially a man of God, and thus open him up for further cispicious exploration. It is easy to see, then, the promise in combining Graybill's reading with Ladin's personal insights as a foundation for a cispicious reading of Jonah.

The final two figures who come to mind are Mordecai and Esther. Both use their own gender, and the preconceptions of those around them, to reveal then destabilise the cultural expectations placed upon them. Mordecai's drag-like performance in the Persian royal court in Esther 8:15 (NRSV) highlights his own playfulness.[16] Meanwhile Esther's status as a high-profile figure assumed to be female provides a much-needed opportunity to explore the juxtaposition between different femininities (especially contrasting Vashti and Esther). As cispicion gains momentum there will be more value in returning to these less prominent figures – but it cannot be limited to finding representation in the margins. By focussing on such central figures as I have highlighted, rather than solely on their marginal counterparts, my analysis aims to open up the genderscape further and to recognize greater plurality.

I have tested the value of my cispicious approach in the context of biblical interpretation. The questions I have asked are not limited to biblical text though.

---

14. Ladin, *Soul of the Stranger*, 1–15.

15. Graybill, *Are We Not Men?*, 132.

16. Katherine Gwyther and Jo Henderson-Merrygold, 'The Disidentification of Mordecai: A Drag Interpretation of Esther 8:15' *Hebrew Studies*, 63 (2022), 119–141. Mordecai attires himself in 'royal robes of blue and white, a great golden crown and a mantle of fine linen and purple' (Esth 8:15). This directly recalls the adornments of the citadel of Susa, with its 'white cotton curtains and blue hangings tied with cords of fine linen and purple to silver rings ... drinks were served in golden goblets' (1:5–7). Mordecai's performance mimics the Persian court itself, and the gendered connotations that accompany both his status and the expectations of palace life.

Halberstam's work has already demonstrated the importance of exploring the portrayal of gender diversity in film and popular culture. Through making the focus on cisnormative presuppositions explicit, my cispicious approach is applicable to other texts and works of literature. The impact of the hermeneutics of cispicion is apparent, having found application in Early Modern Studies by Marjorie Rubright.[17] In the time since Rubright's publication, I have refined my approach further in order to more clearly interlink the narratological strategies used to read texts with my central notion of indecent whimsy. In doing so, I have put low theory more centrally in my own work and see its applicability in other time periods and contexts. Rubright shows the exciting potential for this methodology beyond biblical scholarship, although there is no shortage of biblical material to interrogate.

The theoretical development of the hermeneutics of cispicion in this work provides an invaluable starting point for all this work, but the methodology can be further refined by bringing it into dialogue with others whose gender nonconforming voices are missing. Indecent whimsy has given me the methodological tools to undertake these readings and revealed more than was previously visible. I do also agree with Namaste who stresses that it is even better to read with those who can expand on such stories through their personal experience and insights. Such co-produced interpretations will make cispicious interpretations stronger and richer for the integration of more polyphonous takes on a diverse genderscape. There is further significant opportunity in those conversations to explore whether different insights emerge from readers familiar with the stories as part of a living religious tradition, in contrast with those encountering them as tales from antiquity. Whether the Bible, and its motifs, is familiar – let alone normative – has the potential to elicit radically different interpretations. Even where the text does carry religious authority, there are likely to be differences between Christian and Jewish perspectives. Details such as the familiarity or status of a given character may have a profound impact on how their gender is understood. This may be particularly evident when reading with people with no religious or cultural familiarity with the texts. These open up exciting new avenues for cispicious exploration.

The final area I see for fruitful inquiry is to recognize the value of the contexts from which these stories emerged. The cispicious readings I present here are very much located in the reader response tradition, where today's insights inform the interpretation. However, as trans historians so importantly remind us, diverse genderscapes are not new.[18] By returning to the foundational contexts of the texts

---

17. Marjorie Rubright, 'Transgender Capacity in Thomas Dekker and Thomas Middleton's *The Roaring Girl* (1611)', *Journal for Early Modern Cultural Studies* 19, 4 (2019), 45–74. Rubright cites Henderson-Merrygold, 'Present and Future of Trans Hermeneutics'. She writes, 'Jo Henderson-Merrygold challenges critics, instead, to adopt a "hermeneutics of cispicion: to treat cisnormativity, and its presence in literature, society, and culture, with suspicion; to be suspicious that a given individual is necessarily cisgender (i.e., fixed and/or binary in their gender identity/expression)"' (49).

18. See, for example, Mary Weismantel, 'Towards a Transgender Archaeology: A queer rampage through prehistory', in *The Transgender Studies Reader 2*, ed. Susan Stryker and

I would also bring my approach into dialogue with historical approaches to both the Bible and gender in antiquity. To undertake such work there is a need to reshape the cispicious toolkit for the purpose of historical (re)discovery. This will be an important part of continuing to identify and elevate indigenous perspectives. Here, however, those will come through the particular specificities of the contexts that gave us the stories in the first place.

A Fantastic Genderscape?

I began this project with a short autobiographical reflection on my failures. It seems apt to conclude with another personal reflection. At the end of this cispicious journey I have been able to offer not only a richer genderscape, but one that is plausible and grounded in a deep theoretical understanding of the influence of cisnormativity on that landscape. As I revisit a formative experience from childhood the importance of these strands comes to the fore.

Once upon a time in a very familiar and nearby land – indeed the one in which I grew up – the town was run by pixies. While the town itself is rather staid, the pixies open the door to quite the tantalizing, immersive nonbinary genderscape. These fantastical characters lived across the area but were – and indeed still are – most associated with Pixies' Parlour, a sandstone cave downriver from my hometown. Thanks to Samuel Taylor Coleridge and R. F. Delderfield the legacy of the pixies continues to come alive annually.[19] These pixies were happily settled until the arrival of Christianity, with the resident humans their thralls. A dastardly scheme ensued with the Chief Pixie capturing and casting spells over anyone threatening to strengthen the hold of the church. Their attempts were thwarted and the pixies were forced to retreat to the aforementioned cave. Since that time (or at least since 1954 when Delderfield actually introduced the idea), the pixies have taken their revenge through an annual re-enactment. But there is a tacit understanding that this story is definitely not real. No matter how much the geological feature of Pixies' Parlour offers some credence to the story, it remains clearly a work of fiction. And in the re-enactment of the story the pixies are no

---

Aren Z. Aizura (New York: Routledge, 2013), 319–324; Chris Mowat, 'Engendering the Future: Divination and the Construction of Gender in the Late Roman Republic' (PhD, Newcastle University, 2018).

19. Ray Girvan, 'Coleridge, Pixies' Parlour, and Invented Tradition', JSBlog – Journal of a Southern Bookreader, updated 1 March 2014, accessed 18 October 2019, http://jsbookreader. blogspot.com/2014/03/coleridge-pixies-parlour-and-invented.html. Ray Girvan argues that the story of Ottery's pixies is a relatively recent invention; however, this does not diminish the value of the story in the town's life today. Here I retell it primarily from my own recollection as its significance for me and in this work is based on my own participation in the storyworld. It is that involvement that subsequently informs my reflections and gender and the juxtaposition with the church and biblical counterparts.

more than primary school aged children – Brownies, Cubs, Rainbows, Beavers – in costume and make-up, with adults as the spellbound humans, and the town centre rather than the riverside becomes the stage on which the scripted drama unfurls. It is an act of fantasy and fun, and just as the pixies run screaming from the town centre, the suspended disbelief dissipates as the children return in their usual form. Normal, real life continues from that point on, until the same time the next year.

The tale of the pixies, and its annual show, is in marked contrast with the stories I encountered and performed at church. While I became a participant in this annual ritual through a group that met at the church I attended the storyworlds never mixed. There were different grand tales: stories of our protestant forefathers and mothers whose Devonian idyll was a refuge from seventeenth-century religious and political strife; biblical accounts of our ancestors whose tales accounted for the ways of the world and models for contemporary life; incomprehensible accounts of evangelical revival and the active interventions of God in the world today. These accounts filled my infant and adolescent mind with truths and facts applicable to the world today. Where life differed from that storyworld, it was more on account of the shortcomings of those who did not adhere to a correctly Christian outlook than flaws in the truths inherent to the narrative and historical storyworld. This was the normal, real world to which I returned when not immersed in the fantasy of Pixie Day.

In the real world, informed by the Christian storyworld of my church upbringing, the genderscape was clearly established and demarcated. Their stories were of godly men and women, boys and girls. What was clear was the importance of motherhood and submission to their husbands for the women that the girls would become. Meanwhile the boys were given less clear guidance on how to become men, leaving formation largely in trust to the dominance of male influence. Amongst those inspirational figures – again drawing from both church and biblical forebears – was a broad range of examples of manhood with whom the boys and men could find representation. I, meanwhile, did not quite settle into either one of the bifurcated gender categories easily. Those established, gendered, apparently real-world characters offered little value to me. What remains instead is a sense of disquiet. There were, no doubt, countless factors in my sense of discontinuity, but what strikes me now is the difference between the genderscapes of the biblical and folk storyworlds.

The genderscape of folk stories, of which the tale of Pixie Day is an archetypal example, differs subtly but significantly from that of the biblical and church-based real world. Aged ten, I got to be Chief Pixie, and hold the town hostage. Unlike the church roles, the Chief Pixie was not defined by their gender – the role was an opportunity for me to just be free of gendered expectations writ large in the church contexts. The script changes based on which villainous creature was summoned rather than the sex or gender of the child reading it. The Chief Pixie stands just beyond the clear visibility of the audience with a camouflage net covering the only window into the Pixies' Parlour set: the illusion is a key part of the performance. The effective illusion for me was found in the obfuscation of gender: while it was the combination of a partially hidden, partially visible gender-free pixie-child who captivated the town, it was the possibility of partially hidden, partially visible gender itself that entranced me. Perhaps it was my first encounter with a whimsical, playful, fleeting model of gender free from the constraints of the Christianized real world that contributes to the clarity and warmth of this memory. The will-o'-the-wisp-like gender of the Chief Pixie faded from view as the performance ended, but what endures is the sense that there is gender beyond the strictly bifurcated model. Yet I knew that the stories informing Pixie Day were not real and therefore must fade in the face of the truth of the authorized counterparts I found in church. That sense of a possibility of something different, a glimpse into other genders, dissipated for a long time, but never truly disappeared. Perhaps it, like the Chief Pixie of the story, retreated to a safe cave until it could attempt another – hopefully more successful and enduring – reappearance.

All these years later my understanding of genderscapes has changed markedly. No longer do I have such an inescapable sense of needing to be either/or: male or female, cis or trans, masculine or feminine. Equally, no longer is there such a clear delineation between the fantastic and the factual. What I acknowledge instead is the different power and impact of each story. The pixies of my home town may be whimsical mythical figures, but they have a small sphere of influence. Sarai/h and Esau, meanwhile, carry a mnemohistorical status that gives their (after)lives truth and authority on a global, almost timeless scale. Their stories become real in the way they continue to shape what it means to be gendered today. So here, in my cispicious interpretation, their voices appear anew, in ways that remain credible – and perhaps, over time, influential. In opening up their stories I hope that others will not only see a richer genderscape but will also find encouragement to apply cispicious approaches in other ways and other places.

GLOSSARY

Androcentrism is a term used especially by feminist scholars to describe the primary focus on male perspectives. Men and their experiences are centralized to the exclusion of women and female experiences. It is an outworking of **patriarchy**. Androcentrism is particularly apparent in the ancestral narratives, as the patriarchs and their male heirs dominate the narrator's focus. For further exploration of androcentrism see the discussion of hermeneutics of suspicion in the Introduction and throughout Chapter 2 as Deryn Guest differentiates their approach from their feminist forebears. Confronting and challenging androcentrism, as well as patriarchy, in biblical interpretation features heavily in cited works by Mieke Bal, Athalya Brenner-Idan, J. Cheryl Exum, Esther Fuchs, Elisabeth Schüssler Fiorenza, Susan Niditch, T. Drorah Setel, Phyllis Trible, and Fokkelien van Dijk-Hemmes.

Cisgendering reality, coined by J. E. Sumerau, Ryan Cragun and Lain Mathers, describes 'the processes whereby religions define transgender experience as other'.[1] This can also include the ways 'religious leaders and members socially construct and maintain cisnormative interpretations of the world through their ongoing teachings, rituals, and other faith-related activities'.[2] A particular problem is 'erasing transgender reality in favor of an exclusive focus on a cisnormative world'.[3] It is this specific problem, when traced back through the interpretation of biblical narratives, that I attempt to address in my project.

Cisgenderism is 'the cultural and systematic ideology that denies, denigrates, or pathologizes self-identified gender identities that do not align with assigned gender at birth as well as result behavior, expression, and community. This ideology endorses and perpetuates the belief that cisgender identities and expression are to be valued more than transgender identities and expression and creates an inherent system of associated power and privilege.'[4] **Cisnormativity** is the name given to the system of power and privilege that leads to cisgenderism and the related problem of **transphobia**.

Julia Serano uses the term slightly differently in *Whipping Girl*.[5] She differentiates between discrimination due to not identifying with an anticipated binary **gender**,

---

1. Sumerau, Cragun and Mathers, 'Cisgendering of Reality', 295.
2. Sumerau, Cragun and Mathers, 'Cisgendering of Reality', 296.
3. Sumerau, Cragun and Mathers, 'Cisgendering of Reality', 300.
4. Erica Lennon and Brian J. Mistler. 'Cisgenderism'. *Transgender Studies Quarterly (TSQ)* 1, 1–2 (2014): 63–64: 63.
5. Serano, *Whipping Girl*: 77–93.

e.g. non-binary people or those who 'challenge societal norms with regard to gender expression', from **cissexism**.[6] Serano also reflects that cisgenderism is also tied to 'the gender-entitled belief that all women are (or should be) feminine and men masculine.'[7] (I use this recognition as the core component of my conceptualization of **cisnorms**.) In *Whipping Girl* cissexism describes the discrimination due to being transsexual, which she defines as 'those of us who identify and live as members of the sex other than the one we were assigned at birth'.[8] She subsequently acknowledges how the differences have become somewhat lost and cisgenderism has rather fallen out of common usage in favour of cissexism.[9]

Cisnormativity describes the structural and systematic privileging of those who live and identify as the **sex** and **gender** assigned at birth. It relies upon the assumption that anyone encountered is ordinarily cisgender and so erases trans people and gender nonconformity.[10] As Serano notes, cisnormativity is 'a societal mindset wherein cis/cisgender/cissexual [*sic*] are presumed to be the norm, while trans/transgender/transsexual people and experiences are deemed "abnormal" by comparison (if they are considered at all)'.[11] The outworkings of cisnormativity include **cisgenderism**, **cissexism** and **transphobia**.

Cisnormativity functions as a corollary to **heteronormativity** and **patriarchy** as an ideology that shapes our preconceptions about what is normal, natural and, in the light of biblical interpretation, divinely created (see also **cisgendering reality**). I propose a framework for recognising cisnormativity in Chapter 1. In Chapter 2 I differentiate cisnormativity from heteronormativity. This then forms the basis for a suspicious hermeneutic (see Introduction) that relates specifically to the named ideology of cisnormativity.

Cisnorm is a contraction of cisnormativity which I use to describe common preconceptions about normal, natural **sex** and **gender**. Such norms include the perception that women should be feminine and men masculine (cf. Serano's use of **cisgenderism**) and that people should only ever live as the sex and gender assigned at birth. In other words, gender nonconformity and transness is *not* considered

6. Serano, 'Cissexism and Cis Privilege Revisited'.
7. Serano, *Whipping Girl*, 90.
8. Serano, *Whipping Girl*, xviii, 12–13; Serano, 'Cissexism and Cis Privilege Revisited'. In this later clarification Serano explains that she 'was highlighting the obstacles that are more specifically faced by transsexuals (i.e., those of us who identify and live as members of the sex other than the one we were assigned at birth). I focused on transsexuality because, at the time, it felt like most of the discussion about transgender issues (especially within feminist and queer circles) placed more interest and concern for those who challenge societal norms with regard to gender expression, while often ignoring or outright dismissing issues faced by transsexuals (who primarily defy norms with regard to gender identity and sex embodiment)'.
9. Serano, 'Julia's Trans, Gender, Sexuality, & Activism Glossary!'
10. Serano, *Whipping Girl*, 164–170.
11. Serano, 'Julia's Trans, Gender, Sexuality & Activism Glossary!'

normal or natural: they are not cisnormal. Cisnorms are found at the intersection of Meg-John Barker's description of dominant gender norms in the UK and the different facets of Serano's concept of cissexism. Barker provides a guide to quotidian gender norms, associated with cisnormativity, and recognizes that:

- A person must have a gender – it is not possible to be a person without one.
- That gender is binary: a person can only be a man or a woman.
- Gender remains the same throughout life, based on what was assumed to be at birth based on a person's visible genitalia (i.e., people are assumed to be cisgender – remaining in the gender that was assumed at birth). In some cases their genitalia will have been altered surgically to make them fit cultural norms for a boy or girl.
- Men will be masculine; women will be feminine.[12]

Added to that is the problem of cissexism. Cissexism encompasses traditional sexism (the anti-patriarchal endeavour associated with feminism), oppositional sexism and cisgenderism.[13] Oppositional sexism 'is the belief that female and male are rigid, exclusive categories, each possessing a unique and nonoverlapping set of attributes, aptitudes, abilities and desires'.[14] She continues, 'Oppositional sexists attempt to punish or dismiss those of us who fall outside of gender or sexual norms because our existence threatens the idea that women and men are "opposite" sexes'. It is these very norms, and those that are privileged in traditional and cisgenderism that comprise my conceptualisation of cisnorms. As shown in Chapter 1, and in the case studies of Chapters 3 and 4, diverging from anticipated gender expectations is frequently met with erasure, violence or other punishments, in line with Serano's observations.

Cissexism, like **cisgenderism**, recognises the sexism, discrimination and mistreatment that affects those who do not conform to the expectations of cisnormativity, most notably trans people. The two terms largely function synonymously, which much of the above definition for cisgenderism also apply here. As with the other 'cis' terminology, Serano's attention to language adds further context. For Serano, cissexism 'is the belief that transsexuals' identified genders are inferior to, or less authentic than, those of *cissexuals*'.[15] She contrasts this with the privilege that comes with being cis – or at least of conforming sufficiently to **cisnorms**.[16]

12. Barker, *Gender, Sexual, and Relationship Diversity*, 31. They emphasize how dominant these ideas are in 'mainstream western culture' (8) before noting that this is a contextually and historically formed perspective.

13. Serano, *Whipping Girl*, 11–20.

14. Serano, *Whipping Girl*, 13.

15. Serano, *Whipping Girl*, 11. Emphasis original. When first published Serano preferred use of the term 'cissexual' rather than 'cisgender'. She has subsequently recognized the wider acceptance of 'cisgender' or even 'cis' as the most commonly used contrast to trans. For further discussion, see page 51–55 above.

16. Serano, *Whipping Girl*, 161–193.

Gender (discussed in detail on pages 44–46), in this project, conveys a person's sense of self. Whether this is an internal recognition or encountered in interpersonal relationships it is a way of encountering someone's agency and identity. In the interpretations presented here gender signifies the character's self-expression. This is in contrast with the immediately visible aspects of the character's life that become apparent when we look at them, especially their bodies.

More broadly, gender encompasses the social, psychological, ontological and cultural facets of our identities. It is socially constructed and historically contextual. Gender informs so much about how we relate to one another.[17] It both informs *and* is informed by our sex, so the two concepts are almost inseparable. Considering gender as a (semi-)distinct concept from sex enables us to focus on identity, status, performance, social relationships and roles. The aspects of identity that I privilege in this project become most apparent in social situations and through roles and behaviour. Where gender does not align consistently with the sex assigned at birth, the individual does not conform to **cisnorms**.

Gender criticism is a term that has become inextricable from trans exclusion. It largely supersedes the term 'terf', a trans-exclusionary radical feminist. It traces its roots to the theological and feminist scholarship of Mary Daly and Janice Raymond.[18] Gender criticism has very high-profile celebrity advocates, most notably author J. K. Rowling and former comedy writer Graham Linehan, who do not accept the validity of trans people living out their authentic genders and sexes. The movement has a particularly high level of advocates in the UK in the late 2010s and even at this point in the early 2020s. Its core arguments are antithetical to this project.

Gender Criticism was also a term used in academic gender scholarship that sought to provide a holistic engagement with gender and sex. The main advocate cited here is Deryn Guest, whose monograph *Beyond Feminist Biblical Studies* profoundly shapes this project.[19] Guest's work, along with that of Nicole Ruane and Marco Derks, do not in any way advocate the position of those activists mentioned immediately above.[20] Rather they are seeking new ways address gender diversity within and beyond the cisnormative binary. My term, cispicion, is one option for moving away from the language of gender criticism and its abusive, **cissexist** connotations.

17. See, for example, Kate Bornstein's description of being perceived as a male then later a female salesperson. Bornstein, *Gender Outlaw*, 146. This social interaction is an example of what Julia Serano calls gendering and relates back to cisgender assumption: we regularly use any number of social and embodied cues which then allows us to assign the other a gender. Serano, *Whipping Girl*, 161–193.

18. See also note 1 on page 67, and note 133 on page 102–103 for further discussion and examples.

19. Guest, *Beyond Feminist Biblical Studies*. I discuss this monograph and its contribution to my project in Chapter 2, pages 91–98.

20. Ruane, 'When Women Aren't Enough'; Derks, '"If I Be Shaven"', 554.

Genderfuckery encompasses a rebellious and playful approach to gender diversity. The term has gained a political edge since it was used by Susie Bright to affirm androgyny (as one form of nonconformity).[21] Deryn Guest uses David Bergman's history of the term which traces it back to a 1970s drag troupe and a 1974 article by Christopher Lonc entitled 'Genderfuck and Its Delights'.[22] It has a particular rebelliousness that comes through messing with binary gender codes embedded in cisnorms and in doing so it subverts those very expectations.[23] In this project genderfuck features heavily in the discussion of Guest's work (Chapter 2), and links closely to Jack Halberstam's whimsical approach to gender (Chapter 1).

Heteronormativity describes a set of social norms that privilege different sex relationships and those within them. Those different sexes – male and female – are presented to be oppositional and mutually exclusive. The most privileged sexual relationships are those between one man and one woman, non-heterosexual sexualities are not treated as equivalent – and often not valid at all.[24] The prospect for reproduction underpins heteronormativity with the result that childbearing functions as both a justification for it, and a proof of the validity of its underlying principles.[25]

Heteronormativity intersects with **patriarchy** and **cisnormativity** as it creates privilege and marginalization. **Queer** theory then responds to these structures to provide ways to deconstruct those norms. In turn queer theorists have brought heteronormativity into greater focus. In particular Adrienne Rich is particularly influential for her attention to the compulsory make-up of heterosexuality.[26] Equally, Michel Foucault provided a paradigm-shifting insight into a shape and context to the (European) history of sexuality.[27] The foundation stones lead Lauren

---

21. June Reich traces the term 'Genderfuck' back to Bright's article, ('A Star is Porn.' *On Our Backs*, Oct.–Nov. (1989), 8–9). See June L. Reich, 'Genderfuck: The Law of the Dildo' *Discourse* 15, 1 (1992), 112–127: 112–113.

22. Guest, 'From Gender Reversal', 9. Guest cites David Bergman in *Camp Grounds: Style and Homosexuality* (Amherst, MA: University of Massachusetts Press, 1993), 7. Guest continues to trace the lineage through Reichs and Erin Runions before embarking on their genderfuck reading of Jael's story.

23. Runions, 'Zion is Burning', 93.

24. Hornsby, 'Introduction', 2.

25. Warner, 'Introduction', 9. For Warner, reproduction is so inextricable from heterosexuality he suggests it should more aptly be described as reprosexuality. Warner's term also emphasises the desire for a past and future that also drives the need to reproduce and, in turn, bolsters heterosexuality. See also Edelman, *No Future*. Edelman argues that breaking the reproductive imperative requires a queer acceptance of the death drive. This willingness to embrace finitude and death is, for Edelman, the most queer thing possible as it irrevocably breaks away from heterosexuality and the need to reproduce.

26. Rich, 'Compulsory Heterosexuality', 130–142.

27. Foucault, *History of Sexuality*.

Berlant and Michael Warner to suggest that heteronormativity relies on 'three propositional paradigms', namely:

> those that propose that human identity itself is fundamentally organized by gender identifications that are hardwired into infants; those that equate the clarities of gender identity with the domination of a relatively coherent and vertically stable 'straight' ideology; and those that focus on a phallocentric Symbolic order that produces gendered subjects who live out the destiny of their position.[28]

The persistent focus on two, and only two, sexes means that much gender-diverse scholarship relates most directly to heteronormativity rather than cisnormativity. While they remain closely entwined, heteronormativity continues to draw close attention to matters of sexuality. To distinguish the two, and to allow a more targeted focus on gender, I argue for a need to address cisnormativity specifically. For further discussion of heteronormativity and its complex relationship with this project see Chapter 1, especially Beyond Que(e)rying Gender (p. 42). In Chapter 2 I turn my analysis to Deryn Guest's work, all of which responds to the problem of heteronormativity.

Kyriarchy is a neologism coined by Elisabeth Schüssler Fiorenza to reflect the domination of lords or masters.[29] She proposed it as a more accurate reflection of abusive and exclusionary power dynamics than the term **patriarchy**. Her term recognizes differential power dynamics based on race, class, education, race and ethnicity as well as sex and gender. Discussed in further detail on page 10, a suspicion of the influence of kyriarchy is foundational to Schüssler Fiorenza's feminist hermeneutics of suspicion.

Mnemohistory is a term attributed to Jan Assmann.[30] It describes the complexity inherent in an account of history inextricable from its cultural and remembered forms. In other words, it emphasizes the importance of how history is understood, including what it has meant and does mean for a community, with far less interest in any objective truths. Mnemohistory is a helpful designation for many of the Bible's stories as the historical and contextual information that aids understanding is inextricable from the story itself. Here I also use mnemohistory in recognition of the cultural transmission of those stories and the history contained within. Through such transmission meaning has and insight has both evolved and become authoritative irrespective of the aims of any given author. Mnemohistory thus alludes to the archive-like function of the Bible, where it carries with it generations of insight, commentary and transmission.[31]

---

28. Berlant and Warner, 'Sex in Public' (1998), 552 n.11.
29. Bugg, 'Explanation of Terms (Glossary)', 211.
30. Assmann, 'Collective Memory and Cultural Identity', 125–133.
31. For further discussion of the way biblical discourses, grounding in those texts, function as an archive see Thiem, 'Art of Queer Rejections', 33–56.

Patriarchy describes the societal and systematic privileging of maleness. Following the critical attention of feminist scholars, its presence is particularly visible in the Bible. The Bible is an androcentric collection: in other words, it is 'a man's "book," where women appear for the most part simply as adjuncts of men, significant only in the context of men's activities'.[32] Male perspectives are centralized to the exclusion of accounts of other genders. Phyllis Bird expresses how this appears in a cultural context when she says that 'the Old Testament is a collection of writings by males from a society dominated by males. These portray a man's world. They speak of events and activities engaged in primarily or exclusively like males (war, cult and government) and of a jealously singular God, who is described and addressed in terms usually used for males'.[33] To consolidate male power and privilege, hegemonic masculinity is the pinnacle of desirable manliness.[34] The result is that femininity and womanliness are treated as antithetical to – and indeed a threat to – masculinity. These themes endure from the biblical narratives into the contemporary world. Indeed, Elisabeth Schüssler Fiorenza notes how important it is to engage with the concept and critique it in contemporary society.[35]

The concept of patriarchy warrants some critique though, as it implies a homogeneity to maleness that just is not apparent. While some men are privileged over others, it is not the case that all men hold more power than all women. Schüssler Fiorenza's chosen term of **kyriarchy** is a more nuanced descriptor of the inherent power dynamics. She makes her rationale explicit when she draws attention to both the meaning of patriarchy and its limitations. Patriarchy

> literally means the rule of the father and is generally understood within feminist discourses in a dualistic sense as asserting the domination of all men over all women in equal terms. The theoretical adequacy of patriarchy has been challenged because, for instance, black men do not have control over white wo/men and some women (slave-mistresses) have power over subaltern women and men (slaves).[36]

Despite the limitations of the term, patriarchy continues to stand alongside **heteronormativity** and **cisnormativity** as a significant system of social norms related to gender and sex.

---

32. Phyllis Bird, 'Images of Women in the Old Testament', in *Religion and Sexism: Images of Women in the Jewish and Christian Tradition* ed. Rosemary Radford Ruether (New York: Simon and Schuster, 1974), 41–88, 41.

33. Bird, 'Images of Women', 41–42.

34. Connell, *Masculinities*, 77–79.

35. For example, Schüssler Fiorenza commends Margaret Atwood for the way she brings the problem of patriarchy to a new audience through her novel *The Handmaid's Tale*. Schüssler Fiorenza highlights how language including male-centred language and phallocentric imagery continues to oppress women. See Schüssler Fiorenza, *But She Said*, 2–4.

36. Bugg, 'Explanation of Terms (Glossary)', 212–213.

Queer is a complex and multifaceted term with an array of meanings. In everyday parlance, queer gives name to an identity that does not conform to normative expectations of gender and/or sexuality. In one regard it is used as an umbrella term for people who identify as lesbian, gay, bi, pansexual, trans or any other marginalized gender or sexuality. However it also functions as category in and of itself. In other words, one can describe oneself as being queer on grounds of sexuality without further detail; it can similarly function as a descriptor of gender identity. Queer has historically been used as a term of abuse, but more recently has been reclaimed and is largely used positively.

Despite the use of queer as a noun, and as a proudly worn identity, Lee Edelman cautions that we cannot use the term in that way. He considers it counter to the politics inherent in the term to use it as a term of self-identity: 'queerness can never define an identity; it can only disturb one ... the efficacy of queerness ... lies in its resistance to a symbolic reality'.[37] Those political aims are inherently deconstructive in remit in that they trace their roots through critical theory and gender scholarship such as that of Michel Foucault and Judith Butler, into the sphere of lesbian and gay studies.[38] Indeed Eve Kosofsky Sedgwick, one of the most prominent figures of early queer scholarship, argues that at its core queer denotes 'same-sex sexual object choice, lesbian or gay'.[39] As she continues, she makes the important observation that 'to disavow those meanings or to displace them from the term's [queer] definitional center, would be to dematerialize any possibility of queerness itself'.[40] Sedgwick's insight emphasises how strongly lesbian and gay identity, later expanded into a broader focus on non-heterosexual sexualities, underpins the conceptualization of queer.

Despite this central focus on sexuality, the very reason Teresa de Lauretis has become so associated with popularising the term 'queer' is to distance it from an exclusive focus on specific modes of sexuality.[41] More than that she was acutely aware of the androcentric, white culture that predominated lesbian and gay studies.[42] De Lauretis recognized that there was far greater difference within non-heterosexual sexualities – beyond the bifurcated gender binary identities of gay

---

37. Edelman, *No Future*, 17, 18.
38. Butler, *Gender Trouble*; Foucault, *History of Sexuality*.
39. Eve Kosofsky Sedgwick, *Tendencies* (Durham, NC: Duke University Press, 1993), 8.
40. Sedgwick, *Tendencies*, 8.
41. Teresa de Lauretis, 'Queer Theory: Lesbian and Gay Sexualities, An Introduction', *Differences* 3, 2 (1991): iii–xviii.
42. de Lauretis, 'Queer Theory', iv. She persuasively argues that even the language of gay and lesbian had 'become the standard way of referring to what only a few years ago used to be simply "gay" (e.g., the gay community, the gay liberation movement) or, just a few years earlier still, "homosexual"'. In other words, it as a 'white gay historiography and sociology, which add on women as an afterthought, with little or no understanding of female socio-sexual specificity'.

man or lesbian – and argued for what we now understand to be a more intersectional approach:

> We do not know much about one another's sexual history, experience, fantasies, desire, or modes of theorizing. And we do not know enough about ourselves, as well, when it comes to differences between and within lesbians, and between and within gay men, in relation to race and its attendant differences of class or ethnic culture, generational, geographical, and socio-political location. We do not know enough to theorize those differences.[43]

The aim core to de Lauretis's desire to shift from gay and lesbian studies to queer theory emphasises the need to be aware of the areas of marginalization that become normal (if unintentional) part of a discipline. Similar concerns have subsequently been raised in trans studies and within this project about the attention paid to gender diversity. As the definitions cited here, and those explored in Chapters 1 and 2 highlight, sexuality through the lens of heteronormativity is *the* predominant focus of queer scholarship even though it has sought to expand its remit.

Even though de Lauretis argued for queer scholarship to address exclusionary practice in lesbian and gay scholarship, similar accusations have been made against queer scholarship as the discipline has grown. In a notable critique, Cathy Cohen argues that queer has consolidated rather than deconstructed the very binaries it has sought to destroy. Instead it has created a new dichotomy between all that is queer and all that is not.[44] This is particularly apparent in the relationship between queer and trans scholarship. Heather Love, writing from a trans studies perspective, notes the differences between categories: 'If *queer* can be understood as refusing the stabilizations of both gender and sexuality implied by the categories of gay and lesbian and opening onto a wider spectrum of sexual nonnormativity, *transgender* emerged as a term to capture a range of gendered embodiments, practices, and community formations that cannot be accounted for by the traditional binary.'[45]

---

43. de Lauretis, *Queer Theory*, x. She continues, 'Thus an equally troubling question in the burgeoning field of "gay and lesbian studies" concerns the discursive constructions and constructed silences around the relations of race to identity and subjectivity in the practices of homosexualities and the representations of same-sex desire'.

44. Cathy J. Cohen, 'Punks, Bulldaggers, and Welfare Queens: The Radical Potential of Queer Politics'. *GLQ: A Journal of Gay and Lesbian Studies*, 3, 4 (1997): 437–465, 438. 'Instead of destabilizing the assumed categories and binaries of sexual identity, queer politics has served simply to reinforce simple dichotomies between heterosexual and everything "queer." An understanding of the ways in which power informs and constitutes privileged and marginalized subjects on both sides of this dichotomy has been left unexamined'.

45. Heather Love, 'Queer', *Transgender Studies Quarterly (TSQ)* 1, 1–2 (2014), 172–176: 172–173

Love notes that both communities and their related academic disciplines share a commitment 'their activist investments, dissident methodologies, and their critical interrogation of and resistance to gender and sexual norms' yet they necessarily remain discrete.[46] Despite these commonalities she also emphasizes that some within trans scholarship 'have argued that queer studies has not engaged fully with the material conditions of transgender people but has rather used gender nonnormativity as a sign or allegory of queerness'.[47] This, then shows the limitations of queer's applicability for this project. For further exploration of these themes see, in particular, Chapter 2. In that chapter I explore how approaching gender diversity or non-normativity through a queer-focussed approach limits interpretation as it does not adequately address the impact of **cisnormativity**.

Sex is a complex term that centres around the physical and biological features of being male, female or intersex. It is socially and historically constructed as a way to make sense of biological and anatomical difference. The distinction between the two aspects is contentious, with some theorists like Meg-John Barker preferring to use an amalgamated form (sex/gender) in light of their biopsychosocial approach.[48] However, distinguishing sex from gender helps to draw specific attention to embodiment and bodily sex markers.

Assignation of sex is frequently tied to an appraisal of genitals at birth, but is not solely reliant on that. As discussed in Chapter 1 (p. 43), the understanding of sex has changed throughout time. Thomas Laqueur and Anne Fausto-Sterling emphasize that the lack of a wider sex-scape is not due to a lack of scientific data.[49] In this project there is no equivalent scientific data so textual details provide the only indicators. References to genitalia, such as Esau's penis, or to reproductive capability in Sarai/h's case, indicate primary sex markers. Meanwhile the contrasts between Esau and Jacob's hirsuteness and voice emphasize secondary sex characteristics. Similarly the account of Sarah nursing (breast or chest feeding) Isaac functions as an indicator of sex. Then it is the social construction of those sexes, in antiquity and as understood through our own bodies, that makes them so real and meaningful.

Sex also provides us with a visible representation of our gendered selves. This can correlate with our gender or differ from it. For many it is invaluable to be able to transform your body to enable it to better represent who you are.[50] Yet sex continues to shape how we are received by one another. Embodied sexual characteristics steer acquaintances to gender us one way or another – even in the knowledge those assumptions may be flawed.

46. Love, 'Queer', 172.
47. Love, 'Queer', 174.
48. Barker, *Gender, Sexual, and Relationship Diversity*, 21.
49. Laqueur, *Making Sex*, 243; Fausto-Sterling, 'The Five Sexes'.
50. For further discussion, see Chapter 1, particularly discussions of Viviane Namaste and Jay Prosser's work.

BIBLIOGRAPHY

Ahmed, Sara. *Living a Feminist Life*. Durham, NC: Duke University Press, 2017.
Alter, Robert. *The Art of Biblical Narrative*. London: George Allen & Unwin, 1981.
Alter, Robert. *Genesis: Translation and Commentary*. New York: Norton, 1996.
Althaus-Reid, Marcella. 'Paul Ricoeur and the Methodology of the Theology of Liberation: The Hermeneutics of J. Severino Croatto, Juan Luis Segundo and Clodovis Boff'. PhD, University of St Andrews, 1993. https://hdl.handle.net/10023/2674
Althaus-Reid, Marcella. 'Gustavo Gutiérrez Goes to Disneyland: *Theme Park Theologies* and the Diaspora of the Discourse of the Popular Theologian in Liberation Theology'. In *Interpreting Beyond Borders*, edited by Fernando F. Segovia. The Bible and Postcolonialism, 36–58. Sheffield: Sheffield Academic Press, 2000.
Althaus-Reid, Marcella. *Indecent Theology: Theological Perversions in Sex, Gender and Politics*. London: Routledge, 2000.
Althaus-Reid, Marcella. *The Queer God*. London: Routledge, 2003.
Althaus-Reid, Marcella. 'Preface'. In *We Drink from Our Own Wells*, by Gustavo Gutiérrez. SCM Classics, xxiii–xxix. London: SCM Press, 2012.
Amos, Claire. *The Book of Genesis*. Epworth Commentaries. Peterborough: Epworth, 2004.
Anderson, Bradford A. *Brotherhood and Inheritance: A Canonical Reading of the Esau and Edom Traditions*. Library of Biblical Studies. London: T&T Clark, 2011.
Apostolacus, Katherine. 'The Bible and The Transgender Christian: Mapping Transgender Hermeneutics in the 21st Century'. *Journal of the Bible and its Reception* 5, 1 (2018): 1–29. https://doi.org/10.1515/jbr-2016-0027.
Arnold, Bill T. *Genesis*. The New Cambridge Bible Commentary. Google Play ed. New York: Cambridge University Press, 2009.
Assmann, Jan. 'Collective Memory and Cultural Identity'. *New German Critique* 65, Cultural History/Cultural Studies (1995): 125–133. https://doi.org/10.2307/488538.
Auerbach, Erich. 'Odysseus' Scar'. In *Mimesis: the Representation of Reality in Western Literature*, 3–23. Princeton, NJ: Princeton University Press, 2003.
Bal, Mieke. 'Introduction'. In *Anti-Covenant: Counter-Reading Women's Lives in the Hebrew Bible*, edited by Mieke Bal. The Library of Hebrew Bible/Old Testament Studies, 11–24. Sheffield: Sheffield Academic Press, 1989.
Barker, Meg-John. *Gender, Sexual, and Relationship Diversity (GSRD)*, BACP Good Practice across the Counselling Professions, Lutterworth, Leics: British Association for Counselling and Psychotherapy, 2017.
Berlant, Lauren, and Michael Warner. 'Sex in Public'. *Critical Inquiry* 24, 2: Intimacy (1998): 547–566. https://doi.org/10.1086/448884.
Berlant, Lauren, and Michael Warner. 'Sex in Public'. In *Queer Studies: An Interdisciplinary Reader*, edited by Robert J Corber and Stephen Valocchi, 170–183. Oxford: Blackwell, 2003.
'The Bible: Transgender and Genderqueer Perspectives'. *Journal for Interdisciplinary Biblical Studies* 1, 2 (2020).
Bird, Phyllis. 'Images of Women in the Old Testament'. In *Religion and Sexism: Images of Women in the Jewish and Christian Tradition* ed. Rosemary Radford Ruether, 41–88. New York: Simon and Schuster, 1974.

Boer, Roland. *Knockin' on Heaven's Door: The Bible and Popular Culture.* London: Routledge, 1999.
Boer, Roland. 'Of Fine Wine, Incense and Spices: The Unstable Masculine Hegemony of the Book of Chronicles'. In *Men and Masculinity in the Hebrew Bible and Beyond*, edited by Ovidiu Creangă. The Bible in the Modern World, 20–33. Sheffield: Sheffield Phoenix Press, 2010.
Boer, Roland. 'The Patriarch's Nuts: Concerning the Testicular Logic of Biblical Hebrew'. *Journal of Men, Masculinities and Spirituality* 5, 2 (2011): 41–52.
Boff, Leonardo. *Jesus Christ Liberator: A Critical Christology of Our Time*, Translated by Patrick Hughes. London: SPCK, 1980.
Booth, Robert. 'Transgender Man Loses Appeal Court Battle to be Registered as Father'. *The Guardian*, 29 April 2020. https://amp.theguardian.com/society/2020/apr/29/transgender-man-loses-appeal-court-battle-registered-father-freddy-mcconnell.
Bornstein, Kate. *Gender Outlaw: On Men, Women, and the Rest of Us.* Revised & Updated ed. New York: Vintage, 2016.
Brayford, Susan. *Genesis.* Septuagint Commentary Series. Leiden: Brill, 2007.
Brenner-Idan [Brenner], Athalya. *Colour Terms in the Old Testament.* Journal for the Study of the Old Testament Supplement Series. Sheffield: JSOT Press, 1982.
Brenner-Idan [Brenner], Athalya, ed. *A Feminist Companion to The Latter Prophets.* Sheffield: Sheffield Academic Press, 1995.
Brueggemann, Walter. *Genesis.* Interpretation: A Bible Commentary for Teaching and Preaching. Louisville, KY: Westminster John Knox Press, 1982.
Bugg, Laura Beth. 'Explanation of Terms (Glossary)'. In *Wisdom Ways: Introducing Feminist Biblical Interpretation*, edited by Elisabeth Schüssler Fiorenza, 207–216. Maryknoll, NY: Orbis Books, 2001.
Bullough, Vern L., and Bonnie Bullough. *Cross-dressing, Sex, and Gender.* Philadelphia: University of Pennsylvania Press, 1993, 246.
Butler, Judith. 'Against Proper Objects'. *Differences: A Journal of Feminist Cultural Studies* 9, 4 (1991): 387–407.
Butler, Judith. *Bodies that Matter: On the Discursive Limits of 'Sex'.* New York: Routledge, 1993.
Butler, Judith. *Gender Trouble: Feminism and the Subversion of Identity.* Tenth Anniversary ed. London: Routledge, 1999.
Butler, Judith. *Undoing Gender.* New York: Routledge, 2004.
Butler, Judith. 'My Life, Your Life: Equality and the Philosophy of Non-Violence'. The Gifford Lectures, University of Glasgow, 1–3 October 2018.
Carden, Michael. 'Genesis/Bereshit'. In *The Queer Bible Commentary*, edited by Deryn Guest, Robert E. Shore-Goss [Goss], Mona West and Thomas Bohache, 21–60. London: SCM Press, 2006.
Chapman, Cynthia R. *The House of the Mother: The Social Roles of Maternal Kin in Biblical Hebrew Narrative and Poetry.* The Anchor Yale Bible Reference Library. New Haven, CT: Yale University Press, 2016.
Clines, David J. A. *Interested Parties: The Ideology of Writers and Readers of the Hebrew Bible.* Journal for the Study of the Old Testament Supplement Series. Sheffield: Sheffield Academic Press, 1995.
Clines, David J. A. 'Dancing and Shining at Sinai: Playing the Man in Exodus 32–34'. In *Men and Masculinity in the Hebrew Bible and Beyond*, edited by Ovidiu Creangă. The Bible in the Modern World, 54–63. Sheffield: Sheffield Phoenix Press, 2010.

Cohen, Cathy J. 'Punks, Bulldaggers, and Welfare Queens: The Radical Potential of Queer Politics'. *GLQ: A Journal of Gay and Lesbian Studies* 3, 4 (1997). https://doi.org/10.1215/10642684-3-4-437.

Cohen, Jeffrey Jerome. 'Monster Culture (Seven Theses)'. In *Monster Theory: Reading Culture*, edited by Jeffrey Jerome Cohen, 3–25. Minneapolis, MN: University of Minnesota Press, 1996.

Connell, Raewyn W. *Masculinities*. Cambridge: Polity Press, 1995.

Corber, Robert J, and Stephen Valocchi. 'Introduction'. In *Queer Studies: An Interdisciplinary Reader*, edited by Robert J Corber and Stephen Valocchi, 1–20. Oxford: Blackwell, 2003.

Cornwall, Susannah. 'Apophasis and Ambiguity: The "Unknowingness" of Transgender'. In *Trans/Formations*, edited by Lisa Isherwood and Marcella Althaus-Reid. Controversies in Contextual Theology, 13–40. London: SCM Press, 2009.

Culbertson, Philip L. 'Designing Men: Reading the Male Body as Text'. In *Men and Masculinities in Christianity and Judaism: A Critical Reader*, edited by Björn Krondorfer, 115–124. London: SCM Press, 2008.

Dalley, Stephanie. *Myths from Mesopotamia: Creation, The Flood, Gilgamesh, and Others*. Oxford World Classics. Oxford: Oxford University Press, 1989.

Davidson, Robert. *Genesis 12–50*. The Cambridge Bible Commentary on the New English Bible. Cambridge: Cambridge University Press, 1979.

Davies, Philip R. 'Genesis and the Gendered World'. In *The World of Genesis: Persons, Places, Perspectives*, edited by Philip R. Davies and David J. A. Clines. Journal for the Study of the Old Testament Supplement Series, 7–15. Sheffield: Sheffield Academic Press, 1998.

Day, Georgia. 'Trans-formed by the Spirit: How the Doctrine of Miraculous Conception Reveals Jesus to be an Intersex Trans Man'. *Feminist Theology* 31, 2 (2023): 165–180. https://doi.org/10.1177/09667350221134953

de Lauretis, Teresa. 'Queer Theory: Lesbian and Gay Studies, An Introduction'. *Differences* 3, 2 (1991): iii–xviii.

Derks, Marco. '"If I Be Shaven, Then My Strength Will Go From Me": A Queer Reading of the Samson Narrative'. *Biblical Interpretation* 23, 4–5 (2015): 553–573. https://doi.org/10.1163/15685152-02345p05.

DiPalma, Brian Charles. *Masculinities in the Court Tales of Daniel: Advancing Gender Studies in the Hebrew Bible*. Routledge Studies in the Biblical World. London: Routledge, 2018.

Duncan, Celena M. 'The Book of Ruth: On Boundaries, Love, and Truth'. In *Take Back the Word: A Queer Reading of the Bible*, edited by Robert E. Shore-Goss [Goss] and Mona West, 99–102. Cleveland, OH: Pilgrim Press, 2000.

Edelman, Lee. *No Future: Queer Theory and the Death Drive*. Durham, NC: Duke University Press, 2004.

Eilberg-Schwartz, Howard. *God's Phallus and Other Problems for Men and Monotheism*. Boston, MA: Beacon Press, 1994.

Enke, A. Finn. 'The Education of Little Cis: Cisgender and the Discipline of Opposing Bodies'. In *Transfeminist Perspectives in and beyond Transgender and Gender Studies*, edited by A. Finn [Anne] Enke, 60–77. Philadelphia, PA: Temple University Press, 2012.

Exum, J. Cheryl. *Fragmented Women: Feminist (Sub)Versions of Biblical Narratives*. Cornerstones. Second ed. London: Bloomsbury, 2016.

Fausto-Sterling, Anne. 'The Five Sexes: Why Male and Female Are Not Enough'. *The Sciences* 33, 2 (1993): 20–24.

Feinberg, Leslie. *Transgender Warriors: Making History from Joan of Arc to Dennis Rodman*. Boston, MA: Beacon Press, 1997.

Ferber, Alona. 'Judith Butler on the Culture Wars, JK Rowling and Living in "Anti-Intellectual Times"'. *New Statesman*, 2020, 22 September. https://www.newstatesman.com/international/2020/09/judith-butler-culture-wars-jk-rowling-and-living-anti-intellectual-times.

Fewell, Danna Nolan, and David M Gunn, 'Controlling Perspectives: Women, Men and the Authority of Violence in Judges 4 and 5'. *Journal of the American Academy of Religion*, 58, 3 (1990), 389–411.

Fisk, Anna. 'Sisterhood in the Wilderness: Biblical Paradigms and Feminist Identity Politics in Readings of Hagar and Sarah'. In *Looking Through a Glass Bible: Postdisciplinary Biblical Interpretations from the Glasgow School*, edited by A. K. M. Adam and Samuel Tongue. Biblical Interpretation Series, 113–137. Leiden: Brill, 2014.

Focht, Caralie. 'Butch-Femme Dynamics in Exodus 2–6 and 14: A Lesbian-Focused Character Study'. *Theology & Sexuality* 25, 3 (2019): 188–204. https://doi.org/10.1080/13558358.2020.1721408.

Fokkelman, J. P. 'Genesis'. In *The Literary Guide to the Bible*, edited by Robert Alter and Frank Kermode, 36–55. Cambridge, MA: Harvard University Press, 1987.

Frankel, Ellen. *The Five Books of Miriam: A Woman's Commentary on the Torah*. San Francisco, CA: HarperSanFrancisco, 1998.

Fuchs, Esther. *Feminist Theory and the Bible: Interrogating the Sources*. New York: Lexington Books, 2016.

Girvan, Ray. 'Coleridge, Pixies' Parlour, and Invented Tradition', JSBlog – Journal of a Southern Bookreader, updated 1 March 2014, accessed 18 October 2019, http://jsbookreader.blogspot.com/2014/03/coleridge-pixies-parlour-and-invented.html.

Gordon, Cyrus H. *Before the Bible: The Common Background of Greek and Hebrew Civilisations*. London: Collins, 1962.

Graybill, Rhiannon. *Are We Not Men? Unstable Masculinity in the Hebrew Prophets*. New York: Oxford University Press, 2016.

Greenberg, Steven. *Wrestling with God and Men: Homosexuality in the Jewish Tradition*. Madison, WI: University of Wisconsin Press, 2004.

Gross, Sally. 'Intersexuality and Scripture'. *Theology and Sexuality* 11 (1999): 65–74. https://doi.org/10.1177/135583589900601105.

Guest, Deryn. 'Hiding Behind the Naked Women in Lamentations: A Recriminative Response'. *Biblical Interpretation* 7, 4 (1999): 413–448. https://doi.org/10.1163/156851599X00308.

Guest, Deryn. *When Deborah Met Jael: Lesbian Biblical Hermeneutics*. London: SCM Press, 2005.

Guest, Deryn. 'Looking Lesbian at the Bathing Bathsheba'. *Biblical Interpretation* 16, 3 (2008): 227–262. https://doi.org/10.1163/156851508X27611.

Guest, Deryn. 'From Gender Reversal to Genderfuck: Reading Jael Through a Lesbian Lens'. In *Bible Trouble: Queer Readings at the Boundaries of Biblical Scholarship*, edited by Teresa J. Hornsby and Ken Stone. Semeia Studies, 9–43. Atlanta, GA: SBL Press, 2011.

Guest, Deryn. *Beyond Feminist Biblical Studies*. Bible in the Modern World. Sheffield: Sheffield Phoenix Press, 2012.

Guest, Deryn. 'Troubling the Waters: תהום, Transgender, and Reading Genesis Backwards'. In *Transgender, Intersex, and Biblical Interpretation*, edited by Teresa J. Hornsby and Deryn Guest, 21–44. Atlanta, GA: SBL Press, 2016.

Guest, Deryn. 'Modeling the Transgender Gaze: Performances of Masculinity in 2 Kings 9–10'. In *Transgender, Intersex, and Biblical Interpretation*, edited by Teresa J. Hornsby and Deryn Guest, 45–80. Atlanta, GA: SBL Press, 2016.

Guest, Deryn, Robert E. Shore-Goss [Goss], Mona West and Thomas Bohache, eds. *The Queer Bible Commentary*. London: SCM Press, 2006.

Gutiérrez, Gustavo. *A Theology of Liberation: History, Politics and Salvation*. Translated by Sister Caridad Inda and John Eagleson. London: SCM Press, 1974.

Gutiérrez, Gustavo. *We Drink from Our Own Wells: The Spiritual Journey of a People*. SCM Classics. London: SCM Press, 2012.

Gwyther, Katherine and Jo Henderson-Merrygold, 'The Disidentification of Mordecai: A Drag Interpretation of Esther 8:15' *Hebrew Studies*, 63 (2022): 119–141 https://doi.org/10.1353/hbr.2022.0006.

Haddox, Susan E. '"The Lord is With You, You Mighty Warrior": The Question of Gideon's Masculinity'. *Proceedings of the East Great Lakes and Midwest Biblical Societies* 30 (2010): 70–87.

Haddox, Susan E. 'Favoured Sons and Subordinate Masculinities'. In *Men and Masculinity in the Hebrew Bible and Beyond*, edited by Ovidiu Creangă. The Bible in the Modern World, 2–19. Sheffield: Sheffield Phoenix Press, 2010.

Halberstam, Jack [Judith]. *Female Masculinity*. Durham, NC: Duke University Press, 1998.

Halberstam, Jack [Judith]. *In a Queer Time and Place: Transgender Bodies, Subcultural Lives*. New York: New York University Press, 2005.

Halberstam, Jack [Judith]. *The Queer Art of Failure*. Durham, NC: Duke University Press, 2011.

Hale, C. Jacob. 'Consuming the Living, Dis(re)membering the Dead in the Butch/FtM Borderlands'. *GLQ: A Journal of Lesbian and Gay Studies* 4, 2 (1998): 311–348. https://doi.org/10.1215/10642684-4-2-311.

Hamilton, Victor P. *The Book of Genesis: Chapters 18–50*. NICOT. Grand Rapids, MI: Eerdmans, 1995.

Harding, James E. *The Love of David and Jonathan: Ideology, Text, Reception*. Abingdon, Oxon: Routledge, 2014.

Hartke, Austen. *Transforming: The Bible and the Lives of Transgender Christians*. Louisville, KY: Westminster John Knox Press, 2018.

Heacock, Anthony. *Jonathan Loved David: Manly Love in the Bible and the Hermeneutics of Sex*. The Bible in the Modern World. Sheffield: Sheffield Phoenix Press, 2011.

Henderson-Merrygold, Jo. 'Queer(y)ing the Epistemic Violence of Christian Gender Discourses'. In *Rape Culture, Gender Violence, and Religion: Christian Perspectives*, edited by Caroline Blyth, Katie B. Edwards and Emily Colgan. Religion and Radicalism, 97–117. London: Palgrave, 2018.

Henderson-Merrygold, Jo. 'Gendering Sarai: Reading Beyond Cisnormativity in Genesis 11:29–12:20 and 20:1–18'. *Open Theology* 6, 1 (2020): 496–509. https://doi.org/10.1515/opth-2020-0133.

Henderson-Merrygold, Jo. 'Reading Biblical Embodiment Cispiciously'. In *Embodying Religion, Gender and Sexuality*, edited by Katy Pilcher and Sarah-Jane Page. Gendering the Study of Religion in the Social Sciences, 129–144. London: Routledge, 2021.

Henderson-Merrygold, Jo. 'Jacob—A (Drag) King Amongst Patriarchs'. In *Texts, Contexts and Intertexts of Women and Gender in the Bible*, edited by Zanne Domoney-Lyttle and Sarah Nicholson, 125–140. Sheffield: Sheffield Phoenix Press, 2021.

Herzer, Linda Tatro. *The Bible and the Transgender Experience: How Scripture Supports Gender Variance*. Kindle ed. Cleveland, OH: Pilgrim Press, 2016.

Heyward, [Isabel] Carter. *The Redemption of God: A Theology of Mutual Relation.* Lanham, MD: University Press of America, 1982.

Heyward, [Isabel] Carter. *Our Passion for Justice: Images of Power, Sexuality, and Liberation.* New York, Pilgrim Press, 1984.

Heyward, [Isabel] Carter. *Touching Our Strength: The Erotic as Power and the Love of God,* San Francisco, CA: Harper and Row, 1989.

Hoffner, Harry A., Jr. 'Symbols of Masculinity and Femininity: Their Use in Ancient near Eastern Sympathetic Magic Rituals'. *Journal of Biblical Literature* 85, 3 (1966): 326–334. https://doi.org/10.2307/3264246

Horner, Thomas M. *Jonathan Loved David: Homosexuality in Biblical Times.* Philadelphia, PA: Westminster, 1978.

Hornsby, Teresa J. 'Introduction: The Body as Decoy'. In *Transgender, Intersex and Biblical Interpretation,* edited by Teresa J. Hornsby and Deryn Guest, 1–12. Atlanta, GA: SBL Press, 2016.

Hornsby, Teresa J. 'Gender Dualism, or The Big Lie'. In *Transgender, Intersex and Biblical Studies,* edited by Teresa J. Hornsby and Deryn Guest, 13–20. Atlanta, GA: SBL Press, 2016.

Hornsby, Teresa J. 'The Dance of Gender: David, Jesus, and Paul'. In *Transgender, Intersex, and Biblical Interpretation,* edited by Teresa J. Hornsby and Deryn Guest, 82–93. Atlanta, GA: SBL Press, 2016.

Hornsby, Teresa J., and Deryn Guest, eds. *Transgender, Intersex and Biblical Interpretation.* Atlanta, GA: SBL Press, 2016.

Iantaffi, Alex, and Meg-John Barker. *How to Understand Your Gender: A Practical Guide for Exploring Who You Are.* London: Jessica Kingsley Publishers, 2017.

Iantaffi, Alex, and Meg-John Barker. *Life Isn't Binary: On Being Both, Beyond and In-Between.* London: Jessica Kingsley Publishers, 2019.

Ingraham, Chrys. 'The Heterosexual Imaginary: Feminist Sociology and Theories of Gender'. *Sociological Theory* 12, 2 (1994): 203–219. https://doi.org/10.2307/201865.

Jacob, Benno. *The First Book of the Bible: Genesis.* New York: KTAV Publishing House Inc, 1974.

Jennings Jr., Theodore W. *Jacob's Wound: Homoerotic Narrative in the Literature of the Ancient Israel.* New York: Continuum, 2005.

Joyce, Paul M. 'The Way of the Future? Into Our Second Century'. In *SOTS at 100: Centennial Essays of the Society for Old Testament Study,* edited by John Jarrick, 159–177. London: Bloomsbury T&T Clark, 2017.

Junior, Nyasha. *Reimagining Hagar: Blackness and Bible.* New York: Oxford University Press, 2019.

Kidner, Derek. *Genesis.* Tyndale Old Testament Commentaries. London: Tyndale Press, 1967.

Koch-Rein, Anson. 'Monster'. *Transgender Studies Quarterly (TSQ)* 1, 1–2 (2014): 134–135. https://doi.org/10.1215/23289252-2399821.

Kolakowski, Victoria. 'The Concubine and the Eunuch: Queering up the Breeder's Bible'. In *Our Families, Our Values: Snapshots of Queer Kinship,* edited by Robert E. Shore-Goss [Goss] and Amy Adams Squire Strongheart, 35–49. Binghamton, NY: Harrington Park, 1997.

Kolakowski, Victoria. 'Toward a Christian Ethical Response to Transsexual Persons'. *Theology and Sexuality* 1997, 6 (1997): 10–31. https://doi.org/10.1177/135583589700300602.

Kolakowski, Victoria. 'Throwing a Party: Patriarchy, Gender, and the Death of Jezebel'. In *Take Back the Word: A Queer Reading of the Bible*, edited by Robert E. Shore-Goss [Goss] and Mona West, 103–114. Cleveland, OH: Pilgrim Press, 2000.

Ladin, Joy. *The Soul of the Stranger: Reading God and Torah from a Transgender Perspective*. Waltham, MA: Brandeis University Press, 2019.

Laqueur, Thomas. *Making Sex: Body and Gender From the Greeks to Freud*. Cambridge, MA: Harvard University Press, 1990.

Lennon, Erica, and Brian J. Mistler. 'Cisgenderism'. *Transgender Studies Quarterly (TSQ)* 1, 1–2 (2014): 63–64. https://doi.org/10.1215/23289252-2399623.

Lester, CN. *Trans Like Me: A Journey For All of Us*. London: Virago, 2017.

Lev, Sarra. 'Esau's Gender Crossing: *Parashat Toldot* (Genesis 25:19–28:9)'. In *Torah Queeries: Weekly Commentaries on the Hebrew Bible*, edited by Gregg Drinkwater, Joshua Lesser and David Shneer, 38–42. New York: New York University Press, 2009.

Livingston, Jennie. 'Paris is Burning'. 78 Minutes. USA: Off-White Productions, 1990.

Llewellyn, Dawn. 'Maternal Silences: Motherhood and Voluntary Childlessness in Contemporary Christianity'. *Religion and Gender* 6, 1 (2016): 64–79. https://doi.org/10.18352/rg.10131.

Love, Heather. 'Queer'. *Transgender Studies Quarterly (TSQ)*, 1, 1–2 (2014): 172–176. https://doi.org/10.1215/23289252-2399938.

Macwilliam, Stuart. 'Ideologies of Male Beauty and the Hebrew Bible'. *Biblical Interpretation* 17, 3 (2009): 265–287. https://doi.org/10.1163/156851508X329674.

Marchal, Joseph A. *Appalling Bodies: Queer Figures Before and After Paul's Letters*. New York: Oxford University Press, 2020.

McDonald, Joseph. *Searching for Sarah in the Second Temple Era: Images in the Hebrew Bible, the Septuagint, the Genesis Apocryphon, and the Antiquities*. Scriptural Traces: Critical Perspectives on the Reception and Influence of the Hebrew Bible. London: T&T Clark, 2021.

Mobley, Gregory. 'The Wild Man in the Bible and the Ancient Near East'. *Journal of Biblical Literature* 116, 2 (1997): 217–233. https://doi.org/10.2307/3266221.

Mollenkott, Virginia Ramey. *Omnigender: A Trans-religious Approach*. Revised and Expanded ed. Cleveland, OH: Pilgrim Press, 2007.

Moss, Candida R., and Joel S. Baden. *Reconceiving Infertility: Biblical Perspectives on Procreation and Childlessness*. Princeton, NJ: Princeton University Press, 2015.

Mowat, Chris. 'Engendering the Future: Divination and the Construction of Gender in the Late Roman Republic'. PhD, Newcastle University, 2018. http://theses.ncl.ac.uk/jspui/handle/10443/4859.

Muñoz, José Esteban. *Disidentification: Queers of Color and the Performance of Politics*. Minneapolis, MN: University of Minnesota Press, 1999.

Muñoz, José Esteban. *Cruising Utopia: The Then and There of Queer Futurity*. New York: New York University Press, 2009.

Musa, Aysha Winstanley. 'Jael Is Non-Binary; Jael Is Not A Woman'. *Journal for Interdisciplinary Biblical Studies* 1, 2 (2020a): 97–120. https://doi.org/10.17613/y6zg-7s57.

Musa, Aysha Winstanley. 'Jael's Gender Ambiguity in Judges 4 and 5'. PhD, University of Sheffield, 2020b. http://etheses.whiterose.ac.uk/27692/.

Namaste, Viviane. *Invisible Lives: The Erasure of Transsexual and Transgendered People*. Chicago, IL: The University of Chicago Press, 2000.

Namaste, Viviane. 'Undoing Theory: The "Transgender Question" and the Epistemic Violence of Anglo-American Feminist Theory'. *Hypatia* 24, 3 (2009): 11–32. https://doi.org/10.1111/j.1527-2001.2009.01043.x.

Neff, Samuel. 'Transfigurations: Transgressing Gender in the Bible'. DVD, 103 minutes. Newbeerg, OR: Barclay Press, March 2017. http://www.barclaypressbookstore.com/transfigurations.

Nemesius of Ernesa, *On the Nature of Man,* ed. William Tefler. Philadelphia, PA: Westminster Press, 1955.

Nestle, Joan. 'The Femme Question'. In *The Persistent Desire: A Femme-Butch Reader*, edited by Joan Nestle et al., 138–146. Boston, MA: Alyson Publications, 1992.

Nestle, Joan, Clare Howell and Riki A. Wilchins, eds. *GenderQueer: Voices From Beyond the Binary.* Los Angeles, CA: Alyson Books, 2002.

Niditch, Susan. 'Genesis'. In *Women's Bible Commentary: Revised and Updated*, edited by Carol A. Newsom, Sharon H. Ringe and Jacqueline E. Lapsley, 27–45. Louisville, KY: Westminster John Knox Press, 2012.

O'Connor, Kathleen M. 'Lamentations'. In *Women's Bible Commentary*, edited by Carol A. Newsom, Sharon H. Ringe and Jacqueline E. Lapsley, 278–282. Louisville, KY: Westminster John Knox Press, 2012.

Patterson, GPat, and Leland G. Spencer. 'Toward Trans Rhetorical Agency: A Critical Analysis of Trans Topics and Rhetoric and Composition and Communication Scholarship', *Peitho* 20, 4 (2020): https://cfshrc.org/article/toward-trans-rhetorical-agency-a-critical-analysis-of-trans-topics-in-rhetoric-composition-and-communication-scholarship/

Pearce, Ruth, and Francis Ray White. 'Beyond the Pregnant Man: Representing Trans Pregnancy in *A Deal With The Universe*'. *Feminist Media Studies* 19, 5 (2019): 764–767. https://doi.org/10.1080/14680777.2019.1630925.

Plaskow, Judith. 'Transing and Gendering Religious Studies'. *Journal of Feminist Studies in Religion* 34, 1 (2018): 75–80. https://doi.org/10.2979/jfemistudreli.34.1.10.

Power, Shannon. 'Lesbian Kicked Out of the Bowling Alley Because She Used the Women's Restroom'. *GayStarNews*, 22 October 2018. https://www.gaystarnews.com/article/lesbian-kicked-out-of-bowling-alley-because-she-used-the-womens-restroom/#gs.6QJqWNvx.

Prosser, Jay. *Second Skins: The Body Narratives of Transsexuality.* New York: Columbia University Press, 1998.

Queen, Carol, and Lawrence Schimel, eds. *Pomosexuals: Challenging Assumptions About Gender and Sexuality.* San Francisco, CA: Cleis Press, 2001.

Radford Ruether, Rosemary. *Womanguides: Readings toward a Feminist Theology, with a new preface.* Boston, MA: Beacon Press, 1996.

Rashkow, Ilona N. *Taboo or not Taboo: Sexuality in the Hebrew Bible.* Minneapolis, MN: Fortress Press, 2000.

Reich, June L. 'Genderfuck: The Law of the Dildo' *Discourse* 15, 1 (1992), 112–127. https://www.jstor.org/stable/41389251.

Rich, Adrienne. 'Compulsory Heterosexuality and Lesbian Existence'. In *Feminism and Sexuality: A Reader*, edited by Stevi Jackson and Sue Scott, 130–142. Edinburgh: Edinburgh University Press, 1996.

Ricoeur, Paul. *Freud and Philosophy: An Essay on Interpretation*, translated by Denis Savage. New Haven, CT: Yale University Press, 1970.

Ricoeur, Paul. *The Conflict of Interpretations: Essays in Hermeneutics,* edited by Don Ihde. Northwestern University Studies in Phenomenology & Existential Philosophy. Evanston: Northwestern University Press, 1974.

Riggs, Damien W., Carla A. Pfeffer, Ruth Pearce, Sally Hines, and Francis Ray White. 'Men, Trans/Masculine, and Non-binary People Negotiating Conception: Normative

Resistance and Inventive Pragmatism'. *International Journal of Transgender Health* (2020): 1–13. https://doi.org/10.1080/15532739.2020.1808554.

Rosenberg, Gil. *Ancentral Queerness: The Normal and the Deviant in the Abraham and Sarah Narratives*. Hebrew Bible Monographs. Sheffield: Sheffield Phoenix Press, 2019.

Ross, Samuel. 'A Transgender Gaze at Genesis 38'. *Journal for Interdisciplinary Biblical Studies* 1, 2 (2020): 25–39. https://doi.org/10.17613/wbs2-qj93.

Ruane, Nicole J. 'When Women Aren't Enough: Gender Criticism in Feminist Bible Interpretation'. In *Feminist Interpretation of the Hebrew Bible in Retrospect: III. Methods*, edited by Susanne Scholz. Recent Research in Biblical Studies, 243–260. Sheffield: Sheffield Phoenix Press, 2016.

Rubright, Marjorie. 'Transgender Capacity in Thomas Dekker and Thomas Middleton's *The Roaring Girl* (1611)'. *Journal for Early Modern Cultural Studies* 19, 4 (2019): 45–74. https://doi.org/10.1353/jem.2019.0037.

Runions, Erin. 'Zion is Burning: Genderfuck and Hybridity in Micah and *Paris Is Burning*'. In *How Hysterical: Identification and Resistance in the Bible and Film*, 93–114. New York: Palgrave Macmillan, 2003.

Sabia-Tanis [Tanis], Justin. 'Eating the Crumbs That Fall from the Table: Trusting the Abundance of God'. In *Take Back the Word: A Queer Reading of the Bible*, edited by Robert E. Shore-Goss [Goss] and Mona West, 43–54. Cleveland, OH: Pilgrim Press, 2000.

Sabia-Tanis [Tanis], Justin. *Trans-Gender: Theology, Ministry and Communities of Faith*. Eugene, OR: Wipf & Stock, 2018 [2003].

Said, Edward. *Orientalism*. New York: Pantheon, 1978.

Sandars, N. K. *The Epic of Gilgamesh*. Penguin Classics. Revised ed. Harmondsworth, Middlesex: Penguin 1972.

Sawyer, Deborah F. 'Biblical Gender Strategies: the Case of Abraham's Masculinity'. In *Gender, Religion and Diversity: Cross-Cultural Perspectives*, edited by Ursula King and Tina Beattie, 162–171. London: Continuum, 2004.

Schept, Susan. 'Hesed: Feminist Ethics in Jewish Tradition (Genesis 12, 24)'. In *Reading Genesis: Beginnings*, edited by Beth Kissileff, 83–91. London: Bloomsbury T&T Clark, 2016.

Schneider, Tammi J. *Sarah: Mother of Nations*. New York: Continuum, 2004.

Schüssler Fiorenza, Elisabeth. *In Memory of Her: Feminist Practices of Biblical Interpretation*. New York: Crossroad, 1983.

Schüssler Fiorenza, Elisabeth. *Bread Not Stone: The Challenge of Feminist Biblical Interpretation*. Boston, MA: Beacon Press, 1984.

Schüssler Fiorenza, Elisabeth. *But She Said: Feminist Practices of Biblical Interpretation*. Boston, MA: Beacon Press, 1992.

Schüssler Fiorenza, Elisabeth. *Bread Not Stone: With a New Afterword*. The Challenges of Feminist Biblical Interpretation. Boston, MA: Beacon Press, 1995.

Schüssler Fiorenza, Elisabeth. *Wisdom Ways: Introducing Feminist Biblical Interpretation*. Maryknoll, NY: Orbis Books, 2001.

Sedgwick, Eve Kosofsky. *Tendencies*. Durham, NC: Duke University Press, 1993.

Segundo, Juan Luis. *The Liberation of Theology*. Maryknoll, NY: Orbis Books, 1976.

Serano, Julia. 'Cissexism and Cis Privilege Revisited. Part 1: Who Exactly Does "Cis" Refer To?'. Whipping Girl, 2014, accessed 1 October 2019, http://juliaserano.blogspot.co.uk/2014/10/cissexism-and-cis-privilege-revisited.html.

Serano, Julia. *Whipping Girl: A Transsexual Woman on Sexism and the Scapegoating of Femininity*. Second ed. Berkeley, CA: Seal Press, 2016.

Serano, Julia. *Excluded: Making Feminist and Queer Movements More Inclusive*. Berkeley, CA: Seal Press, 2013.

Serano, Julia. 'Julia's Trans, Gender, Sexuality, & Activism Glossary!' JuliaSerano.com, [no date], accessed 3 June 2020, http://www.juliaserano.com/terminology.html.

Setel, T. Drorah. 'Prophets and Pornography: Female Sexual Imagery in Hosea'. In *Feminist Interpretation of the Bible*, edited by Letty M. Russell Philadelphia, PA: Westminster Press, 1985. http://www.womencanbepriests.org/classic/russ_cnt.asp.

Sherwood, Yvonne. 'Hagar and Ishmael: The Reception of Explusion'. *Interpretation: A Journal of Bible and Theology* 68, 3 (2014): 286–304. https://doi.org/10.1177/0020964314535544.

Shildrick, Margrit. *Embodying the Monster: Encounters with the Vulnerable Self*. London: Sage, 2002.

Shore-Goss [Goss], Robert E., and Amy Adams Squire Strongheart, eds. *Our Families, Our Values: Snapshots of Queer Kinship*. Binghamton, NY: Harrington Park, 1997.

Shore-Goss [Goss], Robert E., and Mona West, eds. *Take Back the Word: A Queer Reading of the Bible*. Cleveland, OH: Pilgrim Press, 2000.

Skinner, John. *A Critical and Exegetical Commentary on Genesis*. The International Critical Commentary. Edinburgh: T&T Clark, 1910.

Smit, Peter-Ben. *Masculinity and the Bible: Survey, Models, and Perspectives*. Brill Research Perspectives. Leiden: Brill, 2017.

Smith, S. H. '"Heel" and "Thigh": the Concept of Sexuality in the Jacob-Esau Narratives'. *Vetus Testamentum* 40, 4 (1990): 464–473. https://doi.org/10.1163/156853390X00154.

Snorton, C. Riley. *Black on Both Sides: A Racial History of Trans Identity*. Minneapolis, MN: University of Minnesota Press, 2017.

Speiser, E. A. *Genesis*. The Anchor Bible Commentary. Garden City, NY: Doubleday, 1964.

Spencer-Hall, Alicia, and Blake Gutt. *Trans and Genderqueer Subjects in Medieval Hagiography*. Amsterdam: Amsterdam University Press, 2021.

Spillers, Hortense J. 'Mama's Baby, Papa's Maybe: An American Grammar Book'. *Diacritics* 17, 2 (1987): 64–81. https://doi.org/10.2307/464747

Stiebert, Johanna. 'The Maligned Prophet: Prophetic Ideology and the "Bad Press" of Esau'. In *Sense and Sensitivity: Essays on Reading the Bible in Memory of Robert Carroll*, edited by Alastair G. Hunter and Philip R. Davies. The Library of Hebrew Bible/Old Testament Studies, 33–48. Sheffield: Sheffield Academic Press, 2002.

Stiebert, Johanna. *First-Degree Incest and the Hebrew Bible: Sex in the Family*. The Library of Hebrew Bible/Old Testament Studies. London: Bloomsbury T&T Clark, 2016.

Stone, Ken. 'Queer Commentary and Biblical Interpretation: An Introduction'. In *Queer Commentary and the Hebrew Bible*, edited by Ken Stone, 11–34. London: Sheffield Academic Press, 2001.

Stone, Ken. 'The Garden of Eden and the Heterosexual Contract'. In *Bodily Citations: Religion and Judith Butler*, edited by Ellen T. Armour and Susan M. St Ville, 48–70. New York: Columbia University Press, 2006.

Stone, Ken. 'Bibles That Matter: Biblical Theology and Queer Performativity'. *Biblical Theology Bulletin* 38, 1 (2008): 14–25. https://doi.org/10.1177/01461079080380010301.

Stone, Sandy. 'The *Empire* Strikes Back: A Posttranssexual Manifesto'. In *The Transgender Studies Reader*, edited by Susan Stryker and Stephen Whittle, 221–235. New York: Routledge, 2006 [1987].

Strassfeld, Max. 'Transing Religious Studies'. *Journal of Feminist Studies in Religion* 34, 1 (2018): 37–53. https://doi.org/10.2979/jfemistudreli.34.1.05.

Strassfeld, Max. *Trans Talmud: Androgynes and Eunuchs in Rabbinic Literature.* University of California Press, 2022.
Strudwick, Patrick. 'A High Court Judge Has Ruled that "Mother" No Longer Means "Woman"'. *Buzzfeed,* 10 October 2019. https://www.buzzfeed.com/patrickstrudwick/mother-no-longer-means-woman-judge-rules.
Strudwick, Patrick. 'A Trans Dad Will Now Go To The Supreme Court To Be Named The Father On His Child's Birth Certificate'. *Buzzfeed,* 29 April 2020. https://www.buzzfeed.com/patrickstrudwick/trans-dad-supreme-court-named-father.
Stryker, Susan. 'My Words to Victor Frankenstein Above the Village of Chamounix: Performing Transgender Rage'. *GLQ: A Journal of Lesbian and Gay Studies* 1, 3 (1994): 237–254. https://doi.org/10.1215/10642684-1-3-237.
Stryker, Susan. '(De)Subjugated Knowledges: An Introduction to Transgender Studies'. In *The Transgender Studies Reader,* edited by Susan Stryker and Stephen Whittle, 1–17. New York: Routledge, 2006.
Stryker, Susan. *Transgender History.* New York: Seal Press, 2008.
Sumerau, J. E., Ryan T. Cragun and Lain A. B. Mathers. 'Contemporary Religion and the Cisgendering of Reality'. *Social Currents* 3, 3 (2016): 293–311. https://doi.org/10.1177/2329496515604644.
Tate, Shirley Anne. *Black Beauty: Aesthetics, Stylization, Politics.* London: Routledge, 2009.
Thiem, Yannik [Annika]. 'No Gendered Bodies without Queer Desire: Judith Butler and Biblical Gender Trouble'. *Old Testament Essays* 20, 2 (2007): 456–470. https://doi.org/10520/EJC85873.
Thiem, Yannik [Annika]. 'The Art of Queer Rejections: The Everyday Life of Biblical Discourse'. *Neotestamentica* 48, 1 (2014): 33–56.
Thomas, Ebony Elizabeth. *The Dark Fantastic: Race and the Imagination from Harry Potter to the Hunger Games.* Kindle ed. New York: New York University Press, 2019.
Thompson, Holly. 'The Reception of Esther: A Genderqueer/Non-Binary Reading of the Ancient Texts and in Modern Scholarship'. DPhil. University of Oxford. 2021, https://ora.ox.ac.uk/objects/uuid:f263f6cd-ff25-4497-9a28-1c04c2113578
Toscano, Peterson. 'Transfigurations Study Guide'. PetersonToscano.com, Updated 13 April, 2018, https://petersontoscano.com/portfolio/transfigurations/.
'Trans*/Religion'. *Transgender Studies Quarterly (TSQ)* 6, 3 (2019).
'Transing and Queering Feminist Studies and Practices of Religion.' *Journal of Feminist Studies in Religion* 34, 1 (2018) Special Issue.
Trible, Phyllis. 'Depatriarchalizing in Biblical Interpretation'. *Journal of the American Academy of Religion* 41, 1 (1973): 30–48. https://doi.org/10.1093/jaarel/XLI.1.30.
Trible, Phyllis. *God and the Rhetoric of Sexuality.* Philadelphia, PA: Fortress Press, 1978.
Trible, Phyllis. *Texts of Terror.* SCM Classics. London: SCM Press, 2002.
Valentine, Katy E. 'Examining Scripture in Light of Trans Women's Voices'. In *The Oxford Handbook of Feminist Approaches to the Hebrew Bible,* edited by Susanne Scholz. Oxford Handbooks, 509–524. New York: Oxford University Press, 2021.
van Dijk-Hemmes, Fokkelien. 'Sarai's Exile: A Gender-Motivated Reading of Genesis 12.10–13.2'. In *A Feminist Companion to Genesis,* edited by Athalya Brenner-Idan [Brenner]. The Feminist Companion to the Bible, 222–234. Sheffield: Sheffield Academic Press, 1993.
Vawter, Bruce. *A Path Through Genesis.* London: Sheed & Ward, 1957.
Vawter, Bruce. *On Genesis: A New Reading.* London: Geoffrey Chapman, 1977.
Vermes, Geza, *The Dead Sea Scrolls in English.* Sheffield: JSOT Press, 1987.

von Rad, Gerhard. *Genesis: A Commentary*. Old Testament Library. Revised ed. London: SCM Press, 1972.
Vorster, Johannes N. 'The Queering of Biblical Discourse'. *Scriptura* 111, 3 (2012): 602–620. https://doi.org/10.7833/111-1-39.
Wamue, G., and M. Getui, eds. *Violence Against Women: Reflections by Kenyan Women Theologinas*. Nairobi:L Acton, 1996.
Warner, Michael. 'Introduction: Fear of a Queer Planet. *Social Text* 29 (1991): 3–17. https://www.jstor.org/stable/466295.
Weems, Renita J. *Just A Sister Away: A Womanist Vision of Women's Relationships in the Bible*. Kindle ed. San Diego, CA: LuraMedia, 2005.
Weismantel, Mary. 'Towards a Transgender Archaeology: A queer rampage through prehistory'. In *The Transgender Studies Reader 2*, edited by Susan Stryker and Aren Z. Aizura, 319–324. New York: Routledge, 2013.
Wenham, Gordon J. *Genesis 16–50*. Word Biblical Commentary. Google Play ed. Dallas, TX: Word Books, 2000.
West, Mona. 'The Book of Ruth: An Example of Procreative Strategies for Queers'. In *Our Families, Our values: Snapshots of Queer Kinship*, edited by Robert E. Shore-Goss [Goss] and Amy Adams Squire Strongheart, 51–60. Binghamton, NY: Harrington Park Press, 1997.
West, Mona. 'Ruth'. In *The Queer Bible Commentary*, edited by Deryn Guest, Robert E. Shore-Goss [Goss], Mona West and Thomas Bohache, 190–194. London: SCM Press, 2006.
Westermann, Claus. *Genesis 12–36*. Translated by John J. Scullion. A Continental Commentary. London: SPCK, 1985.
Westermann, Claus. *Genesis*. Translated by David E. Green. Edinburgh: T&T Clark, 1987.
Wiegel, Rebecca E. 'Trans Historiography and the Problem of Anachronism: Eunuchs and other Non-Men in Matt 19:1–14'. Society of Biblical Literature Annual Meeting, Denver, CO, 19 November 2018.
Wilchins, Riki A. *Read My Lips: Sexual Subversion and the End of Gender*. Ithaca, NY: Firebrand Books, 1997.
Wilcox, Melissa M. 'Religion is Already Transed; Religious Studies is Not (Yet) Listening'. *Journal of Feminist Studies in Religion* 34, 1 (2018): 84–88. https://doi.org/10.2979/jfemistudreli.34.1.12
Wittig, Monique. 'The Straight Mind'. In *The Straight Mind: And Other Essays*, 21–32. Boston, MA: Beacon Press, 1992.
Wolf, Mark J. P. *Building Imaginary Worlds: The Theory and History of Subcreation*. New York: Routledge, 2012.
Woolstenhulme, Katie Jayne. 'The Role and Status of the Biblical Matriarchs in Genesis Rabbah'. PhD, Durham University, 2017. http://etheses.dur.ac.uk/12197/.

INDEX OF REFERENCES

Genesis
1	100–101	16:1–9	128–129
1–2	101	16:1–16	129–136
2	9–10	16:2	133
10	120	16:3–4	144
10:32	121 n29	16:4	129, 138 n87, 138
11	116, 139	16:5	129, 132, 137
11:7–8	121	16:5–6	133, 136
11:10–32	121 n29	16:6	129, 133
11–12	114	16:7–14	132
11:26–30	154 n10	16:8	134
11:26–32	121	16:9	132, 134
11:27–21:12	24	16:15	135
11:27–23:2	12, 113–160	17	136, 139
11:27–31	118–119	17:2	151
11:29	118 n22, 118	17:15	116
11:29–12:20	113 n1, 117–130	17:15–22	136
11:29–31	113, 116, 117–120, 125, 142	17:16	138
		17:17	137
		17:19	136
11:30	117, 119–120	18	139, 143, 146
12	116, 120, 126–128, 129, 131, 134, 139, 149	18:1–14	143
		18:6	136
12:1–3	121	18:8	136
12:5	120, 121	18:9	136–137
12:7–8	121, 126	18:9–15	136–139
12:10–20	113, 120–128, 123, 125, 141, 144	18:10	139
		18:11	137, 143, 145
12:11–13	121, 123	18:12	137, 138
12:14–15	123	18:12–13	137
12:14–16	122	18:13–15	137, 148
12:17	122	18:14	143
12:18–19	122	18:15	139, 149
12:20	122	18:16–33	139
13	131	19	139
14:17–24	131	20	116, 126 n46
15	131	20–21	139–149
16	114, 137, 138, 143, 148	20:1	138 n87
16–18	114, 128–139	20:1–2	141
16:1–2	133, 136	20:1–7	140–141
16:1–3	129, 132	20:1–18	113 n1, 149–150
16:1–6	131–132	20:1–20	116, 168

20:2	141	25:29	163, 166
20:3	116, 141	25:29–30	163
20:3–7	141	25:29–34	136–137 n85, 155, 162–168, 177, 179, 185
20:5	141		
20:8–18	141–142	25:30	165, 170
20:10–13	142	25:32	165, 166, 170, 176
20:12	142	25:34	168
20:13	142	26	126 n46
20:16	142, 143 n90	26:1–33	168
20:17–18	142, 143, 145	26:8	138 n87
21	116	26:11	138 n87
21:1	128, 143	26:17–18	138 n87
21:1–2	144–145	26:20	138 n87
21:1–3	116–117, 139	26:34–35	168–170, 177, 181
21:1–8	147, 149–150	27	24, 161, 169, 190
21:1–14	144	27:1	171
21:4	146	27:1–4	171
21:6–7	146	27:1–17	171–174
21:8	147	27:1–46	170–181, 177–181
21:9–20	147	27:3	160 n39, 171–172
21:9–21	129–130	27:3–4	173
21:10	116–117, 147–148	27:5	172
21:11	148	27:5–17	172
21:12	148	27:5–29	136–137 n85
21:15–19	148	27:9	176
21:19–20	149	27:9–10	173
22	148, 190	27:11	173
22:20–23	118 n22	27:11–12	172, 173
23:1–2	149	27:12	174
23:1–20	138 n87	27:15	176
23:2	117	27:16	172
23:3–20	149	27:18	176
24	118 n22	27:18–30	174–177
24:15	118 n22, 154 n10	27:19	176
24:24	118 n22	27:20	176
24:47	118–119 n22	27:22	176
25	177, 190	27:22–23	176
25:19–23	154	27:23	174, 176–177
25:19–26	154–160	27:27	176
25:19–34	153–162, 182	27:31	176
25:25	151, 153, 154–155, 172	27:31–32	176 n83, 178
25:25–26	154–155	27:31–46	178–181
25:25–33:17	12	27:33–34	178–179, 180
25:26	172	27:34–35	179
25:27	136–137 n85	27:36	179
25:27–28	154, 160–162	27:37–40	179
25:27–34	176	27:39–40	180
25:28	172, 179	27:41	179, 180

27:41–42	183	*Judges*	
27:41–45	179	3:24	159 n33, 160 n37
27:46	179	4–5	79–80, 87–88
28–31	184	5:26	88
28:6	181	14:6–16:30	195
28:6–9	181–182	16:17	155
28:7	181	19–20	180 n93
28:8	181		
28:9	181	*Ruth*	
28:24–30	153–154	1–4	79
29:5–6	118–119 n22		
32:1–22	183	*1 Samuel*	
32:6	183	16:12	155, 156
33	153, 181, 186, 190, 192	16ff	114, 131 n64, 193
33:1–4	183	17:42	155, 156
33:1–17	182–185	24:3	160 n37
33:3	183	24:5	159 n33
33:6	183		
33:6–7	183	*2 Samuel*	
33:8	183	11:2	81–82
33:9	183	14:26	155
33:13	183		
33:14	183	*1 Kings*	
33:14–17	183	1–2	114, 131 n64, 193
33:15	183		
34:7	180 n93	*2 Kings*	
34:13–26	180 n93	9:2	105
35:16–20	192	9–10	105–107, 172 n73
35:18	192	9:14	105
35:29	184	9:24	106
36	184–185	9:30–37	106
36:1–41	183		
36:2–3	168–169 n69	*Esther*	
37:2–36	192	8:15	196
42–45	192		
		Song of Songs	
Exodus		5:4	88 n79
32	114, 131 n64	5:10	156
34	114, 131 n64		
		Isaiah	
Leviticus		3:16–17	97 n111
13:19	156 n15	6:2	159 n33
13:24	156 n15	7:20	159 n33
13:42–43	156 n15	47:2	159 n33
		51:1–2	128 n54
Deuteronomy		53	134 n80
22:5	67	57:8	88 n79

Jeremiah
  5:31   88 n79
  49:8–10   181 n95
  50:15   88 n79

Lamentations
  1   96
  4:7 156

Ezekiel
  16   97 n111
  23   97 n111

Jonah
  2   196
  4   196

Malachi
  2–3   181 n95

Romans
  9:13   181 n95

Hebrews
  12:16   181 n95

1QapGen
  XX   124

INDEX OF AUTHORS AND KEY THEMES

Ahmed, Sara, 67 n1
Alter, Robert, 167, 169
Althaus-Reid, Marcella,
   11–14, 18–20, **30–40**,
   40–42, 63–65
   Indecent Theology,
   36–37, 40
   The Queer God, **36–40**
Anderson, Bradford A., 156,
   164
androcentrism, 9–12,
   81–83, 91–92
Arnold, Bill T., 119–120,
   133

Barker, Meg-John, 45–46
beauty, 113–114, 120–125,
   134–135, 141,
   149–150, 155–157
Berlant, Lauren, and
   Michael Warner, 94
*Beyond Feminist Biblical
   Studies, see* Guest,
   Deryn
binaries, 1–2, 46–47, 49–51,
   76–77, 85–87,
   99–100, 101, 162,
   186, 191–192
birthright, 162–170,
   178–179
bodies. *see* embodiment
Boer, Roland, 159
Bornstein, Kate, 3–4, 85–86
Brayford, Susan, 165, 177
Brenner-Idan, Athalya, 164
butchness, 21–24, 72–75,
   79, 81–85, 88–91,
   98–99, 110–111
Butler, Judith, 14, 19–20,
   44–52, 55–57, 77, 87,
   92

Carden, Michael, 128, 161
Chapman, Cynthia, 147
childlessness, 119–120,
   125–128
cis, 1–2, 12–14, 17–18,
   26–27, 52–55
cisgender. *see* cis
cisnormativity, 1–2,
   12–15, 17–20, 24–27,
   32–33, 36–42, 50–62,
   69–70
cisnorms, 40 n84. *see
   also* cisnormativity
cissexism, 52–55
cisgendering reality, *see*
   Sumerau, J. E., Ryan
   Mathers and Lain
   Cragun
cispicion, 6, 12–15, 17–20,
   29–30, 40–41, 63–65,
   67–71, 74–75, 84,
   110–111, 187–200
Clines, David J. A., 114–116,
   130–135, 138,
   148–149, 155–156,
   193–194
Connell, Raewyn W., 22
   n14, 156

Davidson, Robert, 183–184
Derks, Marco, 73–74
drag, 24, 170–181
   kinging, 24

Edelman, Lee, 28
Eilberg-Schwartz, Howard,
   130–132, 159, 195
embodiment, 19–20, 36–38,
   42–48, 55–65, 70,
   99–100, 103–104,
   106–107, 121–124,
   146–147, 151–186,
   189, 191–192,
   195–196
Enkidu, 157–159, 160, 162,
   172
Epic of Gilgamesh. *see*
   Enkidu
euphemisms, 87–88,
   159–160
Exum, J. Cheryl, 126,
   129–130, 132

failure, 12–15, 17–20,
   40–41, 162–168
Feinberg, Leslie, 67,
   85–86
female masculinity, 2–4,
   72–92, 130–135
   Female Masculinity
   (Halberstam). *see*
   Halberstam, Jack
femininity, 23–25, 45–46,
   83, 88–89, 106–107,
   109–111, 113–114,
   116–128, 133–135,
   137–150, 152–153,
   160–161, 165, 173,
   187–188, 190–195
feminism, 78–79, 81–98,
   110–111
*From Gender Reversal to
   Genderfuck, see*
   Guest, Deryn

gender, 42
gender diversity, 12–15,
   17–19, 28–30, 41–42,
   50–51, 67–71, 91–98,
   108–110, 188–198
genderqueer, 87–91, 94–98,
   100–104, 110–111

Graybill, Rhiannon, 195–196
Gross, Sally, 68, 127–128, 145
Guest, Deryn, 12, 14, 26, **68–111**, 135, 187–188, 190, 193–194
  Beyond Feminist Biblical Studies, 73, **91–98**
  From Gender Reversal to Genderfuck, **84–91**, 98, 101, 106, 111
  Looking Lesbian at the Bathing Bathsheba, **81–84**, 85, 89, 91, 102
  Modeling the Transgender Gaze, 99, **105–108**
  Transgender, Intersex and Biblical Interpretation, 69, 71, 74, **98–110**
  Troubling the Waters, 99, **101–104**, 109
  When Deborah Met Jael, **75–81**, 81–85, 89, 91, 94, 96, 102
Gutiérrez, Gustavo, 8

hair, 153–157, 166–167, 171–172, 174–177
Halberstam, Jack [Judith], 2, 13, 15, 18–20, **20–30**, 40–42, 50, 58, 63–65, 74, 75–76, 80, 85–86, 90–91, 104, 105, 107–109, 110, 113–114, 116, 117–118, 122–123, 127–128, 136, 142, 148, 149, 152, 162–163, 184, 185, 187–197
  Female Masculinity, **20–25**, 27, 85–86, 90–91
  The Queer Art of Failure, **28–30**, 40, 195

In a Queer Time and Place, **25–28**
Hamilton, Victor, 160, 167–168
hermeneutics of suspicion, **6–12**
heteronormativity, 26–30, 41–42, 46–47, 50–51, 71–84, 90–111
Hornsby, Teresa J., 46–47, 99–101
Hornsby, Teresa J. and Deryn Guest, 69, 98–101. *see also Transgender, Intersex and Biblical Interpretation*
hypermasculinity, 170–171

indecency, 13–14, 30–41. *see also* Althaus-Reid, Marcella
Indecent Theology, see Althaus-Reid, Marcella
indecent whimsy, 13–14, 40–41
Ingraham, Chrys, 95

Jacob, Benno, 168

Kolakowski, Victoria, 68–69, 71

Ladin, Joy, 69, 195–196
Laqueur, Thomas, 43–44
lesbian, 46–47
Lev, Sarra, 162, 166
liberation theology, 7–12, 33–35
Looking Lesbian at the Bathing Bathsheba, see Guest, Deryn
low theory, 13, 20, **28–30**, 40–41, 62, 64, 80, 91, 104, 113–114, 116, 188–190, 195, 197. *See also The Queer Art of Failure*

masculinity, 76–77, 87–92, 105–110, 114–117, 128–139, 149–150, 151–165, 170–174, 177, 184–186, 187–191, 193–195
Modeling the Transgender Gaze, see Guest, Deryn
Mollenkott, Virginia Ramey, 68, 128
monster theory, 102–104
Moss, Candida and Joel S. Baden, 125
motherhood, 125–128
Muñoz, José Esteban, 21 n10

Namaste, Viviane, 14, 19–20, 41, 48–49, 54–55, **60–62**, 64, 68, 90, 98, 152, 187–188, 192, 197
Niditch, Susan, 156
nonbinary, 109–110

patriarchy. *see* androcentrism
penis, 87–88, 154–156, 159–160
Plaskow, Judith, 70–71
pregnancy, 35, 125–128, 143–146
Prosser, Jay, 14, 19–20, 41–42, 44–45, 49, 54, **55–60**, 61–68, 76, 90, 97–98, 152, 166, 187, 189

queer, 11–14, 25–42, 47–64
  biblical studies, 67–69, 71–75, 84–91, 101–102, 193–194, 195
  theology, 30–40
  theory, 25–30, 41–42, 47–52, 54–57, 59–64, 85–87, 94–96, 109, 110–111

Index of Authors and Key Themes   229

Queer Art of Failure, The,
see Halberstam,
Jack
Queer God, The, see
Althaus-Reid,
Marcella
*Queer Time and Place, In
a,* see Halberstam,
Jack

Rashkow, Ilona, 165–166
retcon, 116–117, 139–149.
see also Wolf,
Mark J. P.
Rich, Adrienne, 47–48, 77
Ricoeur, Paul, 6–12, 44
Rubright, Marjorie, 197
ruddiness, 155–158,
184–185

Sabia-Tanis, Justin, 68, 71
Sawyer, Deborah, 131
Schept, Susan, 147
Schussler Fiorenza,
Elisabeth, 8–12
Segundo, Juan Luis, 7–8
Serano, Julia, 14, 19–20, 42,
44–46, 49, **52–55**, 59,
62, 64, 90, 100,
113–114, 124, 128,
149, 187, 189
sex, 43–44
Shildrick, Margrit, 102
Skinner, John, 184
Smith, S. H., 159
somatics. *see* embodiment
Spencer-Hall, Alicia and
Blake Gutt, 70
Stiebert, Johanna, 156, 159
Stone, Ken, 72
Stone, Sandy, 67
Strassfeld, Max, 70–71, 102
Stryker, Susan, 42, 51–52,
54, 55, 63
Sumerau, J. E., Ryan
Mathers and Lain
Cragun, 69–70

Tate, Shirley Anne, 123
trans, 17–20, 22–23, 25–27,
41–43, 125
biblical studies, 68–71,
73–74, 85–86, 88–89,
110–111, 121,
122–125. *see also
Transgender, Intersex
and Biblical
Interpretation*
theory, 26–27, 41–43,
48–49, **51–63**, 63–65,
67–68
transphobia, 52–54, 67
n1, 70–71, 102–103
*Transgender, Intersex and
Biblical
Interpretation. see*
Guest, Deryn
Trible, Phyllis, 8–9, 148,
191
Troubling the Waters, see
Guest, Deryn

Valentine, Katy, 145, 193
Vawter, Bruce, 184
von Rad, Gerhard, 157–158,
161, 163–164,
175–176, 183

Wenham, Gordon, 129, 132,
134
Westermann, Claus, 119,
164, 182–183, 184
When Deborah Met Jael, see
Guest, Deryn
Wilchins, Riki, 85–86
Wilcox, Melissa M., 71
Wolf, Mark J. P., 139–140

www.ingramcontent.com/pod-product-compliance
Lightning Source LLC
Chambersburg PA
CBHW051521230426
43668CB00012B/1693